Above: Bonner makes a penalty save against Romania at 1990 World Cup.

IRELAND'S GREATEST

60 Years of Football Heroes - Over 300 Player Profiles

DEAN HAYES

Appletree Press

First published in 2006 by
Appletree Press Ltd
The Old Potato Station
14 Howard Street South
Belfast BT7 1AP

Tel: +44 (0) 28 90 24 30 74
Fax: +44 (0) 28 90 24 67 56
Email: reception@appletree.ie
Web site: www.appletree.ie

A catalogue record for this book is available from the British Library.

Ireland's Greatest – 60 Years of Football Heroes

ISBN-10: 0 86281 995 4
ISBN-13: 978 0 86281 995 8

Desk & Marketing Editor: Jean Brown
Copy-Editor: Jim Black
Designer: Stuart Wilkinson
Production Manager: Paul McAvoy

9 8 7 6 5 4 3 2 1

AP3324

Author's Note
All details are believed correct and while every effort has been made to ensure accuracy, information can not be guaranteed.
In the event of any error the publisher and author would welcome any further information and offer their sincere apologies.

CONTENTS

INTRODUCTION

This 'Who's Who' of Republic of Ireland footballers revisits the many contrasting post-war experiences of the national side through its lifeblood – the players. Some are great, some good, some less than good, but all have one thing in common: all have pulled on the green shirt and taken to the field to represent their country.

A total of 318 players have appeared for the Republic of Ireland in the post-war period. They appear here in chronological order – that is, in the order they made their international debut. There are of course, matches where a number of players made their debut at the same time and in such cases they are listed alphabetically. Should you be unsure of the decade in which a particular favourite played, there is an index at the back of the book for easy reference.

In the statistics section at the head of each player's entry, match dates are listed according to the year that marked the end of the season in which the game was played. Every post-war game is included in the book up to the end of the qualifying rounds for the 2006 World Cup Finals.

For each player, I have aimed to provide the following information: full name, recognised position, period as a Republic of Ireland player, date and place of birth, date of death, career details, breakdown of appearances and goals scored for the Republic of Ireland and biography.

This book is a collection of statistics and biographies. But I hope it is more than that: it is a celebration of the great game. Since international football resumed in 1946, a number of Republic of Ireland records have been broken, anniversaries marked and personal bests established. These include the record for the longest gap between a first and second cap when Alex Stevenson who had won his first cap against Holland in May 1932, was recalled to the national side for the game against England in September 1946! The Republic also became the first country outside of the United Kingdom to beat England on their home soil when they won 2-0 at Goodison Park in 1949. Jimmy Holmes became the youngest player to appear for the Republic of Ireland when at the age of 17 years 200 days, he made his debut against Austria in May 1971, whilst Steve Staunton was the first Republic of Ireland player to register 100 international caps.

Every game and every championship brings a new chapter. The story will continue.

Dean P Hayes

Left: David O'Leary scores a vital penalty against Romania to take Ireland to the World Cup quarter-finals in 1990.

THE 1940s

The Republic of Ireland's last match before the Second World War was against Germany in Bremen in May 1939. To the bitter resentment of Britain and Northern Ireland, the Republic stayed neutral during the hostilities. Germany's sporting punishment for her wartime aggression was to be barred from FIFA and therefore from competing in the next World Cup. Hostilities prevented the competition in Brazil in 1942, and the tournament's earmarked successor four years later was a non-starter.

At the end of the fighting came news from across the Irish Sea that the British Associations had mended their fences with FIFA and had condescended to rejoin, taking part in the World Cup for the first time. This spelled trouble for the Emerald Isle, because the two Irelands were now embarked on a quest for what was the same prize. They would now have to put a stop to their habit of selecting players from north and south of the border.

Politically, the split from Britain was finalised in 1949 when the Republic of Ireland declared its intention to leave the Commonwealth. In footballing terms, the friction with Northern Ireland continued a while due to both Dublin and Belfast seeking exclusive rights to the use of the word 'Ireland'.

The Republic of Ireland were alloted to a World Cup pool with Sweden and Finland in the only European section (other than the British one of the four home countries) to comprise more than two nations.

Ireland might have been celebrating the birth of the Republic but they had little to celebrate on the football pitch. Since the war ended, they had played 10 matches, seven of them against Portugal or Spain, who had likewise stayed neutral during the hostilities – even so, the Republic must have been sick of the sight of them!

The breakthrough came on 30 September 1946 when the Republic entertained England who two days earlier had beaten Northern Ireland 7-2 in Belfast. The Republic were just eight minutes from a draw when Tom Finney pounced to score the game's only goal.

The new era brought down the curtain on Republic of Ireland sides dominated by Irish-based players. With the exception of the Johnny Careys, Tommy Eglingtons and Peter Farrells – of whom there were not that many – the selectors had to scour the English lower divisions in search of eligible players to represent the Republic.

However, towards the end of the failed World Cup bid, the Republic of Ireland beat England 2-0 at Goodison Park. The result entered the nation's folklore, though in England little significance was attached because nine of the Republic's side played in the Football League!

Alex Stevenson

Position	Inside-forward
Born	Alexander Ernest Stevenson, Dublin, 9 August 1912
Died	1985
Clubs	

Dolphin; Glasgow Rangers; Everton; Bootle; St Patrick's Athletic

International Caps	7

Matches

Year	Opponent	Result	Score	G
1932	Holland	won	2-0	
1947	England	lost	0-1	
1947	Spain	won	3-2	
1947	Portugal	lost	0-2	
1948	Portugal	lost	0-2	
1948	Spain	lost	1-2	
1949	Switzerland	lost	0-1	

Hailed as one of the finest ball-players of his generation, Alex Stevenson's control was near perfect, his stocky body able to withstand the sometimes ruthless tackling of his contemporaries. But it was his brain that made him a truly great player and he graced the Everton team either side of World War Two.

Stevenson was discovered by Glasgow Rangers coach Arthur Dixon playing junior football with the Dolphin club in Dublin. Dixon signed him for the Ibrox club in 1931.

It was with Rangers that he rose to stardom, helping them win two successive Scottish League Championships. His love of Rangers was such that it took a good deal of coaxing before Everton could persuade him to leave Ibrox in January 1934.

At Goodison he struck up an awe-inspiring partnership with fellow countryman Jackie Coulter – the impish pair tore many defences to shreds with their speedy interplay and remarkable understanding of each other's intentions. Alex Stevenson went on to score 90 goals in 271 games for the Blues – respectable figures for a man not employed primarily as a scorer – and won a League Championship winners' medal in 1938-39, the last pre-war season.

He left Everton in 1949 to join non-League Bootle. He later returned to Ireland and in 1953-54, when he was 41 years old, was turning out for St Patrick's Athletic in the League of Ireland.

His 'two Ireland' international career, like his Everton career, straddled the Second World War. He won the first of his seven caps for the Republic of Ireland when playing with Dolphin in a 2-0 defeat of Holland in Amsterdam in May 1932 and didn't play again until the Republic met England in Dublin in September 1946 – a gap of 14 years, which is the longest gap between winning first and second Irish caps.

Bill Gorman

Position	Full-back
Born	William Charles Gorman, Sligo, 13 July 1911
Died	December 1978
Clubs	

Shettleston Juniors; Bury; Brentford; Deal Town

International Caps	13

Matches

Year	Opponent	Result	Score	G
1936	Switzerland	won	1-0	
1936	Hungary	drew	3-3	
1936	Luxembourg	won	5-1	
1937	Germany	won	5-2	
1937	Hungary	lost	2-3	
1938	Norway	drew	3-3	
1938	Czechoslovakia	drew	2-2	
1938	Poland	lost	0-6	
1939	Switzerland	won	4-0	
1939	Poland	won	3-2	
1939	Hungary	drew	2-2	
1947	England	lost	0-1	
1947	Portugal	lost	0-2	

Bill Gorman's speed off the mark and enthusiasm combined to make him one of the finest defenders in the game and earned him 13 full caps for the Republic of Ireland and four for Northern Ireland.

His qualification for both the North and the South came about by chance: he had made a premature entry into the world while his parents – father was Scottish, mother was English – were on holiday in Sligo!

Gorman's international career straddled the Second World War. He made his debut for the Republic of Ireland in the 1-0 defeat of Switzerland in March 1936 and was a regular in the Irish defence when war broke out in 1939. The prematurely balding full-back was 35 years old when he won his last cap for the Republic against Portugal in May 1947.

He was brought up in Clydebank and played his early football for Shettleston Juniors before moving south to play for Second Division Bury. He made 52 league appearances for the Shakers before joining Brentford for a fee of £7,000 in December 1938. The Bees were enjoying the only period of First Division football in their history. By signing players of the calibre of Bill Gorman, the Griffin Park club hoped to stay at the top. However, it wasn't to be and in 1946-47 they were relegated to the Second Division.

The hostilities carved a huge chunk out of Bill Gorman's career, as it did for many other players and when he left Griffin Park in October 1950 to take over as player-manager of Kent League side Deal Town, his total of Football League appearances for the Bees amounted to just 125.

Tommy Breen

Position	Goalkeeper
Born	Thomas Breen, Drogheda, 27 April 1917
Died	1988

Clubs

Newry Town; Belfast Celtic; Manchester United; Belfast Celtic; Linfield; Shamrock Rovers; Glentoran

International Caps	5

Matches

Year	Opponent	Result	Score	G
1937	Switzerland	won	1-0	
1937	France	won	2-0	
1947	England	lost	0-1	
1947	Spain	won	3-2	
1947	Portugal	lost	0-2	

A splendid and fearless goalkeeper, Tommy Breen had originally played Gaelic football, from which he developed the art of safe handling and long kicking. He joined Belfast Celtic from Newry Town with defender Johnny Feehan in the early 1930s and was without doubt 'one of the most outstanding players to appear for the legendary Belfast club'.

He won Irish League Championship medals with Celtic in 1932–33 and 1935–36 before leaving Celtic Park towards the end of this latter season, to join Manchester United.

He opened his League campaign in England in most inauspicious circumstances: after less than a minute of his debut against Leeds United at Elland Road he had to pick the ball out of the net! Breen, who was United's sixth goalkeeper in as many seasons, helped the club win promotion to the First Division in 1937–38. He made 71 appearances for the Old Trafford club by September 1939 when League football was abandoned because of war.

The outbreak of hostilities saw him leave Old Trafford and return to Belfast, having been given permission by United to resume his career at Celtic Park. When the war ended he went south to play for Shamrock Rovers.

Before the war, Breen had won nine caps as Northern Ireland keeper in the old Home International Championships. He had made his debut for the Republic of Ireland in the 1-0 defeat of Switzerland in May 1937 and kept another clean sheet for his second cap the following week when the Republic beat France 2-0 in Paris. After that, the Republic's goalkeeping responsibilities were handled by Southend United's George McKenzie – Tommy Breen had to wait until September 1946 for his third cap. His fifth and final call up to the national side came almost exactly ten years after his first, against Portugal in May 1947.

Johnny Carey

Position	Defender
Born	John James Carey, Dublin, 23 February 1919
Died	August 1995

Clubs

St James's Gate; Manchester United

International Caps	29
International Goals	3

Matches

Year	Opponent	Result	Score	G
1938	Norway	drew	3-3	
1938	Czechoslovakia	drew	2-2	
1938	Poland	lost	0-6	
1939	Switzerland	won	4-0	
1939	Poland	won	3-2	1
1939	Hungary	drew	2-2	1
1939	Hungary	drew	2-2	
1939	Germany	drew	1-1	
1946	Portugal	lost	1-3	
1946	Spain	won	1-0	
1947	England	lost	0-1	
1947	Spain	won	3-2	
1947	Portugal	lost	0-2	
1948	Portugal	lost	0-2	

Matches Continued

Year	Opponent	Result	Score	G
1948	Spain	lost	1-2	
1949	Switzerland	lost	0-1	
1949	Belgium	lost	0-2	
1949	Portugal	won	1-0	
1949	Sweden	lost	1-3	
1949	Spain	lost	1-4	
1950	Finland	won	3-0	
1950	England	won	2-0	
1950	Finland	drew	1-1	
1950	Sweden	lost	1-3	
1951	Norway	drew	2-2	1
1951	Argentina	lost	0-1	
1951	Norway	won	3-2	
1953	France	drew	1-1	
1953	Austria	won	4-0	

The undisputed architect of Manchester United's 'second coming' in the years after World War Two was Matt Busby, but his right-hand man and representative on the pitch was Johnny Carey.

The genial Irishman had an illustrious playing career at club and international level, which was followed by a successful but largely under-rated series of managerial appointments. Above all else though, Carey had an unrivalled reputation for sportsmanship, which won the respect of team-mates and opponents and made him a natural choice as captain.

Dublin-born Carey joined United from the local St James's Gate club in November 1936 for just £250. He was spotted by United's chief scout at the time, Louis Rocca, who had gone to watch another player. It was allegedly only Carey's third game of football but Rocca was so keen that the 17-year-old was signed before he even had time to take off his boots! In 1937-38 he helped United win promotion to the First Division and appeared in 53 games before the war intervened. After army service, he returned to a bomb-devastated Old Trafford and began a seven-year run with the first of Busby's great sides.

He captained United's 1948 FA Cup-winning team and the one which finally lifted the League Championship in 1951-52 after several near misses. By the time he retired in 1953, Carey had made 344 appearances and scored 18 goals for United.

He was also capped 29 times by the Republic of Ireland – including leading his country to a famous 2-0 win over England at Goodison Park in 1949 – and played seven times for Northern Ireland. Carey also captained the Rest of Europe against Great Britain in 1947 and was voted 'Footballer of the Year' in 1949 and 'Sportsman of the Year' in 1950.

Carey was a man so versatile that he figured in nine different positions for the Reds, ten if you include the occasion he pulled on the goalkeeper's jersey when Jack Crompton was taken ill at an away match. He was also versatile on the international stage, appearing in seven different positions for the Republic of Ireland.

After hanging up his boots, he could have stayed at Old Trafford in a coaching role but he chose to move into management with Blackburn Rovers. Things went well at Ewood, Carey taking them into the First Division. This success led to his appointment as Everton manager in 1958. This was the one club in which he failed to make a big impact – he was famously fired by chairman John Moores in a London taxi! From Merseyside he went to Brisbane Road and guided Leyton Orient into the top flight for the first and only time. He then had five seasons in charge of Nottingham Forest, taking them to the FA Cup semi-final and runners-up spot in Division One in 1966-67. Carey's last job in football was a second, less happy spell at Blackburn which ended in 1971.

He left football for a textile machine company and ended his working days in 1984 in the Treasurer's Office of Trafford Borough Council. His retirement was spent in Bramall, Cheshire, where he could indulge his passion for golf and make regular visits to his beloved Old Trafford.

Kevin O'Flanagan

Position	Winger
Born	Kevin Patrick O'Flanagan, Dublin, 10 June 1919

Clubs

Bohemians; Arsenal; Barnet; Brentford

International Caps	10
International Goals	3

Matches

Year	Opponent	Result	Score	G
1938	Norway	drew	3-3	1
1938	Czechoslovakia	drew	2-2	
1938	Poland	lost	0-6	
1939	Poland	won	3-2	
1939	Hungary	drew	2-2	
1939	Hungary	drew	2-2	2
1939	Germany	drew	1-1	
1947	England	lost	0-1	
1947	Spain	won	3-2	
1947	Portugal	lost	0-2	

Dr Kevin O'Flanagan was one of the most talented sportsmen of the pre-war years. Not only was he excellent at athletics – the Irish sprint champion in 1941 and long jump champion on four occasions between 1938 and 1943 – but he was also an accomplished tennis player and single-figure handicap golfer!

Quite amazingly he found time to add team sports to his remarkable repertoire of individual skills. He was captain of Bohemians when they won the Irish Cup in 1945 and after taking up a medical appointment in Middlesex, he signed as an amateur for First Division Arsenal, for whom he made 17 appearances either at outside-right or centre-forward. Many's the time when a team-mate was injured, he would quickly be in attendance! At the same time as turning out for the Gunners, he was playing top-class rugby union with London Irish.

Not surprisingly, his busy schedule limited his availability for Arsenal. In 1949 after a spell playing non-League football for Barnet, he joined Second Division Brentford for whom he made half-a-dozen appearances before an ankle injury ended his playing days.

As an international, Kevin O'Flanagan was doubly honoured, playing for his country at both rugby and soccer. O'Flanagan scored on his debut for the Republic of Ireland in the 3-3 draw with Norway in November 1937, and went on to win a total of 10 caps, seven before the hostilities as a Bohemians player and three during his Arsenal days.

Following his premature retirement from the game, he returned to medical practice in Ireland. O'Flanagan was also team doctor to the Irish National Olympic side for three years and was a member of the International Olympic Committee for the 1992 Olympic Games in Barcelona.

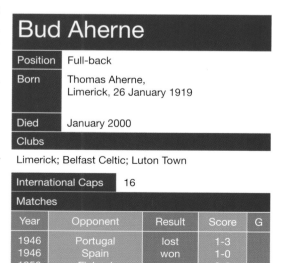

Bud Aherne

Position	Full-back
Born	Thomas Aherne, Limerick, 26 January 1919
Died	January 2000

Clubs

Limerick; Belfast Celtic; Luton Town

International Caps	16

Matches

Year	Opponent	Result	Score	G
1946	Portugal	lost	1-3	
1946	Spain	won	1-0	
1950	Finland	won	3-0	

Matches Continued				
Year	Opponent	Result	Score	G
1950	England	won	2-0	
1950	Finland	drew	1-1	
1950	Sweden	lost	1-3	
1950	Belguim	lost	1-5	
1951	Norway	drew	2-2	
1951	Argentina	lost	0-1	
1951	Norway	won	3-2	
1952	West Germany	won	3-2	
1952	West Germany	lost	0-3	
1952	Austria	lost	0-6	
1952	Spain	lost	0-6	
1953	France	drew	1-1	
1954	France	lost	3-5	

Thomas Aherne, known to everyone as 'Bud', played senior hurling for his native Limerick and played in the South East Cork junior championship with Carrigaline while stationed with the army at Fort Camden, Crosshaven. But football was his first love and he began his career with his home-town club Limerick before in 1945 moving north to play for Belfast Celtic.

A quick player with excellent positional sense, he made his debut for the Republic of Ireland in their first post-war international against Portugal in Lisbon, in a team which contained ten debutants and Johnny Carey.

With Belfast Celtic, he won an Irish League Championship medal in 1947-48 to add to the Irish Cup winners' medal he'd won the previous season. Whilst at Belfast, he was a regular in the Irish League representative side and was also one of only a handful of players to represent both 'Irelands'. He was a member of the Belfast Celtic side which achieved an unexpected victory over Scotland, who had been dubbed the 'wonder team of 1949'. The Scots, who were Home International Champions, met the Irish club in America's Triboro Stadium. Despite believing they had little to fear, the Scots lost 2-0.

In March 1949 Aherne joined Luton Town for a fee of £6,000 and claimed a first team place almost immediately. It proved a shrewd piece of business by the Hatters for he became a cult figure, as the Kenilworth Road faithful admired his tough tackling and intelligent use of the ball. Aherne made 267 League appearances for the Hatters and made a telling contribution to their promotion-winning season of 1954-55, when the club entered the First Division for the first time in their history.

Whilst with Luton, Aherne played in the Republic side which inflicted England's first home defeat by an overseas side at Goodison Park in September 1949 – it was the second of 13 consecutive appearances in the national side. His last appearance came in a World Cup qualifier against France in October 1953, a match the Irish lost 5-3.

Aherne left Luton in 1961 to become coach to the London Spartan League club, Vauxhall Motors.

Ned Courtney

Position	Goalkeeper
Born	Edward Courtney, Dublin

Clubs	
Cork United; Cork Athletic	

International Caps	1

Matches				
Year	Opponent	Result	Score	G
1946	Portugal	lost	1-3	

Goalkeeper 'Ned' Courtney was a Gaelic player who though born in Dublin, joined the army and settled in Cork.

Courtney, an army captain as well as a brave, reliable keeper, played in goal for the Cork Gaelic team before signing for League club Cork United in 1945. He won a League Championship medal with United in 1945-46, his performances leading to him making his full international debut in dramatic fashion in June 1946. He was driven by army lorry from Cork to Dublin in an emergency when Tommy Breen, the Shamrock Rovers' keeper cried off from the international side to play Portugal in Lisbon.

Though it proved to be his only cap, Courtney became part of the Republic's footballing history. When he was injured after half-an-hour, attempting to prevent Portugal's third goal in a 3-1 defeat, he was replaced in goal by Con Martin, who thus became the Republic's first-ever substitute goalkeeper.

Ned Courtney enjoyed his best years with Cork Athletic, who replaced United in the late 1940s. He won back-to-back League Championship medals with Athletic in 1949-50 and 1950-51, and between 1951 and 1953 played in three successive FAI Finals. He was a Cup winner in 1951, and played in the 1-1 draw with Dundalk in the 1952 Final. He missed the replay which Athletic lost 3-0 through injury, and spent most of the 1952-53 season in retirement, having lost his place in the side to Healy and then after making a comeback, to Waters. But he was between the posts in the 1953 FAI Cup Final success in which Sunderland and England legend Raich Carter played at inside-right for Cork.

Tommy Eglington

Position	Outside-left
Born	Thomas Joseph Eglington, Dublin, 15 January 1923
Died	18 February 2004

Clubs

Shamrock Rovers; Everton; Tranmere Rovers

International Caps	24
International Goals	2

Matches

Year	Opponent	Result	Score	G
1946	Portugal	lost	1-3	
1946	Spain	won	1-0	
1947	England	lost	0-1	
1947	Spain	won	3-2	
1947	Portugal	lost	0-2	
1948	Portugal	lost	0-2	
1949	Switzerland	lost	0-1	
1949	Portugal	won	1-0	
1949	Sweden	lost	1-3	
1951	Norway	drew	2-2	
1951	Argentina	lost	0-1	
1952	West Germany	won	3-2	
1952	West Germany	lost	0-3	
1952	Austria	lost	0-6	
1952	Spain	lost	0-6	
1953	France	drew	1-1	
1953	Austria	won	4-0	1
1954	France	lost	3-5	
1954	Luxembourg	won	4-0	1
1954	France	lost	0-1	
1955	Norway	won	2-1	
1955	Holland	won	1-0	
1955	West Germany	lost	1-2	
1956	Spain	drew	2-2	

One of Everton's greatest-ever servants, Tommy Eglington also stands out as one of the early greats of Irish football. One of only a handful of players who have appeared for both Northern Ireland and the Republic, he was a member of the Irish side which recorded an historic 2-0 victory over an England side – appropriately enough at Goodison Park – in 1949. They became the first overseas side to defeat England on English soil.

Eglington was the Republic's regular outside-left for a decade in the immediate post-war years. During that time he won 24 caps, scored two goals and was national team captain on two occasions.

Like many of his contemporaries, he excelled at hurling and Gaelic football during his schooldays, but it was as one of the finest match-winning left wingers in the game of football that he came to be remembered.

Tommy Eglington joined Everton in the summer of 1946 in a double transfer deal involving the Blues' other immediate post-war great, Peter Farrell. The double deal, which cost Everton £10,000 has often been described as the best piece of business in the club's history. Elegant and unruffled, with an explosive burst of pace and a thundering shot, Eglington had been with Shamrock Rovers for just one season (that of 1945-46) when he ended the campaign as the Hoops' leading scorer with 11 goals before leaving for Goodison Park.

Eglington made his League debut for the Toffees in a 3-2 home win over Arsenal in September 1946, going on to claim a regular place for the next 11 seasons – all but three of which were spent in the First Division. Following Everton's relegation at the end of the 1950-51 season they were promoted back to the top flight in 1953-54, having finished runners-up to Leicester City on goal difference. During this spell at the lower level, Eglington guaranteed himself a place in the pages of Everton's history. On 27 September 1952 he almost single-handedly demolished Doncaster Rovers at Goodison Park, scoring five Toffees goals in a 7-1 win. He ended that season as the club's leading scorer in the Football League with 14 goals in 39 games.

A player with intricate close control and stunning shooting power, Eglington left Everton for Tranmere Rovers in the summer of 1957. For a little over three seasons he gave the Wirral-based club the same wholehearted service that he had given the Blues, before finally hanging up his boots and returning to his native Dublin, where for many years he ran a butcher's shop.

Peter Farrell

Position	Wing-half
Born	Peter Desmond Farrell, Dublin, 16 August 1922
Died	16 March 1999
Clubs	Shamrock Rovers; Everton; Tranmere Rovers; Hdyhist Town
International Caps	28
International Goals	3

Matches

Year	Opponent	Result	Score	G
1946	Portugal	lost	1-3	
1946	Spain	won	1-0	
1947	Spain	won	3-2	
1947	Portugal	lost	0-2	
1948	Portugal	lost	0-2	
1948	Spain	lost	1-2	
1949	Switzerland	lost	0-1	
1949	Portugal	won	1-0	
1949	Spain	lost	1-4	
1950	England	won	2-0	1
1950	Finland	drew	1-1	1
1950	Sweden	lost	1-3	
1951	Argentina	lost	0-1	
1951	Norway	won	3-2	1
1952	West Germany	won	3-2	
1952	West Germany	lost	0-3	
1952	Austria	lost	0-6	
1952	Spain	lost	0-6	
1953	France	drew	1-1	
1954	Austria	won	4-0	
1954	France	lost	3-5	
1954	France	lost	0-1	
1955	Norway	won	2-1	
1955	Holland	won	1-0	
1955	West Germany	lost	1-2	
1956	Yugoslavia	lost	1-4	
1956	Spain	drew	2-2	
1957	England	lost	1-5	

Above: Peter Farrell (right)

Peter Farrell's career coincided with that of Tommy Eglington, for after playing with Shamrock Rovers as a schoolboy, the two of them joined Everton in a combined deal which cost the Blues £10,000 spread over two years. Like his close friend Eglington, Farrell enjoyed 11 seasons with Everton, during which time he became something of a living legend on Merseyside – in fact, he is one of the few footballers to have a street named after him – Farrell Close!

His debut for Everton was postponed until late November 1946 because of an injury he sustained playing tennis! After that, he was a virtual ever-present in the Everton side – never dropped, he went on to make 453 League and Cup appearances.

On the international front, Farrell appeared at left-half for Northern Ireland in seven internationals between September 1946 and March 1949, while he was a regular in the Republic of Ireland side from 1946 to 1957, making a total of 28 appearances. He scored one of the goals in the Republic's epic 2-0 defeat of England at Goodison Park in September 1949, making them the first overseas team to beat England on home soil. Farrell also achieved the unusual distinction of captaining his country in his first international against Portugal, an honour bestowed on him in a further 11 internationals.

Peter Farrell was captain when the Blues dropped down to Division Two in 1950-51 for only the second time in their history. However, their fall from grace was short-lived, for three seasons later they found their way back into the top flight. An inspiration to all around him and very popular on the field, Farrell was also something of a hero off it, mixing freely with the club's supporters in a down-to-earth manner.

In October 1957, less than six months after Eglington left Everton for Tranmere Rovers, Peter Farrell embarked on the same short journey across the River Mersey to link up yet again with his close friend and colleague. He was immediately appointed captain at Prenton Park. Although his three seasons on the Wirral were not the happiest of his career, he continued to play as enthusiastically as ever, more than justifying Tranmere's £2,500 investment in a player heading towards the end of his career.

Farrell left Tranmere at the end of 1960 to join Welsh non-League side Hydhist Town as player-manager, later returning to Ireland to continue in management before working in broadcasting with RTÉ in Dublin.

Jimmy McAlinden

Position	Centre-forward
Born	James McAlinden, Belfast, 31 December 1917
Died	15 November 1993
Clubs	

Belfast Celtic; Portsmouth; Stoke City; Southend United; Glenavon

International Caps	2

Matches				
Year	Opponent	Result	Score	G
1946	Portugal	lost	1-3	
1946	Spain	won	1-0	

Jimmy McAlinden started out with Belfast Celtic, scoring many valuable goals including the two that beat Bangor in the replayed Irish Cup Final in 1938 and clinched Celtic's second successive League and Cup double. His rapidly developing skills didn't go unnoticed across the water and almost every top flight club manager braved the Irish Sea to see his talents first hand.

Consequently in the summer of 1938, McAlinden was on his way to high-flying First Division side Portsmouth for a fee of £6,000. He immediately won a first team place and in his first season at Fratton Park, he won an FA Cup winners' medal after Pompey beat Wolverhampton Wanderers 4-1. During the club's run to the final, McAlinden scored seven goals in their six games.

When the Second World War broke out in 1939, McAlinden returned to Belfast Celtic and won two more Irish Cup winners' medals in 1941 and 1944. He also represented the Irish League, appearing for them against the Army and Combined Service teams.

When the hostilities ended, he returned to Portsmouth but after a total of 60 League games and 15 goals he was transferred to

Stoke City in September 1947. The move was not an unmitigated success and after 12 months he moved back south, this time to Southend United for £6,000.

The talented forward had the distinction of being capped four times by Northern Ireland as well as appearing twice on the Republic's Iberian tour of the summer of 1946.

At Southend, he was appointed the club's captain, giving the Roots Hall side excellent service and ended his League career with 218 games for them, though he missed 11 games through suspension in 1950 over illegal payments he had allegedly received.

On leaving Southend United, he ventured into management as player-boss at Glenavon whom he led to a League and Cup double. Amongst his honours as a manager, he prized the knowledge that he nurtured Martin O'Neill at Distillery, whom he later transferred to Nottingham Forest and a European Cup winners' medal. O'Neill scored two goals to pave the way for Distillery's 3-0 win over Derry City in the 1971 Irish Cup Final. McAlinden later managed Drogheda United in the League of Ireland.

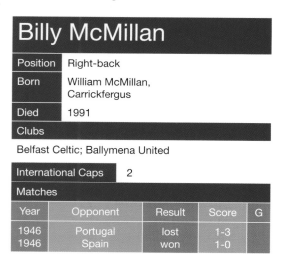

Billy McMillan

Position	Right-back
Born	William McMillan, Carrickfergus
Died	1991
Clubs	

Belfast Celtic; Ballymena United

International Caps	2

Matches				
Year	Opponent	Result	Score	G
1946	Portugal	lost	1-3	
1946	Spain	won	1-0	

An outstanding full-back in the Belfast Celtic side of the 1930s and 1940s, he had joined the club when they were a dominant force in Irish League football. Between 1937 and 1940, McMillan won successive Irish League Championship medals with the club and then added another in 1948. He also won four Irish Cup winners' medals in 1942, 1943, 1944 and 1947.

In June 1946 Billy McMillan was chosen to replace Cork United's Billy Hayes, whose leg injury kept him out of the Republic's Iberian tour. He had originally been listed to travel as a reserve, but made his international debut alongside Celtic team-mates Bud Aherne and Jackie Vernon in a 3-1 defeat against Portugal. He kept his place in the side for the Republic's next match the following week, and had an outstanding game in the 1-0 victory over Spain in Seville in front of General Franco.

Having played for the IFA in Victory Internationals against England, Scotland and Wales in 1946, he also played against the Football League in 1947 and 1948.

McMillan was a member of the Belfast Celtic team which drew 1-1 with Linfield on 27 December 1948, when Celtic's Jimmy Jones had his leg broken when attacked by spectators – the incident all but spelt the end of Belfast Celtic in Irish League football. However, they did tour the United States in the summer of 1949 and McMillan, along with Aherne and McAlinden was outstanding in a 2-0 defeat of Scotland.

When Belfast Celtic withdrew from football, Billy McMillan was appointed player-manager of Ballymena United but remained there for only a couple of seasons before drifting out of the game.

Con Martin

Position	Defender/Goalkeeper
Born	Cornelius Joseph Martin, Dublin, 20 March 1923
Clubs	

Drumcondra; Glentoran; Leeds United; Aston Villa

International Caps	30
International Goals	6

Matches

Year	Opponent	Result	Score	G
1946	Portugal	lost	1-3	
1946	Spain	won	1-0	
1947	England	lost	0-1	
1947	Spain	won	3-2	
1948	Portugal	lost	0-2	
1948	Spain	lost	1-2	
1949	Switzerland	lost	0-1	
1949	Belgium	lost	0-2	
1949	Portugal	won	1-0	
1949	Sweden	lost	1-3	
1949	Spain	lost	1-4	1
1950	Finland	won	3-0	2
1950	England	won	2-0	1
1950	Finland	drew	1-1	
1950	Sweden	lost	1-3	1
1950	Belgium	lost	1-5	
1951	Argentina	lost	0-1	
1952	West Germany	lost	0-3	
1952	Austria	lost	0-6	
1952	Spain	lost	0-6	
1954	France	lost	3-5	
1954	France	lost	0-1	
1954	Luxembourg	won	1-0	
1955	Norway	won	2-1	1
1955	Holland	won	1-0	
1955	Norway	won	3-1	
1955	West Germany	lost	1-2	
1956	Yugoslavia	lost	1-4	
1956	Spain	drew	2-2	
1956	Holland	won	4-1	

The versatility of dual Irish international Cornelius Martin is legendary, for he played in every position at senior level, including goalkeeping appearances for the Republic of Ireland and Aston Villa.

The father of Republic of Ireland international Mick Martin of Manchester United and Newcastle United, he was a fine all-round athlete, excelling in Gaelic football, basketball and soccer.

He began his career with Drumcondra before moving to Irish League club Glentoran where he won his first cap and in doing so, became the Republic's first-ever substitute. In June 1946 he came off the bench to play in goal for the injured Ned Courtney of Cork United, in the friendly against Portugal in Lisbon.

Con Martin, who went on to win 30 caps for the Republic of Ireland and made six appearances for Northern Ireland, was without doubt the best utility player of the era. He played in no fewer than five different positions for his country – goalkeeper, right- and left-back, right-half and in his more usual position of centre-half. In addition to this, he captained the Republic on five occasions and netted six goals.

In January 1947 he left the Oval for Leeds United with the Elland Road club paying £8,000 for his services. However, he arrived too late to save the Yorkshire club from relegation to Division Two. With Leeds hard-up for cash, they sold him to Aston Villa for £10,000 in October 1948.

He enjoyed his best days at Villa Park, playing at left-back in his first two seasons with the club before starting the 1951-52 First Division campaign as the club's goalkeeper! He went on to play between the posts for Villa on 26 occasions, eventually making 194 League appearances in eight seasons with the club.

Jackie O'Reilly

Position	Winger
Born	John O'Reilly, Cobh, Co. Cork, 7 May 1914

Clubs

Cork Bohemians; Cobh Wanderers; Cobh Ramblers; Cork United; Norwich City; Cork United

International Caps	2
International Goals	1

Matches

Year	Opponent	Result	Score	G
1946	Portugal	lost	1-3	1
1946	Spain	won	1-0	

Jackie O'Reilly played his early football with Cork Bohemians, Cobh Wanderers and Cobh Ramblers before joining League of Ireland club Cork United in the summer of 1935. However, he was an all-round athlete – a Cork County Cup winner at rugby who only missed out on a place in Ireland's Olympic swimming team because of an allergy!

With Cork United, he was an FAI Cup runner-up in 1936, when they lost the final 2-1 to Shamrock Rovers. Shortly after that final, he left Cork to join Norwich City and although he netted a couple of goals on his Football League debut for the Canaries, most of his time at Carrow Road was spent as understudy to Billy Warnes. Relegated to Norwich's reserves, he scored 17 goals in 12 games before returning to Cork United in 1939, having scored 11 goals in 33 League outings for the East Anglian club (1936-38).

On his return, he was part of a brilliant Cork United side which dominated League of Ireland football in the 1940s. He won five League Championship medals with Cork United and one in 1949-50 with the renamed Cork Athletic. O'Reilly also played in a further five FAI Cup Finals in the post-war era, scoring a record seven Cup Final goals. He was a winner with Cork United in 1941 and 1947 and a runner-up in 1942 and 1943 and a runner-up with Cork Athletic in 1950.

O'Reilly, who represented the League of Ireland on eight occasions, was capped when international football resumed after the Second World War, scoring the Republic's first goal against Portugal on 16 June 1946.

On hanging up his boots, he emigrated to Mississauga in the Canadian province of Ontario.

Paddy Sloan

Position	Inside-forward/Wing-half
Born	Joseph Walter Sloan, Lurgan, 30 April 1920
Died	19 January 1993

Clubs

Glenavon; Manchester United; Arsenal; Sheffield United; Milan; Torino; Udinese; Brescia; Norwich City; Peterborough United; Rabat FC (Malta); Hastings United; Leamington Lockheed; Bath City

International Caps	2
International Goals	1

Matches

Year	Opponent	Result	Score	G
1946	Portugal	lost	1-3	
1946	Spain	won	1-0	1

Paddy Sloan's career spanned four decades, in which he played for no less than 14 clubs in five countries, including some of the greatest names in European football.

He began his career in the Irish League with Glenavon, from whom he signed for Manchester United in September 1937. He spent two seasons at Old Trafford but on being unable to break into the Reds' League side, he joined Tranmere Rovers. When war broke out, Sloan returned to Glenavon and when they resigned from the Regional League, he had a brief spell with Glentoran before joining the RAF. He served in Europe during the hostilities and then spent the 1944-45 season with Fulham before returning to Prenton Park for the first post-war campaign of 1945-46.

In May 1946 he joined Arsenal and was immediately switched from inside-forward to wing-half. He won two caps for the Republic of Ireland in 1946 against Portugal and Spain, netting the winner over the latter side in Madrid. He also played for Northern Ireland against Wales in April 1947.

Following the signings of Alex Forbes and Archie Macauley, he lost his place in the Arsenal side and moved to Sheffield United. In the summer of 1948, Sloan became one of the first players to be transferred to the Italian League. In just over three years in Italy, he turned out for Milan, Torino, Udinese and Brescia before signing for Norwich City.

After a handful of games for the Canaries, he played for Peterborough United.

In July 1954 he became player-coach of Maltese club Rabat FC and later held similar positions with Hastings United, Leamington Lockheed and Bath City.

After a spell coaching in Turkey, he emigrated to Australia in 1963 and became coach at Melbourne club Juventus. Paddy Sloan later became Chairman of the National Coaches Association.

Jackie Vernon

Position	Centre-half
Born	John Joseph Vernon, Belfast, 26 September 1918
Died	June 1981
Clubs	

Dundela; Belfast Celtic; West Bromwich Albion; Crusaders

International Caps	2

Matches

Year	Opponent	Result	Score	G
1946	Portugal	lost	1-3	
1946	Spain	won	1-0	

Like a number of Irish soccer stars, Jackie Vernon learnt his football in the Gaelic code. Following a series of impressive displays for Dundela, he rejected the advances of Liverpool and opted to play for local Irish League side, Belfast Celtic.

During the war years, Jackie Vernon won every honour possible with the legendary Belfast side. In 1940 he was a member of the side, which for the fifth time won the Irish League and added the City and Gold Cups to their title success. Celtic were also regional League Champions in 1941 and 1942 and won the Irish Cup in 1941, 1943 and 1944.

He made two appearances for the Republic of Ireland as a Belfast Celtic player on an Iberian tour in 1946. But probably his greatest achievement on the international scene was his inclusion in the Great Britain side which played the Rest of Europe in a Victory International at Hampden Park in 1947.

In February 1947, Jackie Vernon joined West Bromwich Albion for a club record fee of £10,000 – but the winter was so bad, he had to wait five weeks before making his debut! After taking a little while to settle in to the faster pace of English football, Vernon was acknowledged as one of the finest centre-backs in the country. In six seasons at the Hawthorns, he made 190 League appearances and in 1948-49 helped Albion win promotion to Division One as runners-up to Fulham.

Vernon left the Albion in 1952 – the Midlands club continued to pay him a salary for a further two years. He continued to play part-time football with Crusaders of Belfast, whilst running his family's butchery business in the city.

Dave Walsh

Position	Centre-forward
Born	David John Walsh, Waterford, 28 April 1923
Clubs	

Shelbourne; Limerick; Linfield; West Bromwich Albion; Aston Villa; Walsall; Worcester City

International Caps	20
International Goals	5

Matches

Year	Opponent	Result	Score	G
1946	Portugal	lost	1-3	
1946	Spain	won	1-0	
1947	Spain	won	3-2	2
1947	Portugal	lost	0-2	
1948	Portugal	lost	0-2	
1948	Spain	lost	1-2	
1949	Switzerland	lost	0-1	
1949	Portugal	won	1-0	
1949	Sweden	lost	1-3	1
1949	Spain	lost	1-4	
1950	England	won	2-0	
1950	Finland	drew	1-1	
1950	Sweden	lost	1-3	
1951	Norway	drew	2-2	1
1951	Argentina	lost	0-1	
1951	Norway	won	3-2	
1952	Spain	lost	0-6	
1953	Austria	won	4-0	
1954	France	lost	3-5	1
1954	France	lost	0-1	

A most unorthodox opportunist, Dave Walsh first attracted attention as a prolific scorer during his junior career in his native Waterford. After serving both Shelbourne and Limerick in the League of Ireland, netting 13 goals as the latter club's top scorer in 1942-43, he moved north to play for Belfast club Linfield in the Irish League.

In three years at Windsor Park, Walsh collected Irish Cup winners and runners-up medals before in 1945-46 scoring 60 goals as Linfield won the Irish League Championship.

In the summer of 1946, Dave Walsh became West Bromwich Albion's first signing after the Second World War when they paid £3,500 for his services. He started his Football League career in spectacular style, scoring in his first six games for the Albion – a new club record. In all, Walsh scored 94 League goals in 165 games for the Baggies and in 1948-49 helped the club win promotion to the First Division.

In the immediate post-war era, the sturdy, powerful centre-forward was Northern Ireland's first-choice No.9 and scored five goals in nine starts. He scored as many goals for the Republic of Ireland, albeit over a longer period of time, in 20 games from June 1946 to November 1953.

After selling their star striker Trevor Ford to Sunderland, Albion's neighbours Aston Villa earmarked Dave Walsh as the Welsh international's replacement and in December 1950, they got their man for a fee of £25,000. He spent four-and-a-half seasons at Villa Park, scoring 37 goals in 108 First Division games.

He later ended his League career in the Midlands with a brief spell at Walsall. In the summer of 1956, Walsh joined non-League Worcester City but within a year, a serious knee injury had forced his retirement. On leaving the game, he ran a sports shop and newsagents at Droitwich before retiring to Torquay in 1984.

Paddy Coad

Position	Wing-half/Forward
Born	Patrick Coad, Waterford, 1920
Clubs	

Corinthians; Waterford; Glenavon; Shamrock Rovers; Waterford

International Caps	11
International Goals	3

Matches

Year	Opponent	Result	Score	G
1947	England	lost	0-1	
1947	Spain	won	3-2	1
1947	Portugal	lost	0-2	
1948	Portugal	lost	0-2	
1948	Spain	lost	1-2	
1949	Switzerland	lost	0-1	
1949	Belgium	lost	0-2	
1949	Portugal	won	1-0	1
1949	Sweden	lost	1-3	
1951	Norway	won	3-2	1
1952	Spain	lost	0-6	

Midfield general Paddy Coad joined Waterford from Corinthians in 1937, before a year later moving north to play for Glenavon. He had only been there a matter of weeks when war broke out and he returned to Waterford.

In 1941 in a dispute over bonuses Coad – along with his Waterford team-mates – refused to play in a 'Test Match' against Cork United which would have decided the winner of that year's League Championship.

In January 1943, Coad signed for Shamrock Rovers – he was to remain with the Hoops until 1959. In fact, he became such an influential player at Milltown that the team in the 1950s earned the nickname 'Coad's

Colts'. With Rovers, Coad played in seven FAI Cup Finals, being on the winning side in 1944, 1945, 1948 and 1956. Coad, who was club captain in the 1950s, led the club to three League of Ireland Championships in 1953-54, 1956-57 and 1958-59 after which he returned to his home-town club Waterford. He had scored 126 League of Ireland goals and netted 41 goals in the FAI Cup competition – testimony to his ability on the field.

In September 1946, Coad cut short his honeymoon to make his international debut for the Republic of Ireland against England in Dublin. Over the next five years, Coad won a further ten caps for his country. His three goals against Spain (won 3-2) in March 1947, Portugal (won 1-0) in May 1949 and Norway (won 3-2) in May 1951 meant that every time he found the net, the Republic won!

In 1983, Paddy Coad was awarded the PFA of Ireland Merit Award for his services to the game in the Republic of Ireland.

Billy Hayes

Position	Full-back
Born	William Edward Hayes, Cork, 7 November 1915
Died	22 April 1987
Clubs	

Sheffield St Vincents; Huddersfield Town; Burnley

International Caps	2

Matches

Year	Opponent	Result	Score	G
1947	England	lost	0-1	
1947	Portugal	lost	0-2	

Although he was born in Cork, full-back Billy Hayes was brought up in Sheffield. After representative honours for Sheffield

and England schoolboys, he was signed as an amateur by Huddersfield Town in 1932 from junior club, Sheffield St Vincents.

He turned professional in April 1933 and made his First Division debut against Derby County in August 1934, although it wasn't until 1937 that he established himself as the Terriers' first-choice right-back.

He quickly made a big impression and was selected by Northern Ireland for the match against England in Belfast in October 1937. Hayes missed only one of Huddersfield's games in 1938-39 and was in the Town side beaten at Highbury in the FA Cup semi-final of March 1939 by Portsmouth, the eventual trophy winners in that last season before war was declared. Hayes continued after the war from where he had left off, and made his second full international debut against England, this time for the Republic of Ireland in Dublin in September 1946 – a narrow 1-0 win for the English on this occasion.

After four more seasons in Huddersfield's side, in which he took his total of League and Cup appearances to 195, Billy Hayes was suddenly transferred to Burnley in 1950. He was already well acquainted with the Burnley players at the time, as for many years he had lived in Accrington where he owned a garage and had trained regularly at Turf Moor. In the twilight of his career, he made just a dozen appearances for the Clarets before being released in May 1952.

Billy Hayes, who was a top-class golfer, winning the Professional Footballers Golf Championship in 1949, devoted himself to his business interests in Accrington for many years. He died in hospital in the town in 1987 following a fall.

Michael O'Flanagan

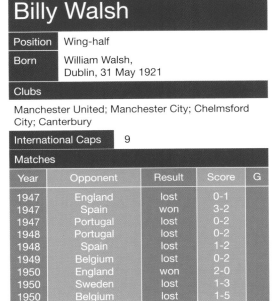

Position	Winger
Born	Michael O'Flanagan, Dublin, 29 September 1922

Clubs

Bohemians; Belfast Celtic

International Caps	1

Matches

Year	Opponent	Result	Score	G
1947	England	lost	0-1	

After spells playing junior football with Kenilworth Home Farm and St Patrick's CYMS, Michael O'Flanagan signed for Bohemians in 1939, making his way into the first team a couple of years later.

A first team regular with the famous amateur club, he won many trophies with the Bohs – perhaps the club's best achievement being the winning of the Inter-City Cup in 1945. The cup was competed for on a home-and-away basis between clubs from the North and South. But the northern teams were strengthened by some of the best English professionals who were stationed in the North during the Second World War. Even so, in 1945 Bohemians defeated the famous Belfast Celtic 3-2 on aggregate to lift the trophy.

In September 1946, he was called up to replace the injured Dave Walsh for the match against England in Dublin – it proved to be his only appearance for the national side in a match England won 1-0, courtesy of a Tom Finney goal.

In 1947 he joined Lansdowne Rugby Club, playing in the same side as his brother Dr Kevin O'Flanagan. Two years later he won a cap against Scotland in what was Ireland's Triple Crown-winning season!

One of his best game in a Bohemians shirt came in May 1948 when a Bohs select XI beat Manchester United 2-1.

In 1949, O'Flanagan was invited by Belfast Celtic to replace the injured Jimmy Jones on Celtic's famous North American tour of that year. He played in all ten of Celtic's games on the tour, including the famous 2-0 defeat of Scotland.

Billy Walsh

Position	Wing-half
Born	William Walsh, Dublin, 31 May 1921

Clubs

Manchester United; Manchester City; Chelmsford City; Canterbury

International Caps	9

Matches

Year	Opponent	Result	Score	G
1947	England	lost	0-1	
1947	Spain	won	3-2	
1947	Portugal	lost	0-2	
1948	Portugal	lost	0-2	
1948	Spain	lost	1-2	
1949	Belgium	lost	0-2	
1950	England	won	2-0	
1950	Sweden	lost	1-3	
1950	Belgium	lost	1-5	

Billy Walsh holds a quite unique international record in that he was honoured by three countries!

Having left Dublin at the age of seven to live in Manchester, he represented England schoolboys on three occasions, won five Northern Ireland caps in successive internationals between October 1947 and November 1948 and won nine Republic of Ireland caps in the immediate post-war era.

On leaving school, he landed an office job before in 1935 joining Manchester United as an apprentice. A year later he became an apprentice at Manchester City, signing professional forms in the summer of 1938. During the Second World War he 'guested' for several clubs and towards the end of the hostilities he was turning out for City on Saturday afternoons and working down the pit for the rest of the week.

Walsh, who won a Second Division Championship medal in 1946-47, clocked up 109 League appearances for City before leaving Maine Road in April 1951 to become player-manager with Chelmsford City. Within months he had left to take up a similar position at Canterbury prior to emigrating to Australia.

Walsh, who was hugely popular with the Irish players and supporters, had his best performance in a Republic shirt in the side which defeated England 2-0 at Goodison Park in 1949 – England's first home defeat by a foreign team. 'Billy Walsh was in one of his cheekiest moods, going into tackles with real dash, coming out with the ball, dribbling through and passing with an accuracy that sent shivers through the English defence'.

John McGowan

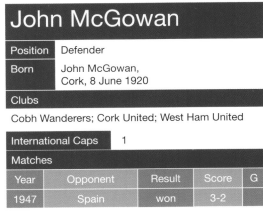

Position	Defender
Born	John McGowan, Cork, 8 June 1920

Clubs

Cobh Wanderers; Cork United; West Ham United

International Caps	1

Matches

Year	Opponent	Result	Score	G
1947	Spain	won	3-2	

Defender John McGowan was a member of Cork United's outstanding team which dominated League of Ireland football in the 1940s.

During that decade, McGowan collected honours galore – including five League Championship medals of which three were won in succession between seasons 1940–41 and 1942–43 and two back-to-back in 1944–45 and 1945–46. McGowan, who had joined Cork from Cobh Wanderers, also played in four FAI Cup Finals, emerging with winners' medals in 1941 and 1947.

Towards the end of that 1946–47 season McGowan, who had played at both right-back and centre-half for the Inter-League team, made his only full international appearance for the Republic, wearing the No.2 shirt in a 3-2 home win over Spain.

Shortly after making his international debut McGowan, along with Cork United team-mate Tommy Moroney, was transferred to West Ham United. When he arrived at Upton Park, he was bereft of boots and had to break in a new pair, which caused his feet to blister! This meant that he missed his Football League debut for the Hammers. To add insult to injury he damaged his knee and later had to have two cartilage operations. Whilst Moroney became a big hit with the London club, McGowan failed to get his career off the ground at Upton Park.

In 1952 he returned to Ireland to coach Cork Hibs for a spell before drifting out of the game.

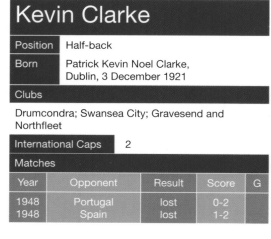

Kevin Clarke

Position	Half-back
Born	Patrick Kevin Noel Clarke, Dublin, 3 December 1921
Clubs	

Drumcondra; Swansea City; Gravesend and Northfleet

International Caps	2

Matches

Year	Opponent	Result	Score	G
1948	Portugal	lost	0-2	
1948	Spain	lost	1-2	

Hailing from the Dublin suburb of Santry, Kevin Clarke began his senior career with local club Drumcondra. A cool, stylish half-back, he played in three FAI Cup Finals with the Drums and was on the winning side on two occasions. In 1943 he played at left-back as the Drums beat Cork United. Three years later, he lined up at centre-half as Drumcondra beat Dublin rivals Shamrock Rovers 2-1. His other appearance in an FAI Cup Final came in 1948 when their opponents were again the Hoops, but this time the scoreline was reversed.

When Drumcondra won the League Championship in 1947–48, Kevin Clarke was outstanding. His consistent displays led to him representing the League of Ireland and in May 1948, winning two full international caps for the Republic of Ireland in away defeats by Portugal and Spain.

In November 1948 Clarke left Drumcondra to join Swansea City. Although the (then) Vetch Field club went on to win the 1948–49 Third Division (South) Championship, he only appeared in 10 League games.

On leaving the Swans, Clarke joined non-League Kent side Gravesend and Northfleet, with whom he spent a couple of seasons.

A steeplejack by trade, his son Charlie played for the club in 1965-66, one of the rare occasions of father and son playing for Fleet.

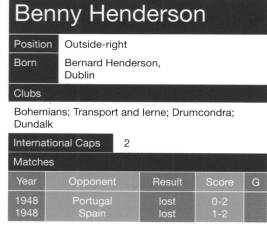

Benny Henderson

Position	Outside-right
Born	Bernard Henderson, Dublin
Clubs	

Bohemians; Transport and Ierne; Drumcondra; Dundalk

International Caps	2

Matches

Year	Opponent	Result	Score	G
1948	Portugal	lost	0-2	
1948	Spain	lost	1-2	

Reputedly the tallest winger in the League of Ireland, Benny Henderson had brief spells with St Paul's, Bohemians, Transport and Ierne before moving to Drumcondra in the summer of 1945.

Equally at home on either wing, he possessed one of the strongest shots in the League. In ten seasons with Drumcondra, Henderson won two League of Ireland Championship medals – in 1947-48 and 1948-49 – and played in four FAI Cup Finals.

Though often described as unpredictable, he was one of the greatest match-winners Drumcondra has ever known. In 1946 he scored the winner in the Drums' 2-1 FAI Cup Final victory over Shamrock Rovers. Two years later he netted the consolation goal, but missed a last-minute penalty as the Hoops reversed the 1946 scoreline. In 1954 he was a winner again as Drumcondra beat St Patrick's Athletic. Old acquaintances were renewed in 1955 as the Drums and Shamrock Rovers lined-up for the Final – Rovers winning 1-0.

In May 1948, Henderson scored twice and made two goals in the League of Ireland's 5-2 defeat of the Defence Forces – not surprisingly he was named 'Man-of-the-Match'. This display clinched his place in the Republic's squad for the Iberian tour later that month, on which he won caps against Portugal and Spain. An enigmatic player, he later ended his career with a brief spell at Dundalk.

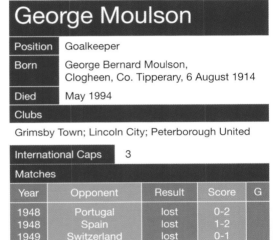

George Moulson

Position	Goalkeeper
Born	George Bernard Moulson, Clogheen, Co. Tipperary, 6 August 1914
Died	May 1994
Clubs	

Grimsby Town; Lincoln City; Peterborough United

International Caps	3

Matches				
Year	Opponent	Result	Score	G
1948	Portugal	lost	0-2	
1948	Spain	lost	1-2	
1949	Switzerland	lost	0-1	

George Moulson, whose family had moved from Tipperary to Grimsby in the 1920s, was the younger brother of Con Moulson, who himself won five caps for the Republic of Ireland in the 1930s, while on the books of Lincoln City and Notts County.

George Moulson was bought out of the Army by Grimsby Town, who desperately needed his services. He put pen to paper, signing for the Mariners in the summer of 1936. His first-team opportunities at Blundell Park were limited owing to the fine form of England international keeper George Tweedy. But when Tweedy was laid low by 'flu, the way was clear for Moulson to make his first-class debut in the ill-fated 1939 FA Cup semi-final against Wolves at Old Trafford. He had hardly touched the ball when he was involved in a collision with Wolves' forward Dickie Dorsett. Moulson suffered concussion and took no further part in the game – 10-men Grimsby Town lost 5-0.

During the Second World War, Moulson played regularly for the Mariners – 103 appearances – and made 102 'guest' appearances for Lincoln City.

It was April 1947 – more than ten years after signing for the club – that Moulson made his Football League debut. It proved to be his only league outing for the Mariners and in June 1947 he joined Lincoln City. In 1947-48 he was in outstanding form as the Imps won the Third Division (North) Championship, his displays leading to three full caps for the Republic of Ireland.

Moulson was in goal for three consecutive games between May and December 1948 and though he was never on the winning side, he gave a series of solid displays.

After one more season at Sincil Bank, he lost his place to Arthur Jepson and left to end his career at then Midland League club, Peterborough United.

Tommy Moroney

Position	Wing-half
Born	Thomas Moroney, Cork, 10 November 1923
Died	16 May 1981
Clubs	

Cork United; West Ham United; Evergreen United

International Caps	12
International Goals	1

Matches				
Year	Opponent	Result	Score	G
1948	Spain	lost	1-2	1
1949	Portugal	won	1-0	
1949	Sweden	lost	1-3	
1949	Spain	lost	1-4	
1950	Finland	won	3-0	
1950	England	won	2-0	
1950	Finland	drew	1-1	
1950	Belgium	lost	1-5	
1951	Norway	drew	2-2	
1951	Norway	won	3-2	
1952	West Germany	won	3-2	
1954	France	lost	3-5	

A member of the great Cork United side which swept all before them in the 1940s, wing-half Tommy Moroney won League of Ireland Championship medals in 1944-45 and 1945-46 and an FAI Cup winners medal in 1947, scoring one of the two goals in the defeat of Bohemians in the replayed final.

Moroney, a former amateur international who represented the League of Ireland during his Cork days, was also played rugby for Munster. There is little doubt that he would have been capped at rugby but for cancellation of internationals during the war years.

During the summer of 1947, Leeds United, West Ham United and a number of other English clubs were interested in acquiring the services of Tommy Moroney. It was the Hammers who won the day, though there was a touch of farce about the actual transfer deal! Moroney and his Cork team-mate John

McGowan arrived at Upton Park a week after the other players had begun training because of 'passage and passport delays' and came without their boots. Cork United refused to post them and they had to break in new ones!

In spite of this, Moroney did enough to impress in his trial game and claimed a first team place almost immediately. He spent his entire Football League career at Upton Park, making 148 Second Division appearances in six seasons with the club.

Whilst with the Hammers, he marked his international debut with the Republic's goal in the 2-1 defeat by Spain in Barcelona in May 1948. He won his second cap the following May and from then until October 1951 he was a regular in the Republic's defence. He played in his 11th international in the 3-2 defeat of West Germany in October 1951 but then waited two years for another call from the Irish selectors. By this time, he had returned to Ireland to play for Evergreen United when he was recalled for the World Cup qualifier with France in October 1953. The 5-3 defeat by the French, in which Tommy Moroney played most of the game at outside-right, was his last for his country.

On hanging up his boots, he managed Cork Celtic.

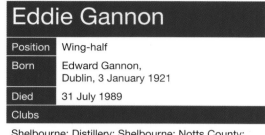

Eddie Gannon

Position	Wing-half
Born	Edward Gannon, Dublin, 3 January 1921
Died	31 July 1989
Clubs	

Shelbourne; Distillery; Shelbourne; Notts County; Sheffield Wednesday; Shelbourne

International Caps	14

Matches

Year	Opponent	Result	Score	G
1949	Switzerland	lost	0-1	
1949	Belgium	lost	0-2	
1949	Portugal	won	1-0	
1949	Sweden	lost	1-3	
1949	Spain	lost	1-4	
1950	Finland	won	3-0	
1951	Norway	drew	2-2	
1952	West Germany	lost	0-3	
1952	Austria	lost	0-6	
1954	Luxembourg	won	4-0	
1954	France	lost	0-1	
1955	Norway	won	2-1	
1955	Norway	won	3-1	
1955	West Germany	lost	1-2	

After spells with Shelbourne and Distillery, wing-half Eddie Gannon rejoined his first club where he was a League of Ireland Championship winner in 1943-44. That season, Shelbourne narrowly failed to achieve the 'double', losing the FAI Cup Final 3-2 to local rivals Shamrock Rovers.

In August 1946, Eddie Gannon was transferred to Notts County and his performances for the Meadow Lane club led to him winning the first of 14 full caps for the Republic of Ireland against Switzerland in December 1948. After three seasons with County, for whom he made 108 league appearances, he was transferred to Sheffield Wednesday, with the Owls' boss Eric Taylor paying £15,000 for his services.

There is no doubt that Eddie Gannon spent the best years of his career at Hillsborough. A wing-half of genuine quality, he scored very few goals himself but certainly created

plenty for those around him. Gannon played a major role in the club's promotion from Division Two in 1949-50 and after they had lost their top flight status the next season, in their Second Division winning season of 1951-52. When Wednesday reached the FA Cup semi-finals in 1954, only to lose 2-0 to Preston North End, Eddie Gannon was once again the major driving force. After he had appeared in 204 league games for Sheffield Wednesday, he returned in 1955 to his former club Shelbourne as player-manager.

Gannon, who won his last three caps whilst at Shelbourne, later ended his involvement with the game following a spell as manager of Dublin junior club, Bolton Athletic.

Rory Keane

Position	Full-back
Born	Thomas Roderick Keane, Limerick, 31 August 1922
Clubs	

Limerick; Swansea Town

International Caps	4

Matches

Year	Opponent	Result	Score	G
1949	Switzerland	lost	0-1	
1949	Portugal	won	1-0	
1949	Sweden	lost	1-3	
1949	Spain	lost	1-4	

A tough, traditional defender, Rory Keane played his early football for home-town team Limerick in the early 1940s, prior to joining Swansea Town in June 1947.

He was badly injured on his debut for the Welsh club in their match with Leyton Orient but made a full recovery to become an important member of the Swans' side for the next six seasons. His impressive form, during the early stages of the club's Third Division (South) Championship-winning season of 1948-49, led to him winning full international honours.

However, Keane's full international debut was for Northern Ireland in November 1948 when he partnered Johnny Carey in a 3-2 defeat by Scotland at Hampden Park. He made his Republic of Ireland debut the following month against Switzerland before having his best game at this level in a 1-0 win over Portugal in May 1949. He appeared in two more games that summer but following the defeats by Portugal and Sweden, he lost his place to Bud Aherne.

In early 1950, Rory Keane badly fractured his leg and though he returned to first team action the following season, he was never the same player. Keane appeared in 164 league games for the Swans and though he failed to score for the club, he did execute a number of goal-line clearances to prevent near-certain goals. In the FA Cup fourth round tie against the mighty Arsenal at Highbury in the 1949-50 season, he punched the ball over the bar from a Lewis header when it was almost over the line! Unfortunately the Gunners scored from the resultant penalty and went on to win 2-1.

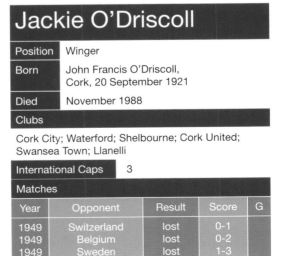

Jackie O'Driscoll

Position	Winger
Born	John Francis O'Driscoll, Cork, 20 September 1921
Died	November 1988
Clubs	

Cork City; Waterford; Shelbourne; Cork United; Swansea Town; Llanelli

International Caps	3			
Matches				
Year	Opponent	Result	Score	G
1949	Switzerland	lost	0-1	
1949	Belgium	lost	0-2	
1949	Sweden	lost	1-3	

Winger Jackie O'Driscoll spent nine very successful years in League of Ireland football before trying his luck in the Football League.

After starting out as a 17-year-old with Cork City in 1938, he joined Waterford and was a member of the Blues' side which lost the 1941 FAI Cup Final to Cork City's successor, Cork United. He then spent the following season with Shelbourne before signing for Cork United in 1942.

In five years with his home-town club, O'Driscoll won three League of Ireland Championship medals (1942-43, 1944-45 and 1945-46) and two FAI Cup winners medals in 1943 and 1947. Jackie O'Driscoll was one of three players in the Cork United cup-winning side of 1947 who secured contracts with Football League clubs just weeks after the final. John McGowan and Tommy Moroney signed for West Ham United, whilst Jackie O'Driscoll joined Swansea Town for a 'substantial four-figure fee'.

Possessing great pace and a powerful shot, O'Driscoll replaced Swansea's Welsh international winger Ernie Jones, who was sold to Tottenham Hotspur to make way for him. The same month that he put pen to paper, O'Driscoll was a member of the League of Ireland side which took on the Football League. In 1948-49, O'Driscoll's crosses provided Richards and McCrory with plenty of goal opportunities as the Swans went on to win the Third Division (South) Championship.

Not surprisingly, his performances during the course of that successful campaign led to him being honoured at full international level by both Northern Ireland and the Republic of Ireland, for whom he won his first cap in the 1-0 defeat by Switzerland in December

1948. He was also a member of the Northern Ireland team which contested the 1948-49 Home International Championship and though he played in all three games, he was never on the winning side!

Inevitably his performances at club and international level attracted the attention of the bigger clubs but just when it seemed he would move to the top flight, he badly damaged an ankle which was to end his League career. At the end of the 1951-52 season after which he had scored 26 goals in 117 league games, he left to play for Llanelli, who were then playing in the Southern League.

Brendan Carroll

Position	Centre-forward
Born	Brendan Carroll, Bray, Co.Wicklow
Clubs	

Bray Wanderers; Shelbourne; Transport

International Caps	2			
Matches				
Year	Opponent	Result	Score	G
1949	Belgium	lost	0-2	
1950	Finland	won	3-0	

Despite suffering the curse of many of his fellow professionals – he was one-footed – there were many followers of the game who in the late 1940s, regarded Brendan Carroll as potentially the best centre-forward in the League of Ireland.

Carroll started out with his local club Bray Wanderers where his prolific marksmanship soon attracted interest from a host of other clubs. In the summer of 1947, Carroll signed for Shelbourne and in his first two seasons with the club, was their leading scorer. In 1949 he was a League of Ireland representative player and in the same year helped Shels to the FAI Cup Final where they lost 3-0 to Dundalk.

Carroll, who possessed great speed from a standing start, did well on his international debut in the 2-0 defeat by Belgium in April 1949, but was replaced by a fit-again Dave Walsh for the Republic's next match against Portugal. Carroll's second run out for his country came in the 3-0 World Cup qualifying victory over Finland in September 1949. He had looked extremely dangerous, coming close to scoring himself as well as laying on chances for Fitzsimons and Desmond, when he was injured after 25 minutes and replaced by Shamrock Rovers' Paddy Daly.

Carroll later left Shelbourne to play for the 1950-51 season with Transport.

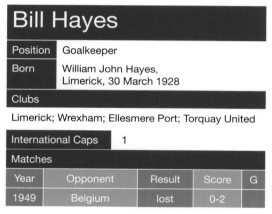

Bill Hayes

Position	Goalkeeper
Born	William John Hayes, Limerick, 30 March 1928
Clubs	

Limerick; Wrexham; Ellesmere Port; Torquay United

International Caps	1

Matches

Year	Opponent	Result	Score	G
1949	Belgium	lost	0-2	

Goalkeeper Bill Hayes played his early football for his home-town club Limerick. His displays between the posts in the first season of football after the war led to him winning Amateur International honours and representing the League of Ireland.

In April 1949, the Limerick keeper became the country's fifth post-war goalkeeper when he took over from George Moulson for the visit of Belgium. Though he had a sound

game and couldn't be faulted for the goals, Belgium ran out 2-0 winners.

The following summer, Hayes left Limerick to join Wrexham but after just 14 appearances for the Robins in the Third Division (North), he left the Racecourse Ground to play non-League football for Ellesmere Port.

Then in August 1952 he was given the chance to resurrect his Football League career by Torquay United. He didn't have the best of debuts for the Gulls as they were beaten 7-2 by Coventry City! He didn't play again until the last dozen games of that 1952-53 season, after which he established himself as the Devon club's first-choice keeper. He remained at Plainmoor for another couple of seasons but having appeared in 54 league games, he drifted into the local West Country non-League scene, playing for a number of sides.

Kit Lawlor

Position	Forward
Born	John Christopher Lawlor, Dublin, 3 December 1922
Clubs	

Shamrock Rovers; Drumcondra; Doncaster Rovers; Drumcondra; Dundalk

International Caps	3

Matches

Year	Opponent	Result	Score	G
1949	Belgium	lost	0-2	
1951	Norway	drew	2-2	
1951	Argentina	lost	0-1	

A crafty player with the tendency to slow up the game and with the ability to score from long range, Kit Lawlor followed in the footsteps of his father, who was a goal-getting centre-forward with Talbot United and Mullingar.

A former employee of O'Rourkes Bakery, Kit Lawlor had played in the Bakery League and for Bradmola. Having then joined Shamrock Rovers, he later had two successful spells with Drumcondra in between which he spent a stint in the Football League with Doncaster Rovers.

His first spell with Drumcondra lasted for four seasons from the summer of 1946 and yielded two League of Ireland Championship medals in 1947-48 and 1948-49. Lawlor, who was the club's leading scorer in both of those campaigns, also won an FAI Cup winners' medal in 1946 when Drumcondra overcame Dublin rivals Shamrock Rovers 2-1. The same teams contested the 1948 final but this time the scores were reversed.

Prior to leaving Drumcondra for Doncaster Rovers, Lawlor made his full international debut for the Republic of Ireland when he played in the 2-0 defeat by Belgium in April 1949. His other two caps – both won in friendly matches – came after he had made the switch to Doncaster.

Lawlor spent five seasons at Belle Vue during which time he scored 46 goals in 128 Second Division games.

On his return to Drumcondra, he played in the 1957 FAI Cup Final and again Shamrock Rovers provided the Drums' opposition. The Drums won 2-0 to exact revenge for their defeat of nine years earlier. Another League of Ireland Championship medal was added to his collection in 1957-58 before Kit Lawlor, whose son Mick also played international football for the Republic, moved to Dundalk where he ended his career.

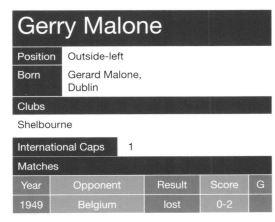

Gerry Malone

Position	Outside-left
Born	Gerard Malone, Dublin

Clubs

Shelbourne

International Caps	1

Matches

Year	Opponent	Result	Score	G
1949	Belgium	lost	0-2	

Lar O'Byrne

Position	Left-back
Born	Lar O'Byrne, Dublin

Clubs

Shamrock Rovers; St Patrick's Athletic; Transport

International Caps	1

Matches

Year	Opponent	Result	Score	G
1949	Belgium	lost	0-2	

Peter Corr

Position	Outside-right
Born	Peter Joseph Corr, Dundalk, Co. Louth, 26 June 1923

Clubs

Dundalk; Preston North End; Everton; Bangor

International Caps	4

Matches

Year	Opponent	Result	Score	G
1949	Portugal	won	1-0	
1949	Spain	lost	1-4	
1950	England	won	2-0	
1950	Sweden	lost	1-3	

There is little doubt that left-winger Gerry Malone was Shelbourne's most consistent player throughout his 12 seasons with the League of Ireland club.

Malone, who was often described as slow, but who in fact was a skilful dribbler, played for Shelbourne from 1944 to 1956. The scorer of a number of both vital and spectacular strikes, he was the Shels' leading scorer in seasons 1945-46 and 1955-56. In a dozen seasons with Shelbourne, he netted 68 league goals. During that time, he helped the Reds to win the League of Ireland Championship in 1946-47 and 1955-56. He also played in two FAI Cup Finals for Shelbourne but was never on the winning side. In 1949, Shelbourne were beaten by Dundalk and two years later they lost 1-0 to Cork Athletic in the replayed final.

Gerry Malone was most definitely a surprise selection for the Republic of Ireland side to play Belgium in Dublin in April 1949. Though the Belgians won 2-0, Malone provided Brendan Carroll (his striking partner at Shelbourne) with a number of pin-point crosses as the Irish sought to get back on terms. It proved to be Gerry Malone's only cap.

Tough-tackling left-back Lar O'Byrne was a member of the Shamrock Rovers side in the seasons immediately after the end of the Second World War. During that time he helped the Hoops to the FAI Cup Final and was rated one of the best full-backs in the League of Ireland.

His consistent displays for the Hoops led to the former Leinster League player making his full international debut for the Republic of Ireland against Belgium in Dublin in April 1949. One of four debutants, he couldn't prevent the visitors from returning to the continent with a 2-0 victory – the Republic's first defeat at the hands of the Belgians.

O'Byrne had a promising international debut and even made a couple of goal-line clearances and a last-ditch tackle late in the game. However, it proved to be the only international appearance of a player who later turned out for St Patrick's Athletic and Transport in the early 1950s.

A former Co. Louth Gaelic player, Peter Corr began his football career with League of Ireland club Dundalk, where his impressive displays on the wing led to him joining Preston North End in April 1947.

Most of his only season at Deepdale was spent as understudy to the mercurial Tom Finney but even when he was chosen for the League side, he suffered with injuries. As a result, by the time he moved on to Everton in the summer of 1948, he had managed just three appearances.

On his arrival at Goodison Park, he teamed up with fellow Irishmen Tommy Eglington, Peter Farrell and Alex Stevenson and together they formed a formidable attacking quartet, bursting with both ability and flair.

Despite his undoubted ability – he had an outstanding turn of speed which enabled him to lose his marker and provide pin-point crosses – he was no more than an occasional player in the Toffees' First Division side. He made just 24 appearances in his two seasons with the club, but won four full caps for the Republic of Ireland during this time, including being a member of the historic Irish side which defeated England 2-0 on his then home ground of Goodison Park in September 1949.

Shortly after this, Corr left Merseyside to end his playing days back in Ireland with Bangor.

Tommy Godwin

Position	Goalkeeper
Born	Thomas Fergus Godwin, Dublin, 20 August 1927
Died	8 August 1996
Clubs	

Home Farm; Shamrock Rovers; Leicester City; Bournemouth

International Caps	13

Matches

Year	Opponent	Result	Score	G
1949	Portugal	won	1-0	
1949	Sweden	lost	1-3	
1949	Spain	lost	1-4	
1950	Finland	won	3-0	
1950	England	won	2-0	
1950	Finland	drew	1-1	
1950	Sweden	lost	1-3	
1950	Belgium	lost	1-5	
1951	Norway	drew	2-2	
1956	Holland	won	4-1	
1957	England	drew	1-1	
1958	Denmark	won	2-0	
1958	Poland	drew	2-2	

Tommy Godwin began his senior career in the League of Ireland with Home Farm before joining Shamrock Rovers. A master of the high ball and no mean shot-stopper, he represented the League of Ireland during his early days with the Hoops. In the 1948 FAI Cup semi-final he broke his leg – this not only ruled him out of the final but also prevented him from winning further representative honours.

Having won his first cap for the Republic of Ireland in a 1-0 win over Portugal in May 1949, he kept his place in the side for the next 18 months until replaced by the new Shamrock Rovers' keeper Fred Kiernan.

Godwin, who by this time had played for Leicester City, was now with Bournemouth. His outstanding form for the Cherries led to him winning an international recall in 1956 and the last of his 13 caps two years later!

He was earning a living as a carpenter and keeping goal for Shamrock Rovers when he starred in the Republic's shock 2-0 win over England at Goodison Park and within days he had signed for Leicester City. During his time at Filbert Street, his place was constantly under threat from Scottish international keeper-to-be Johnny Anderson. Indeed, City's confidence in the younger keeper led to Godwin's departure to Bournemouth in June 1952. He then spent ten seasons at Dean Court, making 357 league appearances, all in the Third Division (South) and in the Third Division from 1958.

On retirement he stayed close to Dean Court and worked as a parks supervisor for Bournemouth Corporation.

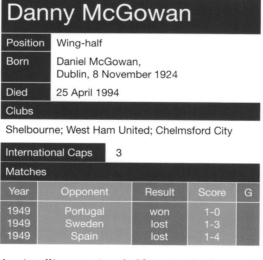

Danny McGowan

Position	Wing-half
Born	Daniel McGowan, Dublin, 8 November 1924
Died	25 April 1994
Clubs	

Shelbourne; West Ham United; Chelmsford City

International Caps	3

Matches

Year	Opponent	Result	Score	G
1949	Portugal	won	1-0	
1949	Sweden	lost	1-3	
1949	Spain	lost	1-4	

An intelligent wing-half or inside-forward, Danny McGowan made his debut for his home-town club Shelbourne in April 1946. In 1946-47, his first full season with the club, he won a League of Ireland Championship

medal, his form leading to representative honours for the League of Ireland against the Football League in May 1947.

A year later, on the advice of former West Ham United star Charlie Walker, Danny McGowan was on his way to Upton Park. After crossing St George's Channel, he improved out of all recognition – he scored on his Hammers' debut against Lincoln City – and at the end of his first season with the London club, played for the Republic of Ireland against Portugal.

Outstanding in a 1-0 win for the Irish, he kept his place in the side for the next two internationals before losing his place to Middlesbrough's Peter Desmond.

He went on to play for West Ham for six seasons, scoring eight goals in 82 league outings. A fine club man, he was given a free transfer by Hammers' boss Ted Fenton and ended his playing days in the Southern League with Chelmsford City.

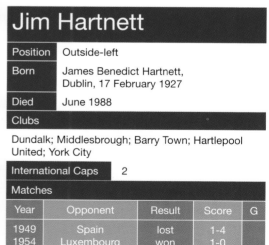

Jim Hartnett

Position	Outside-left
Born	James Benedict Hartnett, Dublin, 17 February 1927
Died	June 1988
Clubs	

Dundalk; Middlesbrough; Barry Town; Hartlepool United; York City

International Caps	2

Matches

Year	Opponent	Result	Score	G
1949	Spain	lost	1-4	
1954	Luxembourg	won	1-0	

After beginning his career in the League of Ireland with Dundalk, winger Jim Hartnett's displays for the club's reserve side, soon led to him displacing Joe O'Brien in the first team.

Despite displaying delightful ball skills, there was some surprise in April 1948 when Hartnett was chosen for the League of Ireland side to face the Scottish League, as he was thought to be on the small side and lacking experience.

Two months later he became the fifth Dundalk player to leave Oriel Park and cross St George's Channel in a little over a year when he signed for First Division Middlesbrough for a four-figure fee.

Within days of putting pen to paper, he won his first full cap in the 4-1 defeat by Spain at home. Almost five years later, whilst still with Middlesbrough, he got his second and final call-up for the Republic's World Cup qualifier against Luxembourg at the Municipal Stadium in that country. The inexperienced Irish side contained six debutants – it was Hartnett who provided the cross for George Cummins to score the game's only goal.

In six seasons at Ayresome Park, Hartnett made just 48 league appearances – shortly after the Luxembourg game, he left the League game to join Welsh non-League club Barry Town. In September 1957, Hartlepool United gave him another chance at League level but he couldn't hold down a regular first-team place and moved on to York City where he ended his career.

THE 1950s

The Republic of Ireland's form in the years following the lesson painfully inflicted upon them by Sweden prior to the 1950 World Cup Finals, showed more low spots than high. Ireland looked particularly fragile away from home, where they found themselves beaten 5-1 by Belgium, 3-0 by Germany, 6-0 by Austria and 6-0 again, this time by Spain. Two of these defeats were later reversed in Dublin – with soon-to-be World Champions Germany beaten 3-2 and Austria defeated 4-0.

When FIFA convened to announce the draw for the 1954 World Cup, the Republic found themselves in the same group as France and Luxembourg. France were developing into one of Europe's more enterprising sides, having drawn 2-2 with England at Wembley and beaten World Champions West Germany 3-1. They had also got off to a flying start in the World Cup with a 6-1 defeat of Luxembourg away from home.

The 1954 World Cup campaign would see a new Republic of Ireland team, one without the services of that magnificent captain Johnny Carey. He was by now the Republic's team coach, some might even have said manager, except that the selectors continued to pull the strings. The new skipper was Everton's Peter Farrell. He was one of seven players – the others being Tommy Eglington, Arthur Fitzsimons, Con Martin, Tommy Moroney, Reg Ryan and Davy Walsh – who were embarking on their second World Cup quest.

Ireland's first match in the World Cup against the French brought a feast of football. The then largest crowd to cram into Dalymount Park (45,000) saw Ireland go down 5-3 to a side that they were accustomed to beating. The fact of the matter was that their opponents rose to the big occasions when the Republic could not!

Despite beating Luxembourg, home and away, the Republic lost 1-0 in the return against the French at Parc des Princes, Paris and so failed to reach the finals.

It was only in 1954 that FIFA finally bowed to the reality of the Republic's existence – a good five years after Dublin's proclamation of a republic, the world's governing body of the sport agreed to refer to its footballers as representing 'The Republic of Ireland'. The new designation was employed for the first time in the home match against Norway in November 1954, a match the Republic won 2-1.

Between the 1954 and 1958 World Cup qualifying matches, the Republic played just seven games, yet strung together a series of results to suggest that they could possibly win through to the finals. They beat Norway twice, Holland twice and in a heroic display in Hamburg, went down narrowly 2-1 to the World Cup holders Germany. The Republic's other defeat prior to the 1958 qualifiers was a 4-1 home defeat to Yugoslavia – the first time Ireland had entertained a team from a communist country. In fact, interventions from church and state came close to the game being cancelled. The draw for the qualifiers saw the Republic grouped with England and Denmark – the whole of the Republic looked forward to two tussles with their mighty neighbours – and who knows, the Republic had won at Goodison the last time the two countries met!

Having beaten Denmark 2-1, the Republic travelled to Wembley for their first game on the hallowed turf – this followed one of the country's greatest wins when they beat World Champions Germany 3-0. Sadly, there was to be no repeat performance as the Republic of Ireland, who were 4-0 down at half-time, were beaten 5-1. Manchester United's Tommy Taylor netted a hat-trick to add to his treble in the previous group match against Denmark. Just 11 days later, the Republic faced England at Dalymount Park – if Ireland could win at home, then beat the Danes away, they would force England into a play-off.

Dalymount Park's previous record attendance had been set against France in the 1954 World Cup qualifiers but for the return against England, the ground was bursting at the seams with 47,600 crammed inside. The Republic got the start they wanted when Alf Ringstead netted after only three minutes and though England had chances to draw level, the Irish still led 1-0 as the game entered its final minute. Tom Finney's cross was met by Atyeo, who buried the ball into the net. The whole of Dalymount went silent – in fact, one Irish newspaper went as far as to insist that the silence could be heard in O'Connell Street!

Paddy Daly

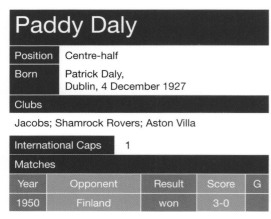

Position	Centre-half
Born	Patrick Daly, Dublin, 4 December 1927

Clubs

Jacobs; Shamrock Rovers; Aston Villa

International Caps	1

Matches

Year	Opponent	Result	Score	G
1950	Finland	won	3-0	

At the peak of his career, Paddy Daly was regarded as the best centre-half in the League of Ireland.

He had joined Shamrock Rovers from Jacobs in early 1949. Strong in the air and solid on the ground, his displays won him selection for the League of Ireland representative side. He won his only full international cap for the Republic of Ireland when he replaced the injured Brendan Carroll of Shelbourne after just 25 minutes in the 3-0 defeat of Finland in a World Cup qualifier in September 1949. Daly's appearance on the field of play at Dalymount Park that day was shrouded in controversy, however. By bringing off the bench a substitute, the FAI had unknowingly infringed the rules of the World Cup tournament, which at the time prohibited players being replaced.

Two months later, Daly was a member of the Shamrock Rovers side which played Aston Villa at Villa Park in a friendly. After impressing that day, he became the subject of many transfer enquiries from leading English clubs. As it turned out, he actually ended up at Villa Park as the Villans secured the signature of Daly and his Shamrock Rovers team-mate Ossie Higgins for a total cost of £15,000.

Though he spent a good number of years at Villa Park, he only made three Football League appearances before dropping out of first-class football.

Peter Desmond

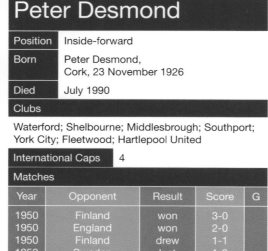

Position	Inside-forward
Born	Peter Desmond, Cork, 23 November 1926
Died	July 1990

Clubs

Waterford; Shelbourne; Middlesbrough; Southport; York City; Fleetwood; Hartlepool United

International Caps	4

Matches

Year	Opponent	Result	Score	G
1950	Finland	won	3-0	
1950	England	won	2-0	
1950	Finland	drew	1-1	
1950	Sweden	lost	1-3	

When inside-forward Peter Desmond began his League of Ireland career with Waterford in 1947-48, he was an Irish soldier. A tremendous worker who possessed a very powerful shot, he spent the next season with Shelbourne and was a member of the Shels side beaten 3-0 by Dundalk in the 1949 FAI Cup Final.

Within weeks of that final Desmond, along with his Shels team-mate Arthur Fitzsimons, had crossed the water to join First Division Middlesbrough.

A former League of Ireland representative player, he won four full caps for the Republic of Ireland in consecutive internationals between September and November 1949. His run in the international side included the Republic's 2-0 win over England at Goodison Park in September 1949, when the Irish became the first non-British team to defeat the English at home.

It was shortly after this game that Desmond finally made Middlesbrough's First Division side. Possessing great pace, it was surprising that he only made two league appearances for Boro before being transferred to Southport in August 1950.

He made a dozen appearances for the Sandgrounders, finding the net on two occasions before being allowed to join York City. Most of his time at Bootham Crescent was spent in the reserve side. Playing in the Midland League, Desmond regularly found the net. Following a spell at non-League Fleetwood Town, he returned to League action, albeit for one game with Hartlepool United.

Arthur Fitzsimons

Position	Inside-forward
Born	Arthur Gerard Fitzsimons, Dublin, 16 December 1929

Clubs

Shelbourne; Middlesbrough; Lincoln City; Mansfield Town

International Caps	26
International Goals	7

Matches

Year	Opponent	Result	Score	G
1950	Finland	won	3-0	
1950	Belgium	lost	1-5	
1952	West Germany	won	3-2	1
1952	West Germany	lost	0-3	
1952	Austria	lost	0-6	
1952	Spain	lost	0-6	
1953	France	drew	1-1	
1953	Austria	won	4-0	
1954	France	lost	3-5	
1954	Luxembourg	won	4-0	1
1954	France	lost	0-1	
1955	Holland	won	1-0	
1955	Norway	won	3-1	1
1955	West Germany	lost	1-2	
1956	Yugoslavia	lost	1-4	1
1956	Spain	drew	2-2	1
1956	Holland	won	4-1	2
1957	Denmark	won	2-1	
1957	West Germany	won	3-0	

Year	Opponent	Result	Score	G
Matches Continued				
1957	England	lost	1-5	
1957	England	drew	1-1	
1958	Denmark	won	2-0	
1958	Poland	drew	2-2	
1958	Austria	lost	1-3	
1959	Poland	drew	2-2	
1959	Czechoslovakia	lost	0-4	

A product of the great football nursery at Johnville, for whom he played at centre-forward, Arthur Fitzsimons was honoured by the Irish minors as an outside-right. He switched to inside-forward when he joined Shelbourne in 1946. His consistency led to him winning representative honours for the League of Ireland. Just weeks after playing for the Shelbourne side beaten 3-0 by Dundalk in the 1949 FAI Cup Final, he was transferred to First Division Middlesbrough with Peter Desmond in a joint deal worth £18,000.

Despite not being given his first team debut by Boro manager David Jack, Fitzsimons made the first of 26 appearances for the Republic of Ireland in a 3-0 defeat of Finland in September 1949. During the course of his international career he found the net seven times, including two goals in the Republic's 4-1 win over Holland in May 1956.

Skilful and pacy, Fitzsimons often over-elaborated with the ball and on many occasions when playing for Middlesbrough would blast his shot over the bar. This caused his Boro team-mate Brian Clough to bellow: 'You make the bloody goals and I'll score them'. Nevertheless, the lightly-built forward scored 51 goals in 231 League and Cup games, with a best of 14 in 1955-56.

On leaving Boro in March 1959 he had a brief spell with Lincoln City where he made the last of his international appearances. He then transferred to his final League club, Mansfield Town. Although he went

on to score 23 goals in 62 League games, he couldn't prevent the Stags from being relegated to the Fourth Division in his first season at Field Mill.

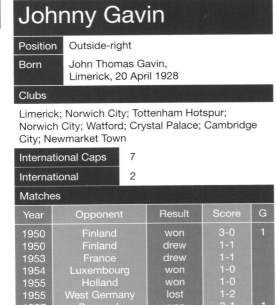

Johnny Gavin

Position	Outside-right
Born	John Thomas Gavin, Limerick, 20 April 1928
Clubs	Limerick; Norwich City; Tottenham Hotspur; Norwich City; Watford; Crystal Palace; Cambridge City; Newmarket Town
International Caps	7
International	2

Matches				
Year	Opponent	Result	Score	G
1950	Finland	won	3-0	1
1950	Finland	drew	1-1	
1953	France	drew	1-1	
1954	Luxembourg	won	1-0	
1955	Holland	won	1-0	
1955	West Germany	lost	1-2	
1957	Denmark	won	2-1	1

A diminutive winger, Johnny Gavin joined Norwich City of the Third Division (South) from his home-town League of Ireland club Limerick in August 1948 for a fee of £1,500.

After a difficult first season in which he won the first of seven caps for the Republic of Ireland, scoring in a 3-0 defeat of Finland, Gavin settled down well to life at Carrow Road. In 1950-51, Gavin was ever-present and the Canaries' leading scorer with 17 goals as the East Anglian club finished runners-up to Nottingham Forest. The following season he scored 19 goals including hat-tricks in the wins over Bristol City, Torquay United and Gillingham. In 1952-53 he was Norwich's joint-top scorer with 20 goals, and netted his fourth hat-trick for the Canaries against Reading.

By the time of his transfer to Tottenham Hotspur in October 1954, Gavin had already won four caps for the Republic of Ireland. He soon became the first Spurs player to represent the Republic, adding two more caps to his collection.

Gavin became a great crowd favourite at White Hart Lane with his speed, strength and positional sense and soon began to find the back of the net. However, when Spurs manager Jimmy Anderson sought to sign the Norwich defender Maurice Norman to bolster a leaky defence, the Canaries would only do business if Gavin was part of the deal.

Returning to Carrow Road in November 1955, Gavin went on to score 132 League and Cup goals including four in a 7-2 win over Southend United, win one more cap and represent the Third Division (South) against the Third Division (North).

In July 1958 he joined Norwich's Third Division rivals Watford. He later finished his senior career at Crystal Palace before playing for Cambridge City and Newmarket, where he was player-coach. Later in life, he was a publican for several years and also a painter and decorator.

Tommy O'Connor

Position	Winger
Born	Thomas O'Connor, Dublin

Clubs
Shamrock Rovers

International Caps	4

Matches

Year	Opponent	Result	Score	G
1950	Finland	won	3-0	
1950	England	won	2-0	
1950	Finland	drew	1-1	
1950	Sweden	lost	1-3	

Speedy winger Tommy O'Connor first attracted attention during the early part of the 1948-49 season when playing for Shamrock Rovers. Unfortunately an injury just before Christmas that season kept him out of the game for several months. There is little doubt that this caused him to lose a certain amount of confidence in his own play. When he returned to first-team action, he not only failed to recapture his earlier form but also had great difficulty in holding down a regular place.

Even so, he was selected for the Republic of Ireland side to face Finland in September 1949. He turned out to be the surprise packet in the 3-0 win over the Finns in this World Cup qualifier, and not surprisingly he retained his place in the national side for the next game against England.

It was a wise move by the Irish selectors to prefer him over both Tommy Eglington and Jackie O'Driscoll, for O'Connor went on to provide the crosses which led to both goals in the Republic's 2-0 win.

O'Connor, who also won representative honours for the League of Ireland, won two further caps against Finland and Sweden later that year.

On leaving Shamrock Rovers, Tommy O'Connor played his football in the Leinster Senior League.

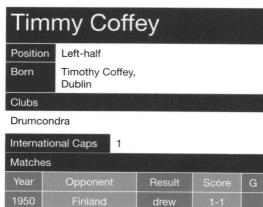

Timmy Coffey

Position	Left-half
Born	Timothy Coffey, Dublin

Clubs
Drumcondra

International Caps	1

Matches

Year	Opponent	Result	Score	G
1950	Finland	drew	1-1	

Predominantly left-footed, Timmy Coffey's best years were spent in the League of Ireland with Drumcondra in the late 1940s and early 1950s.

After winning a League of Ireland Championship medal with the Drums in 1948-49, his form during the early part of the following season was such that it saw him selected for the Republic of Ireland against Finland in Helsinki in a World Cup qualifying match in October 1949.

Coffey only came into the reckoning because of an injury to Manchester City's Willie Walsh. Unfortunately, Coffey was played out of position at right-half. Though he put in a solid display, even supplying the pass from which Peter Farrell scored the Republic's goal in a 1-1 draw, it proved to be his only appearance for the national side.

He was back in his normal position of left-half the following month as the League of Ireland took on their Scottish counterparts. He continued to be an important member of the Drumcondra side and towards the end of his career in 1954, he won an FAI Cup

winners' medal, courtesy of a St Patrick's Athletic own-goal — the only goal of the game!

Reg Ryan

Position	Inside-forward
Born	Reginald Alphonso Ryan, Dublin, 30 October 1925
Died	13 February 1997

Clubs
Nuneaton Borough; Coventry City; West Bromwich Albion; Derby County; Coventry City

International Caps	16
International Goals	3

Matches

Year	Opponent	Result	Score	G
1950	Sweden	lost	1-3	
1950	Belgium	lost	1-5	
1951	Norway	drew	2-2	
1951	Argentina	lost	0-1	
1951	Norway	won	3-2	
1952	West Germany	won	3-2	
1952	West Germany	lost	0-3	
1952	Austria	lost	0-6	
1952	Spain	lost	0-6	
1953	France	drew	1-1	
1953	Austria	won	4-0	
1954	France	lost	3-5	1
1954	Luxembourg	won	4-0	1
1954	France	lost	0-1	
1955	Norway	won	2-1	1
1956	Spain	drew	2-2	

Having played Gaelic football for his school, Reg Ryan left Dublin for Coventry at the age of eight. He began his football career with non-League Nuneaton Borough. In March 1943 while still retaining his amateur status, he joined Coventry City — two years later, he was snapped up by West Bromwich Albion.

In 1948-49 he helped Albion regain the First Division status they had lost before the war. Early the following season he would have won his first cap for the Republic of Ireland against Finland in Helsinki, but the Albion management refused to release him.

He didn't have long to wait however, for the following month (November 1949) he replaced the injured Tommy Moroney in the side to face Sweden. At international level Reg Ryan, who played once for Northern Ireland before southern players were barred from the Home International Championship, appeared 16 times for the Republic of Ireland. One of his three goals for the national side was a penalty against Luxembourg in October 1953 – the Republic's 100th goal in international competition.

Back at the Hawthorns, Ryan helped Albion finish runners-up in the League Championship, four points behind Wolverhampton Wanderers in 1953-54. He won an FA Cup winners' medal after a 3-2 defeat of Preston North End, when the inside-forward was the game's outstanding player.

In the summer of 1955 Ryan joined Derby County for a fee of £3,000. His first job was to instill some spirit back into a Derby side that had sunk to rock bottom. He soon improved team morale and was the link between County manager Harry Storer and the players. In his first year at the Baseball Ground he played for the Third Division (North) team against the Third Division (South) whilst in 1956-57 he captained the Rams to promotion as champions of the Third Division (North).

In September 1958 he moved to Coventry City and helped the Sky Blues win promotion in his first season. In November 1960 he hung up his boots and took up a post organising Coventry's pools. He took up a similar position with West Bromwich Albion a year later before being appointed the club's chief scout in 1962, a position he held for 14 years.

Mattie Clarke

Position	Full-back
Born	Matthew Clarke, Dublin

Clubs

Shamrock Rovers; Dundalk

International Caps	1

Matches

Year	Opponent	Result	Score	G
1950	Belgium	lost	1-5	

An employee of the Guinness Brewery, full-back Mattie Clarke is remembered as one of the League of Ireland's outstanding defenders of the 1940s.

When he joined Shamrock Rovers in the summer of 1938, Clarke was a centre-forward. In one of his early games for the club, he netted a netted a quickfire hat-trick!

He was to spend 12 seasons with Shamrock Rovers, the first two in the club's reserve side before winning a regular place in the League team. Able to play in either full-back berth, Clarke was a resolute and most consistent operator who always displayed tremendous enthusiasm. He won a League of Ireland Championship medal with Rovers in 1938-39, and played in five FAI Cup Finals in 1940, 1944, 1945, 1946 and 1948.

Clarke captained the Hoops in the 1946 final – the only of his five appearances when he did not collect a winners' medal!

After an almost unbroken run of representative appearances for the League of Ireland, he was called up to the full international side to face Belgium in May 1950. Replacing the injured Johnny Carey, he was part of an Irish side beaten 5-1 by the Belgians: he never represented his country again. Shortly after making his international debut, Clarke, who

was Shamrock Rovers' longest-serving player – the club made him a special presentation for his loyalty – left to join Dundalk. He played in his last FAI Cup Final in 1952 when he led Dundalk to victory after a replay – a game in which he not only played at centre-half, but according to most reports had 'the game of his life'!

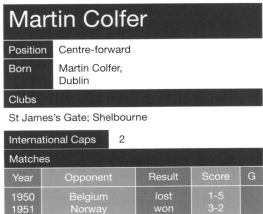

Martin Colfer

Position	Centre-forward
Born	Martin Colfer, Dublin

Clubs

St James's Gate; Shelbourne

International Caps	2

Matches

Year	Opponent	Result	Score	G
1950	Belgium	lost	1-5	
1951	Norway	won	3-2	

A former outside-right with St James' Gate, Martin Colfer joined Shelbourne midway through the 1948-49 season and was soon switched to centre-forward.

The first FAI Cup tie Colfer played in during that campaign was the final, which Shelbourne lost 3-0 to Dundalk. Colfer, who hit the woodwork and was unlucky not to get his name on the scoresheet on a couple of occasions, found himself in the starting line-up only because of an injury to Mattser Cranley.

Over the next couple of seasons, Colfer was Shelbourne's leading scorer and in May 1950 he was called up for his first full cap for the Republic of Ireland.

Over the last few weeks of the 1949-50 season, Colfer wasn't his usual model of consistency. Though when on form he could be a match-winner, he had a disappointing international debut in a 5-1 defeat by Belgium in Brussels. He won a second cap a year later in a 3-2 win over Norway but still failed to get on the scoresheet.

For Shelbourne though, Colfer continued to score on a regular basis. In 1951 he played in another losing FAI Cup Final side when Cork Athletic overcame the Dublin side by a single goal in the replay. Colfer helped the Reds win the League of Ireland Championship in 1952-53 and in seven seasons with the club he scored a total of 40 League goals.

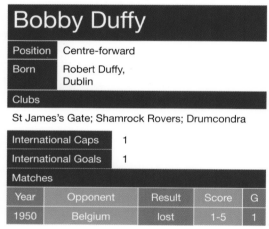

Bobby Duffy

Position	Centre-forward
Born	Robert Duffy, Dublin

Clubs				
St James's Gate; Shamrock Rovers; Drumcondra				

International Caps	1			
International Goals	1			

Matches				
Year	Opponent	Result	Score	G
1950	Belgium	lost	1-5	1

An old-fashioned type of centre-forward, Bobby Duffy played his early football for St James's Gate before entering League of Ireland football with Shamrock Rovers in 1949.

Initially he was unable to break into the Hoops' first team and it was only following the transfer of Ossie Higgins to First Division Aston Villa in November 1949 that he made his debut.

His rise was meteoric, for within four months he had played twice for the League of Ireland representative side against their Irish League counterparts. Duffy finished the 1949-50 season as Shamrock Rovers' leading scorer with 11 goals.

It was this kind of form that prompted the Republic of Ireland selectors to name Duffy ahead of West Bromwich Albion's Davy Walsh in the Irish side to face Belgium in Brussels in May 1950. Though it proved to be Bobby Duffy's only international cap, he did score the Republic's consolation goal after 72 minutes, this after Belgium had put five past Tommy Godwin.

By the start of the 1953-54 season, Duffy had left the Hoops and was playing for Drumcondra, though he spent most of that campaign playing junior football. However, injuries saw him return to the side at the end of the season for the FAI Cup Final victory over St Patrick's Athletic.

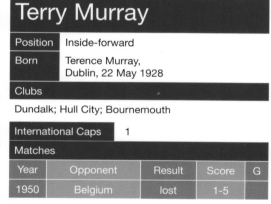

Terry Murray

Position	Inside-forward
Born	Terence Murray, Dublin, 22 May 1928

Clubs				
Dundalk; Hull City; Bournemouth				

International Caps	1			

Matches				
Year	Opponent	Result	Score	G
1950	Belgium	lost	1-5	

A former clerk with the Irish Transport Company, inside-forward Terry Murray began his first-class career with League of Ireland club Dundalk in the summer of 1948.

His impressive displays for Dundalk led to him winning representative honours for the League of Ireland on seven occasions. In May 1950, Terry Murray was one of four League of Ireland players who made their full international debut for the Republic of Ireland in the friendly against Belgium in

Brussels. The national side lost 5-1 and of those debutants only Martin Colfer played for the Republic again.

A stockily-built player, Murray could be a match-winner on his day and this attracted the attention of a number of Football League clubs. In October 1951 Hull City paid £6,000 for his services, but in almost three seasons at Boothferry Park he made only 32 appearances. Whilst with the Tigers he was a member of the FAI team that played Glasgow Celtic at Dalymount Park in April 1953.

Almost a year later, Murray left Hull to join Bournemouth as a replacement for Len Gaynor, who had departed for south coast rivals Southampton. Despite giving everything he had, running himself into the ground, Murray parted company with the Cherries after just one season at Dean Court.

Sean Fallon

Position	Defender/Centre-forward
Born	Sean Fallon, Sligo, 31 July 1922

Clubs				
Sligo Rovers; Glenavon; Glasgow Celtic				

International Caps	8			
International Goals	2			

Matches				
Year	Opponent	Result	Score	G
1951	Norway	drew	2-2	
1952	West Germany	won	3-2	
1952	West Germany	lost	0-3	
1952	Austria	lost	0-6	
1952	Spain	lost	0-6	
1953	France	drew	1-1	1
1955	Norway	won	3-1	
1955	West Germany	lost	1-2	1

Though Sean Fallon's name is synonymous with Scottish giants Glasgow Celtic, he played his early football in and around his native Sligo with Sligo St Mary's, Longford Town, McArthur's FC and Sligo Distillery. In 1947-48 he had a season playing for Sligo Rovers in the League of Ireland. He spent the following campaign in the Irish League with Glenavon before in March 1950 beginning an association with Celtic that lasted almost 30 years.

Though he scored an own goal on his debut in a 2-2 draw at Clyde, he was to become Celtic's 'iron man' of the 1950s.

After making his full international debut for the Republic of Ireland against Norway in November 1950, he went on to win eight caps, five at full-back and three in the No.9 shirt. As a centre-forward, he went against the French 'like a battering ram' at Dalymount in November 1952 and scored after 20 minutes in a 1-1 draw. He also found the net in his final game for his country against West Germany in November 1955.

Celtic rewarded his wholehearted endeavour with the club captaincy. His left arm was chronically susceptible to cracks and breaks and he had to surrender the skipper's role most of the time to his deputy Jock Stein. A broken collarbone against Hearts in October 1953 kept him out for much of the 1953-54 double-winning season. He went off in the 65th minute but then returned with his arm in a sling to play out the match at outside-left!

In his eight seasons as a player at Parkhead, he made 254 League and Cup appearances and won Scottish Cup winners' medals in 1951 and 1954, and Scottish League Cup winners' medals in 1957 and 1958, when Celtic beat Rangers 7-1.

A knee injury ended his career, after which he held a variety of posts at Parkhead including that of first team coach (1959-61), assistant-

manager, acting manager and chief scout. He was responsible for signing Tommy Gemmell, Lou Macari, David Hay, Danny McGrain, Kenny Dalglish and Paddy Bonner!

He left Glasgow to become assistant-manager at Dumbarton in 1978, later taking over the reins before in 1986 becoming a director at Clyde. Fiercely proud of his connections with Celtic, Sean Fallon was awarded a testimonial dinner by the Glasgow club in October 1993.

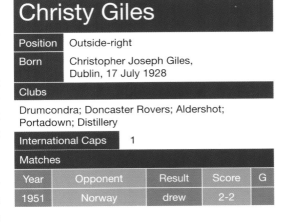

Christy Giles

Position	Outside-right
Born	Christopher Joseph Giles, Dublin, 17 July 1928
Clubs	

Drumcondra; Doncaster Rovers; Aldershot; Portadown; Distillery

International Caps			1	

Matches				
Year	Opponent	Result	Score	G
1951	Norway	drew	2-2	

Fiery winger Christy Giles began his career with League of Ireland club Drumcondra and in 1947-48, his first season with the club, he narrowly missed out on a League and Cup double. The Drums won the Championship, only to lose in the FAI Cup Final 2-1 to fellow Dublin outfit Shamrock Rovers. Drumcondra retained their Championship title the following season but then just missed out on a unique treble by finishing runners-up in 1949-50.

At the end of that campaign, Third Division (North) Champions Doncaster Rovers – whose manager then was Peter Doherty, Northern Ireland international forward – were touring the Republic and were so impressed by Giles that they signed him there and then!

In November 1950, Giles made his international debut as the Republic played out a 2-2 draw with Norway. It was to be Giles' only appearance for his country.

A year later, Giles fell foul of the Belle Vue club's authorities when he failed to show for a game against Coventry City. He had left South Yorkshire to visit his sick wife, although Rovers had refused him permission to do so. He returned to Belle Vue a month later, winning his place back in the side but at the end of that 1951-52 season, he left again, never to return.

The Yorkshire club retained his registration until in August 1953 he joined Aldershot. A week later without having appeared for the Shots, Giles returned to Ireland, playing for Irish League clubs Portadown and Distillery.

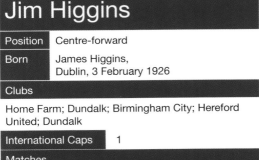

Jim Higgins

Position	Centre-forward
Born	James Higgins, Dublin, 3 February 1926
Clubs	

Home Farm; Dundalk; Birmingham City; Hereford United; Dundalk

International Caps			1	

Matches				
Year	Opponent	Result	Score	G
1951	Argentina	lost	0-1	

A big bustling centre-forward, Jim Higgins started out as a junior with Home Farm in his native Dublin. Such was his reputation as a prolific goalscorer, that he was often called upon to play on both Saturday and Sunday for the club's 'A' and 'B' sides!

In the summer of 1947, Jim Higgins joined Dundalk and though in his first season he wasn't a regular, when he did play, he usually scored. In 1948-49 he was given more of a chance and set the League of Ireland alight with his clever play and his ability to score goals out of nothing.

In November 1949, Higgins along with Dundalk team-mate Eddie O'Hara joined Birmingham City and was immediately drafted into the Blues' First Division side. Unfortunately for the St Andrew's club, his arrival came too late to prevent their relegation to Division Two at the end of that 1949-50 season. Though he scored 12 goals in 50 league games for Birmingham, he is best remembered by older fans for his 45-second goal against Manchester United in February 1951, which took the Blues into the semi-finals of the FA Cup.

Whilst with Birmingham, Jim Higgins won his only cap for the Republic of Ireland, in the 1-0 defeat by Argentina in Dublin in May 1951. In July 1953 he opted for a move to non-League Hereford United, but a year later returned to Ireland to end his career with Dundalk.

At just 5ft 8in, Fred Kiernan was one of the smallest goalkeepers ever to play in the Football League, let alone international football. Despite his lack of inches, Kiernan was a solid and dependable keeper who often produced spectacular saves.

He began his career with Shelbourne, with whom he won a League of Ireland Championship medal and FAI Cup runners-up medal in 1944. He later had spells with Dundalk and Shamrock Rovers. Whilst with the Hoops he won the first of five caps for the Republic of Ireland in the 1-0 defeat by Argentina in May 1951. Kiernan kept his place in the national side for the next four games, which included 3-2 wins over both Norway and West Germany. His fifth and final appearance for his country came a year after his debut. The Irish were beaten 6-0 by Austria in Vienna and Fred Kiernan was replaced by Everton's Jimmy O'Neill.

In October 1951, Kiernan left Shamrock Rovers to join Third Division (South) side Southampton and spent the next five seasons sharing the goalkeeping duties with John Christie, who had just joined the Saints from Ayr United.

Kiernan's best season at The Dell was 1954-55 when he helped Southampton finish third in Division Three (South). He went on to make 132 appearances for the Saints, before leaving the south coast club to end his playing days with non-League Yeovil Town.

Alf Ringstead

Position	Outside-left
Born	Alfred Ringstead, Dublin, 14 October 1927
Clubs	

Northwich Victoria; Sheffield United; Mansfield Town

International Caps	20
International Goals	7
Matches	

Year	Opponent	Result	Score	G
1951	Argentina	lost	0-1	
1951	Norway	won	3-2	1
1952	West Germany	won	3-2	
1952	West Germany	lost	0-3	
1952	Austria	lost	0-6	
1952	Spain	lost	0-6	
1953	Austria	won	4-0	2
1954	France	lost	0-1	
1955	Norway	won	3-1	1
1956	Yugoslavia	lost	1-4	
1956	Spain	drew	2-2	1
1956	Holland	won	4-1	1
1957	England	lost	1-5	
1957	England	drew	1-1	1
1958	Denmark	won	2-0	
1958	Poland	drew	2-2	
1958	Austria	lost	1-3	
1959	Poland	drew	2-2	
1959	Czechoslovakia	won	2-0	
1959	Czechoslovakia	lost	0-4	

Goalscoring winger Alf Ringstead joined Sheffield United from non-League Northwich Victoria in November 1950. A prolific scorer in the Cheshire League, he scored on his Blades' debut in a 2-0 defeat of Coventry City. In fact, he found the net in his first three appearances for the Yorkshire club.

Ringstead was very fast, an excellent header and could shoot hard and accurately with both feet, with the rare quality of fine anticipation.

Early in 1951-52 he netted a hat-trick against Hull City and then later in the season scored twice in a 3-1 win over Wednesday at Hillsborough. The crowd of 65,384 was a record attendance for a Sheffield derby.

Fred Kiernan

Position	Goalkeeper
Born	Frederick William Kiernan, Dublin, 7 July 1919
Died	May 1981
Clubs	

Shelbourne; Dundalk; Shamrock Rovers; Southampton; Yeovil Town

International Caps	5
Matches	

Year	Opponent	Result	Score	G
1951	Argentina	lost	0-1	
1951	Norway	won	3-2	
1952	West Germany	won	3-2	
1952	West Germany	lost	0-3	
1952	Austria	lost	0-6	

Ringstead won his first cap for the Republic of Ireland just six months after arriving at Bramall Lane. He went on to score seven goals in 20 games for the national side including two in a 4-0 win over Austria.

In 1952-53 United were crowned Second Division Champions: they owed their return to the top flight in no small part to the predatory skills and intelligent wing play of Alf Ringstead. During the 1954-5 season, Ringstead scored one of the club's fastest-ever goals with a rising 30-yard volley in the opening seconds as United went 4-0 up after only eight minutes against Newcastle United!

By the time he left Bramall Lane for Mansfield Town in the summer of 1959, Ringstead had scored 101 goals in 247 League games for the Blades. The Stags were in their first season in the new Division Three, having previously played in the old Third Division (North). Unable to rediscover his goalscoring prowess he found the net just three times in 27 outings as Mansfield were relegated to the new Division Four!

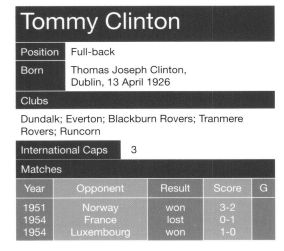

Tommy Clinton

Position	Full-back
Born	Thomas Joseph Clinton, Dublin, 13 April 1926
Clubs	

Dundalk; Everton; Blackburn Rovers; Tranmere Rovers; Runcorn

International Caps		3			
Matches					
Year	Opponent	Result	Score	G	
1951	Norway	won	3-2		
1954	France	lost	0-1		
1954	Luxembourg	won	1-0		

Tommy Clinton was working in the office at Dundalk Railway Station and playing local football when he was invited to join the town's League of Ireland side. Whilst playing for Dundalk, he was spotted by scouts from Everton, who sent their secretary Theo Kelly to the town in March 1948 to sign the player. He put pen to paper, but in the most unusual of circumstances. As Kelly and Tommy Clinton chatted on the platform at Dundalk station, Clinton's train began to move out and he actually signed the contract while hanging out of a lowered carriage window!

He was the rugged type of full-back when he arrived at Goodison Park. Central League wingers soon found that they bred them tough in the Republic of Ireland. Having made his League debut against Burnley in February 1949, he went on to make 80 League and Cup appearances over the next five seasons.

Clinton, who won three caps for the Republic of Ireland whilst with Everton, is unfortunately well-remembered for the penalty he missed in the 1953 FA Cup semi-final against Bolton Wanderers. Everton had been awarded a penalty-kick just before half-time. Clinton blasted the spot-kick wide but it didn't seem to matter because the Blues were 4-0 down at the time. However, thoughts turned to what might have been, as Everton reduced the deficit to 4-3 in the second-half. Bolton then went through to face Blackpool in the famous 'Matthews' Final'.

In April 1955 Clinton joined Blackburn Rovers, but after just half a dozen appearances for Johnny Carey's side, he returned to Merseyside by signing for Tranmere Rovers. He spent a season at Prenton Park before ending his playing days with a spell at non-League Runcorn in the Cheshire League.

Tim Cuneen

Position	Inside-right
Born	Timothy Cuneen, Limerick, 1924
Clubs	

Pike Rovers; Limerick; Coleraine; Limerick

International Caps		1			
Matches					
Year	Opponent	Result	Score	G	
1951	Norway	won	3-2		

Inside-forward Tim Cuneen, who played for Pike Rovers in the Munster League, turned out for Limerick in the League of Ireland during the course of the 1939-40 season and all before he had celebrated his 15th birthday!

A player of great talent, he left Limerick during the early stages of the 1950-51 season to play for Coleraine. Within weeks he returned to his home-town and again turned out for both Pike Rovers and Limerick. Linking well with Sean Cusack, the two Limerick players were selected to represent the League of Ireland. In the match against the Football League in April 1951, they were both outstanding.

Described as an 'artiste with the ball at his feet, he manipulated it with the wizardry of any Mannion', as he continually teased the English defenders.

Cuneen's display in this match contributed a lot to his winning full international honours for the Republic of Ireland against Norway in Oslo the following month. Unfortunately he suffered a bad hip injury in the 42nd minute and was replaced by Shamrock Rovers' Paddy Coad, who went on to net the Republic's winning goal in a five-goal thriller!

Florrie Burke

Position	Centre-half
Born	Florence Burke, Ballintemple, Co.Cork, 1921
Died	July 1995
Clubs	

Cork Athletic; Evergreen United

International Caps	1

Matches

Year	Opponent	Result	Score	G
1952	West Germany	won	3-2	

One of the towering personalities of Irish football, Florrie Burke played minor and junior hurling for Blackrock and was just 17 when he played for Blackrock against Brian Dillons in the City Division Cup Final. After an outstanding performance that day, great things were predicted for him and so it turned out to be, but not in the field of hurling!

After beginning his football career with Rockwell Minors and Blackrock Juniors, Burke joined Cork United in the summer of 1941. Playing as an inside-forward, in his first season of 1941-42 he helped United retain the title they had won the previous season and reach the FAI Cup Final.

Florrie Burke won a further five League Championship medals with Cork United (later Cork Athletic) – in 1942-43, 1944-45, 1945-46, 1949-50 and 1950-51 when as Cork's captain, he led the club to the League and FAI Cup double. Burke also played in the 1947 and 1950 Cup Finals, emerging as a winner and runner-up respectively.

Having moved to centre-half, he was a commanding figure at the heart of the Cork defence – a popular and very sporting figure. He captained the League of Ireland representative side against the Football League, Scottish League and German League sides. On his full international appearance for the Republic of Ireland, he was named 'Man-of-the-Match' in the 3-2 defeat of West Germany.

Burke later became involved in a dispute with Cork Athletic but they were most reluctant to release a player of his calibre. In a rather curious arrangement under the rules of the time, Burke was farmed out to Evergreen United, but as a retained player of Cork Athletic, he could not play for the Turner's Cross side in the League. The FAI Cup was a different matter, and in 1953 just after playing for an FAI XI against Glasgow Celtic, he faced his employers in the Cup Final, which Athletic won 2-1 in the replay.

Dessie Glynn

Position	Centre-forward
Born	Desmond Glynn, Dublin, 7 June 1928
Clubs	

Clifton United; Drumcondra; Shelbourne

International Caps	2
International Goals	1

Matches

Year	Opponent	Result	Score	G
1952	West Germany	won	3-2	1
1955	Norway	won	3-1	

Having won a host of medals with Dublin junior club Johnville, including an FAI Youth Cup winners' medal in 1946, Dessie Glynn joined Clifton United prior to signing for League of Ireland side Drumcondra in January 1949.

In his first season, he helped Drumcondra win the League Championship. In so doing, Glynn appeared in every position bar that of goalkeeper.

His form for the Drums was such that in early October 1951 he was selected for the League of Ireland XI to play the Football League. Despite a 9-1 defeat, Dessie Glynn was the only member of that team asked to make the step up to full international level. In order to make his debut against West Germany in October 1951, Glynn was forced to cancel his honeymoon! However, it was certainly worth it as he scored the winning goal in the historic 3-2 home defeat of the side which three years later would be crowned world champions. Glynn won his second cap in the 3-1 victory over Norway in Oslo in May 1955.

Glynn also played in two FAI Cup Finals with the Drums, collecting a winners' medal in 1954 and a runners-up medal the following season. Deadly in front of goal, he was the Drums' leading scorer in six of eight seasons with the club, netting 96 league goals.

In the summer of 1956, he joined Shelbourne. In his first season he was their top scorer with 12 goals. Midway through the following season he was hospitalised for nine months with tuberculosis, a condition which effectively ended his playing career, though he later coached in New York.

Shay Gibbons

Position	Centre-forward
Born	Seamus Gibbons, Dublin, 19 May 1929
Clubs	

Home Farm; Bohemians; St Patrick's Athletic; Holyhead Town; Cork Hibernians; Dundalk

International Caps	4

Matches

Year	Opponent	Result	Score	G
1952	West Germany	lost	0-3	
1954	Luxembourg	won	4-0	
1956	Yugoslavia	lost	1-4	
1956	Spain	drew	2-2	

Shay Gibbons seemed to have an outstanding career ahead of him as a Gaelic midfielder before he opted for the Association game. He had captained Parnell's in a Dublin junior final, was in the Parnell's team in the 1950 Dublin final when they were beaten by St Vincent's, and at the age of 17 sat on the substitute's bench for the Dublin senior team.

However, it was to soccer that he turned, first playing as a centre-half for Home Farm and later Bohemians' youth teams. Though he switched to centre-forward and went on to become the League of Ireland's most prolific striker in the 1950s, he left the League scene for a little while, preferring to play for Whitehall Rangers in the Athletic Union League – helping them to win the Leinster Junior Cup. After a handful of appearances for Bohemians, he left in 1950 and joined St Patrick's Athletic.

In 1950-51 they won the Leinster Senior League and the following season were elected to the League of Ireland. Surprisingly in their first season in the competition, they were crowned champions! In that 1951-52 season, Gibbons scored 26 goals in 22 games, his marksmanship leading to the first of four full caps for the Republic of Ireland, against West Germany in May 1952. Though he failed to find the net in any of his international appearances, he was again the League of Ireland's leading scorer in 1952-53, when his total of 22 goals included five against Cork Athletic – he also had a 'goal' ruled out.

Gibbons spent four more seasons with St Pat's, topping the club's scoring charts three times. In two of those campaigns – 1954-55 and 1955-56 – he was also the League of Ireland's leading scorer and St Pat's were League Champions. In that 1954-55 season, Gibbons set a new club scoring record with 28 goals.

After a brief spell with Holyhead Town, he played for League newcomers Cork Hibs, before ending his career with Dundalk, where he was again top scorer in his only season with the club.

Frank O'Farrell

Position	Wing-half
Born	Francis O'Farrell, Cork, 9 October 1927
Clubs	

Cork United; West Ham United; Preston North End; Weymouth

International Caps	9
International Goals	2

Matches

Year	Opponent	Result	Score	G
1952	Austria	lost	0-6	
1953	Austria	won	4-0	1
1954	France	lost	3-5	1
1955	Holland	won	1-0	
1955	Norway	won	3-1	
1956	Yugoslavia	lost	1-4	
1956	Holland	won	4-1	
1958	Denmark	won	2-0	
1959	Czechoslovakia	lost	0-4	

Though Frank O'Farrell will probably be remembered more for his achievement as a manager than for his prowess as a player, he did win nine caps for the Republic of Ireland.

He began his first-class playing career with West Ham United, less than six months after his predecessor in the Cork United side, Tommy Moroney had joined the Upton Park club. A competent and polished wing-half, O'Farrell was drilled in the Hammers' football philosophy in the Football Combination where he played over fifty games before making his League debut in December 1950.

He first came under the international spotlight during his time in West Ham's reserves. His performance for the Football Combination XI which played the Brussels League in 1952 impressed the Republic's selectors. In May of that year, he won his first full cap in the 6-0 defeat by Austria in Vienna. Within a year he won his second cap – the opposition was again Austria, but the outcome was completely different as the Republic exacted revenge in the form of a 4-0 victory. O'Farrell played his part in the win by scoring his first international goal. He also scored in his next outing, a 5-3 defeat by France, going on to play his last international match against Czechoslovakia in May 1959.

By then, O'Farrell had joined Preston North End, having signed for the Lilywhites in November 1956. He scored on his debut in a 3-1 win over Manchester City and went on to play in 17 games before he was on the losing side. In 1957-58 he was an important member of the North End side that finished runners-up in the First Division, five points behind champions Wolverhampton Wanderers.

On leaving Deepdale he joined Southern League Weymouth as player-manager. His League management career began with Torquay United and later Leicester City, whom he took to the FA Cup Final in 1969 and the Second Division title in 1970-71. He later managed Manchester United, followed by a spell as coach to the Iranian national side and Cardiff City before ending his managerial career back at Torquay United.

Jimmy O'Neill

Position	Goalkeeper
Born	James Anthony O'Neill, Dublin, 13 October 1931

Clubs

Bulfin United; Everton; Stoke City; Darlington; Port Vale

International Caps	17

Matches

Year	Opponent	Result	Score	G
1952	Spain	lost	0-6	
1953	France	drew	1-1	
1953	Austria	won	4-0	
1954	France	lost	3-5	
1954	Luxembourg	won	4-0	
1954	France	lost	0-1	
1955	Norway	won	2-1	
1955	Holland	won	1-0	
1955	Norway	won	3-1	
1955	West Germany	lost	1-2	
1956	Yugoslavia	lost	1-4	
1956	Spain	drew	2-2	
1957	Denmark	won	2-1	
1958	Austria	lost	1-3	
1959	Poland	drew	2-2	
1959	Czechoslovakia	won	2-0	
1959	Czechoslovakia	lost	0-4	

The son of a professional golfer, Jimmy O'Neill was spotted playing for Dublin junior club Bulfin United by scouts from Everton and taken to Goodison Park for trials. In the early 1950s Goodison Park offered an especially demanding starting point for a young goalkeeper's career.

Ted Sagar, one of the greatest names in Toffee history was approaching retirement – the hunt was on for a replacement. There was certainly no shortage of candidates with the likes of Albert Dunlop and Harry Leyland pushing for a place. After being given his senior baptism during the club's relegation season of 1950-51, O'Neill became firmly established during three years in the Second Division wilderness before playing a prominent part in the 1953-54 promotion campaign.

Despite a disastrous international debut when he had to pick the ball out of the net six times in the thrashing by Spain in Madrid in June 1952, O'Neill went on to make 17 full appearances for the Republic.

An acrobatic shot-stopper, O'Neill was a breathtaking entertainer but there were occasions when his confidence appeared to desert him. Ironically, one of his most memorable games for Everton came in a home thrashing by Arsenal in September 1958, when he was blameless for all six Gunners' goals and single-handedly saved his side from further humiliation.

After being replaced by Albert Dunlop, O'Neill was rescued from Central League football by Stoke City who paid £5,000 for his services in the summer of 1959. He was ever-present as the Stanley Matthews-inspired Potters retained their place in the top flight in 1962-63. Subsequent stints in the League's lower reaches with Darlington and Port Vale completed a very creditable career.

Sean Cusack

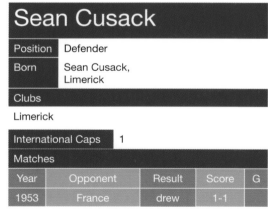

Position	Defender
Born	Sean Cusack, Limerick

Clubs

Limerick

International Caps	1

Matches

Year	Opponent	Result	Score	G
1953	France	drew	1-1	

Versatile defender Sean Cusack began his career with his home-town club Limerick in 1947. They turned out to be his one and only League club. In nine seasons with them, he scored 30 goals – moreover, he was the club's leading scorer in 1948-49, albeit with just six goals!

Able to play in a variety of positions, Cusack's form led to him joining Limerick team-mate Tim Cuneen in the League of Ireland side to face the Football League in April 1951. Starting the game at left-half, Sean Cusack thwarted the might of the right flank of the English side. When Florrie Burke's injury caused a reshuffle, the Thomondgate man moved to the left-back berth where he was again the League of Ireland XI's best player.

Most deservedly, he won full international honours in November 1952, when he lined-up alongside fellow Limerick-born players Bud Aherne and Johnny Gavin for the match against France at Dalymount Park. Despite giving a good account of himself in a 1-1 draw, Cusack never appeared for the Republic again.

He returned to Limerick, continuing to give of his best and in 1953 won his only honour at domestic level when Limerick won the Shield.

Shay Dunne

Position	Full-back
Born	Seamus Dunne, Wicklow, 13 April 1930

Clubs

Drogheda United; Wicklow Town; Shelbourne; Luton Town; Yiewsley; Dunstable Town

International Caps	15

Matches

Year	Opponent	Result	Score	G
1953	France	drew	1-1	
1953	Austria	won	4-0	
1954	France	lost	3-5	
1954	Luxembourg	won	4-0	
1956	Spain	drew	2-2	
1956	Holland	won	4-1	
1957	Denmark	won	2-1	
1957	West Germany	won	3-0	
1957	England	drew	1-1	
1958	Denmark	won	2-0	

<table>
<tr><td colspan="5">Matches Continued</td></tr>
</table>

Year	Opponent	Result	Score	G
1958	Poland	drew	2-2	
1958	Austria	lost	1-3	
1959	Poland	drew	2-2	
1960	West Germany	won	1-0	
1960	Sweden	lost	1-4	

Schooled in the art of the Republic's national code, Shay Dunne turned out at minor and junior level for the Co. Wicklow Gaelic football team before turning his attention to the Association game.

After playing as a junior at Drogheda United, Dunne joined Wicklow Town before in 1949 signing for League of Ireland side Shelbourne. After less than a season at Milltown, Dunne was transferred to Luton Town, making his Football League debut in a 6-1 home win over West Ham United on Boxing Day 1951.

For over a decade, Shay Dunne formed a formidable full-back pairing with fellow Irishman Bud Aherne. He won the first of 15 full international caps for the Republic of Ireland against France in November 1952. When the Republic beat Denmark 2-1 in a World Cup qualifier in Dublin in October 1956, Dunne captained the Irish side.

On the domestic front, he was ever-present when the Hatters won promotion to the First Division in 1954-55, for the first time in their history. Unfortunately injury forced him to miss the 1959 FA Cup Final against Nottingham Forest which Luton lost 2-1. After 323 League and Cup appearances for the Hatters, Shay Dunne left Kenilworth Road to join Southern League side Yiewsley, who were at the time managed by former Newcastle United and England legend Jackie Milburn.

In 1964 after three seasons with Yiewsley, Dunne joined Dunstable Town, helping them gain entry to the Southern League. He hung up his boots in 1968 and three years later returned to his native Wicklow where he worked as a design draughtsman.

Robin Lawler

Position	Defender
Born	Joseph Frederick Lawler, Dublin, 28 August 1925
Died	17 April 1998
Clubs	

Home Farm; Distillery; Transport ; Drumcondra; Belfast Celtic; Fulham; Yiewsley

International Caps	8

Matches				
Year	Opponent	Result	Score	G
1953	Austria	won	4-0	
1954	Luxembourg	won	4-0	
1954	France	lost	0-1	
1955	Norway	won	2-1	
1955	Holland	won	1-0	
1955	Norway	won	3-1	
1955	West Germany	lost	1-2	
1956	Yugoslavia	lost	1-4	

Christened Joseph but known as Robin, Lawler, like many of his compatriots was reared in the Gaelic code.

He played his early football for the Home Farm club in Dublin before in 1943 at the age of 18, moving north to Belfast to play for Distillery. Two seasons later he was on the move again, returning to his native Dublin to play for Transport FC and Drumcondra. In 1945 he signed for the famous Belfast Celtic, then with Celtic team-mates Johnny Campbell and Hugh Kelly, Lawler signed for Fulham in a £30,000 transfer deal in March 1949.

Having won Irish League representative honours whilst with Belfast Celtic, he spent three seasons in Fulham's reserve side before becoming the club's regular left-back midway through the 1952-53 season.

Towards the end of that campaign, Lawler won the first of eight caps for the Republic of Ireland in a 4-0 defeat of Austria. In doing so, he became the first Fulham player to achieve international honours for the Republic. He was his country's regular left-back over the next two or three years until losing his place to Noel Cantwell.

Lawler, who was noted for his long throw-ins, became one of the Cottager's most consistent players in the 1950s. He helped Fulham win promotion to the First Division in 1958-59 but then an unfortunate run of injuries cost him his place in the Cottager's top-flight side of the early 1960s. Having appeared in 299 games for Fulham, he left Craven Cottage for Southern League side Yiewsley before injuries forced his retirement after just one season.

Noel Cantwell

Position	Left-back
Born	Noel Eucharia Cantwell, Cork, 28 December 1932
Died	September 2005
Clubs	

Cork Athletic; West Ham United; Manchester United

International Caps	36
International Goals	14

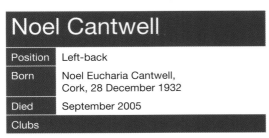

Matches				
Year	Opponent	Result	Score	G
1954	Luxembourg	won	4-0	
1956	Spain	drew	2-2	
1956	Holland	won	4-1	
1957	Denmark	won	2-1	
1957	West Germany	won	3-0	1
1957	England	lost	1-5	
1957	England	drew	1-1	
1958	Denmark	won	2-0	
1958	Poland	drew	2-2	
1958	Austria	lost	1-3	
1959	Poland	drew	2-2	2

Matches Continued				
Year	Opponent	Result	Score	G
1959	Czechoslovakia	won	2-0	1
1959	Czechoslovakia	lost	0-4	
1960	Sweden	won	3-2	
1960	Chile	won	2-0	1
1960	Sweden	lost	1-4	
1961	Norway	won	3-1	
1961	Scotland	lost	1-4	
1961	Scotland	lost	0-3	
1962	Czechoslovakia	lost	1-3	
1962	Czechoslovakia	lost	1-7	
1962	Austria	lost	2-3	1
1963	Iceland	won	4-2	2
1963	Iceland	drew	1-1	
1963	Scotland	won	1-0	1
1964	Austria	won	3-2	2
1964	Spain	lost	0-2	
1964	England	lost	1-3	
1965	Poland	won	3-2	
1965	Spain	won	1-0	
1966	Spain	lost	1-4	
1966	Spain	lost	0-1	
1966	Austria	lost	0-1	
1966	Belgium	won	3-2	2
1967	Spain	drew	0-0	
1967	Turkey	lost	1-2	1

Above: Noel Cantwell

Noel Cantwell joined West Ham United from Cork Athletic in the summer of 1952. Together with John Bond he formed one of the best full-back pairings ever seen at Upton Park.

The 1953-54 season began well for the Hammers and Cantwell but not for the Republic of Ireland. A disastrous World Cup qualifier defeat at the hands of France in October 1953 led the selection committee to make a number of changes for the next match against Luxembourg. In his first match for the national side, Cantwell played at centre-half but performed commendably in a 4-0 win. However, it turned out to be his only contribution to the 1954 qualifying campaign, and it was over two years before he won his second cap. That came in a friendly against Spain at Dalymount Park in November 1955 and following an outstanding game at left-back, he became a fixture in the national side.

He was later chosen to replace Peter Farrell as the Republic's captain. He led the side out for the first time against England in a World Cup game at Dalymount Park in May 1957. Alf Ringstead had given the Republic the lead. Cantwell stretching to clear presented a simple chance to John Atyeo, and the 1-1 draw ended the Republic's hopes of reaching the 1958 World Cup Finals.

In 1957-58 he led the Hammers to the Second Division title and the following season he was ever-present in the club's first season back in the top flight. His achievements at Upton Park were recognised in his native land when he was voted Ireland's 'Footballer of the Year' for 1958-59.

When he joined Manchester United for £29,000 in November 1960, it was a record fee for a full-back. Signed by Matt Busby as

part of his team re-building in the aftermath of the Munich tragedy, Cantwell followed in a long line of fine captains and led the side to victory in the 1963 FA Cup Final over Leicester City.

Back on the international scene, the Irish selectors decided that they needed to add a physical presence to the side's lacklustre forward line. Asked to lead the attack, Cantwell responded in typical fashion – cracking home a 40-yarder against Austria in April 1962. Having picked up his bronze statuette for reaching 25 caps, a landmark he celebrated with a goal against Scotland, he had a one-game spell as Republic of Ireland manager. Without doubt, the highlight of Cantwell's international career came on 13 October 1963 during a European Nations game against Austria. With the scores level at 2-2, the Republic were awarded a last-minute penalty. The Dalymount crowd erupted as Cantwell slotted home his second goal to earn the Republic a quarter-final tie against Spain.

Towards the end of his career, Cantwell concentrated on the coaching side and many expected he would succeed Matt Busby at Old Trafford. Instead, he surprised everyone by replacing Jimmy Hill at Coventry, leading them into Europe. In 1972 he took over as manager of Peterborough United but quit the English game in 1977 to enjoy brief spells in the NASL. He later returned to Peterborough but parted company with the club in 1989. A former PFA Chairman, he was a double international, having also played cricket for his country.

George Cummins

Position	Inside-forward
Born	George Patrick Cummins, Dublin, 12 March 1931
Clubs	

St Patrick's Athletic; Everton; Luton Town; Cambridge City; Hull City

International Caps	19
International Goals	5

Matches

Year	Opponent	Result	Score	G
1954	Luxembourg	won	4-0	
1954	Luxembourg	won	1-0	1
1955	Norway	won	2-1	
1955	Norway	won	3-1	2
1955	West Germany	lost	1-2	
1956	Yugoslavia	lost	1-4	
1956	Spain	drew	2-2	
1958	Denmark	won	2-0	1
1958	Poland	drew	2-2	1
1958	Austria	lost	1-3	
1959	Poland	drew	2-2	
1959	Czechoslovakia	won	2-0	
1959	Czechoslovakia	lost	0-4	
1960	Sweden	won	3-2	
1960	Chile	won	2-0	
1960	West Germany	won	1-0	
1960	Sweden	lost	1-4	
1961	Scotland	lost	1-4	
1961	Scotland	lost	0-3	

An inside-forward with plenty of ability, George Cummins started out with St Patrick's Athletic before signing for Everton in November 1950. After a year in the Merseyside club's reserve side, he played in the same First Division team as fellow Irishmen Tommy Clinton, Don Donovan, Peter Farrell and Jimmy O'Neill. Unable to win a regular place Cummins moved on to Luton Town in August 1953 for a fee of £12,000.

After just two games for the Hatters – the first a 4-4 draw with Oldham Athletic – Cummins was dropped, having difficulty with the cramped conditions of Kenilworth Road as compared to the wide open spaces of Goodison Park. He wasn't too long in winning back his first team place and almost immediately made his international debut for the Republic of Ireland in a 4-0 defeat of Luxembourg in a World Cup qualifier. In the return leg in Luxembourg, he scored his first goal for the national side – it was enough to take all the points on the day. He went on to score five goals in 19 internationals during his time with the Hatters.

In 1954-55 he helped Luton win promotion to the First Division for the first time in their history and in 1959 picked up an FA Cup runners-up medal as the Hatters went down 2-1 to Nottingham Forest. Noted for his high work-rate, Cummins suffered a number of knee injuries during his time at Kenilworth Road and missed virtually the whole of the 1960-61 season. Though he failed to show sufficient signs of recovery in the club's reserve team, he did appear in the League side towards the end of the campaign. However, in the match against Leeds United, he refused to switch positions and was fined by the club and ostracised by members of the first team.

Having scored 21 goals in 186 League games, he was given a free transfer and joined non-League Cambridge City – this after turning down three Football League clubs! He returned to Football League action in 1962-63, ending his playing days with a spell at Hull City.

Liam Munroe

Position	Forward
Born	Liam Munroe, Dublin
Clubs	

Shamrock Rovers

International Caps	1

Matches

Year	Opponent	Result	Score	G
1954	Luxembourg	won	4-0	

Able to play in a variety of forward positions, Liam 'Mousie' Munroe was a most determined player. His early performances for Shamrock Rovers led to him winning representative honours for the League of Ireland.

His display against the Welsh League during the early part of 1953 was outstanding – it seemed only a matter of time before he was elevated to full international status.

Even so, his call-up to the national side in preference to the experienced Sheffield United winger Alf Ringstead raised a few eyebrows. The Republic's opponents in this World Cup qualifier were Luxembourg and despite the inclusion of other debutants Noel Cantwell and George Cummins, the Irish won 4-0. Despite his lack of height, Munroe was a glutton for work and tried extremely hard against Wagner, the best defender in the Luxembourg team. Originally selected to play on the right-wing, he switched places with Shay Gibbons, a quarter-of-an-hour from time and with Munroe leading the forward line, the Republic's attack gathered new power.

Unlucky not to win further caps, he continued playing for Shamrock Rovers and in 1953-54 helped the Hoops win the League Championship.

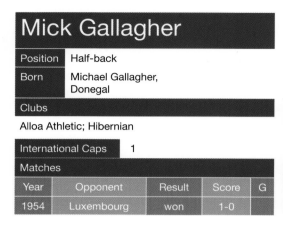

Mick Gallagher

Position	Half-back
Born	Michael Gallagher, Donegal
Clubs	

Alloa Athletic; Hibernian

International Caps	1

Matches

Year	Opponent	Result	Score	G
1954	Luxembourg	won	1-0	

One of the more unlikely-looking footballers to have played the professional game, with thick-set legs and very long shorts, Mick Gallagher played with Rosses GAA club before beginning his soccer career in Glasgow. Having impressed with Alloa Athletic, he joined Hibernian in the summer of 1951 for a fee of £5,000. At Easter Road, he formed part of the club's unsung half-back line that supported Hibs' 'Famous Five' forward line of the early 1950s.

He helped Hibs win two successive Scottish League Championships in 1951–52 and 1952–53 when he laid on numerous goalscoring opportunities for the likes of Gordon Smith, Eddie Turnbull, Lawrie Reilly, Willie Ormond and Bobby Johnstone. It could have been three League titles but for Rangers pipping them by superior goal difference of one in 1953-54.

Gallagher's success for Hibs brought him to the attention of the Republic of Ireland selectors. In March 1954 he became the first Scotland-based player to be picked for the Republic of Ireland since Joe O'Reilly and the legendary Paddy Moore some twenty years earlier.

A fine half-back, Gallagher was one of half-a-dozen debutants in an Irish side that beat Luxembourg 1-0 in a World Cup qualifier in March 1954 – unbelievably it proved to be his only cap.

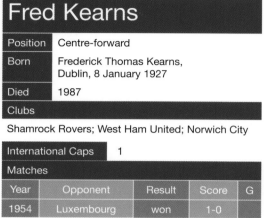

Fred Kearns

Position	Centre-forward
Born	Frederick Thomas Kearns, Dublin, 8 January 1927
Died	1987
Clubs	

Shamrock Rovers; West Ham United; Norwich City

International Caps	1

Matches

Year	Opponent	Result	Score	G
1954	Luxembourg	won	1-0	

A prolific goalscorer with Shamrock Rovers, centre-forward Fred Kearns soon attracted the attention of a number of Football League clubs, particularly West Ham United. The Hammers' chief scout Ben Ives crossed the water in the summer of 1949 to sign Shelbourne's Danny McGowan and Shamrock Rovers' Fred Kearns, having been impressed with both players on a previous visit to the Republic.

West Ham United had in the past signed a number of players from Ireland – John Carroll, Tommy Moroney and Frank O'Farrell, all of whom had adapted to the English game.

There was an added bonus: unlike their English contemporaries, the Irishmen were exempt from National Service and so were able to devote themselves entirely to the game.

A player with a good physique, Kearns impressed in his early days with the club before a series of injuries restricted his first team appearances. However, in March 1954, towards the end of his time at Upton Park, he was one of six debutants in a Republic of Ireland side that beat Luxembourg 1-0 in a World Cup qualifier.

In the close season, having scored 14 goals in 43 Second Division outings for the Hammers, he was transferred to Norwich City. Despite scoring a goal every other game for the Canaries – 11 in 24 Third Division (South) matches – he left Carrow Road after a season.

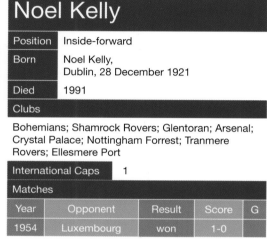

Noel Kelly

Position	Inside-forward
Born	Noel Kelly, Dublin, 28 December 1921
Died	1991
Clubs	

Bohemians; Shamrock Rovers; Glentoran; Arsenal; Crystal Palace; Nottingham Forrest; Tranmere Rovers; Ellesmere Port

International Caps	1

Matches

Year	Opponent	Result	Score	G
1954	Luxembourg	won	1-0	

A scheming inside-forward, Noel Kelly learned his trade in his native Dublin with Bohemians and Shamrock Rovers prior to joining Irish League side Glentoran. His performances for the Belfast club led to him signing for Arsenal for a fee of £650 in September 1947.

A regular in the Gunners' Combination League side, he made just one appearance for the North London club before moving to Crystal Palace in March 1950 for £8000. He spent just one season at Selhurst Park, scoring five goals in 42 League games before he was on the move again, this time to Nottingham Forest.

Kelly then spent a couple of seasons kicking his heels in Forest's reserve side before in

December 1953 being given his debut against Everton, the side he appeared against in his only game for Arsenal. He went from strength to strength during the remainder of that campaign and in March 1954 won his one and only full international cap for the Republic of Ireland against Luxembourg. It was Kelly who provided the pass for George Cummins to score the game's only goal.

Back at Forest, he was a revelation but after scoring 11 goals in 48 League games, he left the City Ground to become player-manager of Tranmere Rovers. Replaced by Peter Farrell after two fairly innocuous seasons in charge at Prenton Park, he became player-manager of Ellesmere Port and later managed Holyhead Town and Northwich Victoria.

Pat Saward

Position	Wing-half
Born	Patrick Saward, Cork, 17 August 1928
Died	20 September 2002
Clubs	

Crystal Palace; Buckingham Town; Millwall; Aston Villa; Huddersfield Town

International Caps	18

Matches

Year	Opponent	Result	Score	G
1954	Luxembourg	won	1-0	
1957	England	lost	1-5	
1957	England	drew	1-1	
1958	Denmark	won	2-0	
1958	Poland	drew	2-2	
1958	Austria	lost	1-3	
1959	Poland	drew	2-2	
1959	Czechoslovakia	won	2-0	
1960	Sweden	won	3-2	
1960	Chile	won	2-0	
1960	West Germany	won	1-0	
1960	Sweden	lost	1-4	
1961	Wales	lost	2-3	
1961	Norway	won	3-1	
1961	Scotland	lost	1-4	
1962	Austria	lost	2-3	
1963	Iceland	won	4-2	
1963	Iceland	drew	1-1	

Though he was born in Co. Cork, Pat Saward was raised in London. As a youngster he turned out for Crystal Palace on amateur forms. Moving on to Buckingham Town, he was spotted by Millwall and signed for the Third Division (South) club in the summer of 1951.

A talented left-half, he nonetheless suffered barracking by a section of Millwall supporters, in spite of Lions' manager Charlie Hewitt appealing in his column in the matchday programme for the player to be given a fair chance. Sadly, his pleas fell on deaf ears and in August 1955 after making 120 appearances for Millwall, Saward left The Den to join Aston Villa for a fee of £16,000.

By then, he had made the first of his 18 full international appearances for the Republic of Ireland against Luxembourg. His international career spanned eight years, his proudest moment coming on 11 May 1960 when he captained the Republic to an historic 1-0 win over West Germany in Dusseldorf.

His stirring performances for Villa helped them win the FA Cup in 1957 and the Second Division Championship in 1959-60, following their relegation the previous season.

In March 1961 he was transferred to Huddersfield Town where he ended his playing career prior to being appointed coach of Coventry City. Pat Saward's first managerial job was at Brighton and Hove Albion who finished runners-up in Division Three in 1971-72. His side played attacking football but after a poor start to the 1973-74 season he was sacked. He later coached the Saudi Arabian club AL-NASR before running a holiday business in Minorca.

Tommy Scannell

Position	Goalkeeper
Born	Thomas Scannell, Youghal, 3 June 1925
Died	1992
Clubs	

Grays Athletic; Tilbury; Southend United

International Caps	1

Matches

Year	Opponent	Result	Score	G
1954	Luxembourg	won	1-0	

Larger-than-life goalkeeper Tommy Scannell joined Southend United as an amateur after a Shrimps' scout had seen him perform miracles for non-League Tilbury in an FA Cup tie against Barking in November 1949.

Whilst working his way up through the ranks, he was fined by the FA as a result of enquiries into the affairs of his first club, Grays Athletic! Finding himself third in the pecking order behind Bert Hankey and Frank Nash, the situation became even more urgent when Southend signed Bristol City keeper Frank Coombs.

However, Scannell made his first team debut in December 1950, and was the club's first-choice keeper for the next five seasons, including playing in Southend's last-ever game at the Greyhound Stadium in May 1955.

Tommy Scannell played for an FA XI against Glasgow Celtic in 1953. In March 1954 he became the second Southend United goalkeeper to represent the Republic of Ireland – after the club's most capped player, George McKenzie – when he played in place of Everton's Jimmy O'Neill in a 1-0 defeat of Luxembourg. Despite keeping a clean sheet, it was his only appearance for the national side.

Scannell, who played in 98 League games for Southend United was forced to retire at the end of the 1954-55 season through injury.

Tommy Traynor

Position	Left-back
Born	Thomas Joseph Traynor, Dundalk, 22 July 1933

Clubs

Dundalk; Southampton

International Caps	8

Matches

Year	Opponent	Result	Score	G
1954	Luxembourg	won	1-0	
1962	Austria	lost	2-3	
1963	Iceland	won	4-2	
1963	Iceland	drew	1-1	
1963	Scotland	won	1-0	
1964	Austria	drew	0-0	
1964	Austria	won	3-2	
1964	Spain	lost	1-5	

One of the game's most uncompromising defenders, Tommy Traynor began his playing career with League of Ireland side Dundalk, with whom he represented the Republic of Ireland at amateur level. Possessing electrifying pace, Traynor was wanted by both Chelsea and Manchester City. It was Southampton who won the race for his signature, owing in no small measure to the persuasive powers of the Saints' Republic of Ireland keeper, Fred Kiernan.

Traynor made his Southampton debut in a 3-0 defeat at Brentford during the course of the club's relegation season of 1952-53. He soon gained a regular place in the Saints' defence, earning a reputation as a merciless tackler who was feared by the opposition. He won his first full cap for the Republic of Ireland in the 1-0 defeat of Luxembourg in March 1954 but had to wait another eight years before pulling on the green shirt in a game against Austria in April 1962.

Traynor played an important role in the Saints' Third Division Championship-winning season of 1959-60. In 1965-66, his final season at The Dell prior to retirement, he helped Southampton win promotion to the top flight for the first time in their history. During the course of the 1963-64 season, Traynor passed Albert Shelley's League appearance record for the Saints, going on to have 433 league games.

Towards the end of the club's promotion-winning season into Division One, he had virtually retired but his influence and presence at the club was an inspiration in itself. His contribution to Saints' re-emergence as one of the quality sides of the 1960s was considerable. As a reward for his long and loyal service, Traynor was given a prestigious testimonial against Dutch side Twente Enschede.

On parting company with the club he became a checker at Southampton Docks, but still maintained his interest in the game by helping in the organisation of the Tyro Junior League.

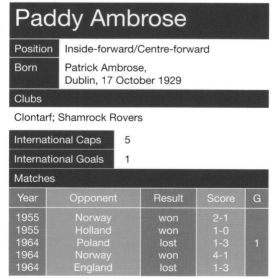

Paddy Ambrose

Position	Inside-forward/Centre-forward
Born	Patrick Ambrose, Dublin, 17 October 1929

Clubs

Clontarf; Shamrock Rovers

International Caps	5
International Goals	1

Matches

Year	Opponent	Result	Score	G
1955	Norway	won	2-1	
1955	Holland	won	1-0	
1964	Poland	lost	1-3	1
1964	Norway	won	4-1	
1964	England	lost	1-3	

In his first game for junior club Clontarf, Paddy Ambrose netted a hat-trick – a performance witnessed by Jimmy Dunne, manager of Shamrock Rovers. Though he was keen to secure his services, Paddy Ambrose was a reluctant footballer!

His first loves were Gaelic football and racing pigeons and it took Dunne over a year to persuade Ambrose to agree terms. Clauses about his hobbies of hurling and pigeon racing had to be incorporated into the contract. Ambrose put pen to paper in the summer of 1949, remaining on the books of Shamrock Rovers until 1973.

He began his career as an inside-forward but midway through the 1953-54 season, switched to centre-forward. Having represented the League of Ireland on a number of occasions, Ambrose finally made his full international debut in the 2-1 home victory over Norway in November 1954. Though he retained his place for the Republic's next match against Holland – a Jack Fitzgerald goal giving the Irish another win – he had to wait nine years for his next cap!

That came against Poland in May 1964 when he scored the Republic's goal in a 3-1 defeat and played in three consecutive internationals.

A strong, determined and totally unselfish player, Ambrose won every domestic honour the Irish game has to offer. He won League Championship medals in 1953-54 (when he was top scorer), 1956-57, 1958-59 and 1963-64; FAI Cup winners' medals in 1955, 1956, 1962 (when he scored twice in the Hoops' 4-1 defeat of Shelbourne in the final) and 1964.

Ambrose, who was also capped as an amateur against England in 1959, was forced to end his playing days because of a recurring ankle injury in 1964. He continued to coach at Glenmalure Park until 1973.

Don Donovan

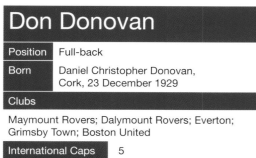

Position	Full-back
Born	Daniel Christopher Donovan, Cork, 23 December 1929

Clubs

Maymount Rovers; Dalymount Rovers; Everton; Grimsby Town; Boston United

International Caps	5

Matches

Year	Opponent	Result	Score	G
1955	Norway	won	2-1	
1955	Holland	won	1-0	
1955	Norway	won	3-1	
1955	West Germany	lost	1-2	
1957	England	lost	1-5	

One of the game's most versatile players, Don Donovan was discovered purely by chance by First Division Everton, during the Merseyside club's pre-season tour of Ireland in 1949. Manager Cliff Britton and a small band of directors took an evening stroll in Cork and ended up watching a local amateur cup-tie.

Donovan was playing at inside-right for Maymount Rovers and did enough to impress the watching English contingent. Britton immediately contacted the youngster's family and invited their talented son to join Everton's junior school. He began as an inside-forward with the 'B' team, but developed at such pace that he soon graduated to the Toffees' League side.

He was tried at wing-half and took to the new position like a natural. Exceptionally good in the air and commanding on the ground, he helped Everton win promotion in 1953-54.

Donovan won the first of his five full caps for the Republic of Ireland in November 1954, playing at right-back in the 2-1 defeat of Norway. He kept his place in the side for the Republic's next three games – wins over Holland and Norway and a 2-1 defeat by West Germany in Hamburg in May 1955. Donovan's last appearance for his country came two years later in a World Cup qualifier against England at Wembley.

Having succeeded Peter Farrell as Everton captain, Donovan's first of only two goals for the club was a spectacular strike from fully 35 yards when Everton were fighting against relegation in 1955-56. They defeated Manchester United 5-2 at Old Trafford and so halted United's run of 26 League games without defeat.

In August 1958 Donovan was back in the Second Division, having joined Grimsby Town for a fee of £10,000. Immediately appointed as the Mariners captain, he missed very few games in his time at Blundell Park but couldn't prevent their relegation to Division Three in 1958-59. Two seasons later he helped them win promotion, going on to appear in 236 games before leaving to become player-manager of Boston United in the summer of 1965.

Paddy Fagan

Position	Winger
Born	Fionan Fagan, Dublin, 7 June 1930

Clubs

Transport; Hull City; Manchester City; Derby County; Altrincham; Norwich Victoria; Ashton United

International Caps	8
International Goals	5

Matches

Year	Opponent	Result	Score	G
1955	Norway	won	2-1	
1960	Sweden	won	3-2	
1960	Chile	won	2-0	
1960	West Germany	won	1-0	1
1960	Sweden	lost	1-4	1
1961	Wales	lost	2-3	2
1961	Norway	won	3-1	1
1961	Scotland	lost	0-3	

Fionan Fagan or 'Paddy' as he was more commonly known, was playing for Transport FC in his native Dublin when his talents were spotted by Hull City. After joining the Tigers, he scored twice in 26 games before his transfer to First Division Manchester City on Christmas Eve 1953.

The winger who was equally at home on either flank, had his best season in terms of goals scored in 1954-55, finding the net 11 times in 42 games. Though he appeared in that season's FA Cup Final defeat at the hands of Newcastle United, he was missing from the City side in the following campaign when they beat Birmingham 3-1 to lift the trophy.

Close control and pin-point crosses were the main features of his play. He won eight full caps for the Republic of Ireland, the first against Norway in November 1954. In doing so, he became the first player to follow his father into the Irish team – Jack 'Kruger' played against Italy in 1926. Five years later in November 1959, Fagan won his second cap in the 3-2 defeat of Sweden. He kept his place in the Republic side until the summer of 1961, by which time he had scored in four consecutive internationals – including the only goal of the game against West Germany in Dusseldorf in May 1960.

Fagan had scored 35 goals in 164 League and Cup games for Manchester City when in March 1960 he was transferred to Derby County for a fee of £8,000. In 1960-61 he was voted the Republic's 'Player of the Year', but he spent most of his time at the Baseball Ground in Derby's Central League side. In the summer of 1961, Fagan left the Rams to take up the post of player-manager of non-League Altrincham before playing for a number of clubs including Northwich Victoria and Ashton United.

Jack Fitzgerald

Position	Centre-forward
Born	Jack Fitzgerald, Waterford, 3 April 1930

Clubs

Bohemians; Waterford; Cork Hibernians

International Caps	2
International Goals	1

Matches

Year	Opponent	Result	Score	G
1955	Holland	won	1-0	1
1956	Holland	won	4-1	

Hailing from one of Munster's most famous footballing families – his brothers Denny, Paul, Peter, Ned and Tom all turned out for Waterford and their father was an international selector – he was a wing-half with Bohemians when they won the FAI Cup in 1947.

He first played for Waterford during the 1949-50 season after which he went to work in England for a year. After returning to the club in readiness for the start of the 1951-52 season, his career really began to take off, following a switch to centre-forward in an injury crisis. As a centre-forward he certainly made the most of his pace, chasing every ball: this coupled with two good feet and heading ability made him a handful.

In 1952-53 he was a member of Waterford's Shield-winning side – the tall blond target man netting a number of important goals. Fitzgerald was the scourge of the League of Ireland defences throughout the 1950s and beyond. In his 13 seasons with the club he was top-scorer in eight, netting a total of 122 goals.

He scored the only goal of the game on his international debut as the Republic of Ireland beat Holland 1-0 in May 1955. He was injured for the Republic's next game but returned to action for the game against the Dutch in Rotterdam, helping his side to complete the double with an emphatic 4-1 win.

Perhaps the most surprising feature of his career with Waterford was his lack of domestic honours. In fact, his only major honour was an FAI Cup runners-up medal gained after a replay against St Patrick's Athletic in 1959. At the end of the 1963-64 campaign, Waterford had to seek re-election to the League and the long-serving Fitzgerald was released. The former milkman then played one more season in the League with Cork Hibs and after topping their goalscoring charts, decided to retire.

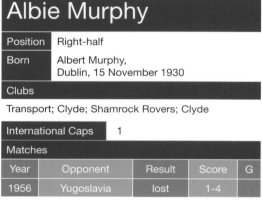

Albie Murphy

Position	Right-half
Born	Albert Murphy, Dublin, 15 November 1930

Clubs

Transport; Clyde; Shamrock Rovers; Clyde

International Caps	1

Matches

Year	Opponent	Result	Score	G
1956	Yugoslavia	lost	1-4	

Albie Murphy was one of the most promising players to appear in the League of Ireland in the years following the Second World War.

His displays for Transport led to him winning representative honours for the League of Ireland against the Scottish League in November 1949. Within a matter of weeks, he was transferred to Scottish League side Clyde, but at the end of that 1949-50 season he returned to Ireland and played for a season with Shamrock Rovers.

He then rejoined the Bully Wee and developed into one of the most consistent and skilful players in the Scottish League.

With Clyde he won a couple of Division Two Championship medals in 1951-52 and 1956-57. He was on the winning side in two Scottish Cup Finals; in 1955 when the mighty Celtic were beaten 1-0 after a replay and three years later when Hibernian were defeated by a single goal.

One of his best seasons at Clyde was 1955-56 when his displays led to his single full international cap. Displacing experienced internationals Don Donovan and Shay Dunne, Murphy wore the No.2 shirt in the match against Yugoslavia in Dublin but was on the losing side as the Republic were beaten 4-1.

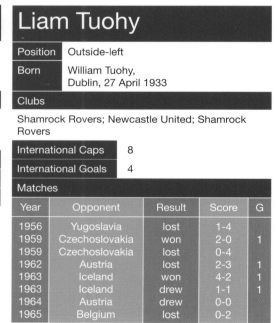

Liam Tuohy

Position	Outside-left
Born	William Tuohy, Dublin, 27 April 1933

Clubs

Shamrock Rovers; Newcastle United; Shamrock Rovers

International Caps	8
International Goals	4

Matches

Year	Opponent	Result	Score	G
1956	Yugoslavia	lost	1-4	
1959	Czechoslovakia	won	2-0	1
1959	Czechoslovakia	lost	0-4	
1962	Austria	lost	2-3	1
1963	Iceland	won	4-2	1
1963	Iceland	drew	1-1	1
1964	Austria	drew	0-0	
1965	Belgium	lost	0-2	

A ball-playing winger with an eye for goal, Liam Tuohy had topped the Under-21 scoring charts for Shamrock Rovers. It was certainly no surprise when at the age of 20 he made the breakthrough into the Hoops' first team. It wasn't long before he was a fixture in Paddy Coad's successful Rovers team of the early 1950s.

In his second season at Milltown, Tuohy

impressed enough to win selection for the League of Ireland XI. Elevation to the Republic of Ireland side followed in October 1956. In the absence of the injured Tommy Eglington, he was chosen for the match against Yugoslavia at Dalymount Park. Over three years passed between his first and second caps, but with his great rival Joe Haverty unavailable for the Republic's debut in the European Nations Cup, the Shamrock Rovers winger lined up to face Czechoslovakia in April 1959. Tuohy certainly made his mark, scoring the Republic's first goal in a 2-0 win.

Despite his good form for the Hoops – winning League Championship medals in 1953-54, 1956-57 and 1958-59, as well as playing in four FAI Cup Finals including scoring the single goal that beat Drumcondra in 1955 – he found himself on a three-year break from international football.

In May 1960 Tuohy was transferred to Newcastle United for a fee of £9,500. He had been attracting interest from Football League clubs for many years and made a good start at St James's Park, showing plenty of spirit. But then like many of his team-mates, he suffered when the Magpies became entangled in a relegation dog-fight during 1960-61. Tuohy was a regular the following season but then lost his place to Jimmy Fell, and returned to Dublin as player-coach for Shamrock Rovers.

Prior to his return to Ireland, he scored in consecutive internationals against Austria and Iceland (twice). Even this rich vein of scoring was not enough to persuade the selection committee and he was replaced by Haverty for the next game at home to Scotland.

Back with the Hoops, he added another League of Ireland Championship medal

to his collection in 1963-64, and won two further FAI Cup medals in 1964 and 1965 after victories in replayed finals over Cork Celtic and Limerick.

Voted the Soccer Writers of Ireland 'Personality of the Year' for 1965-66, Liam Tuohy was the national team manager between 1971 and 1973. Though his rein was short, he did much to lift the Republic of Ireland team out of the doldrums. He retired from the post to pursue his business interests as manager of an ice cream firm, later managing Shelbourne and coaching the Irish youth team until in 1986 Jack Charlton dispensed with his services.

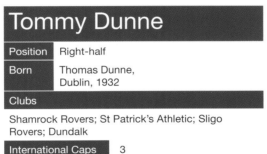

Tommy Dunne

Position	Right-half
Born	Thomas Dunne, Dublin, 1932

Clubs	
Shamrock Rovers; St Patrick's Athletic; Sligo Rovers; Dundalk	

International Caps	3

Matches				
Year	Opponent	Result	Score	G
1956	Holland	won	4-1	
1957	Denmark	won	2-1	
1957	West Germany	won	3-0	

An attack-minded wing-half, capable of taking a firm grip on proceedings in the middle of the park, he began his senior career as an inside-forward with Shamrock Rovers in 1951. However, when the Hoops won the League of Ireland Championship in 1953-54, Tommy Dunne was playing in the Leinster Senior League, though he had been retained by Rovers as a player.

At the end of that season he left Milltown, joining St Patrick's Athletic for a nominal fee – it was one of the best deals done by the Inchicore club.

The son of Jimmy Dunne, who played for Arsenal in the 1930s, he helped St Patrick's wrest the League Championship crown from Rovers in 1954-55, and helped them retain it the following season.

Dunne's form for St Pat's saw him win full international honours. Starting with the game against Holland in May 1956, he played in three successive winning Republic of Ireland sides.

He later won selection for the League of Ireland XI, while as captain of St Patrick's Athletic he led the club to success in two FAI Cup Finals in 1959 and 1961. In the summer of 1964, he left St Pat's to join Sligo Rovers. Two years later he was on the move again, this time to Dundalk whom he helped win the League Championship in 1966-67.

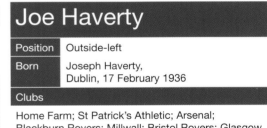

Joe Haverty

Position	Outside-left
Born	Joseph Haverty, Dublin, 17 February 1936

Clubs	
Home Farm; St Patrick's Athletic; Arsenal; Blackburn Rovers; Millwall; Bristol Rovers; Glasgow Celtic; Shelbourne; Chicago Spurs (U.S.)	

International Caps	32
International Goals	3

Matches				
Year	Opponent	Result	Score	G
1956	Holland	won	4-1	1
1957	Denmark	won	2-1	
1957	West Germany	won	3-0	1
1957	England	lost	1-5	
1957	England	drew	1-1	
1958	Denmark	won	2-0	
1958	Poland	drew	2-2	
1958	Austria	lost	1-3	
1959	Poland	drew	2-2	
1960	Sweden	won	3-2	
1960	Chile	won	2-0	
1961	Wales	lost	2-3	
1961	Norway	won	3-1	
1961	Scotland	lost	1-4	1
1961	Scotland	lost	0-3	

Matches Continued				
Year	Opponent	Result	Score	G
1962	Czechoslovakia	lost	1-3	
1962	Czechoslovakia	lost	1-7	
1963	Scotland	won	1-0	
1964	Austria	won	3-2	
1964	Spain	lost	1-5	
1964	Poland	lost	1-3	
1964	Norway	won	4-1	
1964	England	lost	1-3	
1965	Poland	won	3-2	
1965	Spain	won	1-0	
1966	Spain	lost	1-4	
1966	Spain	lost	0-1	
1966	West Germany	lost	0-4	
1966	Austria	lost	0-1	
1966	Belgium	won	3-2	
1967	Turkey	won	2-1	
1967	Spain	lost	0-2	

Standing only 5ft 3in, winger Joe Haverty was one of the smallest players in the Football League during the 1950s and '60s. Having played his early football with Home Farm and St Patrick's Athletic, he joined Arsenal in July 1954, just two months after collecting an FAI Cup runners-up medal with St Pat's.

The skilful Dubliner made his debut for the Gunners the following month at Everton, though it was to be another two years before he was to earn a settled run in the side. He impressed with his tight control and crossing ability and dribbled his way into all but the hardest hearts on the Highbury terraces. Inevitably the affection sometimes wore a trifle thin, when the Irishman overdid his impudent trickery and brought promising attacks to a standstill.

Haverty made his international debut for the Republic of Ireland in the 4-1 victory over Holland in Rotterdam in May 1956, marking the event with a spectacular scissors-kick goal. He wasted little time in adjusting to the rigours and demands of international football, and proceeded to make the No.11 shirt his own. A second goal followed in his third international, a friendly match against West Germany. Two in three was certainly

a misleading strike-rate, as the diminutive Dubliner scored just once more in a further 29 internationals spread over ten years!

Despite his lack of goals, Haverty played in all of the Republic's qualifying matches for the 1958, 1962 and 1966 World Cups. His trickery earned him several spells on the sidelines and limited his number of international appearances. The most notable occasion came during the Republic's match against England at Dalymount Park in May 1964. England right-back George Cohen had had enough of being given the runaround by Haverty. He administered a tackle that not only brought a premature end to his match but also broke his ankle!

On the domestic front, Haverty left Arsenal in the summer of 1961, joining Blackburn Rovers for a fee of £17,500. He was at Ewood Park for less than a season. After losing his place to Mike Harrison, who had just arrived from Chelsea, he left to play for the newly-crowned champions of the Fourth Division, Millwall.

He enjoyed his time at The Den, running rings round the Third Division defences. In December 1964 Haverty joined his fourth and final Football League club – Bristol Rovers – before joining Glasgow Celtic for whom he made just one appearance.

He then headed home to play for Shelbourne. His reputation as one of the game's great nomads was increased with his move to American club, Chicago Spurs. On hanging up his boots, he helped Arsenal's chief Irish scout Bill Darby in the search for new talent for Highbury.

Billy Whelan

Position	Inside-forward
Born	William Augustine Whelan, Dublin, 1 April 1935
Died	6 February 1958
Clubs	
Home Farm; Manchester United	
International Caps	4

Matches				
Year	Opponent	Result	Score	G
1956	Holland	won	4-1	
1957	Denmark	won	2-1	
1957	England	lost	1-5	
1957	England	drew	1-1	

Known as Billy or Liam, Whelan was a ball-playing inside-forward of the highest calibre, who joined Manchester United from Home Farm as an 18-year-old in the summer of 1953. His ball control was a delight to witness and his overall command of the game's skills was a model for any young footballer to study. He made his United debut in a 2-0 win at Preston North End in March 1955 and scored his first goal the following week on his home debut as Sheffield United were beaten 5-0.

Having helped United win the League Championship in 1955-56, he made his full international debut for the Republic of Ireland in the 4-1 defeat of Holland in Rotterdam in May 1956, at a time when away victories for the national side were at a premium.

In 1956-57 United retained the League Championship, and were runners-up to Aston Villa in that season's FA Cup Final. He had a major say in keeping the title at Old Trafford that season with a remarkable 26 goals in 39 League appearances, including a hat-trick in a 3-1 win at Burnley. Whelan netted another treble on the opening day of the 1957-58 season as United won 3-0 at Leicester City.

The artist of the pre-Munich United side, he was vying for the No.8 shirt with Bobby Charlton at the time of the Munich air disaster. Charlton had played in the last seven league games before the crash. Although Whelan did not play in the game against Red Star Belgrade, he was a member of the squad that made that trip and was one of those who lost their lives.

In his relatively short playing career, Billy Whelan, who averaged a goal in every other match, achieved more than most players achieve in a lifetime in the game.

Dermot Curtis

Position	Centre-forward
Born	Dermot Patrick Curtis, Dublin, 26 August 1932

Clubs

Shelbourne; Bristol City; Ipswich Town; Exeter City; Torquay United; Exeter City; Bideford; Elmore

International Caps	17
International Goals	8

Matches

Year	Opponent	Result	Score	G
1957	Denmark	won	2-1	1
1957	West Germany	won	3-0	
1957	England	lost	1-5	1
1957	England	drew	1-1	
1958	Denmark	won	2-0	1
1958	Poland	drew	2-2	1
1958	Austria	lost	1-3	1
1959	Poland	drew	2-2	
1960	Sweden	won	3-2	2
1960	Chile	won	2-0	1
1960	West Germany	won	1-0	
1960	Sweden	lost	1-4	
1961	Norway	won	3-1	
1961	Scotland	lost	1-4	
1962	Austria	lost	2-3	
1963	Iceland	drew	1-1	
1964	Austria	drew	0-0	

Centre-forward Dermot Curtis was a prolific goalscorer for Shelbourne before Bristol City manager Pat Beesley paid £5,000 for his services in November 1956 to replace Jimmy Rogers.

The previous month he had made his full international debut for the Republic of Ireland. He marked the occasion with his side's first goal in the 2-1 home victory over Denmark in a World Cup qualifying game. Curtis eventually took his international tally to eight goals in 17 appearances, including two goals in the 3-2 defeat of Sweden in November 1959.

With Bristol City, Curtis netted 16 goals in 26 Second Division outings alongside John Atyeo, prior to joining Ipswich Town in September 1958. At Portman Road he successfully deputised in either inside-forward berths and though he found the net fairly regularly – 17 goals in 41 games – these were spread over four seasons as he featured in the successes under Alf Ramsey.

He moved to Exeter City in August 1963, forming a notable goalscoring partnership with Alan Banks and helping the Grecians win promotion in 1963-64. Whilst with the Devon club, Curtis won his 17th and final cap against Austria and in doing so, became the first Exeter City player to achieve full international honours. After the Grecians had slipped back into the League's basement at the end of 1965-66, Curtis decided to move on.

He joined local rivals Torquay United, who had just won promotion to the Third Division. After just a dozen games for the Plainmoor club, he rejoined Exeter. Subsequently with Bideford and Elmore where he was player-manager, he later returned to his trade as a sheet-metal worker prior to working as a roofer.

Gerry Mackey

Position	Defender
Born	Gerard Mackey, Dublin, 10 June 1933

Clubs

Shamrock Rovers; King's Lynn

International Caps	3

Matches

Year	Opponent	Result	Score	G
1957	Denmark	won	2-1	
1957	West Germany	won	3-0	
1957	England	lost	1-5	

A strong and versatile defender excelling in both full-back positions and at centre-half, he began his playing days with Johnville in the Dublin Schoolboys league. Six years later, he fulfilled his boyhood ambition of playing for Shamrock Rovers.

Though his League of Ireland career of eight years may appear brief in comparison to that of other players, he achieved much more than most. Mackey captained the Hoops, won League Championship medals in 1953-54, 1956-57 and 1958-59 and played in four successive FAI Cup Finals between 1955 and 1958. He collected winners' medals in the Shield Competition, the Leinster Cup, the Dublin City Cup and the President's Cup.

A former schoolboy and youth international captain, he also gained international honours at amateur level. After two caps at 'B' international level, he won his first full cap for the Republic of Ireland against Denmark in October 1956. The following month he became one of the few home-based players to achieve the rare distinction of captaining the national side, when he led the Republic to a 3-0 victory over West Germany.

During the course of that 1956-57 season, Mackey captained the League of Ireland XI and led them to much success.

After retiring in 1959 to concentrate on family and business, he turned out for King's Lynn in the Southern League, where it was said he had played 'some of the best football in his career'.

Ronnie Nolan

Position	Right-half
Born	Ronald Nolan, Dublin, 1935

Clubs

Shamrock Rovers; Bohemians

International Caps	10

Matches

Year	Opponent	Result	Score	G
1957	Denmark	won	2-1	
1957	West Germany	won	3-0	
1957	England	drew	1-1	
1958	Poland	drew	2-2	
1960	Chile	won	2-0	
1960	West Germany	won	1-0	
1960	Sweden	lost	1-4	
1962	Czechoslovakia	lost	1-3	
1962	Czechoslovakia	lost	1-7	
1963	Iceland	drew	1-1	

Most of wing-half Ronnie Nolan's career was spent playing with Shamrock Rovers, with whom he won League Championship medals on four occasions – 1953-54, 1956-57, 1958-59 and 1963-64.

Without a shadow of doubt, Nolan's biggest success during his time with the Hoops was in the FAI Cup competition: he played in a remarkable eight finals between 1955 and 1966, collecting winners' medals on six occasions. The 1956 final against Cork Athletic is the match that will stand out from all the rest in the mind of Ronnie Nolan. There was less than a quarter-of-an-hour to play with Rovers 2-0 down: they clawed their way back to be on level terms. With just a minute to go, Nolan came up from left-back to head home the winning goal from an inswinging corner-kick.

His performances that season led to him winning the first of 10 international caps, against Denmark in October 1956. In his first six international games, the Republic of Ireland were undefeated, recording memorable home and away victories over West Germany.

Nolan was a regular for the League of Ireland XI throughout the 1950s and '60s, and a member of the Dublin City select which played Arsenal in 1964. He later played for Rovers' Dublin rivals Bohemians, with whom he won another FAI Cup winners' medal in 1970 after Bohs eventually overcame Sligo Rovers 2-1 in a second replay.

Alan Kelly senior

Position	Goalkeeper
Born	Alan James Alexander Kelly, Dublin, 5 July 1936

Clubs

Drumcondra; Preston North End

International Caps	47

Matches

Year	Opponent	Result	Score	G
1957	West Germany	won	3-0	
1957	England	lost	1-5	
1962	Austria	lost	2-3	
1963	Iceland	won	4-2	
1963	Iceland	drew	1-1	
1963	Scotland	won	1-0	
1964	Austria	drew	0-0	
1964	Austria	won	3-2	
1964	Spain	lost	1-5	
1964	Spain	won	0-2	
1964	Poland	lost	1-3	
1965	Belgium	lost	0-2	
1966	Austria	lost	0-1	
1966	Belgium	won	3-2	
1967	Spain	drew	0-0	
1967	Spain	lost	0-2	
1967	Turkey	lost	1-2	
1967	Czechoslovakia	lost	0-2	
1968	Czechoslovakia	won	2-1	
1968	Poland	drew	2-2	
1969	Poland	lost	0-1	
1969	Austria	drew	2-2	
1969	Denmark	drew	1-1	
1969	Czechoslovakia	lost	1-2	

Matches Continued

Year	Opponent	Result	Score	G
1969	Denmark	lost	0-2	
1969	Hungary	lost	1-2	
1970	Scotland	drew	1-1	
1970	Denmark	drew	1-1	
1970	Hungary	lost	0-4	
1970	Poland	lost	1-2	
1970	West Germany	lost	1-2	
1971	Poland	lost	0-2	
1971	Sweden	drew	1-1	
1971	Sweden	lost	0-1	
1971	Italy	lost	0-3	
1971	Italy	lost	1-2	
1971	Austria	lost	1-4	
1972	Iran	won	2-1	
1972	Ecuador	won	3-2	
1972	Chile	lost	1-2	
1972	Portugal	lost	1-2	
1973	USSR	lost	1-2	
1973	France	won	2-1	
1973	USSR	lost	0-1	
1973	Poland	lost	0-2	
1973	France	drew	1-1	
1973	Norway	drew	1-1	

Alan Kelly Senior is the Republic of Ireland's second most capped goalkeeper after Packie Bonner and only a serious injury in September 1973, playing for Preston North End against Bristol City, prevented him from winning more caps. His early displays between the posts were noted by the scouts attending schoolboy matches. He was snapped up by League of Ireland club Drumcondra, whom he helped win the FAI Cup in 1957, defeating Shamrock Rovers 2-0 in the final.

By the time he signed for Preston North End in April 1958, Kelly had already made his international debut in a 3-0 defeat of West Germany, and he suffered the traumatic experience of losing 5-1 to England in a World Cup tie at Wembley in May 1957. The goals against the Republic were not the fault of Alan Kelly but more that of the outfield players who seemed to freeze on the big occasion! Kelly then had to wait almost five years for his next cap. From then on, his inspired displays made him a regular in the national side.

Alan Kelly's debut for North End (in the FA Cup fourth round tie at Swansea) was a late decision after Fred Else fell ill. It was touch-and-go whether or not he would arrive on time but North End fan Jack Whalley used his own car to take Kelly to Vetch Field. His first two League games for North End saw him concede five goals against both Sheffield Wednesday and Spurs.

During 13 seasons as a player at Deepdale, Alan Kelly experienced all the highs and lows associated with a top-flight club. He saw North End slide from a peak of second place in Division One in 1957-58 to Division Three for the first time in their history at the end of the 1969-70 season. On the other hand, the Lilywhites won the Third Division Championship the following season and were narrowly beaten 3-2 by West Ham United in the 1964 FA Cup Final.

Kelly's consistency is obvious: in five successive seasons from 1966, he missed just five out of a possible 214 league games and was never dropped.

At the time of his injury, Alan Kelly had made 47 international appearances for the Republic of Ireland and until recently was the only keeper to have captained the Republic – a role he performed against the USSR in October 1972. He also took over the international managerial reins for one game against Switzerland in April 1980. He would certainly have added to his cap tally but the shoulder injury he sustained led to serious complications – he lost the power in his right-hand and had to learn to write with his left!

On his retirement, Kelly remained loyal to Preston North End. He became assistant-manager and in 1983 became manager. He resigned the post in February 1985 and was later attached to the coaching staff at Everton. Nowadays he runs goalkeeping clinics in Washington DC but returned to Deepdale in 2001 as guest of honour when the Alan Kelly Town End was opened.

Jimmy McCann

Position	Outside-right
Born	James McCann, Dublin
Clubs	

Clontarf; Shamrock Rovers; Drumcondra; Dundalk

International Caps	1
International Goals	1

Matches

Year	Opponent	Result	Score	G
1957	West Germany	won	3-0	1

It was Paddy Ambrose, Shamrock Rover's prolific goalscorer of the 1950s who discovered winger Jimmy McCann. Whilst recovering from a broken ankle midway through the 1952-53 season, Ambrose was 'regraded' to play junior football with Clontarf – it was here that he spotted McCann. Ambrose tipped off his sponsor club, Shamrock Rovers and McCann later took his place in the great Hoops' side of the 1950s.

Known as 'Maxie', his speed down the flanks and accurate corners and crosses created plenty of openings for his fellow forwards. Not that he didn't score his own fair share of goals – 46 in nine seasons with the Hoops and top-scorer in 1957-58. During his stay with Rovers he won three League of Ireland Championship medals (in 1953-54, 1956-57 and 1958-59) and appeared in four successive FAI Cup Finals between 1955 and 1958, picking up winners' medals in 1955 and 1956.

Unusually, 'Maxie' made his full international debut for the Republic of Ireland before having represented the League of Ireland. He marked his debut by scoring the Republic's third goal in their 3-0 defeat of West Germany in Dublin in November 1956, helping inflict on the Germans their heaviest defeat since they won the World Cup in 1954.

Although it proved to be his only full cap, he did represent the Republic again in two 'B' internationals against Iceland (when he scored the winner in a 3-2 victory) and South Africa in 1958.

Midway through the 1961-62 season, McCann was transferred to Drumcondra. Despite rediscovering his goalscoring touch, he was allowed to join Dundalk where he ended his playing days.

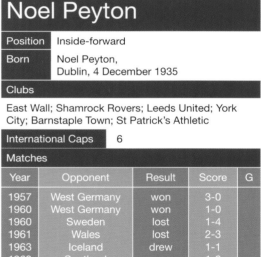

Noel Peyton

Position	Inside-forward
Born	Noel Peyton, Dublin, 4 December 1935
Clubs	

East Wall; Shamrock Rovers; Leeds United; York City; Barnstaple Town; St Patrick's Athletic

International Caps	6

Matches

Year	Opponent	Result	Score	G
1957	West Germany	won	3-0	
1960	West Germany	won	1-0	
1960	Sweden	lost	1-4	
1961	Wales	lost	2-3	
1963	Iceland	drew	1-1	
1963	Scotland	won	1-0	

Inside-forward Noel Peyton joined Shamrock Rovers from junior club East Wall and soon won a regular place in the Hoops' side. He appeared in two FAI Cup Finals, earning a winners' medal in 1956 and a runners-up medal the following year. He also won a League of Ireland Championship medal with the Hoops in 1956-57. By the time he joined Leeds United in January 1958, Peyton had already represented the League of Ireland on five occasions, been capped once at 'B' level and made his full international debut. That came in November 1956 when he was a member of the side that beat World Cup holders West Germany 3-0 in Dublin. Though he added a further five international caps during his stay at Elland Road, he was in and out of the Leeds team.

In just over four years with the Yorkshire club, Peyton scored 20 goals in 117 League and Cup games. At the close of the 1962-63 season – United's third season in Division Two after their relegation at the end of 1959-60 – he joined Fourth Division York City.

A series of injuries severely limited his appearances for the Minstermen and by the time he left Bootham Crescent and moved to non-League Barnstaple Town as player-manager, he had played in just 37 games. He later played for St Patrick's Athletic and though approaching the veteran stage, played for the League of Ireland against the Italian League.

Charlie Hurley

Position	Centre-half
Born	Charles John Hurley, Cork, 4 October 1936

Clubs
Millwall; Sunderland; Bolton Wanderers

International Caps	40
International Goals	2

Matches

Year	Opponent	Result	Score	G
1957	England	drew	1-1	
1958	Denmark	won	2-0	
1958	Poland	drew	2-2	
1958	Austria	lost	1-3	
1959	Czechoslovakia	won	2-0	
1959	Czechoslovakia	lost	0-4	
1960	Sweden	won	3-2	
1960	Chile	won	2-0	
1960	West Germany	won	1-0	
1960	Sweden	lost	1-4	
1961	Wales	lost	2-3	
1961	Norway	won	3-1	
1961	Scotland	lost	1-4	
1961	Scotland	lost	0-3	
1962	Czechoslovakia	lost	1-3	

Matches Continued

Year	Opponent	Result	Score	G
1962	Czechoslovakia	lost	1-7	
1962	Austria	lost	2-3	
1963	Iceland	won	4-2	
1963	Iceland	drew	1-1	
1963	Scotland	won	1-0	
1964	Austria	drew	0-0	
1964	Austria	won	3-2	
1964	Spain	lost	1-5	
1964	Spain	lost	0-2	
1964	Poland	lost	1-3	
1964	Norway	won	4-1	
1965	Spain	won	1-0	
1966	West Germany	lost	0-4	
1966	Austria	lost	0-1	
1966	Belgium	won	3-2	2
1967	Turkey	won	2-1	
1967	Spain	lost	0-2	
1967	Turkey	lost	1-2	
1967	Czechoslovakia	lost	0-2	
1968	Czechoslovakia	won	2-1	
1968	Poland	drew	2-2	
1969	Poland	lost	0-1	
1969	Denmark	drew	1-1	
1969	Czechoslovakia	lost	1-2	
1969	Hungary	lost	1-2	

A living legend. Charlie Hurley was a commanding figure, combining power in the air with an assured touch and the confidence to carry the ball out of defence. Though born in Cork, he moved to live in Hornchurch, Essex when he was seven. He was spotted by Millwall scout Bill Voisey whilst playing with Rainham Youth Centre and signed amateur forms with the club. In October 1953 he turned professional and made his League debut aged 17, ousting fellow Irishman Gerry Bowler from the side. He wasted little time in winning over the notoriously critical Millwall crowd, and became a firm favourite at the Den. Reports of his outstanding displays at the heart of the Lions' defence made their way to the FAI selection committee and in November 1955 he was called into the Republic of Ireland squad for the match against Spain.

A knee injury sustained in a match for the Army Catering Corps, whom he was representing while on National Service, forced him to withdraw from the national squad. However,

eighteen months later he made his international debut against an England side who 11 days earlier had beaten the Republic 5-1. Marking Manchester United centre-forward Tommy Taylor, Hurley was outstanding as the sides played out a 1-1 draw.

Shortly afterwards Hurley, who had made 105 league appearances for Millwall, left the Lions to join Sunderland for a fee of £20,000. His first game for the club could not have been worse as the Wearsiders lost 7-0 at Blackpool and Hurley put through his own goal! His next appearance in Sunderland colours wasn't much better as Burnley beat the north-east club 6-0.

Many Sunderland supporters must have wondered what sort of centre-half manager Alan Brown had signed, but they needn't have worried. Charlie Hurley proved himself over the next 12 seasons to be one of the best central defenders in the country.

At the end of Hurley's first season at Roker Park, Sunderland were relegated from Division One for the first time in their 79-year history. Though they didn't regain that top flight status until 1963-64, Hurley established himself as the team's skipper and defensive kingpin.

His international career had also blossomed during those six years. When the Republic began their European Nations Cup games in 1962, Hurley was appointed team captain. Thereafter, he shared the honour of leading the national side with fellow defender Noel Cantwell. During his 12-year career with the Republic of Ireland he scored two goals, both of which came during a rare appearance at centre-forward in a 4-1 win over Norway in Oslo in May 1964.

Known as 'King Charlie' he went on to play in 402 games for Sunderland, before in the summer of 1969 he was given a free transfer as a thank-you for the loyal service he had shown the club.

He was allowed to negotiate his own contract and joined Bolton Wanderers. After two seasons with the Trotters, he entered management with Reading and took them to promotion from the Fourth Division in 1975-76. Reading were relegated the following year and Hurley resigned, saying that the players were not responding to his methods of management.

Sunderland supporters voted Hurley the 'Player of the Century' in 1979, the club's centenary year. 1989 saw Charlie Hurley rightly admitted to the FAI Hall of Fame.

Mick McGrath

Position	Wing-half
Born	Michael McGrath, Dublin, 7 April 1936
Clubs	

Home Farm; Blackburn Rovers; Bradford Park Avenue; Bangor City

International Caps	22

Matches

Year	Opponent	Result	Score	G
1958	Austria	lost	1-3	
1959	Poland	drew	2-2	
1959	Czechoslovakia	won	2-0	
1959	Czechoslovakia	lost	0-4	
1960	Sweden	won	3-2	
1960	West Germany	won	1-0	
1960	Sweden	lost	1-4	
1961	Wales	lost	2-3	
1962	Czechoslovakia	lost	1-3	
1962	Czechoslovakia	lost	1-7	
1963	Scotland	won	1-0	
1964	Austria	drew	0-0	
1964	Austria	won	3-2	
1964	England	lost	1-3	
1965	Poland	won	3-2	
1965	Belgium	lost	0-2	
1965	Spain	won	1-0	
1965	Spain	lost	1-4	
1965	West Germany	lost	0-4	
1965	Austria	lost	0-1	
1965	Belgium	won	3-2	
1967	Turkey	lost	1-2	

Wing-half Mick McGrath had already established quite a reputation as a schoolboy footballer, following impressive displays in an international under-18 tournament in Germany. Blackburn Rovers' new manager Johnny Carey watched McGrath and Charlie Wade play for an Irish Youth XI against Liverpool FA in 1953. He had been suitably impressed and after keeping an eye on them for almost a year, signed both players from his old club Home Farm in August 1954. Despite some impressive performances in the club's Central League side, he had to wait until April 1956, following an injury to Ken Clayton, before making his debut in a 1-1 draw at Nottingham Forest. It wasn't until 1957-58 when Rovers won promotion to the First Division and McGrath played in every game, that he established himself fully in the Rovers' side.

Shortly after this success, McGrath was called up by the Republic of Ireland side for a two-match tour of Poland and Austria. Johnny Carey had been appointed coach for these games with authority from the selection committee to make changes to the Republic's line-up for the second game against Austria. Carey took the chance to blood the 22-year-old and though the Irish lost 3-1, McGrath had made an impressive debut. He remained an important member of the Republic of Ireland squad for the next nine years, appearing in 22 of the 34 games played during that period.

Along with Ronnie Clayton and Matt Woods, the quiet Irishman helped form one of the most formidable half-back lines in Blackburn's history. He appeared for Rovers in the 1960 FA Cup Final against Wolverhampton Wanderers at Wembley, but had the misfortune to put through his own goal to open the scoring for the Molineux club.

A perfect clubman, Mick McGrath retained his place in the Rovers side under Jack

Marshall until March 1966, when he moved to play for Bradford Park Avenue. He had the unhappy distinction of scoring another own goal on his debut for the Yorkshire club. Not surprisingly he was made captain and was the last Bradford player to win an international cap. After a spell playing non-League football for Welsh club Bangor City in the Northern Premier League, he returned to Ewood Park to help out with Rovers' youth teams before becoming involved in local junior soccer.

Shay Keogh

Position	Defender
Born	Shay Keogh, Dublin
Clubs	

Shamrock Rovers; St Patrick's Athletic

International Caps	1

Matches

Year	Opponent	Result	Score	G
1959	Poland	drew	2-2	

Defender Shay Keogh had quite a chequered career with Shamrock Rovers, whom he joined in 1952. His early displays for the Hoops led to him winning representative honours for the League of Ireland. However, following a bad knee injury, he lost his place in the Shamrock side to Gerry Mackey, who got the international honours which might otherwise have come Shay Keogh's way! On returning to full fitness, he then struggled to make a success of the left-back position, though he did win a League Championship medal in 1953-54 and captain the side to success in the 1955 FAI Cup Final.

Keogh won his favoured centre-half position back at the end of the Championship-winning season of 1957-58 and by the following term when the Hoops retained the title, was back to his brilliant best.

During the early part of that campaign Keogh, who had won a couple of 'B' caps against Romania and Iceland, was called up to make his full international debut against Poland. Despite being a most popular choice, he only managed to get into the side because the Republic's regular centre-half Charlie Hurley couldn't get to Dublin in time! The game itself (which ended 2-2) was described by the local press as a 'drab draw'. Keogh – the only home-based player in the Republic's starting XI – was the only success on the Irish side!

Keogh, whose Rovers career was ended by injury in 1962, later became player-coach of St Patrick's Athletic.

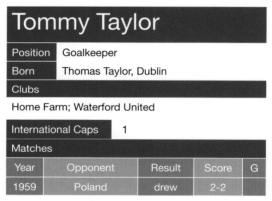

Tommy Taylor

Position	Goalkeeper
Born	Thomas Taylor, Dublin
Clubs	
Home Farm; Waterford United	
International Caps	1
Matches	

Year	Opponent	Result	Score	G
1959	Poland	drew	2-2	

Following a distinguished career in junior football with Home Farm, with whom he won a junior cap, Tommy Taylor joined Waterford United in 1955.

Excellent positional sense, a safe pair of hands and complete control of his penalty area were the attributes which marked Taylor out as a goalkeeper far above the average. He soon made the No.1 jersey his own. In September 1958 he became the first keeper in a first-class match ever to score from inside his own area, netting in a 3-2 Shield victory over Shamrock Rovers.

Taylor, who could have joined virtually any top-flight Football League club instead of Waterford, was the League of Ireland's first-choice keeper for three seasons. Just prior to scoring that goal, he had won a couple of 'B' caps against Iceland and South Africa.

In October 1958, Waterford fans were devastated to hear the news that Tommy Taylor was going to leave the game to take up a building contract in Malta. Ironically, just as he was about to leave, he was called up as the reserve keeper for the Republic of Ireland's match against Poland at Dalymount Park. The score stood at 2-2 when Everton and Republic of Ireland keeper Jimmy O'Neill injured himself in the act of making a brilliant save. With 25 minutes remaining, Tommy Taylor came off the bench to make his full international debut. "Judging by his garb, the Waterford man was quite unprepared. Through no fault of his own, he presented an odd and most un-intentional-like spectacle between the posts," recorded one observer. Nevertheless, he didn't concede a goal as the score remained the same as it had when he came on!

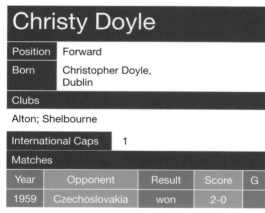

Christy Doyle

Position	Forward
Born	Christopher Doyle, Dublin
Clubs	
Alton; Shelbourne	
International Caps	1
Matches	

Year	Opponent	Result	Score	G
1959	Czechoslovakia	won	2-0	

Versatile forward Christy 'Kit' Doyle was the nephew of Jimmy 'Snowy' Dunne and played his early football for Alton where he was a prolific goalscorer.

His goalscoring exploits led to a number of League of Ireland clubs chasing his signature but it was Shelbourne who secured his services.

Doyle exploded on to the League of Ireland scene in 1957-58. Three seasons with Shelbourne from that campaign, and Doyle was the club's leading scorer on each occasion – scoring a total of 34 league goals in that period.

In April 1959, Doyle was called up to the full Republic of Ireland side to replace injured Dermot Curtis of Ipswich Town. Playing against Czechoslovakia in a preliminary round game for the first European Nations Cup, Doyle had a hand in both goals as the Irish won 2-0. He wasn't retained for the return game in Bratislava, a match the Czechs won 4-0!

Back on the domestic front, Doyle was a member of the Reds side which overcame Cork Hibernians 2-0 in the 1960 FAI Cup Final to lift the Cup for only the second time in the club's history.

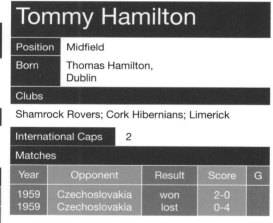

Tommy Hamilton

Position	Midfield
Born	Thomas Hamilton, Dublin
Clubs	
Shamrock Rovers; Cork Hibernians; Limerick	
International Caps	2
Matches	

Year	Opponent	Result	Score	G
1959	Czechoslovakia	won	2-0	
1959	Czechoslovakia	lost	0-4	

Midfield playmaker Tommy Hamilton began his career with Shamrock Rovers, with whom he had seven highly successful seasons. His career at Milltown got off to a flying start in 1955-56: towards the end of the campaign, he scored the winner in the 3-2 FAI Cup Final victory over Cork Athletic. The following season the Hoops won the League of Ireland Championship, and Hamilton topped the club's scoring charts with 15 goals.

Rovers' next success in terms of winning the League title was 1958-59, a campaign in which Hamilton won two full caps for the Republic of Ireland in the European Nations Cup games against Czechoslovakia.

Both games resulted in wins for the home sides – in Dublin, the Republic won 2-0 whilst in Bratislava, the Czechs triumphed 4-0.

In September 1960 Hamilton scored both the Republic's goals in a 2-0 'B' international victory over Iceland.

In 1962 just before that season's FAI Cup semi-final, Hamilton lost his place in the side but an injury to Tony Byrne let him back in and he helped bring about the Hoops' Cup success, scoring twice in the 4-1 defeat of Shelbourne in the final. For his achievements, he was awarded with the 'Soccer Personality of the Year' award. Hamilton also played in the following year's FAI Cup Final against Shelbourne, but by this time he had joined Cork Hibs and finished on the losing side.

Hamilton spent three seasons with the Cork club before in 1965 transferring to their Munster rivals Limerick. As with his previous two clubs, he reached the FAI Cup Final against his former employers, Shamrock Rovers, who triumphed on the day 2-0.

Brendan McNally

Position	Full-back
Born	John Brendan McNally, Dublin, 22 January 1935
Clubs	

Shelbourne; Luton Town

International Caps	3

Matches

Year	Opponent	Result	Score	G
1959	Czechoslovakia	won	2-0	
1961	Scotland	lost	1-4	
1963	Iceland	drew	1-1	

Brendan McNally began his career in Dublin junior football before joining Shelbourne. At the end of the 1955-56 season in which he was the League of Ireland club's most consistent player, he was invited for a trial at Kenilworth Road, the home of Luton Town. That trial turned out to be a friendly game with Fulham in April 1956 and McNally did well enough for Luton to sign him immediately. Considering McNally had only met his team-mates some 45 minutes before kick-off, it was a remarkable achievement!

After putting pen to paper, McNally became the third full-back from the Republic of Ireland on Luton's books, following in the footsteps of Shay Dunne and Bud Aherne.

McNally was a well-built two-footed player who could play in either full-back berth and one who used the ball intelligently.

Luton reached the final of the FA Cup for the first time in 1959. McNally was the right-back in the Hatters' team which went down 2-1 to Nottingham Forest in the Wembley showpiece. An incident at this match left Nottingham Forest's Roy Dwight with a broken leg and saw McNally himself limping badly with a torn cartilage.

Just prior to the final McNally, who had been honoured by the Republic at 'B' level, won the first of three caps when he replaced Luton team-mate Shay Dunne in the game against Czechoslovakia.

In 1959-60, Luton lost their top-flight status and in September 1961 McNally was placed on the transfer list at his own request. He subsequently dropped out of League football having made 164 League and Cup appearances for the Hatters.

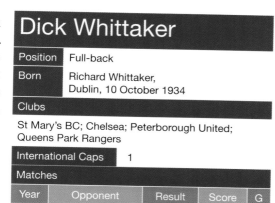

Dick Whittaker

Position	Full-back
Born	Richard Whittaker, Dublin, 10 October 1934
Clubs	

St Mary's BC; Chelsea; Peterborough United; Queens Park Rangers

International Caps	1

Matches

Year	Opponent	Result	Score	G
1959	Czechoslovakia	lost	0-4	

Tough tackling full-back Dick Whittaker was playing junior football for St Mary's Boys Club in his native Dublin when he was spotted by Chelsea. He left Ireland to join the Stamford Bridge club's groundstaff, and in the summer of 1952 signed professional forms for the London club. Though he spent five seasons with Chelsea, he could never win a regular place at full-back due to the fine form of the Sillett brothers – Peter, an England international and John, who later managed Coventry City to FA Cup success.

Always on the fringes of the Chelsea side, he appeared in 48 league games and was at Stamford Bridge when they won the League Championship in 1954-55. Whilst with the Blues, he won his one and only full international cap. He wore the No. 2 shirt in the Republic's second-ever European Nations Cup game against Czechoslovakia in May 1959 – a match the Irish lost 4-0!

In September 1960 he left Chelsea to join Peterborough United who had just been admitted to the Football League. They proceeded to take the Fourth Division by storm, winning promotion as champions in their first season in the Football League. After three seasons with the London Road club, Whittaker left to play for Queen's Park Rangers where he ended his first-class career.

THE 1960s

The Republic of Ireland was one of 17 countries to sign up for a new competition, the European Nations Cup, which was shunned by the likes of Italy, West Germany and England. The European Nations Cup, staged in 1960 and 1964, operated as a straightforward two-legged knockout up to the semi-finals. The Irish had been drawn against Czechoslovakia in a preliminary tie and though they won 2-0 in Dublin, went down 4-0 in Bratislava.

In the games played between the 1958 and 1962 World Cup, the Republic recorded memorable victories over Sweden (3-2) who arrived fresh from defeating England at Wembley and West Germany (1-0) in Dusseldorf.

The teams in the Republic's group for the 1962 World Cup were Scotland and Czechoslovakia. Just weeks before the Irish travelled to Hampden Park, the Scots had been crushed 9-3 at Wembley by England but they bounced back, beating the Republic 4-1. In the return at Dalymount Park, the Scots completed the double. The referee was no Irishman, as he clearly demonstrated towards the end of the game when Fitzgerald was upended well inside the box, and the official gave the Republic a free-kick, a good five yards outside! After losing 3-1 at home to Czechoslovakia, the Irish suffered their heaviest World Cup defeat to that day or since when they were beaten 7-1 in Prague. Four matches, four defeats and 17 goals conceded – these were the Republic's worst-ever figures in the World Cup.

By the time of the 1964 European Nations Cup, numbers entering the competition had swelled with the inclusion of the majority of Europe's major footballing powers. Having beaten Iceland and Austria, the Republic faced Spain for a place in the semi-finals. Sadly, they proved too strong for the boys in green, winning 5-1 in Seville and 2-0 in Dublin.

With the 1966 World Cup Finals being held in England, fans would flood across the Irish Sea should the Republic qualify. Their opponents were Spain and Syria but the latter nation decided to opt out of the competition, leaving the Republic and Spain to fight out a double header. A win for the Irish in their first meeting at Dalymount Park would at least guarantee them a money-spinning play-off. Spain were the better side and it was against the run of play that the Republic of Ireland scored. Johnny Giles was fouled out wide. O'Neill flighted in the free-kick for which Cantwell, playing at centre-forward, Zoco and goalkeeper Iribar rose as one. The Spanish keeper won the race but the ball spilled from his grasp and dropped behind him into the net. Spain pressed hard but the Republic held out for a memorable victory. All the Irish needed in Seville was a draw. Despite taking the lead through Andy McEvoy, the home side won 4-1. The play-off was scheduled for a fortnight later and though Spain again dominated proceedings, the Irish held out until the 79th minute before Ufarte scored the game's only goal.

After finishing third in their 1968 European Championship group, in matches against Czechoslovakia, Turkey and once again Spain, the Republic suffered defeat after defeat with great regularity.

To take part in the next World Cup in Mexico, the Republic found themselves for the first time in a four-team group with Denmark, Hungary and Czechoslovakia. Few gave the Republic much of a chance and so it transpired with their only point coming in a 1-1 home draw with Denmark.

Joe Carolan

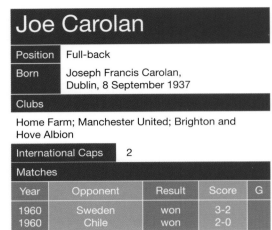

Position	Full-back
Born	Joseph Francis Carolan, Dublin, 8 September 1937

Clubs

Home Farm; Manchester United; Brighton and Hove Albion

International Caps	2

Matches

Year	Opponent	Result	Score	G
1960	Sweden	won	3-2	
1960	Chile	won	2-0	

After a series of impressive performances for Home Farm, full-back Joe Carolan followed in the footsteps of Billy Whelan by signing for Manchester United in February 1956.

Despite his displays in the club's Central League side, he couldn't dislodge the legendary Roger Byrne, or following the Munich disaster, his successor Ian Greaves. His League debut eventually came in November 1958 as United beat Luton Town 2-1. He kept his place in the side for the rest of the season, playing in eight successive victories from debut and only being on the losing side in three of the 23 games. He then proved difficult to displace and missed just one game in 1959-60.

During the early stages of that campaign, Carolan was selected for the full Republic of Ireland side to play Sweden in a friendly, a match the Irish won 3-2. He kept his place for the Republic's next game the following March and was again on the winning side as Chile were beaten 2-0.
Carolan had appeared in 71 games for the Reds before switching his services to Brighton and Hove Albion in December 1960. He spent a couple of seasons at the Goldstone Ground before the determined defender returned to Ireland in the summer of 1962.

Noel Dwyer

Position	Goalkeeper
Born	Noel Michael Dwyer, Dublin, 30 October 1934
Died	January 1993

Clubs

Ormeau; Wolverhampton Wanderers; West Ham United; Swansea City; Plymouth Argyle; Charlton Athletic

International Caps	14

Matches

Year	Opponent	Result	Score	G
1960	Sweden	won	3-2	
1960	Chile	won	2-0	
1960	West Germany	won	1-0	
1960	Sweden	lost	1-4	
1961	Wales	lost	2-3	
1961	Norway	won	3-1	
1961	Scotland	lost	1-4	
1961	Scotland	lost	0-3	
1962	Czechoslovakia	lost	1-3	
1962	Czechoslovakia	lost	1-7	
1964	Poland	lost	1-3	
1964	Norway	won	4-1	
1964	England	lost	1-3	
1965	Poland	won	3-2	

Noel Dwyer was one of a number of promising young goalkeepers on the Molineux staff during the 1950s, having joined Wolverhampton Wanderers from Dublin junior club Ormeau in August 1953.

However, as understudy to England keeper Bert Williams and Malcolm Finlayson, his contribution to Wolves' success during that decade was negligible. Though he spent five years at the club he made just five League appearances, all in 1957-58 when Finlayson was injured.

In December 1958 Dwyer left Molineux to join West Ham United. Although he won a Second Division Championship medal in his first season at Upton Park, he experienced similar difficulties there to those he had with Wolves.

Whilst with the Hammers, Dwyer won the first of 14 full caps for the Republic of Ireland when he played in the 3-2 victory over Sweden in November 1959. Dwyer made his mark at international level in his third game for the national side as the Republic beat the mighty West Germany 1-0 in Dusseldorf. In the months that followed, the West German FA used Dwyer's performance between the posts to illustrate a film on the art of goalkeeping! He played in ten consecutive matches for the Republic of Ireland between November 1959 and October 1961 before losing his place to Preston's Alan Kelly after the 7-1 away defeat by Czechoslovakia.

In August 1960 Second Division Swansea signed Dwyer. It was at the Vetch Field that he established his reputation as a more-than-competent goalminder. In the sixth round of the 1963-64 FA Cup competition, Noel Dwyer played the game of his life to deny Liverpool at Anfield. He made countless saves and even the dependable Ronnie Moran missed a penalty as Swansea won 2-1. Yet in the semi-final, the Dubliner conceded a soft goal to gift Preston North End their winner in a 2-1 defeat.

An acrobatic and stylish keeper, he had made 140 league appearances for the Swans when in January 1965 he replaced Dave MacLaren at Plymouth Argyle. He rounded off his professional career with Charlton Athletic, pulling out of the bigtime due to injury.

Noel Dwyer died in January 1993 after a long battle against cancer. He left a wife, a son and three daughters – one of whom, a former model, was married to former England international, Frank Worthington.

Johnny Giles

Position	Midfield
Born	Michael John Giles, Dublin, 6 November 1940

Clubs

Home Farm; Manchester United; Leeds United; West Bromwich Albion; Shamrock Rovers

International Caps	59
International Goals	5

Matches

Year	Opponent	Result	Score	G
1960	Sweden	won	3-2	1
1960	Chile	won	2-0	
1961	Wales	lost	2-3	
1961	Norway	won	3-1	
1961	Scotland	lost	1-4	
1961	Scotland	lost	0-3	
1962	Czechoslovakia	lost	1-3	1
1962	Czechoslovakia	lost	1-7	
1962	Austria	lost	2-3	
1963	Iceland	won	4-2	
1963	Scotland	won	1-0	
1964	Austria	drew	0-0	
1964	Austria	won	3-2	
1964	Spain	lost	1-5	
1964	Spain	lost	0-2	
1964	Poland	lost	1-3	
1964	Norway	won	4-1	1
1964	England	lost	1-3	
1965	Spain	won	1-0	
1966	Spain	lost	1-4	
1966	Spain	lost	0-1	
1966	Austria	lost	0-1	
1966	Belgium	won	3-2	
1967	Spain	drew	0-0	
1967	Turkey	won	2-1	
1967	Turkey	lost	1-2	
1969	Austria	drew	2-2	
1969	Denmark	drew	1-1	1
1969	Czechoslovakia	lost	1-2	
1970	Scotland	drew	1-1	
1970	Poland	lost	1-2	
1970	West Germany	lost	1-2	
1971	Italy	lost	1-2	
1973	France	won	2-1	
1973	USSR	lost	0-1	
1974	Brazil	lost	1-2	
1974	Uruguay	lost	0-2	
1974	Chile	won	2-1	
1975	USSR	won	3-0	
1975	Turkey	drew	1-1	
1975	Switzerland	won	2-1	
1975	USSR	lost	1-2	
1975	Switzerland	lost	0-1	
1976	Turkey	won	4-0	
1977	England	drew	1-1	
1977	Turkey	drew	3-3	

Matches Continued

Year	Opponent	Result	Score	G
1977	France	lost	0-2	
1977	France	won	1-0	
1977	Poland	drew	0-0	
1977	Bulgaria	lost	1-2	
1978	Bulgaria	drew	0-0	
1978	Turkey	won	4-2	1
1978	Poland	lost	0-3	
1978	Norway	drew	0-0	
1978	Denmark	drew	3-3	
1979	Northern Ireland	drew	0-0	
1979	Denmark	won	2-0	
1979	Bulgaria	lost	0-1	
1979	West Germany	lost	1-3	

Above: Johnny Giles

Johnny Giles was a product of the famous Dublin nursery, Home Farm. He left Dublin at the age of 15 to join Manchester United. After rising through the ranks at Old Trafford, he graduated to the first team in September 1959, making his debut in the 5-1 home defeat by Spurs!

Two months later he was playing for the Republic of Ireland and scored just 16 minutes into the 3-2 defeat of Sweden – at 19 years 304 days old, he was the youngest player to score for the Republic of Ireland.

He won an FA Cup winners' medal in 1963 with Manchester United after the Reds' 3-1 victory over Leicester City. It was his last appearance in a United shirt for he was then surprisingly sold to Leeds United, the Reds' arch-rivals for £32,000. It has been said on many occasions since that the worst decision the Old Trafford club ever made was to let Giles join the Yorkshire side.

A brilliant tactician with one of the game's shrewdest brains, the former winger was transformed by Leeds manager Don Revie into one of the greatest midfield dynamos of the 1960s and even 1970s. In his first season at Elland Road, Giles helped Leeds United win the Second Division Championship, which marked the beginning of the most successful era in the club's history. In the next 10 seasons with the Yorkshire club, Giles won a number of honours including League Championship medals in 1968-69 and 1973-74, an FA Cup winners' medal in 1971-72, a League Cup winners' medal in 1967-68 and UEFA Cup winners' medals in 1967-68 and 1970-71.

Success with Leeds United had an adverse effect upon Giles' international career. Cup runs both domestically and in Europe resulted in a quite hectic fixture schedule. This meant it was not always possible for the Republic of Ireland to gain Johnny Giles' release for international matches. The tension between the midfield maestro and the selection committee was growing. The situation came to a head in 1969, when Giles was inexplicably dropped for the World Cup qualifier against Denmark in Copenhagen. Not even considered good enough to sit on the bench, the situation had become farcical! Giles then reacted by making himself unavailable for the next game and though he soon returned, the Republic's selection committee had made an enemy!

Over the next couple of years, Giles would play a major role in the successful campaign to reform the Republic of Ireland's antiquated selection process.

In the summer of 1975 after playing in 527 League and Cup games for Leeds United, he joined West Bromwich Albion. As player-manager of the Baggies, he took the club into the top flight at the end of his first season. After two seasons at the Hawthorns, he returned to Ireland to play for and manage Shamrock Rovers, guiding the club to victory in the 1978 FAI Cup Final.

Giles had been appointed player-manager of the Republic of Ireland in October 1973. He continued playing until May 1979 – making 59 appearances and captaining his country a record 30 times and then quit as manager the following March.

Afterwards he had brief spells in management with Vancouver Whitecaps and again at West Bromwich Albion in 1984-85. He eventually went into journalism and wrote a regular column in the *Daily Express* – he also works as a pundit for Irish television.

Ambrose Fogarty

Position	Inside-forward
Born	Ambrose Gerald Fogarty, Dublin, 11 September 1933

Clubs	

Bohemians; Glentoran; Sunderland; Hartlepool United; Cork Hibernians; Cork Celtic; Drumcondra

International Caps	11
International Goals	3

Matches				
Year	Opponent	Result	Score	G
1960	West Germany	won	1-0	
1960	Sweden	lost	1-4	
1961	Scotland	lost	1-4	
1962	Czechoslovakia	lost	1-3	
1962	Czechoslovakia	lost	1-7	1
1963	Iceland	won	4-2	1
1963	Iceland	drew	1-1	
1963	Scotland	won	1-0	
1964	Austria	drew	0-0	
1964	Austria	won	3-2	1
1964	Spain	lost	1-5	

Goalscoring inside-forward Ambrose Fogarty was midway through his second season with League of Ireland side Bohemians when in 1955 he moved north to join Irish League club Glentoran.

He soon became a great favourite at the Oval and was a member of the Glentoran side which lost the 1956 Irish Cup Final to Distillery after a three-match marathon. The following year negotiations for his transfer back south were underway, with Cork Hibernians the favourites to secure his signature. However, Sunderland stepped in with a £5,000 bid and Fogarty was on his way to Roker Park.

In his first season, the once-great club were relegated for the first time in their history and the following season a series of niggling injuries meant that he made only three appearances in their first season of Second Division football. He returned to full fitness in 1959-60, his most successful season in goal

terms. He scored 12 goals in 37 games, including a spell of 10 in 12 games midway through the campaign.

His form that season led to the first of 11 caps for the Republic of Ireland, when he played in the 1-0 win over West Germany in Dusseldorf in May 1960.

A regular member of the Sunderland side for the next three seasons, he netted his only hat-trick for the club in December 1961 when Swansea Town were beaten 7-2. He had scored 44 goals in 174 games when in November 1963 he was transferred to Fourth Division Hartlepool United for a 'substantial fee'. He ended his Football League career with 22 goals in 128 league games for the Pool before leaving the Victoria Ground to return to Ireland as player-manager of Cork Hibernians in 1966. Three years later he joined Cork Celtic and in 1970 returned to his native Dublin to end his playing days with Drumcondra.

Maurice Swan

Position	Goalkeeper
Born	Maurice Michael George Swan, Dublin, 27 September 1938

Clubs	

Drumcondra; Cardiff City; Hull City; Dundalk; Drumcondra

International Caps	1

Matches				
Year	Opponent	Result	Score	G
1960	Sweden	lost	1-4	

A most confident and skilful goalkeeper, Maurice Swan had impressed for Drumcondra in his two seasons with the club. It came as no surprise when in the summer of 1960 he signed for First Division newcomers Cardiff City.

Towards the end of his time at Drumcondra, Swan got 45 minutes of international football as a half-time replacement for the injured Noel Dwyer in the Republic of Ireland's game against Sweden in Malmo. The game was already out of the Republic's reach when the debutant keeper took to the field. The Irish were trailing 3-0 but Swan acquitted himself well, making a couple of memorable saves before conceding a last minute goal in a 4-1 defeat.

At Ninian Park, Swan had to share the goalkeeping duties with Ron Nicholls and Welsh international Graham Vearncombe, and it was Boxing Day 1960 before he made his debut in a 1-1 draw at West Bromwich Albion. The following season, a damaged collarbone kept him out of the game for over a year. This had first been damaged when diving at the feet of Newcastle United's Len White the previous season.

In June 1963 Swan left to play for Hull City. His agile anticipation, courage and ability to inspire his colleagues won him many admirers at Boothferry Park. In 1965-66 while with the Tigers, he won a Third Division Championship medal. After 103 League appearances, he returned to Ireland where he played for Dundalk, but by the early 1970s, he was back guarding Drumcondra's goal.

Peter Fitzgerald

Position	Forward
Born	Peter Joseph Fitzgerald, Waterford, 17 June 1937

Clubs

Waterford United; Sparta Club Rotterdam (Holland); Leeds United; Chester City; Waterford

International Caps	5
International Goals	2

Matches

Year	Opponent	Result	Score	G
1961	Wales	lost	2-3	
1961	Norway	won	3-1	2
1961	Scotland	lost	0-3	
1962	Czechoslovakia	lost	1-3	
1962	Czechoslovakia	lost	1-7	

Versatile forward Peter Fitzgerald started out with League of Ireland side Waterford United and in 1958-58, only his second season with the club, he was their leading scorer with 17 goals. He scored the Blues' consolation goal when they went down 2-1 to St Patrick's Athletic in that season's FAI Cup Final.

Shortly after that Cup Final, Fitzgerald linked up with Northern Ireland international Johnny Crossan at the famous Sparta Club of Rotterdam where he spent just over a year.

Meanwhile Leeds United had just been relegated from the First Division and were looking for a quick return to the top flight. The Elland Road club paid out over £50,000 for new players including £7,000 for Peter Fitzgerald. The move was not a success, and over the next season he appeared in just eight League games.

Despite making little impression for United, he won all his five full caps for the Republic of Ireland whilst with the Yorkshire club. He made his debut in the 3-2 defeat by Wales in September 1960. Wales were on their first visit to the Republic and their victory ended the Irish side's eight-match unbeaten run at home. There is little doubt that the highlight of Peter Fitzgerald's international career came in his second game for the Republic against Norway in Dublin in November 1960, when he scored twice in a 3-1 win.

In the summer of 1961, Fitzgerald was transferred to Chester City and the majority of his games for the then Sealand Road club were as a left-winger. He had scored 12 goals in 80 Fourth Division games for the Cestrians before returning to Waterford in 1963 where he won a League of Ireland Championship medal in 1965-66.

Phil Kelly

Position	Full-back
Born	James Philip Vincent Kelly, Dublin, 10 July 1939

Clubs

Sheldon Town; Wolverhampton Wanderers; Norwich City

International Caps	5

Matches

Year	Opponent	Result	Score	G
1961	Wales	lost	2-3	
1961	Norway	won	3-1	
1961	Scotland	lost	0-3	
1962	Czechoslovakia	lost	1-3	
1962	Czechoslovakia	lost	1-7	

Though he was born in Dublin, Phil Kelly was brought up in Birmingham and used to attend evening training sessions at St Andrew's – the home of Birmingham City. However, he slipped through their net, and in September 1957 he signed for Wolverhampton Wanderers, from local junior club Sheldon Town.

When he joined the Molineux club, he was regarded as a central defender, but it wasn't too long before he was converted into a full-back.

Kelly made his League debut for Wolves during their 1958-59 League Championship-winning season but despite some solid displays when called upon, he made just 16 starts in eight seasons with the club.

Though he failed to win a regular place with Wolves, Kelly was called up as the Republic of Ireland's right-back five times between September 1960, when he played in the 3-2 defeat by Wales and October 1961, when he lost out to Manchester United's Tony Dunne.

A cousin of former Everton and Republic of Ireland star Peter Farrell, he eventually left Molineux in the summer of 1967 to join Norwich City. He became a regular in the Canaries' Second Division side, and in four seasons at Carrow Road made 115 league appearances before playing local non-League football.

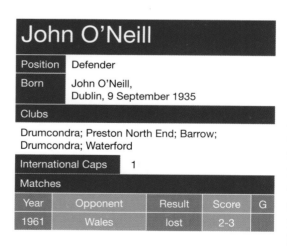

John O'Neill

Position	Defender
Born	John O'Neill,
Dublin, 9 September 1935
Clubs	

Drumcondra; Preston North End; Barrow; Drumcondra; Waterford

International Caps	1
Matches	

Year	Opponent	Result	Score	G
1961	Wales	lost	2-3	

A centre-half in Drumcondra's League of Ireland Championship-winning side of 1957-58, John O'Neill joined Preston North End towards the end of that campaign.

On his arrival at Deepdale, he was immediately switched to full-back, the position in which he made the majority of his 50 appearances for the Lancashire club. Despite an impressive debut in a 2-1 defeat of Arsenal, he found himself in North End's Central League side the following week. He didn't return to first team action until the 1960-61 season.

During the course of this campaign, O'Neill was selected for the Republic of Ireland side to play Wales, a match the Irish lost 3-2 — the country's first home defeat since Yugoslavia's 4-1 victory five years earlier!

North End lost their top-flight status at the end of that 1960-61 season. A spate of niggling injuries saw John O'Neill in and out of the North End side for the next couple of seasons, before he left Preston for Barrow and was immediately moved back to centre-half. In one season with Barrow, O'Neill made 42 appearances before returning to Drumcondra.

In his first season back with his former club, he helped the Dubliners to League Championship success. Midway through the 1965-66 season, he joined the Drums' League of Ireland rivals Waterford.

It was here that O'Neill began to assemble one of the most impressive array of domestic medals of any player in the Irish game. He ended his first campaign with Waterford with a League Championship medal. Over the next decade or so he added a further five League of Ireland Championship medals to his collection. He won a League Cup winners' medal in 1974 and collected FAI Cup runners-up medals in 1968 and 1972 to add to his winners' medal from the same competition with Drumcondra in 1957. Though not prolific, he was the Blues' leading scorer with 16 goals in 1968-69. In his time O'Neill

scored a total of 60 League goals for Waterford as the defender discovered his shooting boots.

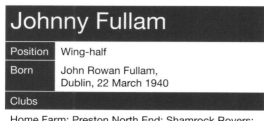

Johnny Fullam

Position	Wing-half
Born	John Rowan Fullam,
Dublin, 22 March 1940
Clubs	

Home Farm; Preston North End; Shamrock Rovers; Bohemians; Shamrock Rovers; Athlone Town

International Caps	11
International Goals	1
Matches	

Year	Opponent	Result	Score	G
1961	Norway	won	3-1	
1964	Spain	lost	0-2	
1964	Poland	lost	1-3	
1964	Norway	won	4-1	
1966	Austria	lost	0-1	
1966	Belgium	won	3-2	1
1968	Poland	drew	2-2	
1969	Poland	lost	0-1	
1969	Austria	drew	2-2	
1969	Denmark	drew	1-1	
1970	Czechoslovakia	lost	0-3	

One of the game's great tacticians, wing-half Johnny Fullam joined First Division Preston North End from Home Farm in October 1958. After spending a season in the club's Central League side, he made his North End debut in a 2-1 win at Newcastle United.

The following season, Fullam established himself in the Preston side. He won the first of 11 caps over a period of nine years when he starred in a 3-1 defeat of Norway. His only international goal came against Belgium in Liege in May 1966 when he netted a 68th minute winner in a 3-2 defeat of the Belgians.

Following North End's relegation to Division Two, Fullam left Deepdale to return to Ireland to join Shamrock Rovers. At Milltown he and Frank O'Neill struck up one of the League of Ireland's great partnerships, helping the Hoops win five FAI Cups. In the 1965 replayed final against Limerick, Fullam netted the winner, whilst his consistent displays in the middle of the park helped Rovers win the League Championship in 1963-64. A knee injury forced him to miss the 1969 FAI Cup Final. His career seemed to be over, but then he was snapped up by Bohemians, who had discarded their amateur status and opened up their doors to professionals.

He captained Bohemians when they won the FAI Cup in 1976 — it was his seventh FAI Cup winners' medal, his second with the Bohs. He also won a League Championship medal with the club in 1974-75 and appeared in three League Cup Finals. Fullam scored for Bohemians in the victory over Finn Harps in 1975 and was on the winning side again in 1977, this time with Shamrock Rovers. He was also a runner-up with the Hoops in 1979 when their opponents in that game were none other than Bohemians.

Twice winner of the Irish Soccer Writers' 'Personality of the Year', Johnny Fullam was just four months short of his 40th birthday when in November 1979 (ten years after he'd been written-off) he helped Athlone Town to victory in the competition. As well as playing football, Fullam was running two successful companies – a motor factors company and an industrial supply company.

Andy McEvoy

Position	Inside-forward
Born	Matthew Andrew McEvoy, Dublin, 15 July 1938
Died	May 1994

Clubs

Bray Wanderers; Blackburn Rovers; Limerick

International Caps	17
International Goals	6

Matches

Year	Opponent	Result	Score	G
1961	Scotland	lost	1-4	
1961	Scotland	lost	0-3	
1963	Scotland	won	1-0	
1964	Austria	won	3-2	
1964	Spain	lost	1-5	1
1964	Spain	lost	0-2	
1964	Poland	lost	1-3	
1964	Norway	won	4-1	1
1964	England	lost	1-3	
1965	Poland	won	3-2	2
1965	Belgium	lost	0-2	
1965	Spain	won	1-0	
1966	Spain	lost	1-4	1
1966	Spain	lost	0-1	
1967	Spain	drew	0-0	
1967	Turkey	won	2-1	1
1967	Czechoslovakia	lost	0-2	

Andy McEvoy joined Blackburn Rovers from Bray Wanderers in the mid-1950s but after a bout of homesickness, he returned to Ireland. Rovers' manager Johnny Carey was determined to sign the young McEvoy and in October 1956 he succeeded when he persuaded him to give the full-time another go.

When he arrived at Ewood Park, McEvoy was an inside-forward but Carey set about converting his new signing into an attacking wing-half. After little success, he moved back to inside-forward where he developed into one of the game's greatest goalpoachers. After a couple of seasons in the club's Central League side, he made his Football League debut in April 1959, scoring twice in a 3-1 defeat of Luton Town. It was the start of a prolific goalscoring career with the Lancashire club.

His progress was rewarded in May 1961 with an international debut for the Republic of Ireland against Scotland at Hampden Park. This was quickly followed by a second cap in Dublin four days later. However, both matches ended in heavy defeats for the Irish and he didn't return to international action until June 1963, when the Republic beat Scotland 1-0. A European Championship match against Spain in Seville in 1964 saw McEvoy take up his preferred position of inside-forward. Although Spain won 5-1, McEvoy grabbed an early goal with a stunning strike. He went on to appear in 17 internationals for the Republic, scoring six goals – a creditable total at a time when the national side was struggling for results.

McEvoy's Blackburn career didn't take off until 1963-64 when he scored 32 goals in 37 games, including four in each of the wins over Spurs (Home 7-2) and Leicester City (Away 5-2) and a hat-trick in the 8-2 win at West Ham United. Only Jimmy Greaves scored more goals that season – in fact, McEvoy was nicknamed the Greaves of the north! He topped Rovers' scoring charts again in 1964-65: his total of 29 goals – including hat-tricks in the defeats of Sheffield United (Home 4-0) and Nottingham Forest (Away 5-2) – saw him finish the First Division's joint leading scorer with Jimmy Greaves.

Rovers were relegated at the end of the 1965-66 season and after spending most of the following season in the reserves, he returned to Ireland. McEvoy, who had scored 103 goals in 213 League and Cup games, drove a tram and played part-time football for Limerick – he won an FAI Cup winners' medal after their victory over Drogheda in 1971. McEvoy, who headed the scoring charts in four of his five seasons with the club, died in Bray in May 1994, aged 56.

Mick Meagan

Position	Full-back
Born	Michael Kevin Meagan, Dublin, 29 May 1934

Clubs

Johnville; Everton; Huddersfield Town; Halifax Town; Drogheda United

International Caps	17

Matches

Year	Opponent	Result	Score	G
1961	Scotland	lost	0-3	
1962	Austria	lost	2-3	
1963	Iceland	won	4-2	
1964	Spain	lost	1-5	
1965	Belgium	lost	0-2	
1966	Spain	lost	1-4	
1966	Spain	lost	0-1	
1966	Austria	lost	0-1	
1966	Belgium	won	3-2	
1967	Spain	drew	0-0	
1967	Turkey	won	2-1	
1967	Spain	lost	0-2	
1967	Turkey	lost	1-2	
1967	Czechoslovakia	lost	0-2	
1968	Czechoslovakia	won	2-1	
1968	Poland	drew	2-2	
1970	Scotland	drew	1-1	

As a schoolboy, Mick Meagan became hooked on soccer after watching the legendary Shamrock Rovers duo of Tommy Eglington and Peter Farrell. Both players left Milltown for Everton in 1946 and six years later after playing for both Rathfarnham and Johnville, Mick Meagan was given the chance to follow his idols to Goodison after impressing in a representative game against a Liverpool district team.

'Chick' as he was known, struggled to establish himself in the Blues' side due to competition for places. He eventually got his chance in the league side in 1957-58, after showing his versatility with polished displays at both wing-half and full-back in the reserves. Thereafter the excellence of Jimmy Gabriel and Brian Harris limited his opportunities but he never complained when out of favour and in May 1961 won the first of 17 caps for the Republic of Ireland.

He made his international debut in the World Cup qualifier against Scotland at Hampden Park and though the Republic lost 4-1, he had done enough to retain his place in the side for the return match at Dalymount Park. Mick Meagan would remain a member of the Republic of Ireland squad throughout the 1960s, though like many of his contemporaries in the English League, he was not always released for matches.

He eventually reaped his reward in the domestic game when in 1962-63 he won a League Championship medal as a full-back, at first replacing the injured Alex Parker on the right and then ousting George Thomson from the left-flank berth on merit. A year later he was on his way out of Goodison in a player exchange deal which brought Huddersfield Town and England World Cup-winner Ray Wilson to Merseyside.

His expert positional play and excellent ball distribution compensated for his lack of pace, and he proved an inspirational signing as Town consolidated their Division Two status. Meagan was made captain at Huddersfield – a job he also enjoyed at his third and final League club, Halifax Town. After a year at The Shay, an Achilles tendon injury brought his professional career to a close.

Meagan returned to his homeland to become player-manager at Drogheda United. It was as a League of Ireland player that he made his 17th and final international appearance against Scotland in September 1969. That game, in which he captained his country for the only time, also marked the beginning of his 12-match stint as national team manager.

Frank O'Neill

Position	Outside-right
Born	Frank Simon O'Neill, Dublin, 13 April 1940

Clubs

Home Farm; Arsenal; Shamrock Rovers; Waterford

International Caps	20
International Goals	1

Matches

Year	Opponent	Result	Score	G
1961	Czechoslovakia	lost	1-3	
1961	Czechoslovakia	lost	1-7	
1965	Poland	won	3-2	
1965	Belgium	lost	0-2	
1965	Spain	won	1-0	
1966	Spain	lost	1-4	
1966	Spain	lost	0-1	
1966	West Germany	lost	0-4	
1966	Austria	lost	0-1	
1967	Spain	drew	0-0	
1967	Turkey	won	2-1	1
1967	Spain	lost	0-2	
1967	Turkey	lost	1-2	
1969	Poland	lost	0-1	
1969	Austria	drew	2-2	
1969	Denmark	drew	1-1	
1969	Czechoslovakia	lost	1-2	
1969	Denmark	lost	0-2	
1969	Hungary	lost	1-2	
1972	Austria	lost	0-6	

Frank O'Neill joined Arsenal from Dublin junior club Home Farm as an amateur in December 1958, signing professional forms the following April. He was a member of the Gunners' reserve side which swept all before them in 1960-61 – the Metropolitan League Championship, League Challenge Cup and Professional Cup. Despite having made only two League appearances for the North London club, O'Neill's performances for the Gunners' second string had sufficiently impressed Shamrock Rovers who paid a record League of Ireland fee to take the winger to Milltown.

He quickly found the measure of League of Ireland football, his wing play bringing him to the notice of the international selection committee during his first season with the Hoops. Following two heavy back-to-back defeats by Scotland, the committee were keen to give Irish-based players a chance.

He was called up for his first full cap for the World Cup qualifier against Czechoslovakia in Dublin in October 1961. The Irish lost that match 3-1, and though he kept his place for the return game in Prague, the Republic went down 7-1! It would be another two-and-a-half years before Frank O'Neill got another chance in a green shirt.

He spent 13 glittering seasons with the Hoops, winning a host of honours including a League of Ireland Championship medal in 1963-64 and seven FAI Cup winners' medals. He won his first cup medal in 1962. This was followed by an incredible run of six consecutive successes in the competition between 1964 and 1969.

His 20th and final international cap came against Austria almost 10 years to the day after his debut. During that time he played his part in a number of notable triumphs – perhaps most famous being his delivery of a free-kick which forced Spain's goalkeeper Iribar to push the ball into his own net, for the single goal which earned a celebrated victory at Dalymount Park in May 1965.

He was appointed player-manager of the Hoops in 1970 and remained in that post for four seasons until he was transferred to Waterford in 1974. He was a member of the side which won Ireland's inaugural League Cup in October 1975 when they beat Donegal side Finn Harps 2-1 in the final.

Tony Dunne

Position	Left-back
Born	Anthony Peter Dunne, Dublin, 24 July 1941

Clubs

St Finbar's; Tara United; Shelbourne; Manchester United; Bolton Wanderers; Detroit Express (U.S.)

International Caps	33

Matches

Year	Opponent	Result	Score	G
1962	Austria	lost	2-3	
1963	Iceland	won	4-2	
1963	Scotland	won	1-0	
1964	Austria	won	3-2	
1964	Spain	lost	0-2	
1964	Poland	lost	1-3	
1964	Norway	won	4-1	
1964	England	lost	1-3	
1965	Poland	won	3-2	
1965	Spain	won	1-0	
1966	Spain	lost	1-4	
1966	Spain	lost	0-1	
1966	Austria	lost	0-1	
1966	Belgium	won	3-2	
1967	Spain	drew	0-0	
1967	Turkey	won	2-1	
1967	Spain	lost	0-2	
1969	Poland	lost	0-1	
1969	Denmark	drew	1-1	
1969	Hungary	lost	1-2	
1970	Hungary	lost	0-4	
1971	Sweden	drew	1-1	
1971	Italy	lost	1-2	
1971	Austria	lost	1-4	
1974	Brazil	lost	1-2	
1974	Uruguay	lost	0-2	
1974	Chile	won	2-1	
1975	Turkey	drew	1-1	
1975	West Germany B	won	1-0	
1975	Switzerland	won	2-1	
1975	USSR	lost	1-2	
1975	Switzerland	lost	0-1	
1976	Turkey	won	4-0	

Tony Dunne was a centre-forward in his junior days in Dublin with St Finbar's and Tara United. He then joined Shelbourne, but a few weeks after winning an FAI Cup winners' medal in April 1960, he was on his way to Manchester United for a knock-down price of £5,000.

Above: Tony Dunne

He worked his way up through the ranks at Old Trafford before claiming a regular first team spot in place of Noel Cantwell midway through the 1961-62 season. That breakthrough signalled the beginning of his career as one of the greatest full-backs the game has ever seen.

With the Republic of Ireland using Noel Cantwell's physical presence at centre-forward, Dunne won the first of his 33 international caps against Austria in Dublin in April 1962. In his early days with the Republic, he was played at right-back, but his best performances at national level came when he was paired with his United team-mate Shay Brennan. He was an important player in the Irish team which narrowly missed out on qualification for the 1966 World Cup Finals. The pinnacle of Dunne's international career came three years later when he was appointed captain of the Republic of Ireland for the first time. This honour came shortly after he had been named Ireland's 'Player of the Year'. Playing alongside his brother Pat, he would skipper his country on four more occasions over the next six years but in June 1972 he fell out with manager Liam Tuohy. He was only recalled after Johnny Giles had taken over as team boss: it was a brief renaissance as he added just five more caps to his tally.

Tony Dunne had 13 seasons at Old Trafford, during which he turned out for the Reds in 530 League and Cup games. He picked up League Championship medals in 1964-65 and 1966-67, an FA Cup winners' medal after United's 3-1 victory over Leicester City in the 1963 final and a European Cup winners' medal in 1968. This match, where the Reds defeated Portuguese champions Benfica 4-1, is regarded by football pundits as one of the greatest displays of Dunne's career.

In April 1973, Tony Dunne was one of six players – including Denis Law – to be freed by United boss Tommy Docherty, and the following August he was transferred to Bolton Wanderers. In five seasons at Burnden Park, Dunne played in 192 League and Cup games. In his final season in the Football League, 1977-78, he won a Second Division Championship medal with the Wanderers.

He then jetted off to the United States to play for Detroit Express in the NASL. Tony Dunne, who still follows the fortunes of the Wanderers, manages the golf driving range he built in Altrincham shortly after hanging up his boots.

Alfie Hale

Position	Inside-forward
Born	Alfred Hale, Waterford, 28 August 1939

Clubs

Waterford; Cork Hibernians; Waterford; Aston Villa; Doncaster Rovers; Newport County; Waterford; St Patrick's Athletic; Limerick; Thurles Town

International Caps	14
International Goals	2

Matches

Year	Opponent	Result	Score	G
1962	Austria	lost	2-3	
1963	Iceland	won	4-2	
1964	Spain	lost	1-5	
1964	Spain	lost	0-2	
1967	Spain	lost	0-2	
1968	Poland	drew	2-2	1
1969	Poland	lost	0-1	
1969	Austria	drew	2-2	1
1969	Denmark	drew	1-1	
1970	Scotland	drew	1-1	
1970	Czechoslovakia	lost	0-3	
1971	Poland	lost	0-2	
1972	Austria	lost	0-6	
1974	Poland	won	1-0	

One of six members of his family to turn out for League of Ireland club Waterford, he was a sharp, quick player with an explosive turn of speed and an eye for goal. After joining Waterford in 1957, he had a brief spell with Cork Hibernians the following season before rejoining his home-town club in readiness for the 1958-59 season in which he was the top-scorer with 18 goals.

As a Waterford player, he won representative honours with the League of Ireland and was in the Irish Olympic side which beat Holland 6-3 in 1960. That Olympic qualifying game saw Hale score a hat-trick, witnessed by Aston Villa manager Joe Mercer who paid £4,500 for his services in June 1960.

Though he had been bought as a replacement for Italy-bound Gerry Hitchens, his progress at Villa Park was hampered by a series of niggling injuries. Rarely seen at first-team level, his displays for the reserves did at least lead to a full international debut against Austria in April 1962. He won the last of his 14 caps against Poland some 12 years later. Hale enjoyed his best spell with the Republic in 1968 when he was capped in four consecutive internationals. This rare extended run in the national side saw him register his two international goals – against Poland in May 1968 and against Austria in November 1968 – both late equalisers at Dalymount Park.

Hale left Villa Park in the summer of 1962, joining Doncaster Rovers for £3,500. He scored 42 goals in 119 league games for the Belle Vue club before moving on to their Fourth Division rivals Newport County in a straight swap deal for Lawrie Sheffield in August 1965. Despite missing a number of games through injury, he scored 21 goals in 34 games in his only season at Somerton Park prior to rejoining Waterford.

Back in Ireland, he helped the Blues to five League of Ireland titles before moving on to Cork Celtic in 1973. He won another League Championship medal in his first season but then left to have brief spells with St Patrick's Athletic and Limerick before deciding to retire. Due to injuries he made a brief comeback with Thurles Town and scored once to earn the remarkable distinction of having scored in four decades – the 1950s, '60s, '70s and '80s!

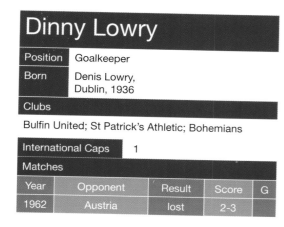

Dinny Lowry

Position	Goalkeeper
Born	Denis Lowry, Dublin, 1936

Clubs
Bulfin United; St Patrick's Athletic; Bohemians

International Caps	1

Matches				
Year	Opponent	Result	Score	G
1962	Austria	lost	2-3	

Goalkeeper Dinny Lowry played his early football with Bulfin United before joining St Patrick's Athletic, where he succeeded the club's first team coach Jimmy Collins between the posts. Described as a 'brilliant young keeper, who has a steadying influence on his defence', Dinny Lowry helped St Pat's win back-to-back League Championships in 1954-55 and 1955-56.

His form during those two campaigns saw the former schoolboy international win representative honours by being selected for the League of Ireland side.

Injuries and a loss of form then hampered his progress, but he bounced back during the 1958-59 FAI Cup campaign which culminated in St Pat's beating Waterford 2-1 in the replayed final and lifting the trophy for the first time. He later appeared in two more FAI Cup Finals with St Pat's, gaining another winners' medal in 1960-61 and a runners-up medal in 1966-67.

Dinny Lowry's only full international cap came in April 1962, when as a 34th minute substitute, he came off the bench to replace the injured Alan Kelly in the 3-2 defeat by Austria.

In March 1969 Dinny Lowry, along with former Dundalk winger Tony O'Connell,

made history by becoming the first professionals to play for Bohemians. Just over a year later, Lowry helped the Bohs to their first FAI Cup success since 1935!

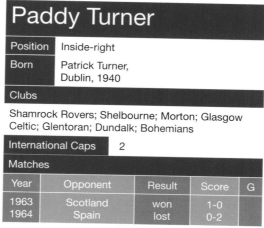

Paddy Turner

Position	Inside-right
Born	Patrick Turner, Dublin, 1940

Clubs
Shamrock Rovers; Shelbourne; Morton; Glasgow Celtic; Glentoran; Dundalk; Bohemians

International Caps	2

Matches				
Year	Opponent	Result	Score	G
1963	Scotland	won	1-0	
1964	Spain	lost	0-2	

Motor mechanic Paddy Turner was a cultured inside-forward, who began his senior career in the League of Ireland with Shamrock Rovers. In his first season with the Hoops, 1958-59, he won a League of Ireland Championship medal.

In the summer of 1960 he was surprisingly allowed to join Rovers' Dublin rivals Shelbourne, and in November 1961 was transferred to Scottish club Morton. He was a huge success at Cappielow Park where his performances attracted scouts from both north and south of the border.

In May 1963 he signed for Celtic. Just 10 days after putting pen to paper, Paddy Turner was in the Republic of Ireland side which beat Scotland 1-0 in Dublin. He won his second cap for the national side in the European Nations Cup game against Spain in April 1964.

At Parkhead, Turner looked to have 'football' stamped all over him following his performance in the Public Trial match.

However, he had made just 14 appearances for the Bhoys when he was dropped for the up-and-coming Bobby Murdoch.

In June 1964 he returned to Ireland to join Belfast club Glentoran in the Irish League, where he spent one season before returning south to sign for Dundalk. Turner had seven seasons at Oriel Park, winning a League Championship medal in 1966-67. He later ended his playing career back in Dublin with Bohemians.

Ray Brady

Position	Centre-half
Born	Thomas Raymond Brady, Dublin, 3 June 1937

Clubs
Transport; Home Farm; Millwall; Queen's Park Rangers; Hastings United

International Caps	6

Matches				
Year	Opponent	Result	Score	G
1964	Austria	drew	0-0	
1964	Austria	won	3-2	
1964	Spain	lost	1-5	
1964	Spain	lost	0-2	
1964	Poland	lost	1-3	
1964	Norway	won	4-1	

The brother of Republic of Ireland legend Liam Brady and Pat Brady, he went on to play for Millwall and Queen's Park Rangers. Ray began his career with League of Ireland club Transport FC before switching to Home Farm.

In 1957 he joined Third Division (South) club Millwall and shortly afterwards was joined by his brother Pat. Though he joined the club as a full-back, Ray Brady's build and height – he stood 6ft – made him ideally suited for a central defensive role and towards the end of the 1960-61 season he made the position his own.

In 1961-62 he helped the Lions win the Fourth Division Championship but after one more season in which he took his total of League appearances to 165, both he and his brother Pat moved across London to Queen's Park Rangers.

Shortly after his arrival at Loftus Road, Ray Brady made his first international appearance for the Republic of Ireland in the scoreless draw with Austria. The first player from Transport to win full international honours, he had an outstanding game in the No.4 shirt and was named 'Man-of-the-Match'. Brady appeared in the Republic's next five games, winning his sixth and final cap in the 4-1 defeat of Norway in Oslo in May 1964.

He spent two seasons at Loftus Road, appearing in 89 Third Division games before leaving to play non-League football for Southern League club, Hastings United.

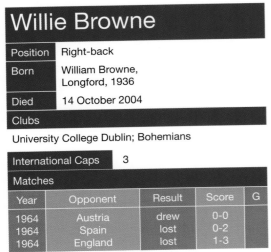

Willie Browne

Position	Right-back
Born	William Browne, Longford, 1936
Died	14 October 2004
Clubs	

University College Dublin; Bohemians

International Caps	3

Matches

Year	Opponent	Result	Score	G
1964	Austria	drew	0-0	
1964	Spain	lost	0-2	
1964	England	lost	1-3	

Full-back Willie Browne was a brilliant amateur player. He played soccer for University College, Dublin, refusing offers to join any of the big Irish clubs.

In October 1958 while still a student, he won 'B' level international honours when he played against South Africa. On completion of his studies, the big defender joined amateur side Bohemians, spending five seasons with the Gypsies between 1961 and 1966.

A former captain of the Irish amateur XI, he represented the League of Ireland on seven occasions and won President's and Leinster Cup winners' medals whilst with the Bohs.

In the last week of September 1963 Browne was involved in two nights of glory for Irish football. Browne made his full international debut for the Republic of Ireland against Austria in Vienna, in a European Nations Cup game known as the 'battle', when the Republic recorded their first-ever scoreless draw. A few days later he was a member of the League of Ireland XI which recorded a remarkable 2-1 victory over the Football League at Dalymount Park. His performance in that game made him the target of a number of clubs across the water but once again, the multi-talented defender resisted all offers. He won two more caps against Spain in April 1964 and against England the following month.

Willie Browne actually delayed his retirement from the game, scheduled for the end of the 1965-66 season, so that he could captain the Republic of Ireland in the European Amateur Tournament that summer.

Ronnie Whelan senior

Position	Inside-forward
Born	Ronald Whelan, Dublin, 17 November 1936
Died	1993
Clubs	

Home Farm; St Patrick's Athletic; Drogheda; Aer Lingus

International Caps	2

Matches

Year	Opponent	Result	Score	G
1964	Austria	drew	0-0	
1964	England	lost	1-3	

The father of former Liverpool captain Ronnie Whelan Junior, Whelan Senior was a gifted inside-forward who played his early football for Stella Maris prior to joining Home Farm. He won numerous honours with Home Farm, who at the time were a junior club. His form led to him having a three-month trial with Chelsea. This didn't work out and he returned to Dublin to join St Patrick's Athletic in 1956.

He spent 12 seasons with St Pat's and was the club's leading scorer in five of those campaigns, netting a total of 89 League goals. St Pat's won the League of Ireland Championship in 1955-56 and in 1958-59 won the FAI Cup, a feat they repeated two seasons later.

Whelan had already represented the League of Ireland XI against the Irish League in March 1961, and scored the winning goal against the Football League a month after making his international debut. That international debut came in the European Nations Cup qualifier against Austria, a game that ended goalless, whilst his second and final appearance came against England in May 1964. Also that year, he was a member of the Dublin XI which played Liverpool.

In the mid-1960s Whelan began to suffer from a spate of niggling injuries. After losing his place in the St Pat's side, he joined Drogheda. Here he had six good seasons, helping them reach the 1971 FAI Cup Final where they lost 3-0 to Limerick. He eventually retired from League of Ireland football in 1973, but continued to play with his employers Aer Lingus in the Leinster Senior League for many seasons.

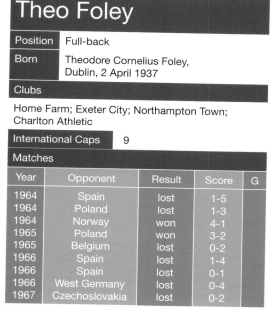

Theo Foley

Position	Full-back
Born	Theodore Cornelius Foley, Dublin, 2 April 1937
Clubs	

Home Farm; Exeter City; Northampton Town; Charlton Athletic

International Caps	9

Matches

Year	Opponent	Result	Score	G
1964	Spain	lost	1-5	
1964	Poland	lost	1-3	
1964	Norway	won	4-1	
1965	Poland	won	3-2	
1965	Belgium	lost	0-2	
1966	Spain	lost	1-4	
1966	Spain	lost	0-1	
1966	West Germany	lost	0-4	
1967	Czechoslovakia	lost	0-2	

A versatile and competitive performer, Theo Foley was one of a number of promising Home Farm youngsters to head to England during the 1950s. His big break did not come with a glamorous top-flight club, but Exeter City of the Third Division (South).

Though he could fill a number of defensive positions, his strength and speed were best used at full-back. He made 154 league appearances for the Devon club before he was transferred to Northampton Town in May 1961.

His six seasons at the County Ground coincided with the most successful era in the club's history. The Cobblers had just won promotion to the Third Division when he joined and two seasons later moved up another rung as Third Division Champions. In 1964-65 they became a First Division club. Foley had by now become a full international, making his debut for the Republic of Ireland against Spain in Seville in March 1964. Occasional appearances followed but the highlight of his international career came when he was made captain for the match against Belgium in March 1965.

Northampton Town's downfall was just as dramatic as their rise. After just one season in the top flight, they dropped to the Third Division in successive seasons. Shortly after the Cobblers lost their Second Division status, Foley was transferred to Charlton Athletic, having made 205 league appearances in a Northampton shirt.

After a handful of appearances for the Addicks, he had spells as George Graham's assistant at Millwall, Queen's Park Rangers and Arsenal. In May 1990 he left Highbury to return to Northampton, this time as the club's manager. Sacked in April 1992 when the club were taken over by new administrators, he later became youth team manager at Fulham and assistant-manager at Southend United.

Freddie Strahan

Position	Centre-half
Born	Frederick Strahan; Dublin
Clubs	

Shelbourne; Rialto

International Caps	5
International Goals	1

Matches

Year	Opponent	Result	Score	G
1964	Poland	lost	1-3	
1964	Norway	won	4-1	
1964	England	lost	1-3	1
1965	Poland	won	3-2	
1966	West Germany	lost	0-4	

A tough-tackling centre-half, Freddie Strahan played a major role in Shelbourne's successes in the 1960s and for much of that decade, he captained the Reds. Playing alongside the likes of Tony Dunne and Paddy Roberts, he was the Reds' skipper when they beat Cork Hibs 2-0 in April 1960 to win the FAI Cup. He also led them to success in the League Championship in 1961-62, missing out on the 'double' by going down 4-1 to Shamrock Rovers in that season's FAI Cup Final. Shelbourne won the Cup again in 1963 with another 2-0 defeat of Cork Hibs.

By the start of the 1963-64 season, Freddie Strahan was the regular centre-half for the League of Ireland XI. Midway through the campaign, his display for the Dublin City select against the mighty Arsenal impressed the international selectors, who called him up for the Republic of Ireland's game against Poland in May 1964. Despite being played out of position at right-half, Strahan rose to the big occasions. Three days later he won his second cap against Norway: playing in his preferred position of centre-half he had an outstanding game in a 4-1 win. Just a fortnight after his international debut, he was preferred to Ray Brady at right-half for the Republic's home game against England. Though the Irish lost 3-1, Freddie Strahan scored a most spectacular goal, especially for a centre-half. With Bobby Moore trailing in his wake, he strode purposefully forward before sending a crisp shot past the despairing dive of England keeper Tony Waiters – it was a strike that any great goalscorer would have been proud of.

In the summer of 1966, an International select played Shelbourne in a benefit match for Strahan, who when his first-class career ended, played in the Leinster Senior League with Rialto.

1963-64 when the Hoops won the League Championship. He helped Rovers win the FAI Cup in 1962 and 1964 when he scored both goals in the replayed final – the winner being a magnificent left-foot drive still talked about by older Shamrock supporters.

His goalscoring exploits for the Hoops led to Bailham representing the League of Ireland – an outstanding debut in the 2-1 defeat of the Football League in October 1963. He also had a good game for the Dublin City select side which played Arsenal in 1964 and later won his one and only full international cap for the Republic of Ireland in the 3-1 home defeat by England in May of that year.

In September 1960 whilst playing in a more forward role, Hennessey scored both the Republic's goals in the 2-1 defeat of Iceland in a 'B' international. Though this alerted the selection committee to Hennessey's attacking talents, four years elapsed before he was called into the full international team as an inside-forward. He made his debut in the 3-2 home victory over Poland in October 1964.

Though he failed to score in any of his five international appearances, he did score a number of spectacular goals for Shelbourne, notably against Sporting Lisbon in the European Cup in 1962. After parting company with the Shels, Jackie Hennessey had a brief spell in the Irish League with Derry City. When he later became unsettled, his old Shelbourne mentor and then-manager of St Patrick's Athletic, Gerry Doyle stepped in to secure his signature. The highlights of his time with St Pat's included a stunning goal in a Fairs Cup-tie against Bordeaux, and a second FAI Cup runners-up medal in 1967 after his side had lost to Shamrock Rovers.

Eddie Bailham

Position	Centre-forward
Born	Edward Bailham, Dublin, 1941
Clubs	

Home Farm; Cork Hibernians; Shamrock Rovers

| International Caps | 1 |

Matches				
Year	Opponent	Result	Score	G
1964	England	lost	1-3	

Big-hearted centre-forward Eddie Bailham earned youth and junior international honours while with Home Farm. He nearly went to Manchester United, having spent the majority of his school holidays at Old Trafford. However, on leaving Home Farm, he had a brief spell with Cork Hibs before in 1960 signing for Shamrock Rovers.

With the Hoops, Eddie Bailham won all the honours the Irish game has to offer. At Shamrock Rovers, Bailham – the type of centre-forward who would shoot on sight – teamed up with Jackie Mooney. Bailham was Rovers' top-scorer in 1961-62 and in

Jackie Hennessey

Position	Wing-half/Inside-forward
Born	John Hennessey, Dublin
Clubs	

Shelbourne; Derry City; St Patrick's Athletic

| International Caps | 5 |

Matches				
Year	Opponent	Result	Score	G
1965	Poland	won	3-2	
1965	Belgium	lost	0-2	
1965	Spain	won	1-0	
1966	West Germany	lost	0-4	
1969	Austria	drew	2-2	

A former schoolboy team-mate of Johnny Giles, Jackie Hennessey was a versatile performer who came into Shelbourne's first team as a fast and skilful inside-forward, before later finding success as a cultured goalscoring left-half.

He spent nine seasons with Shelbourne, during which time he scored 39 league goals and won FAI Cup winners' medals in 1960 and 1963 – beating Cork Hibs on both occasions. Hennessey also won a League Championship medal in 1961-62.

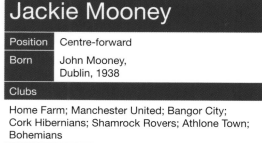

Jackie Mooney

Position	Centre-forward
Born	John Mooney, Dublin, 1938
Clubs	

Home Farm; Manchester United; Bangor City; Cork Hibernians; Shamrock Rovers; Athlone Town; Bohemians

| International Caps | 2 |
| International Goals | 1 |

Matches				
Year	Opponent	Result	Score	G
1965	Poland	won	3-2	1
1965	Belgium	lost	0-2	

Although not particularly tall, centre-forward Jackie Mooney's great strength was his aerial ability. During his early days, he had brief spells with Home Farm, Manchester

United and Welsh club Bangor City before signing for Cork Hibernians. He was their top scorer in 1960-61 and 1961-62 and it wasn't long before Shamrock Rovers secured his services.

At club level, he was one of a number of centre-forwards who preyed on the pin-point crosses of both Liam Tuohy and Frank O'Neill. He was the Hoops' leading marksman in 1962-63, his first season with the club. The following season, Mooney helped Rovers to win the League and Cup double – he was also the League's top goalscorer with 16 goals.

In October 1964 Mooney was given his chance in the Republic of Ireland side alongside Blackburn's Andy McEvoy. The Irish were trailing Poland 2-0 after just 22 minutes when Mooney scored one of the goals in the fight-back to win 3-2. A second cap followed in the Republic's next game against Belgium. When a round of World Cup qualifiers kicked off in the summer of 1965, the Irish selectors decided upon a Cantwell-McEvoy pairing in attack.

Mooney, who won an FAI Cup winners' medal with Shamrock Rovers in 1964-65 then suffered from a number of serious injuries. This caused him to miss three years' football. He eventually he made a comeback to League of Ireland football in 1969 with Athlone, who had been re-elected to the League that year after a 40-year absence. Making an immediate impact, he netted a hat-trick in the 1969 Leinster Senior Cup Final – the club's first senior trophy in 45 years!

He later ended his career with Bohemians and was their top-scorer in 1971-72 before he left to concentrate on his work in the Cargo Department at Dublin Airport.

Fran Brennan

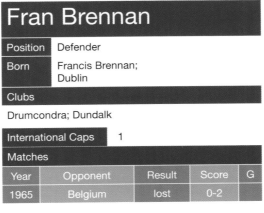

Position	Defender
Born	Francis Brennan; Dublin

Clubs
Drumcondra; Dundalk

International Caps	1

Matches

Year	Opponent	Result	Score	G
1965	Belgium	lost	0-2	

Red-headed Fran Brennan was a tenacious and whole-hearted defender who could operate at both full-back and centre-half. He began his career with Drumcondra whom he helped win the League Championship in 1964-65.

During the course of that season, Brennan won representative honours for the League of Ireland. He was selected for the Republic of Ireland as a replacement for the injured Charlie Hurley in the match against Belgium. He didn't have the best of international debuts as the Republic, severely depleted by injuries and withdrawals, lost 2-0 to a good Belgian side.

Shortly afterwards, he joined Dundalk and in 1966-67 was a part of the Lilywhites' historic season. Dundalk won the League Championship, the Shield, the Top Four Trophy and the Donegal Cup. Fran Brennan was probably the club's most influential player. Brennan's performances at full-back were outstanding – he even had time to support his attack – and one contemporary writer stated that 'he was at the peak of his physical fitness'. Brennan was even caught offside once – quite a feat for a full-back.

An important member of the Dundalk side for a number of seasons, he played his part in the defeat of DOS Utrecht in the Fairs Cup the following season 1968-69.

Ollie Conmy

Position	Winger
Born	Oliver Martin Conmy, Mulrany, 13 November 1939

Clubs
St Paulinus YC; Huddersfield Town; Peterborough United; Cambridge City; Ely City; March Town

International Caps	5

Matches

Year	Opponent	Result	Score	G
1965	Belgium	lost	0-2	
1967	Czechoslovakia	lost	0-2	
1968	Czechoslovakia	won	2-1	
1968	Poland	drew	2-2	
1970	Czechoslovakia	lost	0-3	

Although born in Mulrany, Ollie Conmy was just nine years old when his parents left County Mayo to live in Dewsbury, Yorkshire. Spotted playing for St Paulinus Youth Club by Huddersfield Town, the Terriers gave him his chance at League level. A regular in the Yorkshire club's Central League side, playing mainly on the right-wing, he made his Football League debut against Liverpool in October 1960. He had made just three League appearances in five years when Peterborough United boss Gordon Clarke – who had begun his managerial career at Waterford – took him to London Road in the summer of 1964 for a fee of £2,000.

The switch to East Anglia proved a huge success and it was as a Posh player that he won all five of his full international caps for the Republic of Ireland. In fact, Conmy had never seen the Republic play when he received a surprise call-up to play Belgium at Dalymount Park in March 1965. After the 2-0 defeat it was another two years before he returned to the national side, following Joe Haverty's retirement from the international scene.

He played in both European Nations Cup games against Czechoslovakia – his performance in Prague when he set up Ray Treacy's goal being his best.

Ollie Conmy spent eight seasons at Peterborough, scoring 34 goals in 262 league games. Despite finishing ninth in Division Three in 1967-68, they were relegated for illegal payments. They were still in the Fourth Division when he was freed in 1972. He later played non-League football for Cambridge City, Ely City and March Town.

Shay Brennan

Position	Full-back
Born	James Seamus Anthony Brennan, Manchester, 6 May 1937
Died	9 June 2000
Clubs	

Manchester United; Waterford United

International Caps	19

Matches

Year	Opponent	Result	Score	G
1965	Spain	won	1-0	
1966	Spain	lost	0-1	
1966	Austria	lost	0-1	
1966	Belgium	won	3-2	
1967	Spain	drew	0-0	
1967	Turkey	won	2-1	
1967	Spain	lost	0-2	
1969	Czechoslovakia	lost	1-2	
1969	Denmark	lost	0-2	
1969	Hungary	lost	1-2	
1970	Scotland	drew	1-1	
1970	Czechoslovakia	lost	0-3	
1970	Denmark	drew	1-1	
1970	Hungary	lost	0-4	
1970	Poland	lost	1-2	
1970	West Germany	lost	1-2	
1971	Poland	lost	0-2	
1971	Sweden	lost	0-1	
1971	Italy	lost	0-3	

Manchester-born full-back Shay Brennan became the first of a long line of second-generation Irishmen to play for the Republic. FIFA had relaxed qualification rules to allow players to represent their parents' nation of birth.

Brennan joined Manchester United as a 16-year-old in 1953 and two years later was a member of the FA Youth Cup-winning team. Of all the youngsters called upon to help United in the aftermath of the Munich air disaster, Shay Brennan gave the most mature display when he overcame the intensity of the occasion, and starred as United beat Sheffield Wednesday in the FA Cup fifth round match at Old Trafford in February 1958. What made Brennan's display at outside-left even more remarkable was the fact that he not only scored twice in a 3-0 win but at the time he was a reserve full-back!

Three days after that sensational first team debut, Brennan made his League bow in the home game against Nottingham Forest. He went on to appear in 356 League and Cup games for United – his only League club. He collected two League Championship medals and was a member of the 1968 European Cup-winning team – ample compensation for missing the 1963 FA Cup Final.

He made his first appearance for the Republic of Ireland in the World Cup qualifier against Spain in Dublin in May 1965. The selection of an English-born player brought great debate. The fact that he had been on the brink of an England cap ahead of the 1962 World Cup only intensified matters. Teaming up with Manchester United team-mates Pat and Tony Dunne, Brennan played his part in a celebrated 1-0 victory as the Republic's World Cup campaign got off to a flying start. He retained his place in the national side for the next 18 months, but later found himself on the sidelines when the younger more attack-minded Joe Kinnear got his chance in 1967.

It was inevitable that he would win back his place in the Republic line-up. New national team boss Mick Meagan recalled

Brennan to the side towards the end of the decade, and appointed him team captain for his first World Cup match in charge, against Czechoslovakia.

On leaving Old Trafford, Shay Brennan joined League of Ireland club Waterford United. He continued his winning ways, collecting League Championship medals in 1971-72 and 1972-73. His final success came in October 1973 when Waterford beat Finn Harps 2-1 to lift Ireland's inaugural League Cup competition.

Pat Dunne

Position	Goalkeeper
Born	Patrick Anthony Joseph Dunne, Dublin, 9 February 1943
Clubs	

Everton; Shamrock Rovers; Manchester United; Plymouth Argyle

International Caps	5

Matches

Year	Opponent	Result	Score	G
1965	Spain	won	1-0	
1966	Spain	lost	1-4	
1966	Spain	lost	0-1	
1966	West Germany	lost	0-4	
1967	Turkey	won	2-1	

The younger brother of Manchester United, Bolton Wanderers and Republic of Ireland full-back Tony Dunne, he joined Everton as an apprentice in the summer of 1960 but failed to make the grade at Goodison Park. He returned to his native Dublin to play for Shamrock Rovers.

He won an FAI Cup winners' medal with the Hoops in 1964, this after Rovers had beaten Cork Celtic 2-1 in the replayed final. Shortly afterwards, Manchester United manager Matt Busby paid £10,000 for his services.

His return to the north-west was much more productive this time, for in three seasons at Old Trafford he appeared in 45 league games, plus another 13 in European competitions. In 1965-66 he appeared between the posts in 37 of United's games as they won that season's League Championship.

Dunne had made his full international debut for the Republic of Ireland in the 1-0 World Cup win over Spain in May 1965. His display led to a run of four games in the Republic line-up. With the national side losing three matches in succession, conceding nine goals and failing to qualify for the 1966 World Cup finals, he lost his place to Alan Kelly.

In February 1967 having earlier lost his place at Old Trafford to Northern Ireland's Harry Gregg, he joined Third Division Plymouth Argyle. During four years at Home Park Pat Dunne, one of the best keepers outside of the top flight, made 152 League appearances.

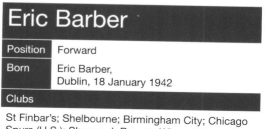

Eric Barber

Position	Forward
Born	Eric Barber, Dublin, 18 January 1942
Clubs	

St Finbar's; Shelbourne; Birmingham City; Chicago Spurs (U.S.); Shamrock Rovers; Wiener Sportclub (Austria); Shelbourne

International Caps	2
Matches	

Year	Opponent	Result	Score	G
1966	Spain	lost	1-4	
1966	Belgium	won	3-2	

Born into a boxing family (his brother Dave was the Irish light-weight champion) he began his career with St Finbar's in Dublin prior to joining Shelbourne in 1958. The following year he was a member of the Shels youth team that won the FAI Cup

and in 1960 helped the club win the senior competition – a feat they repeated in 1963.

A mobile and aggressive centre-forward, he forged a quite formidable partnership up front with Christy Doyle, helping Shelbourne win the League Championship in 1961-62 when he was the club's leading scorer.

Towards the end of the 1964-65 season, he won the first of his two full caps for the Republic of Ireland. Suffering from a bout of toothache, he had a disappointing game in a 4-1 defeat by Spain. Barber's second appearance came almost a year later in a 3-2 win over Belgium. By that time Barber had left Tolka Park to join Stan Cullis's Birmingham City – however, he proved too slow to make any impact on the English scene.

Chicago Spurs ended his nightmare when they paid the St Andrew's club £2,000 to take him to the NASL in the summer of 1967. He then spent the 1969-70 campaign on loan with Shamrock Rovers before having two injury-plagued seasons playing in Austria with Wiener Sportclub. Returning to Ireland in 1972 he rejoined Shelbourne and helped them reach the 1973 FAI Cup Final. Not only did his side lose to Cork Hibs, but he had the indignity of being sent-off!

Eamonn Dunphy

Position	Midfield
Born	Eamonn Martin Dunphy, Dublin, 3 August 1945
Clubs	

Manchester United; York City; Millwall; Charlton Athletic; Reading

International Caps	23
Matches	

Year	Opponent	Result	Score	G
1966	Spain	lost	0-1	
1966	West Germany	lost	0-4	
1967	Turkey	won	2-1	
1967	Spain	lost	0-2	
1967	Turkey	lost	1-2	
1967	Czechoslovakia	lost	0-2	
1968	Czechoslovakia	won	2-1	
1968	Poland	drew	2-2	
1969	Poland	lost	0-1	
1969	Austria	drew	2-2	
1969	Denmark	drew	1-1	
1969	Denmark	lost	0-2	
1969	Hungary	lost	1-2	
1970	Denmark	drew	1-1	
1970	Hungary	lost	0-4	
1970	Poland	lost	1-2	
1970	West Germany	lost	1-2	
1971	Poland	lost	0-2	
1971	Sweden	drew	1-1	
1971	Sweden	lost	0-1	
1971	Italy	lost	0-3	
1971	Italy	lost	1-2	
1971	Austria	lost	1-4	

Whilst Eamonn Dunphy has made a number of significant contributions to the game of football, the majority, if not all, have been made off the pitch!

His playing career began as a 16-year-old apprentice when he joined Matt Busby's Manchester United. Unable to break into the Reds' first team in three years at Old Trafford, he left to join Third Division newcomers York City in August 1965.

His stay at Bootham Crescent was brief – just 22 appearances – but he did win the first of 23 full caps for the Republic of Ireland when he appeared in the World Cup play-off game against Spain in Paris.

In January 1966 he joined Millwall for a fee of £8,000 and turned out to be one of the Lions' shrewdest signings. He helped Millwall win promotion to Division Two in his first season at The Den and became a fixture in the side, going on to make 274 League appearances. Whilst with Millwall, Dunphy added another 22 international appearances to his name, though many believe he only played in so many games due to the regular unavailability of Johnny Giles.

On leaving Millwall in November 1973 he signed for Charlton Athletic, and in 1974-75 helped the Addicks win promotion to Division Two prior to joining Reading. Dunphy then helped Reading win promotion to Division Three in 1975-76. When they dropped back to the Fourth Division the following season, he decided to hang up his boots.

It was off the field that Eamonn Dunphy made his greatest impact on the game. In 1971 he led a players' campaign to replace the Republic's archaic selection committee with a manager/sole selector – his efforts were partially successful as manager Mick Meagan was given a voice at selection meetings! Since retiring as a player, Dunphy has forged a successful career as an author and a journalist. With a number of best-selling books under his belt – notably *Only a Game?* – he now combines regular radio and newspaper work with a role as a television pundit for RTÉ.

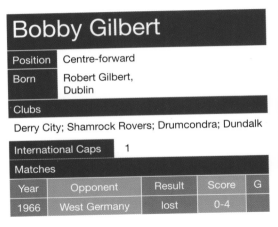

Bobby Gilbert

Position	Centre-forward
Born	Robert Gilbert, Dublin

Clubs

Derry City; Shamrock Rovers; Drumcondra; Dundalk

International Caps	1

Matches

Year	Opponent	Result	Score	G
1966	West Germany	lost	0-4	

Old-fashioned centre-forward Bobby Gilbert played his early football for Derry City, where his impressive displays led to him joining Shamrock Rovers midway through the 1965-66 season. There is no doubt that the big Dubliner, whose strength was in the air, was well served by wingers Frank O'Neill and Liam Tuohy. In his first season with the Hoops, he was their leading scorer with 14 league goals.

This form prompted the Republic of Ireland selectors to draft him into the side to face West Germany in Dublin in May 1966. They decided to switch Ray Treacy from centre-forward to inside-forward to replace the injured Andy McEvoy, and brought in Bobby Gilbert to lead the attack. Unfortunately the Republic were outclassed and Gilbert didn't get a sniff of goal as the Germans won 4-0.

With Shamrock Rovers he played in three successive FAI Cup Finals, winning the lot! They beat Limerick in 1966, St Patrick's Athletic in 1967 and then in 1968 in front of a record crowd of almost 40,000, they defeated Waterford.

Shortly afterwards, Gilbert joined Drumcondra where in his first season, he was the club's leading scorer. A player who

had no frills, just honest power, he later ended his playing days with Dundalk.

John Keogh

Position	Right-back
Born	John Keogh, Dublin, 1942

Clubs

Stella Maris; Shamrock Rovers; Cork Celtic

International Caps	1

Matches

Year	Opponent	Result	Score	G
1966	West Germany	lost	0-4	

One of the first overlapping full-backs in the League of Ireland, Keogh played his early football for Stella Maris prior to joining Shamrock Rovers in 1958 as the Dublin club were embarking on their ninth Championship-winning campaign.

A most reliable defender, he was a key figure in Shamrock Rovers' many successes of the 1960s. He won a League Championship medal with the Hoops in 1963-64 and five FAI Cup winners' medals, the first after a 4-1 defeat of Shelbourne in 1962. There then followed four successive victories between 1964 and 1967. Incredibly after the first three of those finals, Keogh was injured and unable to train before the big day each time. Keogh's run of bad luck seemed to have ended for the 1967 final against St Patrick's Athletic, but not so – he was in hospital having minor cuts to his legs treated, when he fainted, fell and hit his head and needed four stitches! However, he once again recovered and took his place in the No.2 shirt.

Keogh's only international cap for the Republic of Ireland came in May 1966.

A first-half injury to Theo Foley gave him the opportunity to make his debut against West Germany at Dalymount Park. The Republic lost the game 4-0 and with players of the calibre of Tony Dunne, Shay Brennan and Foley ahead of him in the pecking order, there would be no second cap.

In 1968, Keogh left the Hoops to join Cork Celtic. Though he lined-up for them in the 1969 FAI Cup Final against none other than Shamrock Rovers, there was to be no happy ending. The milk salesman scored the own goal which gave his former club a 1-1 draw – the Hoops won the replay 4-1.

Ray Treacy

Position	Forward
Born	Raymond Christopher Patrick Treacy, Dublin, 18 June 1946

Clubs

West Bromwich Albion; Charlton Athletic; Swindon Town; Preston North End; Oldham Athletic; West Bromwich Albion; Shamrock Rovers; Toronto Mets (Canada)

International Caps	42
International Goals	5

Matches

Year	Opponent	Result	Score	G
1966	West Germany	lost	0-4	
1967	Spain	drew	0-0	
1967	Czechoslovakia	lost	0-2	
1968	Czechoslovakia	won	2-1	1
1968	Poland	drew	2-2	
1969	Poland	lost	0-1	
1969	Czechoslovakia	lost	1-2	
1969	Denmark	lost	0-2	
1970	Scotland	drew	1-1	
1970	Denmark	drew	1-1	
1970	Hungary	lost	0-4	
1970	Poland	lost	1-2	
1970	West Germany	lost	1-2	
1971	Poland	lost	1-2	
1971	Sweden	drew	1-1	
1971	Sweden	lost	0-1	
1971	Italy	lost	0-3	
1971	Austria	lost	1-4	
1972	Iran	won	2-1	
1972	Ecuador	won	3-2	
1972	Chile	lost	1-2	
1972	Portugal	lost	1-2	
1973	USSR	lost	1-2	
1973	France	won	2-1	1
1973	USSR	lost	0-1	
1973	Poland	lost	0-2	
1973	France	drew	1-1	
1973	Norway	drew	1-1	
1974	Poland	won	1-0	
1974	Brazil	lost	1-2	
1975	USSR	won	3-0	
1975	West Germany B	won	1-0	
1975	Switzerland	won	2-1	1
1975	Switzerland	lost	0-1	
1976	Turkey	won	4-0	
1976	Norway	won	3-0	
1976	Poland	won	2-0	
1977	France	won	1-0	
1977	Poland	drew	0-0	
1978	Turkey	won	4-2	2
1978	Poland	lost	0-3	
1980	Czechoslovakia	lost	1-4	

Ray Treacy played his junior football for Home Farm. At the age of 15 he left the North Dublin club to sign as an apprentice for First Division West Bromwich Albion. Despite struggling to make an impact at the Hawthorns, Treacy found himself elevated to full international status. He was called into the Republic of Ireland team for the game against West Germany in May 1966. It was certainly a meteoric rise for a player who was still a reserve team player at club level.

With his total of international caps almost equalling in number his first team appearances for Albion, he decided to leave the Hawthorns, and in February 1968 signed for Charlton Athletic for £17,500. The impact on his game following his move to the Addicks was instantaneous. In his first international as a Charlton player, he scored the opening goal in a 2-1 defeat of Czechoslovakia in Prague. A shrewd user of the ball, Treacy was the type of player who created all sorts of problems for the opposition defences. He fitted in well at The Valley and in a little over four seasons, scored 44 goals in 149 League games. The Addicks were relegated at the end of the 1971-72 season. During the summer, Treacy was transferred to Swindon Town.

In a season and a half at the County Ground, he scored 16 goals in 55 league games before leaving to join Preston North End in December 1973. Asked to play in midfield, he was signed too late to prevent North End's relegation to the Third Division and then in 1974-75 suffered endless injuries. He started the 1975-76 campaign with a bang, scoring 11 goals in 27 games – seven in his first nine games of the season before falling out with manager Harry Catterick.

He returned to the Hawthorns for the start of the following season – their new manager Johnny Giles (Treacy's fellow Dublin and Republic of Ireland colleague) took him

an ace penalty-taker – scoring from the spot against Sligo Rovers in the 1978 FAI Cup Final. He played with Toronto Mets in the NASL in 1978-79. After retiring as a player, he enjoyed successful spells in charge of several League of Ireland clubs, most notably with Shamrock Rovers. He led the Hoops to League title success in 1993.

Jimmy Conway

Position	Outside-right
Born	James Patrick Conway, Dublin, 10 August 1946

Clubs	

Bohemians; Fulham; Manchester City

International Caps	20
International Goals	3

Matches

Year	Opponent	Result	Score	G
1967	Spain	drew	0-0	
1967	Turkey	won	2-1	
1967	Spain	lost	0-2	
1968	Czechoslovakia	won	2-1	
1969	Austria	drew	2-2	
1969	Hungary	lost	1-2	
1970	Scotland	drew	1-1	
1970	Czechoslovakia	lost	0-3	
1970	Denmark	drew	1-1	
1970	Hungary	lost	0-4	
1970	Poland	lost	1-2	
1970	West Germany	lost	1-2	
1971	Italy	lost	1-2	1
1971	Austria	lost	1-4	
1974	Uruguay	lost	0-2	
1974	Chile	won	2-1	1
1975	West Germany B	won	1-0	1
1976	Norway	won	3-0	
1976	Poland	won	2-0	
1977	Poland	drew	0-0	

back. In May 1977 he left English football to join Giles as his assistant at Shamrock Rovers. He was the Hoops' leading scorer in two of his three seasons with the club and

One of a family of 17, Jimmy Conway had unsuccessful trials with Leeds United and Manchester United before continuing to play junior football for Stella Maris and serve his apprenticeship as a carpenter.

He later joined Bohemians and in May 1966 he signed for First Division Fulham, in a deal

Above: Ray Treacy

which also saw his Bohs team-mate Turlough O'Connor make the switch to Craven Cottage. Within five months of putting pen to paper, Conway was rewarded with a full international cap against Spain to add to his amateur honours.

A fast and direct winger with an eye for goal, he was one of the links in the Cottagers' trials and tribulations of the 1960s and '70s, surviving their relegation from the top flight to the Third Division. This fall down the leagues brought a most emphatic response from the Dubliner. Fulham's leading scorer with 23 goals in 1969-70, he then played a major role in the Cottagers' promotion-winning campaign of 1970-71.

With Fulham's return to the Second Division assured, Conway celebrated by scoring his first international goal in the 2-1 defeat by Italy in May 1971.

A cartilage injury struck soon after but he fought his way back to full fitness and in 1975 was a member of Fulham's FA Cup Final team – a match the Cottagers lost 2-0 to their fellow Londoners West Ham United.

In the summer of 1976, after scoring 67 goals in 316 League games for Fulham, Conway left Craven Cottage to join First Division Manchester City. His stay at Maine Road was brief and he soon packed his bags to go and play in America.

Tony O'Connell

Position	Outside-left
Born	Anthony O'Connell, Dublin, 1941
Clubs	
Stella Maris; Shamrock Rovers; Dundalk; Bohemians	
International Caps	2
Matches	

Year	Opponent	Result	Score	G
1967	Spain	drew	0-0	
1971	Poland	lost	0-2	

As with a number of his fellow Republic team-mates, winger Tony O'Connell began his career with Stella Maris, before in 1959 joining Shamrock Rovers. He won an FAI Cup winners' medal with the Hoops in 1962. The following year he was the architect of the League of Ireland's 2-1 win over the Football League at Dalymount Park, when he gave seasoned international captain Jimmy Armfield the run-around!

He left Shamrock Rovers to play in Canada and America in 1963-64 – the season that the Hoops won the double! Following his return to Rovers for the start of the 1964-65 season, he was switched to most of the other forward positions – Liam Tuohy was holding down the No.11 shirt. O'Connell won back-to-back FAI Cup winners' medals with Rovers. They defeated Limerick in the replayed 1965 final and then beat the same side 2-0 in 1966, when he was one of the goalscorers. Shortly after this he parted company with Rovers to join Dundalk.

He was then selected for the Republic of Ireland's European Championship tie with Spain in October 1966, a game that ended goalless. O'Connell helped Dundalk win the League Championship, but in March 1969 obtained his release from the Lilywhites. He joined Bohemians as their first professional player.

He was the Bohs' top scorer in 1969-70 and ended the season with his fourth FAI Cup winners' medal after they had beaten Sligo Rovers 2-1 in a second replay, netting the winner. Whilst with Bohemians, he won his second cap, almost four years to the day after his debut. He was a half-time replacement for Mick Lawlor in the side which lost 2-0 to Poland in Dublin. Tony O'Connell later became President of Bohemians.

John Dempsey

Position	Central defender
Born	John Thomas Dempsey, Hampstead, 15 March 1946

Clubs

Fulham; Chelsea; Philadelphia Furies (U.S.)

International Caps	19
International Goals	1

Matches

Year	Opponent	Result	Score	G
1967	Spain	lost	0-2	
1967	Czechoslovakia	lost	0-2	
1968	Czechoslovakia	won	2-1	
1968	Poland	drew	2-2	1
1969	Poland	lost	0-1	
1969	Austria	drew	2-2	
1969	Denmark	drew	1-1	
1969	Czechoslovakia	lost	1-2	
1969	Denmark	lost	0-2	
1970	Hungary	lost	0-4	
1970	West Germany	lost	1-2	
1971	Poland	lost	0-2	
1971	Sweden	drew	1-1	
1971	Sweden	lost	0-1	
1971	Italy	lost	0-3	
1972	Iran	won	2-1	
1972	Ecuador	won	3-2	
1972	Chile	lost	1-2	
1972	Portugal	lost	1-2	

Above: John Dempsey

John Dempsey was a dependable defender who felt no embarrassment about putting the ball into touch whenever danger threatened. He worked as a car insurance salesman before joining Fulham where he was an instant success, earning a regular place in the Cottagers' back four during the 1963-64 season.

It was as a Fulham player that Dempsey received the first of his 19 full caps for the Republic of Ireland, in a 2-0 defeat against Spain in Valencia. The son of Irish parents – his mother came from Kildare, his father from Waterford – John Dempsey was regarded as an oddity in the 1960s: an Englishman playing for the Republic of Ireland!

With Fulham heading for the Third Division, Dempsey opted for a move across West London in exchange for £70,000. In his first season with the Blues, he won an FA Cup winners' medal, and in 1970-71 the club embarked on a successful European Cup Winners' Cup campaign. It was in the replayed final of that competition against Real Madrid that Dempsey enjoyed his most memorable moment in a Chelsea shirt. His superb volley in Athens gave Chelsea a 1-0 lead and they ended up 2-1 winners after extra-time.

At international level there were a number of highs and lows. His only goal for the national side came against Poland at Dalymount Park in May 1968, when he

was pressed into service as an emergency centre-forward by coach Noel Cantwell. A year later in the absence of Charlie Hurley, he was chosen as captain of the Republic of Ireland side to play Denmark in a World Cup qualifier. In November 1969 he became the first Republic of Ireland player to receive his marching orders in a World Cup qualifier, this time against Hungary in Budapest.

Back on the domestic front, Dempsey suffered the first in a catalogue of injuries in August 1972 and made just 31 appearances over the next three seasons. He seemed to have re-established himself in 1975-76 alongside Mickey Droy but a twisted knee cost Dempsey his place. Unable to force his way back into the side, he remained at Stamford Bridge for a further two seasons, before leaving to end his career in America with Philadelphia Furies. On returning to these shores, he became a PE instructor at the Broadfields Centre for the physically and mentally handicapped in Edgware.

Al Finucane

Position	Centre-half
Born	Al Finucane, Limerick, 1943

Clubs

Limerick; Waterford

International Caps	11

Matches

Year	Opponent	Result	Score	G
1967	Turkey	lost	1-2	
1967	Czechoslovakia	lost	0-2	
1969	Czechoslovakia	lost	1-2	
1969	Denmark	lost	0-2	
1969	Hungary	lost	1-2	
1970	Scotland	drew	1-1	
1970	Czechoslovakia	lost	0-3	
1971	Sweden	lost	0-1	
1971	Italy	lost	0-3	
1971	Italy	lost	1-2	
1972	Austria	lost	0-6	

Al Finucane began his career as a right-half with his home-town club Limerick, but it was only when manager Ewan Fenton decided to play him in the centre of defence that his true talents were revealed.

Finucane's reading of the game was immaculate, and over the next two decades he developed into one of the best central defenders in the League of Ireland. He was a runner-up in the FAI Cup Finals of 1965 and 1966 as the Shannonsiders lost both finals to Shamrock Rovers.

At international level Finucane was a regular stand-in for the English-based defenders Hurley and Dempsey, who were often unavailable. He won the first of his 11 caps against Turkey in February 1967. He enjoyed his best run in the national side in 1969 when he appeared in five consecutive line-ups. Four of these matches ended in defeat and the other – Mick Meagan's first match as manager – brought a 1-1 draw against Scotland.

In 1971 he captained Limerick to their first FAI Cup success when they beat Drogheda in the final. Shortly afterwards, Liam Tuohy took over as manager of the Republic of Ireland. For his first game in charge he appointed Finucane as captain. In a team severely depleted by withdrawals, the Republic lost 6-0 against Austria in Linz. Al Finucane's first game as skipper turned out to be his last appearance in the green of the Republic of Ireland.

On leaving Limerick he moved to Waterford where he added to his collection of medals. He won a League Cup winners' medal in 1973, as Waterford beat Finn Harps to win the inaugural competition. After finishing runners-up the previous year, he captained Waterford to victory in 1980's FAI Cup. That same year saw his testimonial: League

of Ireland champions Limerick entertained Cup winners Waterford in his honour. Al Finucane, who captained the League of Ireland in their Golden Jubilee match, won his third FAI Cup winners' medal.

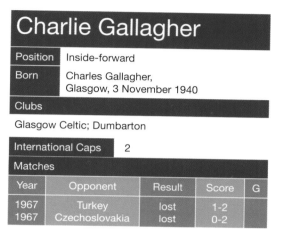

Charlie Gallagher

Position	Inside-forward
Born	Charles Gallagher, Glasgow, 3 November 1940

Clubs

Glasgow Celtic; Dumbarton

International Caps	2

Matches

Year	Opponent	Result	Score	G
1967	Turkey	lost	1-2	
1967	Czechoslovakia	lost	0-2	

A cousin of the former Manchester United and Scotland player Paddy Crerand, the deep-lying inside-forward turned professional with Celtic in March 1959.

Possessing a venomous shot, his highly accurate corners provided a regular source of goals for the Parkhead club. It was from such a set play that Celtic skipper Billy McNeill headed the goal which clinched the 1965 Scottish Cup against Dunfermline Athletic.

To the surprise and delight of Celtic supporters, the Republic of Ireland gave Charlie Gallagher a chance to play international football – his parents were from Donegal. On 22 February 1967 in Ankara, Turkey, he became the first Scots-born player to win a full cap for the Republic of Ireland. In pulling on the green shirt, he became a dual international, for Scotland had capped him at Under-18 level in March 1958.

In February 1968 Gallagher took over Bertie Auld's job of controlling the Bhoys' midfield,

winning balls and feeding the wingers. By the end of the season, he had helped Celtic to their fourth successive Championship.

In the summer of 1970 Charlie Gallagher, who had scored 32 goals in 170 games, left Parkhead to join Dumbarton on a free transfer. At Boghead, he was instrumental in masterminding Dumbarton's Second Division Championship success of 1971-72. Within a year he had decided to retire, later scouting for his beloved Celtic.

Joe Kinnear

Position	Right-back
Born	Joseph Patrick Kinnear, Dublin, 27 December 1946
Clubs	

St Alban's City; Tottenham Hotspur; Brighton and Hove Albion

International Caps	26

Matches

Year	Opponent	Result	Score	G
1967	Turkey	lost	1-2	
1968	Czechoslovakia	won	2-1	
1968	Poland	drew	2-2	
1969	Austria	drew	2-2	
1970	Czechoslovakia	lost	0-3	
1970	Denmark	drew	1-1	
1970	Hungary	lost	0-4	
1970	Poland	lost	1-2	
1971	Sweden	drew	1-1	
1971	Italy	lost	1-2	
1972	Iran	won	2-1	
1972	Ecuador	won	3-2	
1972	Chile	lost	1-2	
1972	Portugal	lost	1-2	
1973	USSR	lost	1-2	
1973	France	won	2-1	
1974	Poland	won	1-0	
1974	Brazil	lost	1-2	
1974	Uruguay	lost	0-2	
1974	Chile	won	2-1	
1975	USSR	won	3-0	
1975	Turkey	drew	1-1	
1975	West Germany B	won	1-0	
1975	Switzerland	won	2-1	
1975	USSR	lost	1-2	
1976	Turkey	won	4-0	

Joe Kinnear moved to London with his family at the age of seven. Having captained Hertfordshire Schoolboys he later joined St Albans City, where he was noticed by Spurs. Though he made his League debut against West Ham United in April 1966, his big breakthrough came in February 1967. Just three days after he had won the first of 26 full caps for the Republic of Ireland against Turkey, Spurs regular full-back Phil Beal suffered a broken arm and was out of action for the rest of the season. Kinnear was the natural replacement. He ended the campaign with an FA Cup winners' medal against Chelsea after Spurs had beaten their London rivals 2-1.

A compact, quick and hard-tackling defender who enjoyed moving up to support the forwards in an era when wingers fell out of favour, Kinnear formed an excellent full-back pairing with Cyril Knowles. Unfortunately in January 1969, he broke his leg – an injury that put him out of the game for almost a year. Joe Kinnear claimed a place in the history books when he became the Republic of Ireland's first-ever substitute in European Championship football, when he replaced Ipswich Town's Tommy Carroll in the 1-1 home draw with Sweden in October 1970.

Back at White Hart Lane, Kinnear played in the League Cup-winning teams of 1971 and 1973 and the successful 1972 UEFA Cup side. Having appeared in 302 games, Kinnear was transferred to Brighton and Hove Albion in the summer of 1975. He only played for the south coast club for a year before retiring.

At first he left football completely but later returned on the management side with a three-week trial as boss of Nepal before assisting Dave Mackay as manager at Doncaster Rovers. He took over as Mackay's successor but after only three months he was dismissed to make way for Billy Bremner. In 1990 he was appointed reserve team coach at Wimbledon, becoming manager in February 1992 after the sacking of Peter Withe. He saved the Dons from almost certain relegation to win a place in the newly-formed Premiership. The 1996-97 season came close to being the greatest in the club's history. He took the Dons to the semi-final stage of both the FA and League Cups and eighth place in the Premiership. Kinnear, who later suffered a heart attack, was replaced by Egil Olsen and on making a full recovery, managed Luton Town and Nottingham Forest.

Turlough O'Connor

Position	Centre-forward
Born	Turlough O'Connor, Athlone Co. Westmeath, 22 July 1946
Clubs	

Limerick; Athlone Town; Bohemians; Fulham; Dundalk; Bohemians; Athlone Town

International Caps	7
International Goals	2

Matches

Year	Opponent	Result	Score	G
1968	Czechoslovakia	won	2-1	1
1972	Austria	lost	0-6	
1972	Iran	won	2-1	
1972	Ecuador	won	3-2	1
1972	Chile	lost	1-2	
1972	Portugal	lost	1-2	
1973	France	won	2-1	

One of eight children of an Irish Army tuba player, Turlough O'Connor's performances for Gentex, his local junior side in his native Athlone, attracted the attention of a number of League of Ireland sides. He had brief spells with Limerick and Athlone Town before signing for Bohemians in February 1965.

Just over a year later, O'Connor and team-mate Jimmy Conway were transferred to Fulham. Though he spent two seasons at Craven Cottage, much of his time was spent on the treatment table as he was forced to undergo two hernia operations.

In spite of these setbacks O'Connor made his full international debut in a much-weakened Republic of Ireland side that faced Czechoslovakia in Prague. They were given little chance against opponents who had won 2-0 in Dublin in their previous meeting. But with just five minutes to go and the score standing at 1-1, O'Connor headed the winning goal! It was a dream debut but because he was struggling at club level, it failed to signal the start of a long international career.

O'Connor returned to Ireland to join Dundalk for a fee of £4,000 and quickly recaptured his scoring form. He won a second cap when he lined up against Austria in Linz and added more caps to his tally during the mini-World Cup in Brazil in 1972. In this competition, he scored a second international goal with the winning strike – a perfect lob from 40 yards – in a 3-2 defeat of Ecuador. Unfortunately, his next appearance against Chile ended rather abruptly when he was sent-off for appealing too strongly for a penalty!

Shortly afterwards he rejoined Bohemians. Over the next six seasons he scored an incredible 106 goals and picked up two League Championship medals. In 1979 O'Connor became player-manager of Athlone Town, leading them to their first League Championship in 1980-81. Later appointed manager of Dundalk, he led them to a League Championship and FAI Cup double in 1987-88 before leaving to manage Bohemians.

Eamonn Rogers

Position	Winger
Born	Edward Eamonn Rogers, Dublin, 16 April 1947
Clubs	

Blackburn Rovers; Charlton Athletic; Northampton Town

International Caps	19
International Goals	5

Matches

Year	Opponent	Result	Score	G
1968	Czechoslovakia	won	2-1	
1968	Poland	drew	2-2	
1969	Poland	lost	0-1	
1969	Austria	drew	2-2	1
1969	Denmark	drew	1-1	
1969	Czechoslovakia	lost	1-2	1
1969	Denmark	lost	0-2	
1969	Hungary	lost	1-2	
1970	Scotland	drew	1-1	
1970	Denmark	drew	1-1	

Matches Continued

Year	Opponent	Result	Score	G
1970	Hungary	lost	0-4	
1971	Italy	lost	0-3	
1971	Italy	lost	1-2	
1971	Austria	lost	1-4	1
1972	Iran	won	2-1	
1972	Ecuador	won	3-2	1
1972	Chile	lost	1-2	1
1972	Portugal	lost	1-2	
1973	USSR	lost	1-2	

Winger Eamonn Rogers turned professional with Blackburn Rovers in May 1965, but the six seasons he spent at Ewood Park saw a steady decline in the fortunes of this once great club.

During his early days with the club, Rogers played alongside future international team-mates Ray Treacy and Terry Conroy in the Republic of Ireland youth team, which finished sixth in the UEFA Finals of 1965.

His League debut for Blackburn Rovers followed shortly afterwards, but at the end of that 1965-66 season the Lancashire club had lost its First Division status.

Though worse was to come, Rogers made his full debut for the Republic of Ireland against Czechoslovakia in Prague – a memorable match that ended in a 2-1 win for the Irish. Rogers was an important member of the national side for the next two years and though he scored his first goal against Austria in his third match, it was 1972 when he found his shooting boots. On the mini-tour of Brazil, he scored in successive games against Ecuador and Chile, going on to score five goals in 19 games – a good record for a winger in a side which went 20 games without victory!

Blackburn continued to struggle in the lower division and in 1970-71 they were relegated to the Third Division. Rogers had proved himself a versatile player with Rovers, but an alleged refusal to play at right-back – he had already played in seven different positions – earned him a reprimand and cost him his place in the side.

In October 1971 after scoring 30 goals in 165 League outings, he joined Second Division Charlton Athletic. In his only season at The Valley, he suffered the ignominy of playing in yet another relegated side! He later ended his League career with a brief spell for Northampton Town.

Tommy Carroll

Position	Right-back
Born	Thomas Roger Carroll, Dublin, 18 August 1942
Clubs	

St Finbar's; Shelbourne; Cambridge City; Ipswich Town; Birmingham City

International Caps	17
International Goals	1

Matches

Year	Opponent	Result	Score	G
1968	Poland	drew	2-2	
1969	Poland	lost	0-1	
1969	Austria	drew	2-2	
1969	Denmark	drew	1-1	
1970	Czechoslovakia	lost	0-3	
1970	Poland	lost	1-2	
1970	West Germany	lost	1-2	1
1971	Sweden	drew	1-1	
1972	Iran	won	2-1	
1972	Ecuador	won	3-2	
1972	Chile	lost	1-2	
1972	Portugal	lost	1-2	
1973	USSR	lost	1-2	
1973	USSR	lost	0-1	
1973	Poland	lost	0-2	
1973	France	drew	1-1	
1973	Norway	drew	1-1	

After beginning his career alongside Tony Dunne and Eric Barber at Shelbourne nursery club St Finbar's, Tommy Carroll was just 15 years old when he joined his elder brother Eddie in the Shel's League of Ireland

on to appear in all of the defensive positions for the Republic, scoring his only goal at this level from the penalty-spot in the 1-1 draw with Sweden in October 1970.

Following Ipswich's promotion to the top flight, competition for places became fierce. Tommy Carroll had to contend with England internationals Mick Mills and Mick McNeill as well as local player Colin Harper for a place in the side.

In November 1971 after impressing on a month's trial, he joined Birmingham City, immediately claiming a first team place and helping the Blues win promotion to the First Division. Sadly though, after little more than a season at St Andrew's, he was forced to retire because of injury.

non-League Altrincham, he returned to Ireland to play for Shamrock Rovers. With the Hoops, Smyth won five FAI Cup winners' medals in successive seasons from 1965 to 1969.

He was at the peak of his form when in October 1968 he won his one and only full cap for the Republic of Ireland, as a substitute during a friendly against Poland. There were just 29 minutes remaining when Smyth came off the bench to replace Preston's Alan Kelly in the 1-0 defeat by the Poles.

He continued to enjoy more success at club level after joining Bohemians, winning League Championship medals in 1974-75 and 1977-78. Smyth, who won two League Cup winners' medals with the Bohs, won further honours after moving to Athlone Town – the last one, another League Cup winners' medal in 1982, just a few months before his 42nd birthday!

side. In seven years at Tolka Park he appeared in every position including goalkeeper, winning a League Championship medal, FAI Cup winners' medal and a President's Cup winners' medal.

In August 1964 he left his native Dublin to play non-League football for Cambridge City where he spent two seasons. During this time he had the distinction of representing the Republic of Ireland at Under-23 level.

In the summer of 1966 he left Cambridge for his first taste of League football with Ipswich Town. In 1967-68, his second season, he helped them win the Second Division Championship.

In May 1968 his efforts at Portman Road were rewarded when he was awarded the first of 17 full caps against Poland. He went

Mick Smyth

Position	Goalkeeper
Born	Michael Smyth, Dublin, 13 May 1940
Clubs	

St Patrick's CYMS; Drumcondra; Barrow; Altrincham; Shamrock Rovers; Bohemians; Athlone Town

International Caps	1

Matches				
Year	Opponent	Result	Score	G
1969	Poland	lost	0-1	

A tall and commanding goalkeeper, Mick Smyth started out with St Patrick's CYMS before joining Drumcondra. Whilst with the Drums he won an FAI Cup runners-up medal in 1961, after losing 2-1 to St Pat's in the final.

The following summer he moved to Fourth Division Barrow. After just a handful of League appearances and a brief spell with

Mick Leech

Position	Centre-forward
Born	Michael Leech, Dublin, 6 August 1948
Clubs	

Ormeau; Shamrock Rovers; Waterford; Shamrock Rovers; Bohemians; Drogheda; St Patrick's Athletic

International Caps	8
International Goals	2

Matches				
Year	Opponent	Result	Score	G
1969	Czechoslovakia	lost	1-2	
1969	Denmark	lost	0-2	
1969	Hungary	lost	1-2	
1972	Austria	lost	0-6	
1972	Iran	won	2-1	1
1972	Ecuador	won	3-2	
1972	Portugal	lost	1-2	1
1973	USSR	lost	1-2	

Though Gaelic football was Mick Leach's first love, he played junior soccer with St Brigid's, from where he moved into the Leinster League with Ormeau. His displays led to a four-month trial with Northampton Town but it was Shamrock Rovers' boss Liam Tuohy who persuaded him to join the Hoops.

He was an FAI Cup-winner in successive years from 1967 to 1969 with Rovers. In 1968-69 Leech helped himself to an unbelievable 56 goals! Though on the small side, he could lead the line well and he seemed able to deliver a goalbound shot from any angle.

It was inevitable that he should receive a call-up to the full international team, but in the match against Czechoslovakia in Dublin, he was kicked out of the game after 44 minutes. Fortunately for a player who had tremendously tight control, he recovered sufficiently to play in the remaining two World Cup fixtures that summer. Leech's two international goals came in the Brazilian Independence Cup in the summer of 1972 against Iran and Portugal.

With Eric Barber becoming the leading scorer with Shamrock Rovers, Leech opted for a move to Waterford but rejoined the Hoops two months later. He scored the only goal of the match against Sligo Rovers in the 1977 League Cup Final. He then helped Bohemians win the 1977-78 League Championship before playing for Drogheda and finally St Patrick's Athletic.

Paddy Mulligan

Position	Right-back
Born	Patrick Martin Mulligan, Dublin, 17 March 1945

Clubs

Home Farm; Bohemians; Shamrock Rovers; Chelsea; Crystal Palace; West Bromwich Albion; Shamrock Rovers; Galway

International Caps	50
International Goals	1

Matches

Year	Opponent	Result	Score	G
1969	Czechoslovakia	lost	1-2	
1969	Denmark	lost	0-2	
1969	Hungary	lost	1-2	
1970	Scotland	drew	1-1	
1970	Czechoslovakia	lost	0-3	
1970	Denmark	drew	1-1	
1970	Hungary	lost	0-4	
1970	Poland	lost	1-2	
1970	West Germany	lost	1-2	1
1971	Poland	lost	0-2	
1971	Sweden	drew	1-1	
1971	Italy	lost	1-2	
1972	Austria	lost	0-6	
1972	Iran	won	2-1	
1972	Ecuador	won	3-2	
1972	Chile	lost	1-2	
1972	Portugal	lost	1-2	
1973	France	won	2-1	
1973	USSR	lost	0-1	
1973	Poland	lost	0-2	
1973	France	drew	1-1	
1973	Norway	drew	1-1	
1974	Poland	won	1-0	
1974	Brazil	lost	1-2	
1974	Uruguay	lost	0-2	
1974	Chile	won	2-1	
1975	USSR	won	3-0	
1975	Turkey	drew	1-1	
1975	Switzerland	won	2-1	
1975	USSR	lost	1-2	
1975	Switzerland	lost	0-1	
1976	Turkey	won	4-0	
1976	Poland	won	2-0	
1977	England	drew	1-1	
1977	Turkey	drew	3-3	
1977	France	lost	0-2	
1977	France	won	1-0	
1977	Poland	drew	0-0	
1977	Bulgaria	lost	1-2	
1978	Bulgaria	drew	0-0	
1978	Norway	drew	0-0	
1978	Denmark	drew	3-3	
1979	England	drew	1-1	
1979	Denmark	won	2-0	

Matches Continued

Year	Opponent	Result	Score	G
1979	Bulgaria	lost	0-1	
1979	West Germany	lost	1-3	
1980	Wales	lost	1-2	
1980	Czechoslovakia	lost	1-4	
1980	Bulgaria	won	3-0	
1980	United States	won	3-2	

After playing his early football with Home Farm, Paddy Mulligan had a couple of games for Bohemians prior to signing for Shamrock Rovers in February 1964. Whilst with the Hoops, Mulligan combined playing with a job as an office furniture salesman.

With Rovers, Mulligan won FAI Cup winners' medals in 1965, 1966, 1967 and 1969 and won the first of his 50 caps for the Republic of Ireland in the ill-tempered World Cup match against Czechoslovakia.

In October 1969 he joined Chelsea for a fee of £17,500 but it took him some time to adapt to the level of fitness expected at Stamford Bridge. The fee was a record for a League of Ireland player. It was still a surprise move for Mulligan, who at 24 was older than most of the footballers who were making their way across the Irish Sea.

It was a long-term injury to Eddie McCreadie that eventually allowed Mulligan to establish himself in the Chelsea side. Despite suffering a spate of niggling injuries, he collected a League Cup runners-up medal in 1972 after the Blues had lost 2-1 to Stoke City. In fact, an injury in the game compelled Mulligan to leave the fray at the interval and his absence is said to have contributed to Chelsea's downfall! Although he was a regular in the Republic of Ireland side, he struggled to hold down a first team place at Stamford Bridge – in September 1972 he jumped at the chance to join Crystal Palace who willingly paid £80,000 for his services.

In September 1975 he was on the move again, this time to West Bromwich Albion who had just appointed Johnny Giles as their manager. In his first season with the club, Mulligan helped the Baggies win promotion to the top flight. He returned to Ireland with Shamrock Rovers in 1977 and later had a spell as player-manager of Galway.

Mulligan, who captained his country on 13 occasions, made the last of his 50 international appearances while on the books of Shamrock Rovers against the United States at Dalymount Park in October 1979.

Eoin Hand

Position	Central defender
Born	Eoin Kevin Joseph Colin Hand, Dublin, 30 March 1946

Clubs

Stella Maris; Swindon Town; Dundalk; Drumcondra; Portsmouth; Shamrock Rovers; Limerick

International Caps	20
International Goals	2

Matches

Year	Opponent	Result	Score	G
1969	Czechoslovakia	lost	1-2	
1970	Poland	lost	1-2	
1970	West Germany	lost	1-2	
1971	Poland	lost	0-2	
1971	Austria	lost	1-4	
1973	USSR	lost	1-2	
1973	France	won	2-1	
1973	USSR	lost	0-1	
1973	Poland	lost	0-2	
1973	France	drew	1-1	
1974	Poland	won	1-0	
1974	Brazil	lost	1-2	
1974	Uruguay	lost	0-2	
1974	Chile	won	2-1	1
1975	Turkey	drew	1-1	
1975	West Germany B	won	1-0	
1975	Switzerland	won	2-1	
1975	USSR	lost	1-2	1
1975	Switzerland	lost	0-1	
1976	Turkey	won	4-0	

Above: Paddy Mulligan

His three seasons at Selhurst Park witnessed a steady decline in the fortunes of Palace, as they dropped from the First to the Third Division in successive seasons.

A tough and uncompromising centre-half, Eoin Hand was somewhat surprisingly used in midfield throughout an international career that saw him win 20 full caps for the Republic of Ireland.

Having played junior football with Dublin's Stella Maris, Hand signed for Swindon Town shortly before his 17th birthday. However, a year later he was released by the Wiltshire club without having appeared in the Robins' League side.

He returned to Ireland, initially with Dundalk before signing for Drumcondra where he was top scorer in each of his two seasons with the club. Whilst with the Drums, Hand was chosen for the League of Ireland side against the Scottish League. After a dominating display at the heart of the defence, Portsmouth paid £5,000 to take him to Fratton Park.

He had two spells at Pompey from 1968 to 1975 and after a spell in South Africa, from 1977 to 1978. Although he appeared in a number of different positions for Portsmouth, he was generally recognised as a strong and determined defender who gave 100% in every game.

Hand won all of his 20 caps whilst with Pompey, the first as a substitute for the injured Mick Leech in a bad-tempered match against Czechoslovakia in Dublin in October 1969. Used more often than not in midfield by the Republic, he gave the back four extra security. Hand was not just a spoiler however, as he proved in the game against France at Dalymount Park in 1972. After chasing what appeared to be a lost cause, he delivered a pin-point cross into the path of Ray Treacy, who scored to give the Republic a first home win for six years! Hand was also a great threat from set pieces and in the match against Chile in 1974, scored with a most memorable header.

Having appeared in 307 League and Cup games during his two spells with Portsmouth, he left Fratton Park and having previously played briefly with Shamrock Rovers, joined Limerick. He scored 11 goals in the club's League Championship success of 1979-80 and was a winner again two years later when Limerick won the FAI Cup for the first time in their history.

Manager of the national team from 1980 to 1985, he later coached in Saudi Arabia and managed St Patrick's Athletic before taking the reins at Huddersfield Town.

Don Givens

Position	Forward
Born	Donald Joseph Givens, Limerick, 9 August 1949

Clubs

Manchester United; Luton Town; Queen's Park Rangers; Birmingham City; Bournemouth (loan); Sheffield United; Xamax Neuchatel (Switzerland)

International Caps	56
International Goals	19

Matches

Year	Opponent	Result	Score	G
1969	Denmark	lost	0-2	
1969	Hungary	lost	1-2	1
1970	Scotland	drew	1-1	1
1970	Czechoslovakia	lost	0-3	
1970	Denmark	drew	1-1	1
1970	Hungary	lost	0-4	
1970	Poland	lost	1-2	1
1970	West Germany	lost	1-2	
1971	Sweden	drew	1-1	
1971	Italy	lost	0-3	
1971	Italy	lost	1-2	
1971	Austria	lost	1-4	
1972	Iran	won	2-1	1
1972	Ecuador	won	3-2	
1972	Portugal	lost	1-2	
1973	France	won	2-1	
1973	USSR	lost	0-1	
1973	Poland	lost	0-2	
1973	France	drew	1-1	
1973	Norway	drew	1-1	
1974	Poland	won	1-0	
1974	Brazil	lost	1-2	
1974	Uruguay	lost	0-2	
1974	Chile	won	2-1	

Matches Continued

Year	Opponent	Result	Score	G
1975	USSR	won	3-0	3
1975	Turkey	drew	1-1	1
1975	West Germany B	won	1-0	
1975	Switzerland	won	2-1	
1975	USSR	lost	1-2	
1975	Switzerland	lost	0-1	
1976	Turkey	won	4-0	4
1976	Norway	won	3-0	
1976	Poland	won	2-0	2
1977	England	drew	1-1	
1977	Turkey	drew	3-3	
1977	France	lost	0-2	
1977	Spain	lost	0-1	
1977	France	won	1-0	
1977	Bulgaria	lost	1-2	1
1978	Bulgaria	drew	0-0	
1978	Norway	drew	0-0	
1978	Denmark	drew	3-3	
1979	N Ireland	drew	0-0	
1979	England	drew	1-1	
1979	Denmark	won	2-0	1
1979	Bulgaria	lost	0-1	
1979	West Germany	lost	1-3	
1980	United States	won	3-2	1
1980	N Ireland	lost	0-1	
1980	Switzerland	won	2-0	1
1980	Argentina	lost	0-1	
1981	Holland	won	2-1	
1981	Belgium	drew	1-1	
1981	Cyprus	won	6-0	
1981	Wales	lost	1-3	
1982	France	won	3-2	

Don Givens captained the Manchester United youth team but had yet to make an appearance in the Red Devils' League side, when he was handed his international debut for the Republic of Ireland in a World Cup match against Denmark in May 1969. Despite a 2-0 defeat, Givens had played well enough to retain his place for the Republic's next match against Hungary in Dublin. It was in this match that Givens scored the first of his 19 international goals, smashing home a Frank O'Neill cross to level the scores. With ten minutes to go, the visitors took the lead and despite Givens coming close to levelling the scores a second time, held on to win 2-1.

Despite his impressive international achievements – scoring four goals in his first seven games – he couldn't force his way into

His commitment to the Republic's cause was never in doubt and he was sent-off twice whilst playing for the national side – against Ecuador in June 1972 and Chile in May 1974. Don Givens also holds the record for scoring the Republic of Ireland's quickest hat-trick. It came in the 4-0 defeat of Turkey in Dublin in October 1975 and took him just nine minutes! This was the first treble scored by a Republic of Ireland player since Paddy Moore 40 years before. For good measure Givens scored the Republic's fourth goal in that game against Turkey. After playing a final game for his country in the epic 3-2 defeat of France in October 1981, he headed the Republic's scoring charts until overtaken by Frank Stapleton.

By now, Givens had joined Birmingham City – his transfer fee soaring to £165,000. He helped the Blues win promotion to the top flight in his first season with the club but following their immediate relegation, he had a loan spell with Bournemouth prior to ending his League career with Sheffield United.

His last kick in the English game before joining Swiss club Xamax Neuchatel was a missed penalty, which resulted in the Blades losing 1-0 to Walsall and thus condemning them to Fourth Division football for the following season!

Above: Don Givens

the United side on a regular basis. In April 1970 he was transferred to Luton Town for £15,000.

After a couple of seasons at Kenilworth Road in which he scored 19 times in 83 League outings, he joined Queen's Park Rangers for £40,000. It was at Loftus Road that Don Givens would enjoy the most settled and productive spell of his career. The dangerous hitman spent six seasons with Rangers, netting 76 times in 242 League games and helping them win promotion to the First Division in 1972-73.

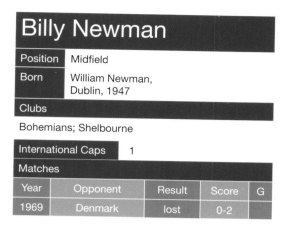

Billy Newman

Position	Midfield
Born	William Newman, Dublin, 1947

Clubs

Bohemians; Shelbourne

International Caps	1

Matches

Year	Opponent	Result	Score	G
1969	Denmark	lost	0-2	

Midfielder Billy Newman was one of the most underrated players in the League of Ireland, having begun his career with Bohemians, where he won both youth and amateur international honours for the Republic of Ireland.

Though he was a little slow over the turf, he was both careful and constructive: among the 12 goals he scored in two seasons with the Bohs, were a number of spectacular strikes. In the summer of 1965 he left Bohemians to join their Dublin rivals Shelbourne.

After some impressive performances for the Shels, Newman was called up into the full Republic of Ireland side. He replaced the unavailable Tony Dunne of Manchester United for the World Cup qualifier against Denmark in Copenhagen in May 1969. The selection committee, who were in dispute with midfielder Johnny Giles, surprised many by turning to Billy Newman. He came into the side at left-half but had been on the field for only 55 minutes of international football when he was substituted by Frank O'Neill of Shamrock Rovers. The Republic, who were trailing 1-0 at the time of the substitution, went on to lose 2-0.

Back at club level, Newman was an FAI Cup runner-up with the Shels in 1973 after they lost the replayed final 1-0 to Cork Hibs.

THE 1970s

The Republic of Ireland's poor results in the 1970 World Cup qualifiers were followed by a similar outcome in the qualifying games for the European Championships of 1972. Their last games in the group stages of this tournament saw them take on Austria, who scored four times at Dalymount Park: it was time for a change of manager. Mick Meagan – who had been in charge for two years – had overseen 12 internationals but the Republic hadn't won any!

His replacement was Liam Tuohy, who knew that one of the national side's greatest problems was lack of preparation before an international match. His first game in charge was the return match with Austria in Linz. Tuohy played six debutants and sent on a seventh off the bench. With the exception of Paddy Mulligan, the side had been selected entirely from players plying their trade in the League of Ireland. The Republic were beaten 6-0! Tuohy made numerous changes for the Brazilian Independence Cup, a tournament in which the Republic had not previously participated. When the Republic beat Iran 2-1 in their opening match, it was their first victory in almost five years – a run of 21 matches without success! They followed it up with a 3-2 defeat of Ecuador before losing to both Chile and Portugal.

It was around this time that the national team began to play some of their international matches at Lansdowne Road and their first game there in modern times was the European Championship game against Italy which the visitors won 2-1. Despite coming to Dublin as World Cup runners-up, they attracted a crowd of just 25,000. Many Irish supporters mourned the loss of Bohemians' grand old stadium at Dalymount Park and especially the famed 'Dalymount Roar' which some viewed was worth a goal start – but it wasn't lost completely as the Irish would alternate between Dalymount and Lansdowne for a number of years to come.

With the 1974 World Cup being held in West Germany, the Republic of Ireland had to get past France and the Soviet Union. Whilst this seemed highly improbable, they were not sure of a place even if they succeeded. The winners of the group were scheduled to play-off against a South American group which comprised Chile and Peru.

Having lost 2-1 at home to the Soviet Union, the situation was desperate. With the Republic now needing to collect five or six points from their three remaining games, many supporters had given up hope. For the home game against France, Tuohy made

Giles captain and brought back the experienced Givens and Mulligan. Jimmy Holmes – just four days past his 19th birthday – became the youngest Republic of Ireland player to appear in a World Cup game. Conroy gave the hosts the lead when his shot smashed into the net via the underside of the bar. The French – up until then the better team – equalised midway through the second-half before Treacy inadvertently scored what proved to be the winning goal. The Republic had won, but sadly never again would Dalymount Park host another World Cup match. Even though the Irish lost the return against the Soviet Union 1-0, they could still head the group if they beat France in Paris and they in turn won in Moscow. It all proved immaterial for despite a spirited showing, they could only draw, Mick Martin netting for the Republic.

The Republic's fourth manager in as many years, Johnny Giles was appointed player-manager in October 1973. His view was that League of Ireland players had neither the fitness nor the know-how to cope with international football: the only League of Ireland player he ever selected in World Cup games was himself, when seeing out his career with Shamrock Rovers!

For the 1976 European Championships, the Republic of Ireland were in the same group as the Soviet Union, Switzerland and Turkey. After completing their six group games, the Republic were top of the table, leaving the Soviet Union to get two points from their remaining two games to pip Ireland at the post – unfortunately, they got them.

Following a 1-1 draw against England at Wembley, the Republic embarked on the qualifying games for the 1978 World Cup Finals. Their opponents were France and Bulgaria. Though the Irish lost 2-0 in Paris, a goal by Liam Brady brought them victory in the return at Lansdowne Road in March 1977. The attendance for this game was put at 48,000 – a record for a football game in Ireland. The Republic needed at least a point from their visit to Bulgaria, but they lost 2-1 in a bad-tempered game which saw two players from each side sent-off. With their hopes hanging by a thread, they had to beat Bulgaria by four goals in Dublin and hope France and Bulgaria play out a draw. As it transpired they were held to a goalless draw by the Bulgarians, and the Republic slid anticlimactically out of the World Cup.

Terry Conroy

Position	Forward
Born	Gerard Anthony Francis Conroy, Dublin, 2 October 1946

Clubs
Home Farm; Glentoran; Stoke City; Bulova (Hong Kong); Crewe Alexandra

International Caps	27
International Goals	2

Matches

Year	Opponent	Result	Score	G
1970	Czechoslovakia	lost	0-3	
1970	Denmark	drew	1-1	
1970	Hungary	lost	0-4	
1970	Poland	lost	1-2	
1970	West Germany	lost	1-2	
1971	Poland	lost	0-2	
1971	Sweden	drew	1-1	
1971	Sweden	lost	0-1	
1971	Italy	lost	0-3	
1973	USSR	lost	1-2	1
1973	France	won	2-1	1
1973	USSR	lost	0-1	
1973	Norway	drew	1-1	
1974	Poland	won	1-0	
1974	Brazil	lost	1-2	
1974	Uruguay	lost	0-2	
1974	Chile	won	2-1	
1975	Turkey	drew	1-1	
1975	West Germany B	won	1-0	
1975	Switzerland	won	2-1	
1975	USSR	lost	1-2	
1975	Switzerland	lost	0-1	
1976	Turkey	won	4-0	
1976	Poland	won	2-0	
1977	England	drew	1-1	
1977	Turkey	drew	3-3	
1977	Poland	drew	0-0	

Terry Conroy played hurling and Gaelic football before deciding to turn to soccer. Playing his early football for Home Farm, he soon attracted scouts from a number of clubs before being signed by Irish League side Glentoran. Displaying his prolific goalscoring ability, he again attracted attention, this time from First Division clubs across the water.

Stoke City won the race for his signature, seeing off competition from Fulham and Newcastle United. Though he scored on his debut against Leicester City in March 1967 it was another two years before he could claim a regular first team place.

Conroy won the first of his 27 caps for the Republic of Ireland in Mick Meagan's second game in charge, against Czechoslovakia in Prague. Although the Irish lost 3-0, he kept his place for the next match. Conroy played in nine consecutive games from his debut but it was under manager Liam Tuohy that he enjoyed his best moments in international football. His first goal at this level came in October 1972 in a World Cup qualifier against the USSR, another in the next game against France.

Conroy spent 11 seasons at the Victoria Ground, scoring 49 goals in 271 League games, exciting Potters' fans with his determined displays. Stoke appeared in a major final for the first time in their 105-year history when they faced Chelsea in the 1972 League Cup Final. Conroy headed the opening goal after just four minutes as the Potters beat the much-fancied Londoners 2-1. Following Stoke's relegation at the end of the 1976-77 campaign, he spent a season in Hong Kong before returning to end his Football League career with Crewe Alexandra.

Kevin Fitzpatrick

Position	Goalkeeper
Born	Kevin Fitzpatrick, Limerick, 1943

Clubs
Limerick

International Caps	1

Matches

Year	Opponent	Result	Score	G
1970	Czechoslovakia	lost	0-3	

Goalkeeper Kevin Fitzpatrick was a member of the Limerick CBS team which won the Munster Colleges Senior Football Championship in 1960. After a string of outstanding displays between the posts in the Limerick 'B' team, he became the club's first-choice keeper midway through the 1962-63 season.

Fitzpatrick went on to become one of the longest-serving players in League of Ireland football in the 1960s and 1970s. A one-club man, he won Munster Cup medals in 1963 and 1977, was a League Cup winner in 1975 and appeared in five FAI Cup Finals, picking up winners' medals in 1971 and 1982. Fitzpatrick also won a League Championship medal in 1979-80 when Republic of Ireland team boss Eoin Hand was their manager.

His one full cap for the national side came in October 1969 when he was selected for the World Cup match against Czechoslovakia in Prague. It was Mick Meagan's first away match in charge of the Republic. A side depleted by injuries and withdrawals lost 3-0, with Czech striker Adamec grabbing a hat-trick. Alan Kelly returned for the next game and Fitzpatrick rejoined Limerick.

His relationship with the club lasted more than two decades for when the club struck a bad patch, he had the courage to take over as manager.

Tony Byrne

Position	Defender
Born	Anthony Brendan Byrne, Rathdowney, 2 February 1946

Clubs

Millwall; Southampton; Hereford United; Newport County

International Caps	14

Matches

Year	Opponent	Result	Score	G
1970	Denmark	drew	1-1	
1970	Poland	lost	1-2	
1970	West Germany	lost	1-2	
1971	Poland	lost	0-2	
1971	Sweden	drew	1-1	
1971	Sweden	lost	0-1	
1971	Italy	lost	0-3	
1971	Italy	lost	1-2	
1971	Austria	lost	1-4	
1973	France	won	2-1	
1973	USSR	lost	0-1	
1973	France	drew	1-1	
1973	Norway	drew	1-1	
1974	Poland	won	1-0	

Having left Ireland with his family to live in England, Tony Byrne joined Third Division Millwall as a junior. After progressing through the ranks he made his League debut for the Lions. It proved to be his only appearance for the London club for in August 1964 he moved to Southampton.

After some impressive displays in the club's reserve side, he had the misfortune to break a leg. It wasn't until April 1967 that he made his Saints debut against Manchester United – and the likes of Best, Law and Charlton at Old Trafford – at the end of the south-coast club's first season in the top flight. Byrne was in and out of the Southampton side for the next seven years, despite winning 14 caps for the Republic of Ireland.

His international debut came in the World Cup match against Denmark in October 1969. The slightly-built defender had an outstanding game – the Danes only breached

the Republic goal once, this a penalty five minutes from time. For the next few years, Byrne was a regular in the Irish squad where his versatility was much valued.

At club level he found his slight build a handicap in Saints' rugged defensive system during their early First Division games. After 93 League appearances he joined Hereford United, then embarking on their third season of League football. After helping the Edgar Street club win the Third Division Championship in 1975-76, he left to end his first-class career with Newport County.

Steve Heighway

Position	Winger
Born	Stephen Derek Heighway, Dublin, 25 November 1947

Clubs

Skelmersdale United; Liverpool; Minnesota Kicks (U.S.)

International Caps	34

Matches

Year	Opponent	Result	Score	G
1971	Poland	lost	0-2	
1971	Sweden	drew	1-1	
1971	Sweden	lost	0-1	
1971	Italy	lost	1-2	
1971	Austria	lost	1-4	
1973	USSR	lost	1-2	
1975	USSR	won	3-0	
1975	Turkey	drew	1-1	
1975	West Germany B	won	1-0	
1975	USSR	lost	1-2	
1976	Turkey	won	4-0	
1976	Norway	won	3-0	
1977	England	drew	1-1	
1977	France	lost	0-2	
1977	Spain	lost	0-1	
1977	France	won	1-0	
1977	Bulgaria	lost	1-2	
1978	Bulgaria	drew	0-0	
1978	Norway	drew	0-0	
1978	Denmark	drew	3-3	
1979	N Ireland	drew	0-0	
1979	Bulgaria	lost	0-1	
1980	Bulgaria	won	3-0	
1980	United States	won	3-2	
1980	N Ireland	lost	0-1	

Matches Continued

Year	Opponent	Result	Score	G
1980	England	lost	0-2	
1980	Cyprus	won	3-2	
1980	Argentina	lost	0-1	
1981	Belgium	drew	1-1	
1981	France	lost	0-2	
1981	Cyprus	won	6-0	
1981	Wales	lost	1-3	
1981	Belgium	lost	0-1	
1982	Holland	drew	2-2	

Above: Steve Heighway

Steve Heighway, who was born in Dublin, did not see a game of football until he moved to England with his parents at the age of 10. He was with Manchester City when he was 17 and although they gave him every opportunity to enjoy a footballer's life, his education always came first. He had done well at school – well enough that he eventually won a place at Warwick University. Even at 21, when most footballers already have five years of a full-time career behind them, Steve Heighway wasn't contemplating turning professional.

He was playing for Skelmersdale United, a club that was earning a growing reputation in the old Amateur Cup when he was signed by Liverpool.

In September 1970 he made his international debut for the Republic of Ireland side against Poland in Dublin, before he'd played in the Liverpool League side!

Heighway brought pace and width to the Liverpool attack, having a two-footed talent which enabled him to cut inside opponents or to pass them on the outside. In the months following his first team debut, he turned the tide in the Merseyside derby with Liverpool 2-0 down. He scored the first from an acute angle and then provided the cross for John Toshack to equalise, before Chris Lawler hit the winner from a Heighway cross. He ended his first campaign with a near post shot that deceived Arsenal keeper Bob Wilson, to give Liverpool the lead in the 1971 FA Cup Final that the Gunners came back to win 2-1. Despite wearing the No.9 shirt, Heighway was a winger with the audacity to take on defenders and confound them, running at them and getting past them time and time again.

He helped the Reds win the European Cup in 1977 and 1978 after victories over Borussia Mönchengladbach and FC Bruges respectively. The same teams provided the opposition in 1973 and 1976 when Liverpool won the UEFA Cup. Four League Championship medals were added to his collection in 1973, 1976, 1977 and 1979 and an FA Cup winners' medal in 1974 when he scored in the 3-0 defeat of Newcastle United.

His success for Liverpool did nothing for the Republic's cause, only serving to restrict Heighway's appearances for the national side. At the close of the decade, he crossed the Atlantic to end his playing days with Minnesota Kicks.

When the position of youth development officer at Anfield became available in 1988 he jumped at the chance to return to his spiritual home. He later became youth team manager and in 1996 led his young charges to success in the FA Youth Cup. According to Bill Shankly, Heighway was 'an individualist who could win a match with one flash of genius'.

Above: Mick Kearns

Mick Kearns

Position	Goalkeeper
Born	Michael Kearns, Banbury, 26 November 1950

Clubs

Oxford United; Plymouth Argyle (loan); Charlton Athletic (loan); Walsall; Wolverhampton Wanderers; Walsall

International Caps	18

Matches

Year	Opponent	Result	Score	G
1971	Poland	lost	0-2	
1974	Poland	won	1-0	
1974	Uruguay	lost	0-2	
1974	Chile	won	2-1	
1976	Norway	won	3-0	
1976	Poland	won	2-0	
1977	England	drew	1-1	
1977	Turkey	drew	3-3	
1977	France	lost	0-2	
1977	Spain	lost	0-1	
1977	France	won	1-0	
1977	Bulgaria	lost	1-2	
1978	Norway	drew	0-0	
1978	Denmark	drew	3-3	
1979	N Ireland	drew	0-0	
1979	England	drew	1-1	
1980	United States	won	3-2	
1980	N Ireland	lost	0-1	

Goalkeeper Mick Kearns began his career with Oxford United. In five years at the Manor Ground he made 67 League appearances. Whilst with the U's, he made his full international debut for the Republic of Ireland against Poland in Dublin, coming off the bench to replace Alan Kelly after 76 minutes. In doing so, Kearns became the youngest goalkeeper (at 19 years 301 days old) ever to play for the Republic.

In October 1972 Kearns was loaned out to Plymouth Argyle with a view to a permanent move: he broke his leg in a training accident and the transfer was put on hold. When he had made a full recovery, he had a brief loan spell with Charlton Athletic before in July 1973 joining Walsall for £12,000.

It was around this time that Alan Kelly retired from international football, leading to a three-way tussle for the No.1 jersey. Both Paddy Roche and Peter Thomas were given chances between the posts but it was Mick Kearns who established himself in the national side. Kearns, who qualified for the Republic through his Mayo-born parents, went on to make 18 international appearances before succumbing to the talents of Fulham's Gerry Peyton. Without doubt his best display for the Republic came in the 1-0 defeat of France at Lansdowne Road in March 1977.

Kearns was Walsall's first-choice keeper for six seasons, clocking up 249 League appearances, but when the Saddlers lost their Third Division status in 1978-79 he left to join Wolverhampton Wanderers.

He saved a penalty on his Wolves debut against local rivals West Bromwich Albion at the Hawthorns, earning his side a point in a goalless draw. Most of his three seasons at Molineux were spent in the shadow of Paul Bradshaw. He later returned to Walsall where he ended his career.

The son of 'Kit' Lawlor, who played for the Republic of Ireland in the 1940s and, '50s, Mick Lawlor was an energetic midfielder who could also play in the forward line.

In over two decades of League of Ireland football, Lawlor won every major domestic honour. Beginning his career with Shamrock Rovers, he scored in every round of the FAI Cup in 1967-68, including the 3-0 defeat of Waterford in the final. He was also in the Hoops side which retained the trophy the following season.

It was whilst playing for Rovers that he won all five of his international caps. With a large number of English-based players crying off from the Republic's games in the early 1970s, Mick Lawlor was one of a number of Irish-based players to take advantage. He made his debut against Poland at Dalymount Park in September 1970. This was cut short when he was injured shortly before half-time and replaced by Tony O'Connell. However, he had done enough to impress – including striking the Polish post with a rasping drive – and kept his place in the side for the Republic's next three games. His fifth and final cap, also against Poland, came after a two-year absence from the national side.

After spending nine seasons with the Hoops, Lawlor spent 1974-75 and 1975-76 with Dublin rivals Shelbourne, top-scoring on both occasions. He then joined Dundalk, where he was to have the most successful era of his career. In 1976-77, his first season with the club, he was again an FAI Cup winner and in 1978 he won a League Cup winners' medal. The following season he helped the Lilywhites win the League Championship and FAI Cup double for the first time in their history. During his time with Dundalk, he had a spell as the club's assistant-manager, later returning to Shelbourne prior to being appointed player-manager of Home Farm.

Paddy Dunning

Position	Centre-half
Born	Patrick Dunning, Dublin, 1951
Clubs	

Shelbourne; Dundalk; Los Angeles Skyhawks (U.S.); University College, Dublin

International Caps	2

Matches				
Year	Opponent	Result	Score	G
1971	Sweden	lost	0-1	
1971	Italy	lost	0-3	

Shelbourne's Paddy Dunning was just 19 years old when in September 1970 he was chosen to play for the League of Ireland against the Scottish League. Normally a centre-half, he played at left-back where he nullified the threat posed by Celtic's flying winger Jimmy Johnstone. The game had been witnessed by national team boss Mick Meagan. He was so impressed by the youngster that he called Dunning into the Republic of Ireland side for two consecutive European Championship qualifiers against Sweden and Italy. Though both games played on foreign soil ended in defeat, he was not criticised for his performances, though he had played his last internationals.

Dunning spent eight seasons at Tolka Park before in 1977 leaving to play for Dundalk. Having just two FAI Cup runners–up medals to show for his time with the Shels, his luck began to improve following his arrival at Oriel Park.

In 1978 he won a League Cup winners' medal, and in the following season of 1978–79 he enjoyed great success, helping the club win the League Championship and the FAI Cup double. Whilst with Dundalk he spent the summers playing for Los Angeles Skyhawks in the NASL. He won more domestic honours with the Lilywhites in the

Mick Lawlor

Position	Midfield/Forward
Born	Michael Lawlor, Dublin, 1948
Clubs	

Shamrock Rovers; Shelbourne; Dundalk; Shelbourne; Home Farm

International Caps	5

Matches				
Year	Opponent	Result	Score	G
1971	Poland	lost	0-2	
1971	Sweden	drew	1-1	
1971	Sweden	lost	0-1	
1971	Italy	lost	0-3	
1973	Poland	lost	0-2	

1980s – League Cup and FAI Cup winners' medals in 1981 and another Championship medal in 1981-82.

He had spent six years with Dundalk when he returned to his native Dublin to join University College, Dublin. He played an important role in the students' greatest hour, when in 1984 they beat their illustrious neighbours Shamrock Rovers to lift the FAI Cup – the only major honour in the club's history.

Noel Campbell

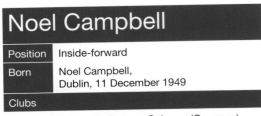

Position	Inside-forward
Born	Noel Campbell, Dublin, 11 December 1949

Clubs
St Patrick's Athletic; Fortuna Cologne (Germany)

International Caps	11

Matches				
Year	Opponent	Result	Score	G
1971	Austria	lost	1-4	
1972	Iran	won	2-1	
1972	Ecuador	won	3-2	
1972	Chile	lost	1-2	
1972	Portugal	lost	1-2	
1973	USSR	lost	1-2	
1973	France	won	2-1	
1975	West Germany B	won	1-0	
1976	Norway	won	3-0	
1977	Spain	lost	0-1	
1977	Bulgaria	lost	1-2	

Red-haired inside-forward Noel Campbell began his career as a goalscoring midfielder with St Patrick's Athletic. After ending the 1968-69 and 1969-70 seasons as the club's leading scorer, he decided it was time to move on.

Ignoring the well-trodden path into English football, he surprisingly opted for a move to Fortuna Cologne in West Germany's Second Division!

He made his full international debut as a half-time substitute for Eamonn Dunphy in the 4-1 defeat by Austria in May 1971 – Mick Meagan's first match in charge. Though he was never a regular in the Republic of Ireland side, he made occasional appearances throughout the 1970s, enjoying his best run in 1972 when he played in all six of the nation's games. However, his 11th and final game saw his international career end on a sour note. Coming on as a 79th minute substitute for Gerry Daly, he received his marching orders just a minute later for his part in a brawl ignited by Tzetkov's challenge on Frank Stapleton and for which four players were dismissed!

Noel Campbell played German football for eight seasons, helping his club win promotion to the Bundesliga via the play-offs. A popular and skilful footballer, he later returned to Ireland to become assistant-manager to Johnny Giles at Shamrock Rovers. When Giles went back to Vancouver Whitecaps, Campbell stepped up to become the Hoops' manager.

Jimmy Dunne

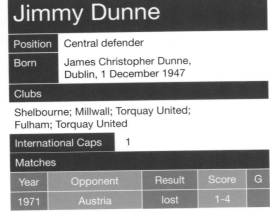

Position	Central defender
Born	James Christopher Dunne, Dublin, 1 December 1947

Clubs
Shelbourne; Millwall; Torquay United; Fulham; Torquay United

International Caps	1

Matches				
Year	Opponent	Result	Score	G
1971	Austria	lost	1-4	

An astute and constructive passer of the ball, Jimmy Dunne's displays for Shelbourne led to Millwall paying the League of Ireland club £1,500 for his services in February 1966.

His Football League career got off to a very slow start as League action eluded him at The Den. It was only after he joined Third Division Torquay United that he got his chance. After three impressive seasons at Plainmoor, Dunne was transferred to Fulham for £15,000 as the Cottagers strove to regain their Second Division status.

It was money well spent, for the big centre-half missed just one game in 1970-71 as Fulham won promotion.

In the close season, Dunne made his international debut for the Republic of Ireland against Austria. On a most miserable Sunday at Dalymount Park, Dunne stretched to intercept a low cross, but only succeeded in turning the ball past Alan Kelly for the most unwelcome of debut goals! The visitors went on to win 4-1 and Jimmy Dunne never wore the green of the Republic again.

Back at Craven Cottage, he continued to be a regular in the Fulham side until 1974 when he decided to emigrate to South Africa. He was back at Craven Cottage less than a year later, and played in the club's reserve side. In April 1976 he rejoined Torquay United, where he ended his career.

Jimmy Holmes

Position	Left-back
Born	James Paul Holmes, Dublin, 11 November 1953

Clubs
Coventry City; Tottenham Hotspur; Vancouver Whitecaps (Canada); Leicester City; Brentford; Torquay United; Peterborough United; Nuneaton Borough

International Caps	30
International Goals	1

Matches				
Year	Opponent	Result	Score	G
1971	Austria	lost	1-4	

Matches Continued				
Year	Opponent	Result	Score	G
1973	France	won	2-1	
1973	USSR	lost	0-1	
1973	Poland	lost	0-2	
1973	France	drew	1-1	
1973	Norway	drew	1-1	
1974	Poland	won	1-0	
1974	Brazil	lost	1-2	
1975	USSR	won	3-0	
	Switzerland	lost	0-1	
1976	Turkey	won	4-0	
	Norway	won	3-0	1
	Poland	won	2-0	
1977	England	drew	1-1	
	Turkey	drew	3-3	
	France	lost	0-2	
	Spain	lost	0-1	
	France	won	1-0	
	Poland	drew	0-0	
	Bulgaria	lost	1-2	
1978	Bulgaria	drew	0-0	
	Turkey	won	4-2	
	Poland	lost	0-3	
	Norway	drew	0-0	
	Denmark	drew	3-3	
1979	Northern Ireland	drew	0-0	
	England	drew	1-1	
	Denmark	won	2-0	
	Bulgaria	lost	0-1	
1981	Wales	lost	1-3	

Jimmy Holmes made his Football League debut for Coventry City in January 1972 – but had already won his first full cap for his country! He was called on as substitute for the Republic of Ireland against Austria in May 1971. Aged just 17 years 200 days, he became the nation's youngest-ever player.

At Coventry he gradually replaced Chris Cattlin and built a reputation as a genuinely classy football-playing full-back, solid in defence, cool and confident in possession.

It was more than a year before Holmes added a second cap to his historic first, but this time the young Dubliner was on from the start, playing an important role in a surprise 2-1 victory over France in a World Cup qualifier at Dalymount Park. Holmes showed his best form for the Republic of Ireland in the 1976 European Championships, when he also became the country's penalty-taker. His first against Turkey was saved by the keeper, he held his nerve and took the next one against Norway to slot home the second goal in a 3-0 win.

Above: Jimmy Holmes

In March 1977 with Spurs sliding towards the Second Division, Holmes joined the North London club for a fee of £100,000. Suffering a spate of injuries, he was unable to prevent Spurs being relegated but over the next two seasons proved his versatility in a variety of defensive positions.

When playing for the Republic against Bulgaria in Sofia in a European Championship qualifier in May 1979, Holmes suffered a broken leg. The injury was serious but it was not helped by the substandard treatment he received from the Bulgarian medical services. It was almost a year before he was able to play again, but by this time Chris Hughton had become established as Spurs' left-back of the future.

Unable to get back into the team, he moved to Vancouver Whitecaps of the NASL. After two years there, in which time he won his 30th and final cap, he returned to England and played on a non-contract basis for Leicester City, Brentford and Torquay United. He then joined Peterborough United as player/assistant-manager before becoming player-manager of Nuneaton Borough. He later had spells as manager of Hitchin Town and Bedworth United before making a new career for himself as a member of the West Midlands police force.

One of the finest defenders to grace League of Ireland football, Mick Gannon started out with Shelbourne where his displays led to full international honours for the Republic of Ireland.

With John Dempsey unavailable, the selectors opted to play Gannon at right-back for the match against Austria in Linz. The game was Liam Tuohy's first as manager and a disaster for the Irish as they went down 6-0!

Despite consistent displays at club level over the following seasons, he was never chosen for the national side again, though he did play representative football for the League of Ireland against the Irish League. With Shelbourne he reached two FAI Cup Finals but was on the losing side on each occasion – going down to Cork Hibs in 1973 in the replay and then two years later being beaten 1-0 by Home Farm.

Gannon left the Shels in 1977 to join Shamrock Rovers. Under Johnny Giles, who tended to play him in midfield, he won an FAI Cup winners' medal – a match in which he was carried off injured after 70 minutes. Whilst with the Hoops, he won a 1979 League Cup runners-up medal and Leinster Senior Cup and Shield winners' medals. Returning to Shelbourne in 1980, he later ended his career with Aer Lingus in the Leinster Senior League.

Versatile defender John Herrick was just 17 when he joined his local League of Ireland club Cork Hibernians prior to the start of the 1970-71 season, a campaign in which the club won the League Championship.

Before the start of the next season, Herrick decided to revert to part-time status, taking up employment with a Cork sports firm. This didn't detract from his displays and he was selected for the League of Ireland Golden Jubilee game. He was also a member of the All-Ireland select side which played Leeds United – both games being played in 1971.

In October of that year he was called up for his first full international against Austria in Linz and thus became the first active Hibs player to be capped – several players had been capped before or after they played for the club. Despite the 6-0 reversal, Herrick took his tally of international caps to three, coming on as substitute for Tommy Carroll in the games against Chile and France – playing a key role in the latter in a 1-1 draw at the Parc des Princes.

In 1971-72 he won an FAI Cup winners' medal with Hibs as a Miah Dennehy hat-trick helped see off Waterford. Lost to the game for a while, in November 1976 he was persuaded to return by Limerick manager Frank Johnson. He contributed greatly to their revival, and became the first Limerick player to be selected as the Irish Soccer Writers' 'Player of the Month'.

Mick Gannon

Position	Right-back
Born	Michael Gannon, Dublin, 2 February 1947
Clubs	

Shelbourne; Shamrock Rovers; Shelbourne; Aer Lingus

International Caps	1
Matches	

Year	Opponent	Result	Score	G
1972	Austria	lost	0-6	

John Herrick

Position	Defender
Born	John Herrick, Cork, 1947
Clubs	

Cork Hibernians; Limerick

International Caps	3
Matches	

Year	Opponent	Result	Score	G
1972	Austria	lost	0-6	
1972	Chile	lost	1-2	
1973	France	drew	1-1	

Mick Kearin

Position	Left-half
Born	Michael Kearin, Dublin, 1948

Clubs

Bohemians; Shamrock Rovers; Bohemians; Athlone Town

International Caps	1

Matches

Year	Opponent	Result	Score	G
1972	Austria	lost	0-6	

All-action midfielder Mick Kearin was a vital member of Shamrock Rovers' successful FAI Cup team of the late 1960s, though he started out with his first club Bohemians as a centre-forward!

He joined the Hoops in the summer of 1966 and found himself playing in all five forward positions and at both right and left-half. He eventually settled into the Rovers' side at left-half – his tigerish tackling proving invaluable for the Milltown club. Kearin, who later captained the club, helped the Hoops to FAI Cup success in three successive seasons between 1967 and 1969. He scored a rare goal in the 4-1 replay victory over Cork Celtic in the last of those finals.

In the League of Ireland Jubilee game in 1971, Mick Kearin was outstanding. Having appeared on the bench in a number of Republic of Ireland matches, he made his one and only international appearance in the disastrous 6-0 European Championship defeat by Austria in Linz. This was Liam Tuohy's first match in charge and with the exception of Chelsea's Paddy Mulligan, the Republic side was made up of League of Ireland players.

At the end of the 1972-73 season, Kearin left the Hoops to rejoin Bohemians. Midway through his first season back with the club, he moved on to Athlone Town where he ended his playing days.

Tommy McConville

Position	Centre-half
Born	Thomas McConville, Dundalk Co. Louth, 1947

Clubs

Dundalk; Waterford; Shamrock Rovers; Dundalk

International Caps	6

Matches

Year	Opponent	Result	Score	G
1972	Austria	lost	0-6	
1973	USSR	lost	1-2	
1973	France	lost	1-2	
1973	USSR	lost	0-1	
1973	Poland	lost	0-2	
1973	France	drew	1-1	

One of the League of Ireland's most versatile and committed defenders, Tommy McConville began his career with his home-town club Dundalk. His displays for the Lilywhites led to him representing the League of Ireland both in the Golden Jubilee match of 1971 and the game against the Football League when Arsenal's John Radford didn't get a look in.

It was his performance in this game that led to Liam Tuohy handing him his first cap for the game against Austria in Linz in October 1971. Despite the 6-0 defeat, McConville became a regular in the Republic side between November 1972 and May 1973 when he took his tally to six caps.

He spent three seasons at Dundalk, helping the club to success in the Shield Competition of 1972. He was linked with a move to Manchester United but in the summer of 1972, he joined Waterford. In his first season with the club, he helped them win the League Championship and the League Cup but shortly afterwards moved to Shamrock Rovers.

Following a couple of disappointing seasons with the Hoops, McConville rejoined Dundalk and in doing so played his part in the club's most successful era. The Lilywhites won the League Championship in 1975-76, 1978-79 and 1981-82, the FAI Cup in 1977, 1979 and 1981 and the League Cup in 1978 and 1981. He gave yeoman service to Dundalk and played an important role. Under the guidance of manager Jim McLaughlin, they became one of the League of Ireland's top club sides. McConville was still playing for Dundalk at the age of 40 but after not fitting into the plans of new manager Turlough O'Connor, he left to take over the reins of Finn Harps.

Mick Martin

Position	Midfield
Born	Michael Paul Martin, Dublin, 9 July 1951

Clubs

Home Farm; Bohemians; Manchester United; West Bromwich Albion; Newcastle United; Vancouver Whitecaps (Canada); Cardiff City; Peterborough United; Rotherham United; Preston North End

International Caps	52
International Goals	4

Matches

Year	Opponent	Result	Score	G
1972	Austria	lost	0-6	
1972	Iran	won	2-1	
1972	Ecuador	won	3-2	1
1972	Chile	lost	1-2	
1972	Portugal	lost	1-2	
1973	USSR	lost	1-2	
1973	USSR	lost	0-1	
1973	Poland	lost	0-2	
1973	France	drew	1-1	1
1973	Norway	drew	1-1	
1974	Poland	won	1-0	
1974	Brazil	lost	1-2	
1974	Uruguay	lost	0-2	

Matches Continued				
Year	Opponent	Result	Score	G
1974	Chile	won	2-1	
1975	USSR	won	3-0	
1975	Turkey	drew	1-1	
1975	West Germany B	won	1-0	
1975	Switzerland	won	2-1	1
1975	USSR	lost	1-2	
1975	Switzerland	lost	0-1	
1976	Turkey	won	4-0	
1976	Norway	won	3-0	
1976	Poland	won	2-0	
1977	England	drew	1-1	
1977	Turkey	drew	3-3	
1977	France	lost	0-2	
1977	Spain	lost	0-1	
1977	France	won	1-0	
1977	Poland	drew	0-0	
1977	Bulgaria	lost	1-2	
1979	Denmark	won	2-0	
1979	Bulgaria	lost	0-1	
1979	West Germany	lost	1-3	
1980	Wales	lost	1-2	
1980	Czechoslovakia	lost	1-4	
1980	Bulgaria	won	3-0	1
1980	United States	won	3-2	
1980	N Ireland	lost	0-1	
1981	France	lost	0-2	
1981	Belgium	lost	0-1	
1981	Czechoslovakia	won	3-1	
1981	West Germany B	lost	0-3	
1982	Holland	drew	2-2	
1982	France	won	3-2	
1982	Algeria	lost	0-2	
1982	Chile	lost	0-1	
1982	Brazil	lost	0-7	
1982	Trinidad & Tobago	lost	1-2	
1983	Holland	lost	1-2	
1983	Spain	drew	3-3	
1983	Malta	won	1-0	
1983	Spain	lost	0-2	

Above: Mick Martin

The son of Con Martin, who won 30 caps for the Republic of Ireland and six for Northern Ireland, as a goalkeeper, defender and midfielder, Mick Martin was also a versatile player.

He began his career in Ireland with Home Farm and Bohemians. He had already made his full international debut when Tommy Docherty, the newly appointed manager of Manchester United paid £20,000 for his signature – at the time, it was a record receipt for a League of Ireland club.

At Old Trafford, he was a regular in the Reds' side in 1972-73 but only appeared occasionally the following season when the club lost their top-flight status.

Despite his difficulties at Old Trafford, Martin continued to command a regular place in the Republic of Ireland line-up and during the managerial tenure of both Liam Tuohy and Johnny Giles, he made more international appearances than any other player. Operating in front of the back four, he was a hardworking individual, the perfect foil for the likes of Liam Brady and Giles.

In September 1975 he left United to join West Bromwich Albion and in his first season at the Hawthorns he helped the Baggies win promotion to the First Division. However, when manager Giles was replaced by Ron

Atkinson, Martin found himself out of the side and in December 1978 he was sold to Newcastle United for £100,000.

Martin became captain at St James Park and spent six seasons in the north-east where his consistent displays won over Newcastle supporters. Just as Arthur Cox's side embarked on an entertaining season which ended in promotion, Martin was left to wander around the country – even North America – to continue his football career.

Mick Martin, who captained the Republic of Ireland in five of his 52 appearances was also dismissed twice while playing for his country. The second occasion, against Bulgaria in June 1977 when he and Noel Campbell were involved in a four-man brawl, signalled the start of a near two-year exile from international football. When Liam Brady became Celtic manager in June 1991 he appointed Martin as the club's coach. On later leaving the game, he went into business on Tyneside, running a sports shop.

Damien Richardson

Position	Forward
Born	Damien John Richardson, Dublin, 2 August 1947

Clubs

Shamrock Rovers; Gillingham; Gravesend; Folkestone; Faversham; Chatham

International Caps	3

Matches

Year	Opponent	Result	Score	G
1972	Austria	lost	0-6	
1973	Norway	drew	1-1	
1980	Czechoslovakia	lost	1-4	

A striker without any obvious weaknesses, Damien Richardson began his career with Shamrock Rovers, and was a regular goalscorer during his time with the Hoops.

He won two FAI Cup medals in 1968 and 1969. Shortly after the '69 final, a move to Preston North End fell through.

His form for the Rovers led to him winning the first of three international caps for the Republic of Ireland when in October 1971 he played in the 6-0 defeat in Austria.

In October 1972 Richardson left Milltown to join Fourth Division Gillingham. He soon claimed a first team place and at the end of his first season at the Priestfield Stadium, he won his second international cap. In doing so, he became the first Gillingham player for 48 years to appear in a full international.

He helped the Gills win promotion to the Third Division in 1973-74 and the following season was voted the club's 'Player of the Year'. Richardson spent nine seasons with the Kent side, scoring 94 goals in 321 League games. He then had spells with a number of non-League clubs in the area, including Gravesend, Folkestone, Faversham and Chatham before returning to the Priestfield Stadium as youth team coach. In May 1989 he succeeded former Spurs boss Keith Burkinshaw as manager. Just over three years later, he again parted company with the club following a poor start to the 1992-93 season.

He then became manager of Cork City but his stay was brief. After an equally short time with Cobh Ramblers, he was appointed boss of Shelbourne.

Paddy Roche

Position	Goalkeeper
Born	Patrick Joseph Christopher Roche, Dublin, 4 January 1951

Clubs

Shelbourne; Manchester United; Brentford; Halifax Town

International Caps	8

Matches

Year	Opponent	Result	Score	G
1972	Austria	lost	0-6	
1975	USSR	won	3-0	
1975	Turkey	drew	1-1	
1975	West Germany B	won	1-0	
1975	Switzerland	won	2-1	
1975	USSR	lost	1-2	
1975	Switzerland	lost	0-1	
1976	Turkey	won	4-0	

A goalkeeper of immense natural ability, Paddy Roche often displayed a lack of confidence, but his early displays for Shelbourne showed none of this and in October 1973 he joined Manchester United for a fee of £15,000.

Roche had already made his international debut for the Republic of Ireland as a member of Liam Tuohy's scratch team that lost 6-0 in Austria. Thankfully, that experience left no lasting scars and he recovered to play in a further seven internationals for the Republic.

Although Roche spent almost nine seasons at Old Trafford, he never really became the Old Trafford club's first-choice keeper. Initially he found himself understudying Alex Stepney and then more often than not, lost out to Gary Bailey. His reputation was somewhat tarnished after a spate of media criticism following a blunder whilst playing for United against Liverpool during the 1975-76 season. However, it was only in August 1982 after being given a free transfer that he left Old Trafford to join Brentford.

Above: Paddy Roche

With the Bees he proved himself a keeper of the highest quality, playing in as many games in 1982-83 as he had done in nine seasons with Manchester United! On losing his place to Trevor Swinburne, he moved on to Halifax Town where he was the Shaymen's first-choice keeper for five seasons. At the end of the 1984-85 season, Roche retired to concentrate on his duties as Halifax Town's Football in the Community Officer.

Miah Dennehy

Position	Winger
Born	Jeremiah Dennehy, Cork, 29 March 1950

Clubs

Cork Hibernians; Nottingham Forest; Walsall; Bristol Rovers, Cardiff City

International Caps	11
International Goals	2

Matches

Year	Opponent	Result	Score	G
1972	Ecuador	won	3-2	
1972	Chile	lost	1-2	
1973	USSR	lost	0-1	
1973	Poland	lost	0-2	
1973	France	drew	1-1	
1973	Norway	drew	1-1	1
1974	Poland	won	1-0	1
1975	Turkey	drew	1-1	
1975	West Germany B	won	1-0	
1976	Poland	won	2-0	
1977	Poland	drew	0-0	

Miah Dennehy, who began his career with Cork Hibs, had great pace and a sharp footballing brain. In 1970-71 he helped them win the League Championship, scoring a hat-trick in a play-off match against Shamrock Rovers. The following season he netted another treble against Waterford in the FAI Cup Final, securing the Cup for Hibs.

Shortly after this triumph, Dennehy was called into Liam Tuohy's squad for the mini-World Cup in Brazil. He made his debut coming off the bench to replace Mick Leech in the 3-2 win over Ecuador. Dennehy remained on the fringes of the national side, making a total of six appearances whilst Tuohy was manager. Having scored in the 1-1 draw with Norway in June 1973, he netted a second in the 1-0 defeat of Poland in October of that year – Johnny Giles' first game in charge of the national side.

By January 1973 Dennehy had parted company with Cork Hibs, as Nottingham Forest manager Dave Mackay paid £20,000 for his services. He settled in well at the City Ground and his performances led to him being named as substitute in the historic All Ireland XI which played Brazil that year – a game in which he came off the bench to play with a broken toe!

Dennehy was a regular first teamer at Forest until the appointment of Brian Clough, after which he was transferred to Walsall. He spent three seasons at Fellows Park, scoring 22 goals in 128 League outings. In the summer of 1978 he moved to Bristol Rovers, later joining Cardiff City. Unable to break into the Bluebirds' side, Dennehy then had a spell in non-League football before returning to Cork to concentrate on junior soccer and hurling with the local St Vincent's GAA club.

Gerry Daly

Position	Midfield
Born	Gerard Anthony Daly, Dublin, 30 April 1954

Clubs

Bohemians; Manchester United; Derby County; Coventry City; Leicester City (loan); Birmingham City; Shrewsbury Town; Stoke City; Doncaster Rovers

International Caps	48
International Goals	13

Matches

Year	Opponent	Result	Score	G
1973	Poland	lost	0-2	
1973	Norway	drew	1-1	
1974	Brazil	lost	1-2	
1974	Uruguay	lost	0-2	
1975	West Germany B	won	1-0	
1975	Switzerland	lost	0-1	
1977	England	drew	1-1	1
1977	Turkey	drew	3-3	1
1977	France	lost	0-2	
1977	France	won	1-0	
1977	Bulgaria	lost	1-2	
1978	Bulgaria	drew	0-0	

Matches Continued

Year	Opponent	Result	Score	G
1978	Turkey	won	4-2	
1978	Denmark	drew	3-3	1
1979	N Ireland	drew	0-0	
1979	England	drew	1-1	1
1979	Denmark	won	2-0	1
1979	Bulgaria	lost	0-1	
1980	N Ireland	lost	0-1	
1980	England	lost	0-2	
1980	Cyprus	won	3-2	
1980	Switzerland	won	2-0	1
1980	Argentina	lost	0-1	
1981	Holland	won	2-1	1
1981	Belgium	drew	1-1	
1981	Cyprus	won	6-0	2
1981	Wales	lost	1-3	
1981	Belgium	lost	0-1	
1981	Czechoslovakia	won	3-1	
1981	West Germany B	lost	0-3	
1981	Poland	lost	0-3	
1982	Algeria	lost	0-2	
1982	Chile	lost	0-1	
1982	Brazil	lost	0-7	
1982	Trinidad & Tobago	lost	1-2	
1983	Holland	lost	1-2	1
1983	Spain	lost	0-2	
1984	Malta	won	8-0	1
1984	Israel	lost	0-3	
1985	Mexico	drew	0-0	
1985	Norway	drew	0-0	
1985	Spain	drew	0-0	
1985	Switzerland	won	3-0	
1986	Switzerland	drew	0-0	
1986	Uruguay	drew	1-1	1
1986	Iceland	won	2-1	1
1986	Czechoslovakia	won	1-0	
1987	Scotland	drew	0-0	

Gerry Daly joined Manchester United from Bohemians for a fee reported to be in the region of £20,000 just before his 19th birthday in April 1973. In his first season at Old Trafford the Reds were relegated to the Second Division. Daly had already made his international debut at that stage for the Republic of Ireland as a substitute in the friendly against Poland shortly after his transfer to England.

Daly proved an effective part of United's midfield which played such attractive football as they stormed to the Second Division title in 1974-75 and reached the FA Cup Final the following season.

At international level, Johnny Giles gave Daly his first start against West Germany 'B'. From September 1976 following his superb performance against England – when he scored from the penalty-spot in a 1-1 draw – he became a regular in the national side for the rest of the decade.

Back at Old Trafford, Daly eventually found himself in dispute with manager Tommy Docherty and in March 1977 he was transferred to Derby County for a fee of £175,000 – a move that made him Ireland's most expensive footballer. Enjoying his football at the Baseball Ground, Daly was shattered six months after putting pen to paper to learn that the Derby board had appointed Docherty to succeed manager Colin Murphy. Although he maintained a first team place, there was an uneasy atmosphere between player and manager. In August 1980 Daly moved to Coventry City for £310,000.

It was around this time that Eoin Hand was appointed coach of the national side – this coincided with Gerry Daly's best run of form in the green shirt. Daly scored three times in Hand's first four games in charge and proved a highly-valued source of both goals and inspiration in a Republic of Ireland side which narrowly missed out on qualification for the 1982 World Cup Finals.

A lack of stability at club level did not help. Following a loan spell at Leicester City, there were transfers to Birmingham City, Shrewsbury Town, Stoke City and Doncaster Rovers: Daly appeared less frequently on Republic of Ireland team sheets. On hanging up his boots, he had a spell as manager of Telford United but is now unable to work because of a back problem.

Left: Gerry Daly

Eamonn Fagan

Position	Defender
Born	Eamonn Fagan, Dublin, 1950
Clubs	

Shamrock Rovers; Athlone Town

International Caps	1

Matches				
Year	Opponent	Result	Score	G
1973	Norway	drew	1-1	

Eamonn Fagan's international career lasted precisely 11 minutes as he came off the bench to replace Ray Treacy in a 1-1 draw against Norway in Oslo in June 1973.

He had started his League of Ireland career in the early 1970s with Shamrock Rovers. His early displays were good enough to earn him two Under-23 caps for the Republic of Ireland, managed by Sean Thomas. Fagan was outstanding at the heart of the Republic's defence in these two games – both against France and ending in 1-1 draws.

A composed defender who could also operate in midfield, Fagan was selected for the full international side by Sean Thomas whose reign as manager – between the appointments of Tuohy and Giles – lasted precisely one match. Though he never wore the green shirt again, Fagan continued to impress for the Hoops until the summer of 1975 when he was transferred to Ambrose Fogarty's Athlone Town.

They had rejoined the League of Ireland in 1969 and were looking to Fagan to provide experience in their back four. Unfortunately his career at St Mel's Park never got off the ground due to a series of injuries and he was forced into premature retirement.

Terry Mancini

Position	Central defender
Born	Terence John Mancini, Camden Town, 4 October 1942
Clubs	

Watford; Port Elizabeth (South Africa); Leyton Orient; Queen's Park Rangers; Arsenal; Aldershot

International Caps	5
International Goals	1

Matches				
Year	Opponent	Result	Score	G
1974	Poland	won	1-0	
1974	Brazil	lost	1-2	1
1974	Uruguay	lost	0-2	
1974	Chile	won	2-1	
1975	USSR	won	3-0	

Above: Terry Mancini

One of the most colourful and popular characters in the Football League during the 1960s and 1970s, Terry Mancini started out with Watford but after five seasons at Vicarage Road, he decided to try his luck in South Africa, and played for two seasons with the Port Elizabeth side.

He was tempted back to the Football League by Orient in November 1967. He spent four seasons at Brisbane Road, appearing in 167 League games and helping the O's win the Third Division Championship in 1969-70.

In October 1971 he moved to Queen's Park Rangers, becoming a great crowd favourite during his three years with the club. He helped the Loftus Road club win promotion from Division Two in 1972-73. Following his displays in the Rangers defence, Mancini became one of the most-unlikely players ever to turn out for the Republic of Ireland.

This son of an Italian father and Irish mother made his debut in Johnny Giles' first game in charge. After impressing in a 1-0 defeat of Poland, Giles kept Mancini in the team for the summer tour of South America. The renowned dressing-room joker was certainly unfazed by his surprise elevation to international football at the age of 31, and scored the Republic's only goal in a 2-1 defeat to world champions Brazil. After playing in four consecutive games, Mancini appeared in his first competitive match for the Republic, a European Championship qualifier in October 1974 against the USSR at Dalymount Park. Though the game ended in a 3-0 win for Giles' side, Mancini was sent-off after 'flooring' Soviet defender Vladimir Kaplichny – it was his last appearance in the green shirt.

He had just joined Arsenal for £20,000, helping the Gunners through two of their worst-ever seasons. Appointed club captain, his only goal for the North London club came in his penultimate appearance, the relegation dogfight with Wolverhampton Wanderers in April 1975. Mancini's strike was enough to take the points, keep Arsenal in the top flight and condemn the Molineux club to Second Division football.

Later given a free transfer, he joined Aldershot. After working as Fulham's assistant-manager, he nowadays runs a car-hire business in New Malden.

Peter Thomas

Position	Goalkeeper
Born	Peter John Thomas, Coventry, 20 November 1944
Clubs	

Coventry City; Waterford

International Caps	2

Matches

Year	Opponent	Result	Score	G
1974	Poland	won	1-0	
1974	Brazil	lost	1-2	

Goalkeeper Peter Thomas began his career with his home-town club Coventry City. He had little opportunity to display his ability due to the outstanding form of Bill Glazier. In fact, his only appearance for the Highfield Road club came in a 3-2 defeat of Cardiff City in the Sky Blues' promotion-winning season of 1966-67.

During the close season he parted company with Coventry, opting for a move to League of Ireland club Waterford. In his first game for the club, he saved a penalty. By the end of the campaign, the club had won the League title. Between 1967-68 and 1972-73 the Kilcohan Park club won five League of Ireland titles. After appearing on the losing

side in three FAI Cup Finals, Thomas was at last on the winning side in 1980 when Waterford defeated St Patrick's Athletic.

In 1969-70, Thomas was named as the Irish soccer writers' 'Personality of the Year' – the first Englishman to win that award.

In 1972 the man from Coventry successfully applied for Irish citizenship. A year later he made his full international debut for the Republic of Ireland, keeping a clean sheet in a 1-0 defeat of Poland. His performance ensured that he kept his place for the next match against Brazil in Rio and though the Republic lost that game 2-1, Thomas was blameless. It was his last appearance at this level, though he continued to be Waterford's first-choice keeper for a total of 15 years.

Liam Brady

Position	Midfield
Born	William Brady, Dublin, 13 February 1956
Clubs	

Arsenal; Juventus (Italy); Sampdoria (Italy); Inter Milan (Italy); Ascoli (Italy); West Ham United

International Caps	72
International Goals	9

Matches

Year	Opponent	Result	Score	G
1975	USSR	won	3-0	
1975	Turkey	drew	1-1	
1975	West Germany B	won	1-0	
1975	Switzerland	won	2-1	
1975	USSR	lost	1-2	
1975	Switzerland	lost	0-1	
1976	Turkey	won	4-0	
1976	Norway	won	3-0	1
1976	Poland	won	2-0	
1977	England	drew	1-1	
1977	Turkey	drew	3-3	
1977	France	lost	0-2	
1977	Spain	lost	0-1	
1977	France	won	1-0	1
1977	Bulgaria	lost	1-2	
1978	Bulgaria	drew	0-0	
1978	Norway	drew	0-0	
1979	N Ireland	drew	0-0	

Matches Continued				
Year	Opponent	Result	Score	G
1979	England	drew	1-1	
1979	Denmark	won	2-0	
1979	Bulgaria	lost	0-1	
1979	West Germany	lost	1-3	
1980	Wales	lost	1-2	
1980	Bulgaria	won	3-0	
1980	England	lost	0-2	
1980	Cyprus	won	3-2	
1981	Holland	won	2-1	
1981	Belgium	drew	1-1	
1981	France	lost	0-2	
1981	Cyprus	won	6-0	
1981	Belgium	lost	0-1	
1982	Holland	drew	2-2	
1982	France	won	3-2	
1982	Chile	lost	0-1	
1982	Brazil	lost	0-7	
1982	Trinidad & Tobago	lost	1-2	1
1983	Holland	lost	1-2	
1983	Iceland	won	2-0	
1983	Spain	drew	3-3	
1983	Malta	won	1-0	
1984	Iceland	won	3-0	
1984	Holland	lost	2-3	1
1984	Malta	won	8-0	2
1984	Israel	lost	0-3	
1984	Poland	drew	0-0	
1985	USSR	won	1-0	
1985	Norway	lost	0-1	
1985	Denmark	lost	0-3	
1985	Italy	lost	1-2	
1985	England	lost	1-2	1
1985	Norway	drew	0-0	
1985	Spain	drew	0-0	
1985	Switzerland	won	3-0	
1986	Switzerland	drew	0-0	
1986	USSR	lost	0-2	
1986	Denmark	lost	1-4	
1986	Wales	lost	0-1	
1987	Belgium	drew	2-2	1
1987	Scotland	drew	0-0	
1987	Poland	lost	0-1	
1987	Scotland	won	1-0	
1987	Bulgaria	lost	1-2	
1987	Belgium	drew	0-0	
1987	Brazil	won	1-0	1
1987	Luxembourg	won	2-0	
1988	Luxembourg	won	2-1	
1988	Bulgaria	won	2-0	
1989	Hungary	drew	0-0	
1989	Hungary	won	2-0	
1990	West Germany	drew	1-1	

Arguably the most talented footballer ever produced by the Republic of Ireland, Liam Brady left Dublin at the age of 15 for North London and Arsenal. He made his League debut for the Gunners against Birmingham City in October 1973 before becoming a regular in the Arsenal side in 1974-75.

That season he won the first of his 72 full caps for the Republic of Ireland, being called into the side for the European Championship qualifier against the USSR. On a memorable afternoon at Dalymount Park, Brady performed with great skill in a 3-0 win, the goals courtesy of a Don Given hat-trick.

With Arsenal in 1976-77, he was instrumental in feeding Malcolm Macdonald and Frank Stapleton for many of the goals they scored that season. In 1977-78 he was a regular in the Arsenal side which reached the League Cup semi-final and the FA Cup Final. In 1978-79 he was back at Wembley with Arsenal when he gave one of the greatest individual performances seen in a Cup Final, helping Arsenal to a last-minute victory over Manchester United. Brady played in a third consecutive FA Cup Final in 1979-80, Arsenal losing 1-0 to West Ham United. The newly-crowned PFA 'Footballer of the Year' was also a member of Arsenal's European Cup Winners' Cup side which lost on penalties to Valencia.

After much speculation and much derision of the Highbury faithful, he was transferred to Juventus of Italy for the ludicrously low sum of £514,000! He spent two seasons in Turin, playing 57 Serie 'A' matches and helping them win the Italian Championship in both seasons.

He was transferred to Sampdoria in 1982, and after two seasons joined Inter Milan in 1984. He had two seasons with Inter before finishing his Italian honeymoon with Ascoli in 1986-87.

In 1985 Brady became the youngest player to record 50 appearances for the national team when he played against England at Wembley.

Above: Liam Brady

The following year his status within Irish football met a new challenge, when the FAI appointed Jack Charlton as manager. Though he tried hard, Brady could never disguise his creative instincts enough for Big Jack. There was one brief period of harmony in the qualifying rounds for the 1988 European Championships. Brady played in all of those games but in the dying minutes of the final group match against Bulgaria, he was sent-off for fouling his marker. The red card combined with a serious knee injury forced him to miss the finals. His international career was almost at an end when in the friendly match against West Germany in September 1989, Charlton substituted him after only 35 minutes! Furious at the humiliation, Brady announced his retirement from international football.

He had returned to England in 1987 to play for West Ham United. Brady made over 100 first team appearances for the Hammers until deciding to call it a day during the summer of 1990.

A year later he became the first manager of Celtic not to have played for the Glasgow giants. He resigned in October 1993 after a string of poor results, later managing Brighton before returning to Highbury as head of Arsenal's youth development programme.

Tony Grealish

Position	Midfield
Born	Anthony Patrick Grealish, Paddington, 21 September 1956

Clubs

Leyton Orient; Luton Town; Brighton and Hove Albion; West Bromwich Albion; Manchester City; Rotherham United; Walsall; Bromsgrove Rovers; Halesowen Harriers

International Caps	45
International Goals	8

Matches

Year	Opponent	Result	Score	G
1976	Norway	won	3-0	
1976	Poland	won	2-0	
1978	Norway	drew	0-0	
1978	Denmark	drew	3-3	1

Matches Continued				
Year	Opponent	Result	Score	G
1979	N Ireland	drew	0-0	
1979	England	drew	1-1	
1979	West Germany	lost	1-3	
1980	Wales	lost	1-2	
1980	Czechoslovakia	lost	1-4	
1980	Bulgaria	won	3-0	1
1980	United States	won	3-2	1
1980	N Ireland	lost	0-1	
1980	England	lost	0-2	
1980	Cyprus	won	3-2	
1980	Switzerland	won	2-0	
1980	Argentina	lost	0-1	
1981	Holland	won	2-1	
1981	Belgium	drew	1-1	1
1981	France	lost	0-2	
1981	Cyprus	won	6-0	1
1981	Wales	lost	1-3	1
1981	Belgium	lost	0-1	
1981	West Germany B	lost	0-3	
1981	Poland	lost	0-3	
1982	Holland	drew	2-2	
1982	Algeria	lost	0-2	
1982	Chile	lost	0-1	
1982	Brazil	lost	0-7	
1982	Trinidad & Tobago	lost	1-2	
1983	Holland	lost	1-2	
1983	Iceland	won	2-0	1
1983	Spain	drew	3-3	
1983	Spain	lost	0-2	
1984	Iceland	won	3-0	
1984	Holland	lost	2-3	
1984	China	won	1-0	
1984	Mexico	drew	0-0	
1985	Mexico	drew	0-0	
1985	USSR	won	1-0	
1985	Norway	lost	0-1	
1985	Denmark	lost	0-3	
1985	Spain	drew	0-0	
1985	Switzerland	won	3-0	1
1986	USSR	lost	0-2	
1986	Denmark	lost	1-4	

Above: Tony Grealish

Despite being born in London, Tony Grealish enjoyed an Irish upbringing as his parents were both involved in the City's Gaelic Athletic Association. As a youngster he had shown great promise as a Gaelic footballer and represented London in the All–Ireland Minor Football Championships.

In 1972 he joined Leyton Orient as an apprentice and shortly afterwards despite his tender years, became a regular in the East London club's first team.

He was only 19 when he was rewarded with a call-up to the Republic of Ireland side for a friendly against Norway in March 1976. Tony Dunne and Joe Kinnear had ended their international careers, so it was in an unfamiliar full-back role that Grealish played his first game, playing his part in a 3-0 victory. He kept his place in the side for the next game against Poland but then found himself left out as Johnny Giles' team made an unsuccessful attempt to qualify for the 1978 World Cup Finals in Argentina.

In the summer of 1979 Grealish was transferred to the O's divisional rivals Luton Town for a fee of £150,000. It was while with the Hatters that Grealish enjoyed his best football with the Republic. Together with Liam Brady and Gerry Daly he formed a top midfield trio – the driving force behind the nation's impressive but ultimately unsuccessful bid to qualify for the 1982 World Cup Finals. He had twice captained the side during the brief reign of Alan Kelly but took over the captain's armband on a regular basis following the appointment of Eoin Hand.

In 1981 he joined Brighton and Hove Albion; two years later he led the Seagulls to their first FA Cup Final. After drawing 2-2 with Manchester United, Brighton lost the replay 4-0. That 1982-83 season also saw the south coast club relegated to Division Two. After one more season at the Goldstone Ground, Grealish joined Johnny Giles' West Bromwich Albion. After one-and-a-half seasons at the Hawthorns, Grealish played for Manchester City and Rotherham United, helping the Millers win the Fourth Division Championship in 1988-89. He finished his League career with Walsall before playing non-League football for a number of clubs including Bromsgrove Rovers and Halesowen Harriers.

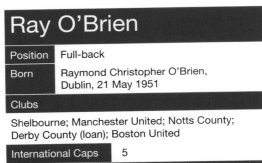

Ray O'Brien

Position	Full-back
Born	Raymond Christopher O'Brien, Dublin, 21 May 1951
Clubs	
Shelbourne; Manchester United; Notts County; Derby County (loan); Boston United	
International Caps	5
Matches	

Year	Opponent	Result	Score	G
1976	Norway	won	3-0	
1976	Poland	won	2-0	
1977	Spain	lost	0-1	
1977	Poland	drew	0-0	
1980	Argentina	lost	0-1	

The son of former Drumcondra wing-half Frank O'Brien, he started out with Shelbourne. Shortly after appearing in the Shels' FAI Cup Final defeat at the hands of

Cork Hibernians in May 1973, he joined Manchester United for £40,000.

After failing to make United's first team, he signed for Notts County for what proved to be a bargain fee of £45,000. At Meadow Lane O'Brien, who was to spend nine seasons with the Magpies, soon won over the County faithful with his commitment and solid defending.

In March 1976 O'Brien won the first of five full caps for the Republic of Ireland, playing alongside fellow debutants Tony Grealish and Micky Walsh in a 3-0 defeat of Norway. He made all his appearances in friendlies. His final cap arrived after an absence of three years, when he came off the bench to replace Tony Grealish in a match against world champions Argentina in the summer of 1980.

His displays for Notts County (despite playing the majority of games at left-back) saw him score more than his fair share of goals. In 1979-80 he topped the club's scoring charts with 10 goals – the first full-back to achieve that distinction.

It was this kind of form that attracted the attention of Brian Clough's Nottingham Forest, but the move across the city never came. Having helped County into the top flight in 1980-81, he spent a couple more seasons at Meadow Lane before a brief loan spell with Derby County, after which he played non-League football for Boston United. Later taking over the managerial reins at the Lincolnshire club, he then held similar positions at both Corby Town and Arnold Town before ending his involvement with the game.

Micky Walsh

Position	Forward
Born	Michael Anthony Walsh, Chorley, 13 August 1954
Clubs	
Chorley; Blackpool; Everton; Queen's Park Rangers; FC Porto (Portugal); Sal Gueiros (Portugal); Espinho (Portugal); Rio Avenue (Portugal)	
International Caps	21
International Goals	3
Matches	

Year	Opponent	Result	Score	G
1976	Norway	won	3-0	1
1976	Poland	won	2-0	
1977	France	lost	0-2	
1977	Poland	drew	0-0	
1979	N Ireland	drew	0-0	
1979	Denmark	won	2-0	
1979	Bulgaria	lost	0-1	
1979	West Germany	lost	1-3	
1981	Belgium	lost	0-1	
1981	Czechoslovakia	won	3-1	
1982	Algeria	lost	0-2	
1983	Holland	lost	1-2	
1983	Spain	drew	3-3	
1983	Spain	lost	0-2	
1984	Iceland	won	3-0	1
1984	Malta	won	8-0	
1984	Poland	drew	0-0	
1984	China	won	1-0	
1985	USSR	won	1-0	1
1985	Norway	lost	0-1	
1985	Denmark	lost	0-3	

Micky Walsh joined Blackpool from non-League Chorley in the summer of 1972 and made his League debut in September 1973 in a draw at Fulham. He was meant to complement Welsh international Wyn Davies up front, but circumstances meant that he moved to outside-left where he was unhappy and struggled to keep his place.

During 1974-75 he became a virtual ever-present, switching from centre-forward to outside-right and he was Blackpool's top-scorer with 12 League goals in an overall tally of only 38. During the course of that season, Walsh scored one of the greatest goals ever seen at Bloomfield Road. It came three

Above: Micky Walsh

with Bob Latchford, but following an injury, couldn't force his way back into the side and joined Queen's Park Rangers. The Loftus Road club were involved in a relegation battle and though Walsh scored three goals in 10 games, it was not enough to save his new club from the drop.

Midway through the 1980-81 season, he quit English football to join Portuguese giants FC Porto. It proved a huge success for him and it was as a Porto player that he enjoyed his best form for the Republic of Ireland. The 1986 World Cup qualifiers saw him make his last contributions in a green shirt. Following spells with Sal Gueiros, Espinho and Rio Avenue, he entered non-League football becoming joint-manager of Diadora club Chertsey Town.

minutes from time in a thrilling game with Sunderland in February 1975, a run from the halfway line that ended with a terrific shot that earned him BBC TV's 'Goal of the Season' award. A strong player with good skill, he netted 17 goals in 1975-76 in an unsuccessful promotion bid, but his best spell came in the next campaign when he teamed up with veteran striker Bob Hatton. Walsh's tally of 26 was the club's highest since Ray Charnley's 30 in 1961-62.

Walsh had made his international debut for the Republic of Ireland against Norway in March 1976, scoring the final goal in a 3-0 win.

Blackpool tried to keep their star forward but after the disastrous 1977-78 season, Walsh, who had scored 76 goals in 194 games, was sold to Everton in a £325,000 deal. Initially he formed a much-feared strike partnership

David O'Leary

Position	Central defender
Born	David Anthony O'Leary, Stoke Newington, 2 May 1958

Clubs

Arsenal; Leeds United

International Caps	68
International Goals	1

Matches

Year	Opponent	Result	Score	G
1977	England	drew	1-1	
1977	France	lost	0-2	
1977	Spain	lost	0-1	
1977	France	won	1-0	
1977	Bulgaria	lost	1-2	
1978	Bulgaria	drew	0-0	
1978	Norway	drew	0-0	
1978	Denmark	drew	3-3	
1979	England	drew	1-1	
1979	Bulgaria	lost	0-1	
1979	West Germany	lost	1-3	
1980	Wales	lost	1-2	
1980	Bulgaria	won	3-0	
1980	N Ireland	lost	0-1	
1980	England	lost	0-2	
1980	Cyprus	won	3-2	
1981	Holland	won	2-1	
1981	Czechoslovakia	won	3-1	
1981	West Germany B	lost	0-3	

Matches Continued

Year	Opponent	Result	Score	G
1981	Poland	lost	0-3	
1982	Holland	drew	2-2	
1982	France	won	3-2	
1983	Holland	lost	1-2	
1983	Iceland	won	2-0	
1983	Spain	lost	0-2	
1984	Israel	lost	0-3	
1984	Poland	drew	0-0	
1984	China	won	1-0	
1985	USSR	won	1-0	
1985	Norway	lost	0-1	
1985	Denmark	lost	0-3	
1985	Israel	drew	0-0	
1985	England	lost	1-2	
1985	Norway	drew	0-0	
1985	Spain	drew	0-0	
1985	Switzerland	won	3-0	
1986	Switzerland	drew	0-0	
1986	USSR	lost	0-2	
1986	Denmark	lost	1-4	
1986	Wales	lost	0-1	
1989	Spain	lost	0-2	
1989	Malta	won	2-0	
1989	Hungary	won	2-0	
1990	West Germany	drew	1-1	
1990	N Ireland	won	3-0	
1990	Malta	won	2-0	
1990	Wales	won	1-0	
1990	USSR	won	1-0	
1990	Finland	drew	1-1	
1990	Turkey	drew	0-0	
1990	Malta	won	3-0	
1990	Romania	drew	0-0 5-4 pen	
1991	Morocco	won	1-0	
1991	Turkey	won	5-0	1
1991	England	drew	1-1	
1991	England	drew	1-1	
1991	Poland	drew	0-0	
1991	Chile	drew	1-1	
1992	Hungary	won	2-1	
1992	Poland	drew	3-3	
1992	Turkey	won	3-1	
1992	Wales	lost	0-1	
1992	Switzerland	won	2-1	
1992	United States	won	4-1	
1992	Albania	won	2-0	
1992	Italy	lost	0-2	
1992	Portugal	won	2-0	
1993	Wales	won	2-1	

Though he was born in Stoke Newington, London, David O'Leary returned to Dublin with his family as a youngster and began his career as a junior with Shelbourne. By the time he was 15, the captain of the Republic of Ireland's schoolboy team was on his way

David O'Leary (R) and Martin O'Neill (L)

back to London to start an apprenticeship with Arsenal.

He wasted little time in settling in at Highbury: Gunners manager Bertie Mee gave him his League debut as a 17-year-old against Burnley in August 1975. O'Leary was to hold down a regular place in the heart of the Arsenal defence for 17 seasons!

O'Leary was only 18 when he was capped at full international level by the Republic of Ireland in a friendly against England at Wembley, playing a key role in a 1-1 draw.

He helped Arsenal to the FA Cup Final of 1978 against Ipswich Town before winning an FA Cup winners' medal against Manchester United the following season. He appeared again at Wembley in the 1980 Final against West Ham United. It was around this time that David O'Leary was considered not only the best centre-back in England, but also in Europe. Throughout his career it was his ability to read the game so well that made his job look so easy. He was unruffled, calm and used the ball as well as any in his position. Allied to these attributes was his speed of thought as well as a great positional sense – it was not often that he was dragged out of position.

Following the appointment of Jack Charlton, O'Leary found himself dropped from the squad for a summer tour of Iceland in 1986. The relationship between the Arsenal defender and manager deteriorated still further when just before the tour, the squad became decimated by withdrawals. Charlton went back to O'Leary to ask if he would join up as a late replacement but he declined. It was the beginning of a two-and-a-half year absence from the national side, when the central defender was at his peak. He missed Euro '88 but returned to the international scene for the qualifiers for Italia '90. It was here in the penalty shoot-out against Romania that O'Leary – on as a substitute for his first appearance at a World Cup Finals – was asked

to take a spot-kick. The scores stood at 4-4 and he needed to beat the Romanian keeper to earn his team a place in the quarter-finals – he coolly sent Lung the wrong way before dispatching the ball into the top right-hand corner of the net. He remained in the Republic of Ireland squad until 1993, contributing to his fifth World Cup qualifying programme!

For Arsenal, O'Leary went on to make a record 558 League appearances, breaking the previous record held by George Armstrong. Towards the end of his days at Highbury, he became a utility player. Injuries and suspensions meant that he could bring the curtain down on his Arsenal career with two Wembley appearances, as the Gunners beat Sheffield Wednesday in the League Cup and FA Cup Finals of 1993.

He then joined Leeds United and after hanging up his boots, remained at Elland Road, first as assistant-manager to George Graham and later as the man in charge. O'Leary was manager of Aston Villa until his replacement Martin O'Neill took over in August 2006.

Frank Stapleton

Position	Forward
Born	Francis Anthony Stapleton, Dublin, 10 July 1956

Clubs

Arsenal; Manchester United; Ajax (Holland); Derby County; Le Havre (France); Blackburn Rovers; Aldershot; Huddersfield Town; Bradford City; Brighton and Hove Albion

International Caps	71
International Goals	20

Matches

Year	Opponent	Result	Score	G
1977	Turkey	drew	3-3	1
1977	France	lost	0-2	
1977	Spain	lost	0-1	
1977	Bulgaria	lost	1-2	
1978	Bulgaria	drew	0-0	
1978	Norway	drew	0-0	
1978	Denmark	drew	3-3	1
1979	N Ireland	drew	0-0	

Matches Continued				
Year	Opponent	Result	Score	G
1979	England	drew	1-1	
1979	Denmark	won	2-0	
1979	West Germany	lost	1-3	
1980	Wales	lost	1-2	
1980	Bulgaria	won	3-0	1
1980	N Ireland	lost	0-1	
1980	England	lost	0-2	
1980	Cyprus	won	3-2	
1981	Holland	won	2-1	
1981	Belgium	drew	1-1	
1981	France	lost	0-2	
1981	Cyprus	won	6-0	1
1981	Belgium	lost	0-1	
1981	Czechoslovakia	won	3-1	1
1981	West Germany B	lost	0-3	
1981	Poland	lost	0-3	
1982	Holland	drew	2-2	1
1982	France	won	3-2	1
1982	Algeria	lost	0-2	
1983	Holland	lost	1-2	
1983	Iceland	won	2-0	1
1983	Spain	drew	3-3	2
1983	Malta	won	1-0	1
1983	Spain	lost	0-2	
1984	Iceland	won	3-0	
1984	Holland	lost	2-3	
1984	Malta	won	8-0	1
1984	Israel	lost	0-3	
1984	Poland	drew	0-0	
1984	China	won	1-0	
1985	Norway	lost	0-1	
1985	Denmark	lost	0-3	
1985	Italy	lost	1-2	
1985	Israel	drew	0-0	
1985	England	lost	1-2	
1985	Norway	drew	0-0	
1985	Switzerland	won	3-0	1
1986	Switzerland	drew	0-0	
1986	USSR	lost	0-2	
1986	Denmark	lost	1-4	1
1986	Uruguay	drew	1-1	
1986	Iceland	won	2-1	
1986	Czechoslovakia	won	1-0	1
1987	Belgium	drew	2-2	1
1987	Scotland	drew	0-0	
1987	Poland	lost	0-1	
1987	Scotland	won	1-0	
1987	Bulgaria	lost	1-2	1
1987	Belgium	drew	0-0	
1987	Luxembourg	won	2-0	
1988	Luxembourg	won	2-1	1
1988	Bulgaria	won	2-0	
1988	Romania	won	2-0	
1988	Yugoslavia	won	2-0	
1988	Norway	drew	0-0	
1988	England	won	1-0	
1988	USSR	drew	1-1	
1988	Holland	lost	0-1	
1989	France	drew	0-0	
1989	Spain	won	1-0	

Matches Continued				
Year	Opponent	Result	Score	G
1989	Malta	won	2-0	
1990	West Germany	drew	1-1	1
1990	Malta	won	3-0	1

Frank Stapleton, who finished his international career as the Republic of Ireland's leading goalscorer, had shown great promise at Gaelic football as a youngster. But after impressing with Dublin-based junior side Bolton Athletic, he began a career as an apprentice with Arsenal in 1972.

Stapleton made his League debut against Stoke City in March 1975, and established himself in the Gunners' side the following season. In 1976-77 he became an automatic choice and formed a great goalscoring partnership with Malcolm Macdonald. He won the first of his 71 caps for the Republic of Ireland in the friendly against Turkey.

After just three minutes, he claimed his first goal and did enough to earn a regular place in the squad for the remainder of Johnny Giles' reign as manager.

Stapleton helped Arsenal to three consecutive FA Cup Finals – 1978-80 – scoring one of the goals in the 1979 FA Cup Final against Manchester United. By this time he had found a new goalscoring partner in Alan Sunderland, and many of the goals he scored were set up by his Republic of Ireland team-mate Liam Brady. Like Brady, Stapleton wanted to leave Highbury after the expiry of his contract, and in August 1981 he joined Manchester United for a tribunal-set fee of £900,000.

He continued at Old Trafford where he'd left off at Highbury and was United's leading scorer in his first three seasons with the club. He was in the United side that lost the 1983 League Cup Final 2-1 to Liverpool and faced

Above: Frank Stapleton

Brighton and Hove Albion in that year's FA Cup Final and replay, which the Reds won 4-0. The first game against Brighton ended in a 2-2 draw. When Stapleton scored

United's first goal, he wrote himself into the history books by becoming the first player to score in the final for two different FA Cup-winning teams.

This was also the year that Eoin Hand chose Stapleton to captain the national side for a European Championship match against Malta. He responded by scoring from the penalty-spot in an 8-0 win.

In the summer of 1987 he was given a free transfer by United as a reward for his long and loyal service. He joined Ajax but spent an unhappy eight months in Amsterdam, requiring a back operation for the removal of a disc. On recovery he continued to prove a potent threat in front of goal for the national side as the Republic qualified for their first major tournament – the 1988 European Championships.

Back on the domestic front he had a loan spell with Derby County before joining French club Le Havre. He failed to settle in France and returned to the north-west of England, spending two seasons with Blackburn Rovers. He later played for Aldershot and had a brief spell with Huddersfield Town before being appointed player-manager of Bradford City. Sacked after failing to steer the Bantams to the Second Division play-offs, Stapleton then had a spell with Brighton before working for a number of clubs in various coaching roles including one as manager of New England Revolution in the new American Soccer League.

Stapleton had ended his international career by netting the only goal of the friendly against West Germany. He followed this in June 1990 with one more against Malta, to make him his country's leading goalscorer.

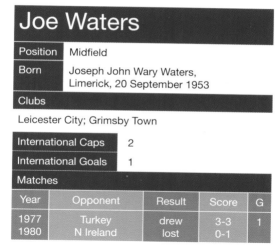

Joe Waters

Position	Midfield
Born	Joseph John Wary Waters, Limerick, 20 September 1953

Clubs

Leicester City; Grimsby Town

International Caps	2
International Goals	1

Matches

Year	Opponent	Result	Score	G
1977	Turkey	drew	3-3	1
1980	N Ireland	lost	0-1	

A skilful and busy midfielder, Joe Waters began his career with Leicester City. Though he struggled to hold down a regular first team place, he will be remembered for his explosive entry into the Foxes side. A last-minute replacement for Alan Birchenall in City's FA Cup quarter-final tie at Queen's Park Rangers, he scored two cracking goals past Phil Parkes before a national television audience.

An astute and energetic prompter on his sporadic returns to the Leicester side after Birchenall's recovery, he earned himself a near immediate call-up to the full Republic of Ireland squad for a South American tour.

In January 1976 Waters left Filbert Street and joined Grimsby Town, initially on loan. The club were preparing to allow him to return to Leicester at the end of his month's loan, but such was the outcry of Mariners fans, his services were secured in a permanent deal costing Grimsby £8,500.

In October 1976 Waters won the first of his two caps for the Republic of Ireland, when he played at right-back against Turkey in Ankara. He marked his debut with the equalising goal in a 3-3 draw!

The Mariners were relegated to the Fourth Division at the end of the 1976-7 season, after which Waters was made captain. An inspirational leader he led the club to promotion in 1978-79. The following season he went one better as the Blundell Park club won the Third Division Championship. He went on to make a record 266 consecutive League appearances between November 1976 and October 1982, going on to score 65 goals in 357 League games for the Mariners.

Waters won his second cap as a replacement for the injured Gerry Daly in the 1-0 defeat to Northern Ireland in November 1979. He left Blundell Park in 1984, moving into a player/coaching role in America. He was still there a decade later, assisting the late Keith Weller with Tacoma Stars in the Major Soccer League.

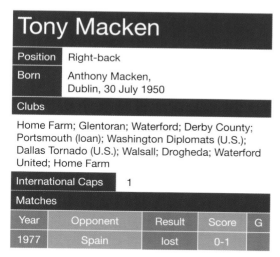

Tony Macken

Position	Right-back
Born	Anthony Macken, Dublin, 30 July 1950

Clubs

Home Farm; Glentoran; Waterford; Derby County; Portsmouth (loan); Washington Diplomats (U.S.); Dallas Tornado (U.S.); Walsall; Drogheda; Waterford United; Home Farm

International Caps	1

Matches

Year	Opponent	Result	Score	G
1977	Spain	lost	0-1	

The Dublin-born utility player began his career with Home Farm before joining Irish League club Glentoran. He helped them win the League Championship in 1971-72, but left the Belfast club to play for Waterford in the League of Ireland ending the season with another Championship medal!

In August 1974 Macken was transferred to Derby County for £30,000. In his time at the Baseball Ground he was used as cover in the Rams' midfield.

While he was with Derby he won his one and only senior cap, in the friendly against Spain in February 1977.

Unable to force his way into the Derby side on a regular basis, he was loaned out to Portsmouth before spending time in the United States with both Washington Diplomats and Dallas Tornado. Macken's former boss at Derby, Dave Mackay, took over as manager of Third Division Walsall in the summer of 1977. In October of that year, he paid the Rams £10,000 to take Macken to Fellow's Park.

In five seasons with the Saddlers, he made 190 League appearances, predominantly at right-back. Despite some impressive displays for Walsall he was unable to earn a recall to international colours. In 1982 Macken returned to Ireland and had spells in the League of Ireland with Drogheda, Waterford United and Home Farm.

Gerry Peyton

Position	Goalkeeper
Born	Gerald Joseph Peyton, Birmingham, 20 May 1956

Clubs
Atherstone Town; Burnley; Fulham; Southend United (loan); Bournemouth; Everton; Bolton Wanderers (loan); Brentford (loan); Chelsea (loan); Brentford; West Ham United

International Caps	33

Matches				
Year	Opponent	Result	Score	G
1977	Spain	lost	0-1	
1978	Bulgaria	drew	0-0	
1978	Turkey	won	4-2	
1978	Poland	lost	0-3	
1979	Denmark	won	2-0	

Matches Continued				
Year	Opponent	Result	Score	G
1979	Bulgaria	lost	0-1	
1979	West Germany	lost	1-3	
1980	Wales	lost	1-2	
1980	Czechoslovakia	lost	1-4	
1980	Bulgaria	won	3-0	
1980	England	lost	0-2	
1980	Cyprus	won	3-2	
1980	Switzerland	won	2-0	
1980	Argentina	lost	0-1	
1981	Holland	won	2-1	
1981	Belgium	drew	1-1	
1981	France	lost	0-2	
1981	Cyprus	won	6-0	
1982	Trinidad & Tobago	lost	1-2	
1985	Mexico	drew	0-0	
1986	Wales	lost	0-1	
1986	Czechoslovakia	won	1-0	
1988	Luxembourg	won	2-1	
1988	Poland	won	3-1	
1989	N Ireland	drew	0-0	
1989	Tunisia	won	4-0	
1990	USSR	won	1-0	
1990	Malta	won	3-0	
1991	Chile	drew	1-1	
1992	United States	won	4-1	
1992	United States	lost	1-3	
1992	Italy	lost	0-2	
1992	Portugal	won	2-0	

Following unsuccessful trials with Coventry City and West Bromwich Albion and after failing to impress at Aston Villa as a junior, Gerry Peyton joined Southern Premier League Atherstone Town.

He was spotted by Burnley scouts and in the summer of 1975 was transferred to the Turf Moor club for £10,000. Following an uncertain start to the 1975-76 season by Alan Stevenson, Peyton was drafted in for his League debut in December 1975, keeping a clean sheet in a goalless draw against Liverpool. Although that season ended in relegation, Peyton had done enough to keep his place until midway through the following season, when he was surprisingly seen as surplus to requirements.

Transferred to Fulham for £35,000, he was an immediate success at Craven Cottage.

His performances were impressive enough to catch the eye of England manager Don Revie. He was called up to join the England Under-21 squad but rejected the opportunity, in the hope that a chance would come along to represent the Republic of Ireland, his parents' birthplace.

He was not disappointed for at the age of 21, he won the first of 33 caps against Spain in Dublin, coming on as a substitute for Walsall's Mick Kearns. For the remainder of the 1970s, the battle for the Republic of Ireland's No.1 jersey was a battle between Peyton and the more experienced Kearns. Peyton could eventually claim victory over Kearns in 1979 when, after outstanding displays against Denmark and Bulgaria, he enjoyed a run of six consecutive matches for the national side. Peyton remained the Republic's first-choice keeper throughout the remainder of Johnny Giles' reign as manager, and played in the first

Above: Gerry Peyton

four games of Eoin Hand's tenancy. He then lost out to Jim McDonagh and later Paddy Bonner. Peyton remained an important part of the squad, and was included in Jack Charlton's final selection for both the 1988 European Championships and the 1990 World Cup Finals.

After almost two years as Fulham's regular last line of defence, Peyton was given a free transfer and joined Bournemouth in the summer of 1986. He was consistency itself as the Cherries stormed to the Third Division Championship and promotion to Division Two for the first time ever. In 1991 at the age of 35 he moved to Everton as cover for Neville Southall but was never able to oust the Welsh international. Following loan spells with Bolton, Norwich, Chelsea and Brentford, he joined West Ham United before taking up a coaching contract in Japan.

of clubs. Following loan spells with non-League Altrincham, Coventry City and Preston North End, he joined Cardiff City, also initially on loan prior to the move being made permanent two months later.

Following Bill Irwin's retirement in 1977 Healey became the Bluebirds' first-choice keeper, having played his part in their promotion back to Division Two in 1975-76.

While at Cardiff, Healey won two caps for the Republic of Ireland. Although he kept a clean sheet on his debut against Poland in April 1977, it was another three years before manager Johnny Giles called upon him again. In February 1980 he replaced the injured Gerry Peyton in the European Championship qualifier against England, for his final 30 minutes of international football.

Two years later, having made 216 League appearances for the Ninian Park club, he was forced into premature retirement following a series of injuries. On ending his involvement with the game, he returned back to Manchester and worked at the local airport.

Matches Continued

Year	Opponent	Result	Score	G
1979	N Ireland	drew	0-0	
1979	England	drew	1-1	
1980	England	lost	0-2	
1980	Cyprus	won	3-2	1
1980	Switzerland	won	2-0	
1981	Holland	won	2-1	1
1981	Belgium	drew	1-1	
1981	France	lost	0-2	
1981	Cyprus	won	6-0	
1981	Poland	lost	0-3	
1982	Holland	drew	2-2	
1982	France	won	3-2	
1983	Holland	lost	1-2	
1983	Iceland	won	2-0	
1983	Spain	drew	3-3	
1983	Malta	won	1-0	
1983	Spain	lost	0-2	
1984	Iceland	won	3-0	
1984	Holland	lost	2-3	
1984	Malta	won	8-0	2
1984	Israel	lost	0-3	
1985	USSR	won	1-0	
1985	Norway	lost	0-1	
1985	Denmark	lost	0-3	
1985	Italy	lost	1-2	
1985	England	lost	1-2	
1985	Norway	drew	0-0	
1986	Switzerland	drew	0-0	
1986	USSR	lost	0-2	
1987	Denmark	lost	1-4	
1987	Belgium	drew	2-2	
1987	Scotland	won	1-0	1
1988	Bulgaria	won	2-0	
1988	Israel	won	5-0	

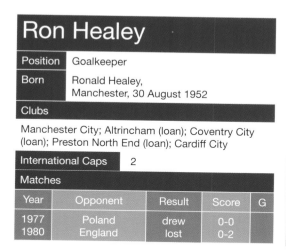

Ron Healey

Position	Goalkeeper
Born	Ronald Healey, Manchester, 30 August 1952
Clubs	

Manchester City; Altrincham (loan); Coventry City (loan); Preston North End (loan); Cardiff City

International Caps	2

Matches

Year	Opponent	Result	Score	G
1977	Poland	drew	0-0	
1980	England	lost	0-2	

Manchester-born goalkeeper Ron Healey began his career with Manchester City where he was understudy to the England international Joe Corrigan. With his opportunities at Maine Road limited – he made 30 First Division appearances in four years with the club – he took the opportunity to go out on loan with a couple

Mark Lawrenson

Position	Defender
Born	Mark Thomas Lawrenson, Preston, 2 June 1957
Clubs	

Preston North End; Brighton and Hove Albion; Liverpool; Tampa Bay Rowdies (U.S.)

International Caps	38
International Goals	5

Matches

Year	Opponent	Result	Score	G
1977	Poland	drew	0-0	
1978	Bulgaria	drew	0-0	
1978	Poland	lost	0-3	
1978	Norway	drew	0-0	

Mark Lawrenson was without doubt one of the most stylish and polished defenders of the modern game, winning almost every honour with Liverpool in the 1980s.

Born just a stone's throw away from Preston North End's Deepdale ground, he followed in his father Tommy's footsteps by joining the Lilywhites, having rejected the opportunity to pursue a cricketing career with Lancashire. At Deepdale, a chance conversation with former Preston favourite Alan Kelly (who was then coach to both North End and the Republic of Ireland) led to Lawrenson, whose mother was born in Waterford, playing for the Irish.

He won the first of 38 caps against Poland in April 1977, but three months later he was on his way to Brighton and Hove Albion for £100,000. He didn't want to leave Deepdale but North End needed the money and so cashed in their most valuable asset. At the time the deal went through, he was on holiday and agreed the transfer in a café on the sea front in Benidorm!

He spent four years on the south coast, helping the Seagulls win promotion to the First Division in 1978-79. In August 1981 Liverpool paid a record-breaking £900,000 for his services.

It was around this time that Lawrenson started to play in midfield for the Republic of Ireland. In Eoin Hand's first game in charge, a World Cup qualifier against Holland in Dublin, he grabbed the winning goal in a 2-1 victory.

With Phil Neal, Alan Hansen and Steve Nicol alongside him, Lawrenson reached the pinnacle of his career with the Reds. He remained a regular in the side in various positions throughout the decade. In doing so, he picked up League Championship and League Cup winners' medals in 1981-82, 1982-83 and 1983-84. He won a European Cup winners' medal in 1984 and in 1985-86 was a double winner when Liverpool won both the League and FA Cup. Another League Championship medal was added to the collection in his last season at Anfield in 1987-88.

At international level Lawrenson scored five goals, including a couple in the record 8-0 home victory over Malta in November 1983. His most memorable contribution was the goal that beat Scotland at Hampden Park in February 1987 and sent the Republic on their way to the 1988 European Championships in Germany. He also captained the national side on his final international appearance, leading them to a 5-0 victory over Israel.

Above: Mark Lawrenson

In April 1988 he took up the offer of a managerial post with Oxford United. After some success he was sacked after a disagreement with the club's directors over the sale of Dean Saunders to Derby County. After a spell as player-coach at Tampa Bay Rowdies, Lawrenson became manager of Peterborough United but is now a prominent television and radio personality.

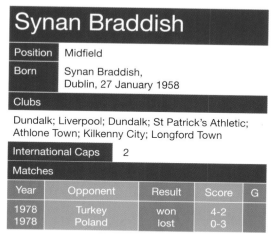

Synan Braddish

Position	Midfield
Born	Synan Braddish, Dublin, 27 January 1958
Clubs	

Dundalk; Liverpool; Dundalk; St Patrick's Athletic; Athlone Town; Kilkenny City; Longford Town

International Caps	2

Matches

Year	Opponent	Result	Score	G
1978	Turkey	won	4-2	
1978	Poland	lost	0-3	

Elegant midfielder Synan Braddish was a product of Dublin junior club Rave Athletic, which in the 1970s was a nursery for League of Ireland club Dundalk. Playing his first game for the Oriel Park club in 1976-77, he ended his first season with an FAI Cup winners' medal.

His performances in the Dundalk midfield led to representative honours in March 1978, when he played for the Republic of Ireland Under-21 side against Northern Ireland. That evening he was outstanding, and the following month he won full international recognition when he played for the Republic in two friendlies against Turkey and Poland.

Also that April he joined Liverpool, just as he was about to sign for Los Angeles Skyhawks. Unfortunately he couldn't force his way into the Liverpool side and the following year he rejoined Dundalk. He played a key role in the club winning the League Cup in 1981-82 – the final being decided by a penalty

shoot-out after two legs and extra-time had failed to provide a goal!

Shortly after this, he left Dundalk to join St Patrick's Athletic where he played for five seasons. He then moved around, playing for Athlone Town, Kilkenny City and Longford Town before ending his involvement with the game.

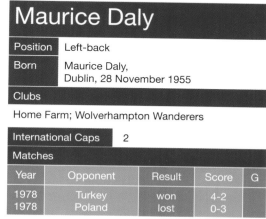

Maurice Daly

Position	Left-back
Born	Maurice Daly, Dublin, 28 November 1955
Clubs	

Home Farm; Wolverhampton Wanderers

International Caps	2

Matches

Year	Opponent	Result	Score	G
1978	Turkey	won	4-2	
1978	Poland	lost	0-3	

Maurice Daly was just 17 years old when he left Home Farm to play in the Football League for Wolverhampton Wanderers. However, his progress at Molineux was slow and the tough-tackling left-back didn't make his debut for the Midlands club until November 1975.

He made a handful of appearances that season but didn't play at all in 1976-77, when the club won promotion to the First Division. He was a regular in the top flight, his displays leading to him winning Under-21 honours for the Republic of Ireland in March 1978 against Northern Ireland.

The following month, Daly played in the friendlies at full international level against Turkey and Poland, as manager Johnny Giles tried to unearth some new talent for the forthcoming European Championship qualifiers. Though he continued to represent

the national side at Under-21 level, playing in the Toulon tournament in May 1978, his contract was cancelled by Wolves during the close season!

Ashley Grimes

Position	Left-back/ Midfield
Born	Augustine Ashley Grimes, Dublin, 2 August 1957
Clubs	

Stella Maris; Bohemians; Manchester United; Coventry City; Luton Town; Osasuna (Spain); Stoke City

International Caps	18
International Goals	1

Matches

Year	Opponent	Result	Score	G
1978	Turkey	won	4-2	
1978	Poland	lost	0-3	
1978	Norway	drew	0-0	
1980	Bulgaria	won	3-0	
1980	United States	won	3-2	
1980	N Ireland	lost	0-1	
1980	England	lost	0-2	
1980	Cyprus	won	3-2	
1981	Czechoslovakia	won	3-1	
1981	West Germany B	lost	0-3	
1981	Poland	lost	0-3	
1982	Algeria	lost	0-2	
1983	Spain	drew	3-3	1
1983	Spain	lost	0-2	
1984	Israel	lost	0-3	
1984	Poland	drew	0-0	
1988	Luxembourg	won	2-1	
1988	Romania	won	2-0	

One of the best left-footed footballers in the Football League, Ashley Grimes served his apprenticeship in his native Dublin with Stella Maris and later Bohemians. In March 1977 a £20,000 fee took him to Manchester United.

The versatile Grimes had unsuccessful trials with the Reds as a schoolboy, but he arrived at Old Trafford having won an FAI Cup winners' medal with the Bohs in 1976.

Within a year of signing for United, Grimes won the first of his 18 caps for the Republic of Ireland as one of six debutants in Johnny Giles' side for the friendly against Turkey. He proved one of the more successful newcomers and enjoyed his best run in the side under Giles – playing in the manager's last five games in charge.

With United, Grimes continued to show his versatility, playing in midfield, on both flanks and in defence. However, midway through the 1982-83 season, Grimes was sent-off at West Ham United for allegedly manhandling the referee – he was charged with bringing the game into disrepute and fined £750. Injury and illness then kept him out of the United side. He had made 107 appearances by the time of his £275,000 transfer to Coventry City in the summer of 1983.

He spent just a year at Highfield Road before moving to Luton Town in a player-exchange deal with the Hatters' full-back Kirk Stephens. He spent five seasons at Kenilworth Road, helping the club win through to both the 1988 and 1989 League Cup Finals. In the 1988 Final against Arsenal, Grimes came off the bench to supply the cross for Brian Stein to score the winner in the 3-2 defeat of the Gunners. A year later, the Hatters went down 3-1 to Nottingham Forest.

By then Grimes' international days were at an end – he had scored in a pulsating European Championship game against Spain in November 1982 when the boys in green pulled back from 3-1 down to level the score. Though there were hopes of an Indian summer following the appointment of Jack Charlton, he made just two further appearances.

In August 1989, Grimes left Luton to play for Spanish club Osasuna before two years later returning to Football League action with Stoke City. He later became Lou Macari's assistant at the Victoria Ground. When the Scottish international left to take over at

Celtic, he took Grimes with him as youth team coach.

Dave Langan

Position	Right-back
Born	David Francis Langan, Dublin, 15 February 1957

Clubs

Derby County; Birmingham City; Oxford United; Leicester City (loan); Bournemouth; Peterborough United

International Caps	26

Matches

Year	Opponent	Result	Score	G
1978	Turkey	won	4-2	
1978	Norway	drew	0-0	
1980	Switzerland	won	2-0	
1980	Argentina	lost	0-1	
1981	Holland	won	2-1	
1981	Belgium	drew	1-1	
1981	France	lost	0-2	
1981	Cyprus	won	6-0	
1981	Wales	lost	1-3	
1981	Belgium	lost	0-1	
1981	Czechoslovakia	won	3-1	
1981	West Germany B	lost	0-3	
1981	Poland	lost	0-3	
1982	Holland	drew	2-2	
1982	France	won	3-2	
1985	Norway	drew	0-0	
1985	Spain	drew	0-0	
1985	Switzerland	won	3-0	
1986	Wales	lost	0-1	
1986	Uruguay	drew	1-1	
1986	Belgium	drew	2-2	
1986	Scotland	drew	0-0	
1987	Poland	lost	0-1	
1987	Brazil	won	1-0	
1987	Luxembourg	won	2-0	
1988	Luxembourg	won	2-1	

After trials with Birmingham City and Manchester United, Dave Langan began his professional career with Brian Clough's Derby County in 1975. After impressing in the club's reserve side, Langan was handed his first team debut (albeit at right-back) by new Rams' boss Colin Murphy. He was an immediate success and maintained his standards in a struggling County side.

Above: Dave Langan

Therefore it wasn't a surprise when he was called into Johnny Giles' Republic of Ireland side for the friendly against Turkey in April 1978. Despite impressing for Derby, Langan won just one more cap under Giles. It wasn't until Eoin Hand took over the reins that he claimed a regular place in the national side.

Langan had pace, tackled well and went forward eagerly, but he became unsettled at the Baseball Ground when, under Colin Addison, relegation from the First Division was increasingly likely. He refused to travel with the team for an FA Cup tie against Bristol City in 1980, then when he did turn up, was sent home and fined. In an attempt to ease Derby's financial problems, Langan was sold to Birmingham City for £350,000. Shortly afterwards a midfield clash during the first half of the Republic of Ireland's friendly with France, left the combative full-back with a knee injury. Suspecting it to be no more than a sprain, he played on for the rest of the game – it proved to be his last international appearance for four-and-a-half years!

His early displays for Birmingham were outstanding but this knee injury put him on crutches, and he missed the whole of the 1983-84 season. He was then given a free transfer: Jim Smith, who had originally taken him to St Andrew's, signed him for Oxford United. Langan not only proved his fitness at the Manor Ground but helped Oxford into the First Division and won back his international place. Langan's pin-point crossing created many goals for his team-mate John Aldridge for both club and country and he helped the U's win the League Cup in 1985-86.

After three appearances for the Republic of Ireland during qualification for the 1988 European Championships, Langan was disappointingly left out of the final squad that travelled to Germany.

On leaving Oxford he had spells with Leicester City, Bournemouth and Peterborough United, before bowing out of League football. Since then, his catalogue of injuries has caused much physical hardship.

Paul McGee

Position	Forward
Born	Paul Gerard McGee, Sligo, 19 June 1954

Clubs

Sligo Rovers; Hereford United; Finn Harps; Sligo Rovers; Queen's Park Rangers; Preston North End; Burnley; Dundalk; Shamrock Rovers; Waterford; Sligo Rovers; Galway; Haarlem (Holland); Derry City; Athlone Town

International Caps	15
International Goals	4

Matches

Year	Opponent	Result	Score	G
1978	Turkey	won	4-2	1
1978	Norway	drew	0-0	
1978	Denmark	drew	3-3	
1979	N Ireland	drew	0-0	
1979	England	drew	1-1	
1979	Denmark	won	2-0	
1979	Bulgaria	lost	0-1	
1980	Czechoslovakia	lost	1-4	1
1980	Bulgaria	won	3-0	
1980	United States	won	3-2	
1980	N Ireland	lost	0-1	
1980	Cyprus	won	3-2	2
1980	Switzerland	won	2-0	
1980	Argentina	lost	0-1	
1981	Belgium	drew	1-1	

Above: Paul McGee

A much-travelled and prolific scorer, Paul McGee moved from Sligo Rovers to Hereford United. After failing to make the grade at Edgar Street, he decided to try his luck in Canada. He later returned to Ireland to play for Finn Harps. After winning an FAI Cup winners' medal, he rejoined Sligo Rovers and in 1976-77 helped them win the League of Ireland Championship.

Football League scouts began to take an interest. Following the goal he scored for the League of Ireland XI against the national side, he joined Queen's Park Rangers in November 1977. He spent two seasons at Loftus Road in and out of the side: after Rangers lost their top-flight status, he found himself surplus to requirements.

Even so, he was with Rangers when he won the first of his 15 caps for the Republic of Ireland against Turkey, scoring the second of his side's goals in a 4-2 win.

In October 1979 he joined Preston North End for a fee of £70,000. During the course of the season he netted in five consecutive games, though four of these games were drawn.

It was while with the Lilywhites that McGee enjoyed his best form in the green shirt of the Republic. Making his World Cup debut against Cyprus in Nicosia – Johnny Giles' last game in charge – he scored twice in a 3-2 win.

After a brief spell on loan with Burnley, he joined the Clarets on a permanent basis – in 1981-82 he helped them win the Third

Division Championship. On losing his place at Turf Moor he returned to Ireland with Dundalk prior to brief spells at Shamrock Rovers, Waterford, Sligo Rovers and Galway. He then joined Dutch club Haarlem before returning to Ireland for periods at both Derry City and Athlone Town.

Gerry Ryan

Position	Winger
Born	Gerard Joseph Ryan, Dublin, 4 October 1955

Clubs

Bohemians; Derby County; Brighton and Hove Albion

International Caps	18
International Goals	1

Matches

Year	Opponent	Result	Score	G
1978	Turkey	won	4-2	
1979	England	drew	1-1	
1979	West Germany	lost	1-3	1
1980	Wales	lost	1-2	
1980	Cyprus	won	3-2	
1980	Switzerland	won	2-0	
1980	Argentina	lost	0-1	
1981	France	lost	0-2	
1981	West Germany B	lost	0-3	
1981	Poland	lost	0-3	
1982	Holland	drew	2-2	
1982	Algeria	lost	0-2	
1982	Chile	lost	0-1	
1982	Brazil	lost	0-7	
1982	Trinidad & Tobago	lost	1-2	
1984	Poland	drew	0-0	
1984	China	won	1-0	
1985	Mexico	drew	0-0	

A winger with flair and an ability to lift crowds, Gerry Ryan began his career with Bohemians in 1975 and helped them to win the FAI Cup the following year. In 1976-77 he appeared in a UEFA Cup fixture against Newcastle United. So impressive was his display that a number of the top Football League clubs chased his signature.

Above: Gerry Ryan

Derby County manager Tommy Docherty brought him to the Baseball Ground at the same time as Fran O'Brien, who failed his medical. It was during his one-year spell with the Rams that Ryan won the first of his 18 caps, when he played in the friendly against Turkey at Lansdowne Road in April 1978.

The following September Ryan moved on to Brighton and Hove Albion in an £80,000 deal. In his first season at the Goldstone Ground, he helped the Seagulls win promotion to the First Division, scoring nine goals in 34 appearances.

On the international front, Ryan claimed his one and only goal in May 1979 – a spectacular effort in a 3-1 defeat at the hands of West Germany. The match against the Germans was a rare appearance in the Republic of Ireland starting line-up, for Ryan won half of his international caps as a substitute.

He was on the bench for Brighton in their drawn 1983 FA Cup Final against Manchester United, coming on for Chris Ramsey. Not only did the Seagulls lose the replay 4-0 but they also had to contend with relegation to Division Two. A broken leg in a match against Crystal Palace in April 1985 brought a premature end to his playing career, though he did later return to Brighton as assistant to Liam Brady.

Noel Synnott

Position	Centre-half
Born	Noel Synnott, Dublin, 1952

Clubs

Ealing; Guildford City; Sligo Rovers; Shamrock Rovers; Waterford

International Caps	3

Matches

Year	Opponent	Result	Score	G
1978	Turkey	won	4-2	
1978	Poland	lost	0-3	
1979	N Ireland	drew	0-0	

A fiercely competitive centre-half, Dublin-born Noel Synnott played his early football in London, initially with Ealing (for whom future Spurs captain Steve Perryman also played) and later Southern League Guildford City.

In 1974 Synnott returned to Ireland to play for Sligo Rovers, before signing for Shamrock Rovers. He was to spend almost 10 years at Milltown and was captain of the Hoops under manager Johnny Giles, who was also in charge of the national side.

Regarded as one of the best central defenders in the League of Ireland, Synnott helped the Hoops beat Sligo Rovers in the League Cup Final of 1976-77. The following year he held the FAI Cup aloft as Shamrock beat the same opposition in the final.

With Johnny Giles deprived of the services of both Mark Lawrenson and David O'Leary, he turned to Synnott and gave him his full international debut in the friendly against Turkey which the Irish won 4-2. He kept his place in the side for the next match against Poland. The following September Synnott made his competitive debut in a goalless European Championship qualifier against Northern Ireland.

He continued to shine for Shamrock Rovers, but in March 1983 disaster struck in the match against Dundalk, when he suffered a badly broken leg and dislocated ankle. The pain and anguish had forced Synnott to the conclusion that he would never play again and he returned to his work as an Aer Lingus fitter.

Later he was asked to manage the company's Leinster Senior League side. After training with them and also Bohemians, he signed for Waterford. In 1986 against all the odds, he lined-up for Waterford in the FAI Cup Final against his old club Shamrock Rovers – the Hoops won 2-0 and Synnott scored an own-goal!

to spend 12 seasons with the club, his only domestic honour came in 1976 when he came off the bench in the FAI Cup Final against Bohemians, a match United lost 1-0.

He represented the League of Ireland XI on five occasions, once playing opposite Diego Maradona in Argentina during the early part of 1978.

In April of that year Clarke made his one and only international appearance for the Republic of Ireland when after 78 minutes he came off the bench to replace captain/player-manager Johnny Giles in a 3-0 defeat against Poland in Lodz.

In the summer of 1980 Clarke joined Drogheda's rivals Dundalk, in a player-exchange deal. He was to spend two very eventful seasons at Oriel Park – winning a League Championship medal in 1981-82. The previous season he had missed Dundalk's first penalty in the League Cup Final shoot-out, after two legs and extra-time had failed to produce a goal between Dundalk and Galway Rovers. Nevertheless, Clarke's Dundalk side went on to win the shoot-out 3-2.

Jerome Clarke

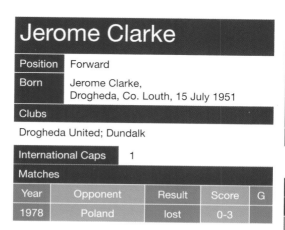

Position	Forward
Born	Jerome Clarke, Drogheda, Co. Louth, 15 July 1951
Clubs	

Drogheda United; Dundalk

International Caps	1

Matches

Year	Opponent	Result	Score	G
1978	Poland	lost	0-3	

Jerome Clarke was a hard-running forward who began his career with his home-town club Drogheda United. Though he was

Eamonn Gregg

Position	Right-back
Born	Eamonn Gregg, Dublin, 1953
Clubs	

Shamrock Rovers; Bohemians; Dundalk; St Patrick's Athletic; Shamrock Rovers; Kilkenny City

International Caps	8

Matches

Year	Opponent	Result	Score	G
1978	Poland	lost	0-3	
1979	Denmark	drew	3-3	
1979	England	drew	1-1	
1979	Denmark	won	2-0	
1979	Bulgaria	lost	0-1	

Matches Continued				
Year	Opponent	Result	Score	G
1979	West Germany	lost	1-3	
1980	Wales	lost	1-2	
1980	Czechoslovakia	lost	1-4	

A resourceful right-sided full-back, Eamonn Gregg joined Bohemians in the summer of 1973, after spending a season playing for Shamrock Rovers.

His time at Bohs coincided with one of the most successful eras in the club's history. They won the League Championship in 1974-75 and 1977-78, the FAI Cup in 1976 and the League Cup in 1975 and 1979.

By the time he won the first of his eight caps for the Republic of Ireland, Gregg was an Under-23 international and had played in three European campaigns with the Bohs. He was called into Johnny Giles' squad for the friendly against Poland in Lodz in April 1978. Despite a 3-0 reverse he had done enough to stay in the Republic's squad for the next 18 months. The right-back position at national level had become something of a problem following the retirement of Joe Kinnear: Gregg filled the void until replaced by Dave Langan. He had appeared in six consecutive games but lost his place after a 4-1 defeat by Czechoslovakia in Prague.

On the domestic scene, Gregg left the Bohs to play for Dundalk and in 1981-82 won another League Championship medal. Following spells with St Patrick's Athletic and again Shamrock Rovers, he became player-manager of Kilkenny City before later managing both Bohemians and Shelbourne.

Cathal Muckian

Position	Forward
Born	Cathal Muckian, Dundalk, Co. Louth, 1952
Clubs	

Drogheda United; Dundalk; Shamrock Rovers; Shelbourne

International Caps	1

Matches

Year	Opponent	Result	Score	G
1978	Poland	lost	0-3	

Austin Hayes

Position	Winger
Born	Austin William Patrick Hayes, Hammersmith, 15 July 1958
Died	December 1986
Clubs	

Southampton; Millwall; Northampton Town; Barnet

International Caps	1

Matches

Year	Opponent	Result	Score	G
1979	Denmark	won	2-0	

moved to play in Sweden but his life was tragically cut short by cancer in December 1986.

Brendan O'Callaghan

Position	Forward/Central defender
Born	Brendan Richard O'Callaghan, Bradford, 23 July 1955
Clubs	

Doncaster Rovers; Stoke City; Oldham Athletic

International Caps	6

Matches

Year	Opponent	Result	Score	G
1979	West Germany	lost	1-3	
1980	Wales	lost	1-2	
1980	United States	won	3-2	
1981	Wales	lost	1-3	
1982	Brazil	lost	0-7	
1982	Trinidad & Tobago	lost	1-2	

Pacy frontman Cathal Muckian began his career with Drogheda United, helping them to the 1976 FAI Cup Final. Without doubt, his best season in terms of goals scored was 1977-78, when he was the club's leading marksman with 21 goals in 30 games.

It was this form that led to manager Johnny Giles naming him in the full Republic of Ireland side to play a friendly against Poland in Lodz towards the end of that campaign. His chances were few and far between, though in the closing stages he almost netted a consolation goal for the Irish in a 3-0 defeat.

Muckian had been working at the Bank of Ireland in Drogheda. When he was promoted to assistant-manager at the Bank's regional office in Dundalk, it seemed logical that he should join the Oriel Park club.

In his first season with his new club, he helped them to the double of League of Ireland Championship and FAI Cup. He continued to display good form the following season but there was still no recall to the national side. In 1980 he was again transferred by the Bank, this time to Dublin. During the course of the 1980-81 season, he turned out for both Shamrock Rovers and Shelbourne before deciding to hang up his boots.

Austin Hayes was a diminutive, nippy forward who never quite broke into the Southampton side on a regular basis, spending many games as a substitute.

The Londoner was shocked to find himself selected for the Republic of Ireland through an ancestral qualification. He played his part in a 2-0 win, setting up the opening goal for Gerry Daly in a European Championship qualifier against Denmark at Lansdowne Road. He became an international footballer whilst in Saints' reserves!

Hayes made his Southampton debut in a European Cup Winners' Cup match, replacing Mick Channon and scoring twice against Carrick Rangers. He will best be remembered at the south-coast club for swinging on a crossbar and breaking it – thus causing the reserve team game to be abandoned!

In February 1981 he was transferred to Millwall for £25,000. In his two seasons at The Den, he proved a most popular player.

In the summer of 1983 he joined Northampton Town and was a regular in the side for two seasons, until becoming one of seven players freed by manager Graham Carr in 1985. After a brief spell with Barnet, he

A tall, powerful target-man, Brendan O'Callaghan was a Yorkshireman, qualified to play for the Republic of Ireland under the parentage rule.

He started his career with Doncaster Rovers and in almost five years at Belle Vue, the player with deceptive pace scored 65 goals in 187 League outings. His scoring feats with the Yorkshire club prompted Stoke City boss Alan Durban to take him to the Victoria Ground for a fee of £40,000 in March 1978.

O'Callaghan had a sensational debut for the Potters, scoring the only goal of the game against Hull City just 10 seconds after coming off the bench! The following season of 1978-79 saw him top the club's goalscoring charts with 17 goals, a total that helped City win promotion to the top flight.

This form led to him being selected as a substitute for the Republic of Ireland's friendly with West Germany in May 1979. O'Callaghan won six caps spread over three years. He was on the winning side only once, in October 1979 when the boys in green beat the United States 3-2.

Towards the end of his time with Stoke, O'Callaghan was moved into the centre of defence. Though he had scored 45 goals in 245 League games for the Potters, it was as a central defender that Oldham Athletic signed him in February 1985. Pitched straight into the Latic's relegation battle, his performances went a long way in helping the Lancashire club avoid the drop. Just ten minutes into the new season of 1985-86, a recurring groin injury forced his withdrawal, and the following January he announced his retirement from the game.

THE 1980s

The Republic of Ireland was drawn in the same group as England and Northern Ireland for the 1980 European Championships along with Bulgaria and Denmark. Unfortunately for the boys in green, England ran away with the group, dropping just one point – a 1-1 draw against the Republic in front of a vast Lansdowne Road crowd of 50,000. Northern Ireland took three points off the Republic to push them down into third place with just two wins from their eight games.

For the 1982 World Cup tournament to be held in Spain, the Irish were grouped with Cyprus, Belgium, Holland and France. Certainly a tough group and one in which they would have to finish in the top two to qualify. Never having played Cyprus before, Paul McGee's eighth minute goal in Nicosia was extremely welcome. Though the score could have been as much as 6-1 to the Republic, the home side never gave up and the Irish won 3-2 to record their first away victory in the World Cup since beating Denmark in 1957. A few weeks after this victory, Johnny Giles resigned as Republic of Ireland team-boss: after Alan Kelly had taken charge for a friendly against Switzerland, Eoin Hand took over the reins. Their next opponents in this World Cup group were Holland, who in the past had lost two World Cup Finals, both to the tournament hosts! Though the Dutch side was in a transitional state, they took the lead and held it until the 79th minute when Gerry Daly levelled the scores. Five minutes later, Brady chipped a free-kick for Mark Lawrenson to score the winner – the Brighton defender had scored in both qualifying matches! The

Republic then drew 1-1 at home to Belgium before losing 2-0 in France. This match is probably best-remembered for its pre-match controversy. Determined that the Republic be permitted to field its strongest side, the FAI compelled FIFA to intervene. English clubs refusing to release players because of League Cup ties found their games postponed – the FAI had won a famous victory.

Now midway through their World Cup qualifying group matches, the Republic hammered Cyprus 6-0, with Gerry Daly netting a hat-trick. A late goal by Ceulmans gave Belgium a 1-0 win over the Irish, before the Republic drew 2-2 against Holland in Rotterdam. Normally that would be hailed as a fantastic result, but it was just what France and Belgium were hoping for. For their final group game, the Republic entertained France in front of a 53,000 crowd at Lansdowne Road. The Irish got off to the best possible start when Mahut, under pressure from Stapleton, put through his own goals after five minutes. Three minutes later the French were level, but goals by Stapleton and Robinson gave the Republic a 3-1 lead at half-time. France had the better of the second-half and though Platini reduced the arrears, the Irish held on to win 3-2. Other results did not go the Republic's way: though they finished level on points with France, they lost out on goal difference.

After a badly-arranged tour of South America, where the Republic lost all three games, the national team embarked on the series of qualification games for Euro '84. Two defeats by Holland and three points dropped against Spain, left the Republic adrift of the pace from the start. Though they ended on a high note with an 8-0 demolition of Malta, Irish supporters were already beginning to turn against the manager. Despite support beginning to fall away, Eoin Hand remained in charge.

In the Republic's qualifying group for the 1986 World Cup in Mexico were Denmark, Norway, Switzerland and the Soviet Union. The Republic's first match was at Lansdowne Road against the much-fancied Soviet Union. Micky Walsh gave the home side the lead and though in the final minute Rodinov smashed a shot against the crossbar and Litovchenko ratted the post from the rebound, the Irish held on to record a famous victory. Unfortunately there followed a lacklustre performance against Norway in Oslo; the home side recorded their second victory in twelve attempts against the Irish. Worse was to come when the Republic were well and truly beaten 3-0 by Denmark, who if they had wanted to, could have won by a much bigger margin. The Republic then gave one of their worst-ever displays in a goalless home draw against Norway. They returned to winning ways with a 3-0 defeat of Switzerland. The return in Berne failed to produce any goals, before the Irish faced the daunting challenge of playing the Soviet Union in Moscow. Unbeaten at home in 19 World Cup matches, they hadn't conceded a goal in 13 of those games and duly beat the Republic 2-0. Denmark – already qualified for the finals – were the Republic's last opponents. Though Frank Stapleton gave the home side an early lead, the Danes came back to win 4-1.

Following the departure of Eoin Hand, Jack Charlton was named as the Republic of Ireland's new manager in February 1986. The former Leeds United and England centre-half could not realistically have expected to qualify for Euro '88, not after the Republic's first five games yielded just five points. But Gary Mackay's late winner for Scotland against Bulgaria took the Republic through. In their opening game against England, Ray Houghton's fifth-minute header, after blunders by Kenny Sansom and Gary Stevens left John Aldridge free to fire in a cross, knocked England back on their heels. Inept performances by England's forwards plus a string of spectacular saves from Packy Bonner sealed England's fate. The Republic then played out a goalless draw with the Soviet Union and only lost 1-0 to Holland, narrowly missing out on a place in the semi-finals. They came back national heroes.

Jerry Murphy

Position	Midfield
Born	Jeremiah Michael Murphy, Stepney, 23 September 1959

Clubs

Crystal Palace; Chelsea

International Caps	3

Matches

Year	Opponent	Result	Score	G
1980	Wales	lost	1-2	
1980	United States	won	3-2	
1980	Cyprus	won	3-2	

Jerry Murphy was a member of Crystal Palace's famous 'Team of the Eighties' youth side, which beat Everton 1-0 to win the FA Youth Cup for the first time in the club's history. They repeated the achievement the following season with another 1-0 victory, this time over Aston Villa.

A former England schoolboy international, Murphy broke into Palace's first team shortly after these successes, and in 1978-79 won a Second Division Championship medal.

He got his chance for the Republic of Ireland whilst still only 19 years old, playing on the left-side of midfield in the friendly against Wales. He did well enough to win two further caps – his third appearance against Cyprus being Johnny Giles' last game in charge. Despite continuing to impress for Palace – going on to score 20 goals in 229 League games – he couldn't win a recall to the national side.

In August 1985, Murphy became Chelsea manager John Hollins' first signing, when he arrived at Stamford Bridge on a free transfer. His early days with the club were punctuated by injuries and these prevented him from winning a regular first team place with the Blues. With injury problems continuing to frustrate his efforts to establish himself, he left the club in the summer of 1988 and dropped out of League football, perhaps wondering what he had done to deserve such misfortune!

John Anderson

Position	Defender
Born	John Christopher Patrick Anderson, Dublin, 7 November 1959

Clubs

West Bromwich Albion; Preston North End; Newcastle United

International Caps	16
International Goals	1

Matches

Year	Opponent	Result	Score	G
1980	Czechoslovakia	lost	1-4	
1980	United States	won	3-2	1
1982	Chile	lost	0-1	
1982	Brazil	lost	0-7	
1982	Trinidad & Tobago	lost	1-2	
1984	China	won	1-0	
1986	Wales	lost	0-1	
1986	Iceland	won	2-1	
1986	Czechoslovakia	won	1-0	
1987	Bulgaria	lost	1-2	
1987	Belgium	drew	0-0	
1987	Brazil	won	1-0	
1987	Luxembourg	won	2-0	
1988	Romania	won	2-0	
1988	Yugoslavia	won	2-0	
1989	Tunisia	won	4-0	

After beginning his career with West Bromwich Albion, right-back John Anderson was not considered good enough for the Baggies' first team, and in August 1979 he joined newly promoted Preston North End for a fee of £40,000.

After making his League debut in a 3-2 defeat of Fulham, Anderson struggled to hold down a regular place in the Preston side and indeed, it was 1981-82 before he fully established himself.

Above: John Anderson

He made his full international debut for the Republic of Ireland as a substitute in a friendly against Czechoslovakia. In the first few years of his international career, Anderson was restricted to a handful of friendlies and tour games. By the time he did line-up for his first competitive game, Jack Charlton was manager.

Anderson left Deepdale in the summer of 1982 to join Newcastle United. It was a costly error by North End manager Gordon Lee, as he went on to become a huge favourite at St James Park. At Newcastle, Anderson soon claimed the right-back berth, and in his second season there (1983-84) helped the Magpies win promotion to Division One after a six-year absence.

At international level, Anderson replaced the injured Langan in the European

Championship qualifiers of 1986 and 1987. He was rewarded with inclusion in the party which travelled to the finals in West Germany in 1988, although he didn't appear in any of the Republic's three matches.

Newcastle played Anderson in all four defensive positions and in midfield. He spent nine seasons in the north-east until an ankle injury forced his retirement in March 1992. Later that summer he was appointed manager of Berwick Rangers but resigned after eight weeks in the job. He later returned to the north-east to work in local radio and assist the Newcastle Kestrels women's football club.

Jeff Chandler

Position	Winger
Born	Jeffrey George Chandler, Hammersmith, 19 June 1959
Clubs	

Blackpool; Leeds United; Bolton Wanderers; Derby County; Mansfield Town (loan); Bolton Wanderers; Cardiff City

International Caps	2

Matches

Year	Opponent	Result	Score	G
1980	Czechoslovakia	lost	1-4	
1980	United States	won	3-2	

Winger Jeff Chandler enjoyed a long and relatively successful career in English football, scoring on his debut for Blackpool against Blackburn Rovers in September 1977. His first full season at Bloomfield Road ended in disappointment when the Seasiders were relegated to the Third Division.

In September 1979 Chandler left Blackpool to play for Leeds United, and within days of putting pen to paper, he had made his full international debut for the Republic of Ireland. He came off the bench to replace Damien Richardson in a 4–1 defeat by

Czechoslovakia in Prague. The following month he started the game against the United States, a match the Irish won 3-2 after being two goals down!

In October 1981 Jeff Chandler crossed the Pennines to join Bolton Wanderers for a fee of £40,000. He was a fixture in the Bolton side for the next four seasons – he bagged 37 goals in two seasons – top-scoring for the club in all competitions during 1984-85 with 20 goals.

In July 1985 Derby County paid a tribunal-set fee of £38,000 to take him to the Baseball Ground, where in his first season he helped them win promotion from Division Three. He failed to command a regular spot in the side at the higher level. After a loan spell with Mansfield Town he rejoined Bolton Wanderers. Disaster struck shortly after his return to Burnden Park when he damaged ligaments in a game against Wigan Athletic. He returned to action the following season and was instrumental in the Wanderers reaching the Sherpa Van Trophy Final at Wembley – his deflected shot giving Bolton the lead in the 4–1 defeat of Torquay United.

He later joined Cardiff City but injury curtailed his appearances and he was forced into premature retirement.

John Devine

Position	Midfield
Born	John Anthony Devine, Dublin, 11 November 1958
Clubs	

Arsenal; Norwich City; Stoke City; IK Start (Norway); Shamrock Rovers

International Caps	13

Matches

Year	Opponent	Result	Score	G
1980	Czechoslovakia	lost	1-4	
1980	N Ireland	lost	0-1	
1981	Czechoslovakia	won	3-1	
1981	West Germany B	lost	0-3	
1982	Holland	drew	2-2	

Matches Continued

Year	Opponent	Result	Score	G
1982	Algeria	lost	0-2	
1983	Spain	drew	3-3	
1983	Malta	won	1-0	
1984	iceland	won	3-0	
1984	Holland	lost	2-3	
1984	Israel	lost	0-3	
1985	USSR	won	1-0	
1985	Norway	lost	0-1	

Above: John Devine

Having begun his career with Arsenal, he spent most of his 10 years at Highbury in the club's reserve side, understudying both Pat Rice and Sammy Nelson.

Devine was playing for the Gunners' reserve side when in September 1979 he won his first cap for the Republic of Ireland in a friendly against Czechoslovakia. He made just one more appearance for the national side before

Eoin Hand took over the managerial reins in 1980.

Back at Highbury following the sale of Rice to Watford, John Devine made the right-back position his own. He ended the 1980-81 season with an FA Cup runners-up medal after Arsenal had been beaten 1-0 by West Ham United.

An injury to Dave Langan meant that he was given an extended run in the national side in his favoured position, and he played in four of the last six qualifiers for the 1984 European Championships.

His performances for Arsenal had become inconsistent and on losing his place to John Hollins, he was given a free transfer and joined Norwich City. He continued to be a regular in Hand's Republic of Ireland side during his time at Carrow Road, but after his form dipped he moved on to Stoke City.

An horrendous injury – his leg broke into five pieces in a game at Brighton – marked the end of his League career. After Stoke he played in Norway with IK Start and then went to India playing and coaching, before in the summer of 1989 returning to his native Dublin to end his career with Shamrock Rovers.

The son of former Republic of Ireland international Don Donovan, he won England schoolboy honours. When the call came, he chose to represent his father's homeland at senior international level.

He was spotted by his father's old club Grimsby Town playing for Louth United of the Midland Counties League, and joined the Mariners as an 18-year-old in August 1976. Despite a promising first season at Blundell Park, Grimsby were relegated to the Fourth Division: over the next couple of seasons, he proved himself the club's best player. In 1977-78 he was Grimsby's top scorer with 14 goals. This prompted Aston Villa to pay £75,000 for his services – at the time Town's record fee.

Shortly after joining Villa, he won his first full cap for the Republic of Ireland against Czechoslovakia but was substituted with seven minutes to play, as an under-strength Irish side went down 4-1 to the Czechs.

In December 1979 he found the net on his Villa debut, but generally found First Division football tough going as he tried to establish himself in the top flight. He played no part in Villa's League Championship-winning season of 1980-81, but won another cap against West Germany 'B'.

After a loan spell at Oxford United, Donovan joined Burnley, but was unable to prevent the Clarets from being relegated to the Third Division at the end of his first season at Turf Moor. He later played for Rotherham United and had a loan spell with Blackpool before a knee injury forced his retirement.

Fran O'Brien

Position	Full-back
Born	Francis O'Brien, Dublin, 1955

Clubs

Bohemians; Philadelphia Fury (U.S.)

International Caps	3

Matches

Year	Opponent	Result	Score	G
1980	Czechoslovakia	lost	1-4	
1980	England	lost	0-2	
1980	Cyprus	won	3-2	

The younger brother of fellow Republic of Ireland international Ray O'Brien, full-back Fran O'Brien started out with Bohemians. He shared in the club's successes of the mid-1970s and was a member of the side that won the Leinster Cup and the President's Cup in three successive seasons and in 1976, the FAI Cup.

He spent a number of summers playing football in America. In March 1978, just as the Gypsies were poised to win the League Championship, he left the Bohs with team-mates Eddie and Pat Byrne to play for Philadelphia Fury in the NASL on a permanent basis.

While in North America Fran O'Brien made history, becoming the first player permanently attached to an American club to be called up by the Republic of Ireland. O'Brien made his full international debut against Czechoslovakia in Prague in September 1979. Although generally regarded as a full-back, he played this game on the left-side of midfield – a position he had held for most of the previous summer in the States. Whilst still a Fury player, he won two further caps for the Republic of Ireland, playing against England and Cyprus in February and March 1980.

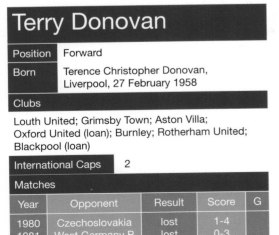

Terry Donovan

Position	Forward
Born	Terence Christopher Donovan, Liverpool, 27 February 1958

Clubs

Louth United; Grimsby Town; Aston Villa; Oxford United (loan); Burnley; Rotherham United; Blackpool (loan)

International Caps	2

Matches

Year	Opponent	Result	Score	G
1980	Czechoslovakia	lost	1-4	
1981	West Germany B	lost	0-3	

Pierce O'Leary

Position	Centre-half
Born	Pierce O'Leary, Dublin, 5 November 1959
Clubs	

Shamrock Rovers; Philadelphia Fury (U.S.); Vancouver Whitecaps (Canada); Glasgow Celtic

International Caps	7

Matches

Year	Opponent	Result	Score	G
1980	Czechoslovakia	lost	1-4	
1980	Bulgaria	won	3-0	
1980	United States	won	3-2	
1980	N Ireland	lost	0-1	
1980	England	lost	0-2	
1980	Argentina	lost	0-1	
1981	Holland	won	2-1	

The younger brother of David O'Leary, he began his career with Shamrock Rovers as a 17-year-old in 1977. The following year he won an FAI Cup winners' medal after the Hoops beat Sligo 1-0 in the final. A week later he left to play in the NASL with Philadelphia Fury.

O'Leary won the first of seven full caps for the Republic of Ireland against Czechoslovakia in September 1979. Over the next twelve months he made six other appearances – taking in both World Cup and European Championship qualifiers. Similar in style to his brother, the two of them played alongside each other twice.

Pierce O'Leary later spent four seasons playing for Vancouver Whitecaps, before joining Scottish giants Glasgow Celtic in November 1984. At the end of his first season at Parkhead, he won a Scottish FA Cup winners' medal, replacing the injured Paul McStay after 74 minutes in the 2-1 defeat of Dundee United. The following season he helped the Bhoys win the League Championship at the last gasp – Hearts had led the table since before the turn of the year

but their unbeaten run of 27 games came to an end at Dundee, whilst Celtic beat St Mirren to pip them for the title.

In August 1986 he skippered Celtic at Highbury in his big brother's testimonial match. He later ran a successful cleaning company in Rutherglen with Paddy Bonner.

Chris Hughton

Position	Full-back
Born	Christopher William Gerard Hughton, Stratford, 1 December 1958
Clubs	

Tottenham Hotspur; West Ham United; Brentford

International Caps	53
International Goals	1

Matches

Year	Opponent	Result	Score	G
1980	United States	won	3-2	
1980	England	lost	0-2	
1980	Switzerland	won	2-0	
1980	Argentina	lost	0-1	
1981	Holland	won	2-1	
1981	Belgium	drew	1-1	
1981	France	lost	0-2	
1981	Cyprus	won	6-0	1
1981	Wales	lost	1-3	
1981	Belgium	lost	0-1	
1981	Poland	lost	0-3	
1982	France	won	3-2	
1983	Holland	lost	1-2	
1983	Spain	drew	3-3	
1983	Malta	won	1-0	
1983	Spain	lost	0-2	
1984	Iceland	won	3-0	
1984	Holland	lost	2-3	
1984	Malta	won	8-0	
1985	Mexico	drew	0-0	
1985	USSR	won	1-0	
1985	Norway	lost	0-1	
1985	Italy	lost	1-2	
1985	Israel	drew	0-0	
1985	England	lost	1-2	
1985	Spain	drew	0-0	
1986	Switzerland	drew	0-0	
1986	USSR	lost	0-2	
1986	Uruguay	drew	1-1	
1986	Iceland	won	2-1	
1987	Belgium	drew	2-2	
1987	Bulgaria	lost	1-2	

Matches Continued

Year	Opponent	Result	Score	G
1988	Israel	won	5-0	
1988	Yugoslavia	won	2-0	
1988	Poland	won	3-1	
1988	Norway	drew	0-0	
1988	England	won	1-0	
1988	USSR	drew	1-1	
1988	Holland	lost	0-1	
1989	N Ireland	drew	0-0	
1989	France	drew	0-0	
1989	Hungary	drew	0-0	
1989	Spain	won	1-0	
1989	Malta	won	2-0	
1989	Hungary	won	2-0	
1990	Wales	won	1-0	
1990	USSR	won	1-0	
1990	Finland	drew	1-1	
1990	Turkey	drew	0-0	
1990	Malta	won	3-0	
1991	Turkey	won	5-0	
1991	Chile	drew	1-1	
1992	Turkey	won	3-1	

Full-back Chris Hughton played for Tottenham Hotspur as a part-time professional for two years, preferring to complete his apprenticeship as a lift engineer before signing full-time.

The move soon paid dividends, for after making his debut against Manchester United, he won the first of his 53 full international caps for the Republic of Ireland. Qualifying on his mother's side, he made his first appearance against the United States in October 1979.

Formerly a winger, he was converted into a fast, overlapping full-back, ever-keen to attack and get a shot in on goal. Capable of playing in either full-back berth, Hughton was a member of the Spurs teams that won the FA Cup in 1981 and 1982, reached the League Cup Final in 1982 and won the UEFA Cup in 1984. The defeat of Anderlecht was probably the highlight of his club career but by then, he had won 19 caps and was a regular in Eoin Hand's Republic of Ireland side.

Having become the first black player to represent the Republic of Ireland, he was a regular member of the national side for 12 years, playing under Alan Kelly, Eoin Hand and Jack Charlton. For both Spurs and the Republic of Ireland, Chris Hughton forged an effective and industrious left-wing partnership with Tony Galvin – the pair were important figures in the Republic's qualification for the 1988 European Championships. Both Spurs men played in all three matches for the boys in green in West Germany. Hughton also travelled to the 1990 World Cup Finals in Italy, but by then he had lost his place in the Spurs team and was struggling somewhat for form.

His great service to the White Hart Lane club was rewarded with a free transfer in June 1990. Although several clubs were interested in acquiring his services, no permanent move was immediately forthcoming. In November 1990 he was loaned to West Ham United to cover for long-term injury victim Julian Dicks, and made the move permanent the following month. He helped the Hammers win promotion from the Second Division in 1990-91 but following Dicks' return from injury, he moved on to Brentford.

His vast experience helped the Bees lift the Third Division title in 1991-92, but shortly afterwards he decided that the time was right to hang up his boots.

He later returned to White Hart Lane to join the coaching staff, prior to being appointed assistant-manager under both Gerry Francis and George Graham. Hughton is currently the North London club's first-team coach.

Above: Chris Hughton

Kevin Moran

Position	Central defender
Born	Kevin Bernard Moran, Dublin, 29 April 1956

Clubs

Manchester United; Sporting Gijon (Spain); Blackburn Rovers

International Caps	71
International Goals	6

Matches

Year	Opponent	Result	Score	G
1980	Switzerland	won	2-0	
1980	Argentina	lost	0-1	
1981	Belgium	drew	1-1	
1981	France	lost	0-2	
1981	Cyprus	won	6-0	
1981	Wales	lost	1-3	
1981	Belgium	lost	0-1	
1981	Czechoslovakia	won	3-1	2
1981	West Germany B	lost	0-3	
1981	Poland	lost	0-3	
1982	France	won	3-2	
1982	Algeria	lost	0-2	
1983	Iceland	won	2-0	
1984	Iceland	won	3-0	
1984	Holland	lost	2-3	
1984	Malta	won	8-0	
1984	Israel	lost	0-3	
1985	Mexico	drew	0-0	
1986	Denmark	lost	1-4	
1986	Iceland	won	2-1	
1986	Czechoslovakia	won	1-0	
1987	Belgium	drew	2-2	
1987	Scotland	drew	0-0	
1987	Poland	lost	0-1	
1987	Scotland	won	1-0	
1987	Bulgaria	lost	1-2	
1987	Belgium	drew	0-0	
1987	Brazil	won	1-0	
1987	Luxembourg	won	2-0	
1988	Luxembourg	won	2-1	
1988	Bulgaria	won	2-0	1
1988	Israel	won	5-0	
1988	Romania	won	2-0	1
1988	Yugoslavia	won	2-0	1
1988	Poland	won	3-1	
1988	Norway	drew	0-0	
1988	England	won	1-0	
1988	USSR	drew	1-1	
1988	Holland	lost	0-1	
1989	N Ireland	drew	0-0	
1989	Spain	lost	0-2	
1989	Hungary	drew	0-0	
1989	Spain	won	1-0	
1989	Malta	won	2-0	1
1989	Hungary	won	2-0	

Matches Continued

Year	Opponent	Result	Score	G
1990	N Ireland	won	3-0	
1990	Malta	won	2-0	
1990	Wales	won	1-0	
1990	USSR	won	1-0	
1990	Malta	won	3-0	
1990	England	drew	1-1	
1990	Egypt	drew	0-0	
1990	Holland	drew	1-1	
1990	Romania	drew	0-0	
			5-4 pen	
1990	Italy	lost	0-1	
1991	Turkey	won	5-0	
1991	Wales	won	3-0	
1991	England	drew	1-1	
1991	Poland	drew	0-0	
1991	Chile	drew	1-1	
1991	United States	drew	1-1	
1992	Poland	drew	3-3	
1992	United States	lost	1-3	
1993	Denmark	drew	0-0	
1993	Spain	drew	0-0	
1993	N Ireland	won	3-0	
1993	Albania	won	2-1	
1994	Lithuania	won	1-0	
1994	Spain	lost	1-3	
1994	Holland	won	1-0	
1994	Bolivia	won	1-0	

Above: Kevin Moran

The name 'Kevin Moran' will be in football's record books forever, but the central defender would gladly opt out of his place in the game's history: the first man to be sent-off in an FA Cup Final. Durham referee Peter Willis was the man who ensured the Irishman's infamy when he controversially dismissed him in the 1985 FA Cup Final against Everton.

Moran was a noted Gaelic footballer, but it was his ability as a soccer player which induced Manchester United boss Dave Sexton to pay a nominal fee to Dublin's Pegasus FC for his transfer in February 1978. The tough-tackling defender made his debut against Southampton in April 1979, becoming a first team regular in 1980-81.

He had by then made his full international debut, called into Ireland's senior team for a friendly against Switzerland during the one-match reign of Alan Kelly in April 1980. The

appointment of Eoin Hand as national coach shortly afterwards did nothing to hinder the United defender's progress, as he played in five of the eight qualifiers for the 1982 World Cup.

Moran's bravery became legendary at Old Trafford as he literally gave blood in the Reds' cause – collecting over 100 stitches in what were mostly facial injuries. As a United player he won two FA Cup winners' medals in 1983 and 1985, although he was denied his medal in the latter final until a few weeks later.

The appointment of Jack Charlton as Republic of Ireland manager in 1986 brought about Moran's best form for the national side. Two years later after a run of three goals in four games, he was appointed captain for the first time. Moran played a major role in the Republic's qualification for the 1988 European Championships, and was included in the squad for the tournament in West Germany, appearing in all three of Ireland's games.

By then he had joined Spanish club Sporting Gijon on a free transfer, later returning to Football League action with Blackburn Rovers. Whilst at Ewood Park, he helped Rovers win their place in the Premiership by beating Leicester City in the Division Two play-off final in May 1992.

Moran remained a key figure throughout the reign of Jack Charlton and was ever-present at Italia '90. Four years later at the age of 38, he was included in the Republic of Ireland squad that travelled to the World Cup in the United States. Unfortunately injury prevented him from adding to his most-impressive collection of international caps. At the end of the tournament, he decided to hang up his boots.

Gary Waddock

Position	Midfield
Born	Gary Patrick Waddock, Kingsbury, 17 March 1962
Clubs	

Queen's Park Rangers; Charleroi (Belgium); Millwall; Queen's Park Rangers; Swindon Town (loan); Bristol Rovers; Luton Town

International Caps	21
International Goals	3
Matches	

Year	Opponent	Result	Score	G
1980	Switzerland	won	2-0	
1980	Argentina	lost	0-1	
1981	Wales	lost	1-3	
1981	Poland	lost	0-3	
1982	Algeria	lost	0-2	
1983	Holland	lost	1-2	
1983	Iceland	won	2-0	
1983	Malta	won	1-0	
1983	Spain	lost	0-2	

Matches Continued

Year	Opponent	Result	Score	G
1984	Iceland	won	3-0	1
1984	Holland	lost	2-3	1
1984	Malta	won	8-0	
1984	Israel	lost	0-3	
1985	Italy	lost	1-2	1
1985	Israel	drew	0-0	
1985	England	lost	1-2	
1985	Norway	drew	0-0	
1985	Spain	drew	0-0	
1986	USSR	lost	0-2	
1990	USSR	won	1-0	
1990	Turkey	drew	0-0	

Above: Gary Waddock

Midfielder Gary Waddock worked his way up through the ranks at First Division Queen's Park Rangers before making his debut as an 18-year-old in 1978-79. A tough-tackling and inspirational midfielder, Waddock started out in the season that Rangers lost their top-flight status. He went on to play an important role in their Second Division Championship-winning season of 1982-83. He was also a member of the side that

lost the 1982 FA Cup Final replay 1-0 to Tottenham Hotspur.

Waddock made his international debut for the Republic of Ireland as a teenager during Alan Kelly's one-match reign as national coach in 1980. His success at club level meant that he earned a regular place in Eoin Hand's team for the qualifying rounds of the 1984 European Championships.

However, he sustained a knee injury that kept him out of the game for more than a year. The injury looked like finishing his career but Waddock refused to accept the medical diagnosis. Against all odds, he fought his way back to fitness. Unfortunately this caused a problem for Waddock and Queen's Park Rangers as the insurance money for his early retirement had already been paid out! While the problem was being resolved, Waddock went to play for Charleroi in the Belgian League before returning to League action in the summer of 1989 with Millwall.

He soon proved his fitness and Jack Charlton recalled him to the national squad for two warm-up matches ahead of Italia '90. However, when the manager announced the final changes to his squad for the tournament, Waddock had been replaced by Alan McLoughlin.

In December 1991 Gerry Francis took Waddock back to his spiritual home at Loftus Road, but he couldn't make the first team. After a loan spell with Swindon, he joined Bristol Rovers. He later played for Luton Town where he was appointed club captain, leading the Hatters to the play-offs in 1996-97. His fighting spirit and high work-rate often lifted an uninspiring Luton side but at the end of the following season, he was one of a number of Luton players released.

Michael Robinson

Position	Forward
Born	Michael John Robinson, Leicester, 12 July 1958

Clubs

Preston North End; Manchester City; Brighton and Hove Albion; Liverpool; Queen's Park Rangers; Osasuna (Spain)

International Caps	24
International Goals	4

Matches

Year	Opponent	Result	Score	G
1981	France	lost	0-2	
1981	Cyprus	won	6-0	1
1981	Belgium	lost	0-1	
1981	West Germany B	lost	0-3	
1981	Poland	lost	0-3	
1982	Holland	drew	2-2	1
1982	France	won	3-2	1
1982	Algeria	lost	0-2	
1982	Chile	lost	0-1	
1983	Holland	lost	1-2	
1983	Iceland	won	2-0	
1983	Spain	drew	3-3	
1983	Malta	won	1-0	
1984	Iceland	won	3-0	1
1984	Holland	lost	2-3	
1984	Israel	lost	0-3	
1985	USSR	won	1-0	
1985	Norway	lost	0-1	
1985	Norway	drew	0-0	
1985	Spain	drew	0-0	
1985	Switzerland	won	3-0	
1986	Denmark	lost	1-4	
1986	Wales	lost	0-1	
1986	Czechoslovakia	won	1-0	

Having shown great promise in Preston North End's youth and reserve teams, Michael Robinson quickly established himself in the Deepdale club's first team, though it seemed that every appearance attracted a posse of scouts from other clubs.

Their interest quickly developed to the point where Manchester City offered £750,000 for his services after he had played just 45 games for Preston. The Deepdale club agreed to let him leave. His time at Maine Road was limited, as he struggled to make an impact at that relatively early stage of his career. A little over twelve months after joining City, he was

Above: Michael Robinson

transferred to Brighton and Hove Albion for less than half the amount he had cost the club in the first place.

Not long after his arrival at the Goldstone Ground, he made his international debut for the Republic of Ireland against France – a match in which he appeared to have a perfectly good goal ruled out. Robinson had won the right to wear the green shirt via an Irish-born grandmother – his call-up to Eoin Hand's side brought the FAI criticism from both the football authorities and the media!

Robinson hit a rich vein of form on the south coast which ultimately led to Liverpool casting their net his way. The Reds paid £200,000 to take him to Anfield and though Robinson had mixed fortunes at the club, he always tried his best whenever selected. He won a League Championship medal as Liverpool clinched their third successive

title; a European Cup winners' medal as a substitute for Kenny Dalglish in the penalties victory over AS Roma in the final and a League Cup winners' medal, again as a substitute.

During the qualification programme for the 1982 World Cup, Robinson gave a match-winning display against France in Dublin, scoring with a powerful drive and setting up a goal for Frank Stapleton in a 3-2 win.

Robinson's last League club prior to joining Osasuna of Spain in 1987 was Queen's Park Rangers, whom he joined for £100,000 in December 1984. Injury forced his retirement after two years with Osasuna but he remained in Spain, where he now enjoys celebrity status as one of the leading television football anchor-men.

Jim McDonagh

Position	Goalkeeper
Born	James (Seamus) Martin McDonagh, Rotherham, 6 October 1952

Clubs

Rotherham United; Bolton Wanderers; Everton; Bolton Wanderers; Notts County; Birmingham City (loan); Gillingham (loan); Sunderland (loan); Wichita (U.S.); Scarborough; Huddersfield Town (loan); Charlton Athletic

International Caps	25

Matches

Year	Opponent	Result	Score	G
1981	Wales	lost	1-3	
1981	Belgium	lost	0-1	
1981	Czechoslovakia	won	3-1	
1981	West Germany B	lost	0-3	
1982	Holland	drew	2-2	
1982	France	won	3-2	
1982	Chile	lost	0-1	
1982	Brazil	lost	0-7	
1983	Holland	lost	1-2	
1983	Iceland	won	2-0	
1983	Spain	drew	3-3	
1983	Malta	won	1-0	
1983	Spain	lost	0-2	
1984	Iceland	won	3-0	

Matches Continued				
Year	Opponent	Result	Score	G
1984	Holland	lost	2-3	
1984	Poland	drew	0-0	
1985	Mexico	drew	0-0	
1985	USSR	won	1-0	
1985	Norway	lost	0-1	
1985	Denmark	lost	0-3	
1985	Spain	drew	0-0	
1985	Switzerland	won	3-0	
1986	Switzerland	drew	0-0	
1986	USSR	lost	0-2	
1986	Denmark	lost	1-4	

Above: Jim McDonagh

Goalkeeper Jim McDonagh has the unusual record of being capped for two different countries.

The Rotherham-born keeper signed for his home-town club in December 1970 and the following year won England youth honours. He was a regular for the Millers and helped them win promotion to Division Three in 1974-75 after two seasons in the Fourth. The following season he lost his place to Tom McAlister after breaking a leg in a game against Chesterfield. McDonagh had a loan spell at Manchester United without playing in the first team, before joining Bolton Wanderers in August 1976, initially on loan.

Within a fortnight he had become the club's first-choice custodian following Barry Siddall's transfer to Sunderland. His consistent performances were a feature of Bolton's successful team of the late 1970s. He conceded only 33 goals in 1977-78 when the Wanderers won the Second Division Championship. Between 1976 and 1980 McDonagh made a club record 161 consecutive League appearances. After the Trotters' relegation from the top flight, he joined Everton for £250,000 in July 1980. It was whilst at Goodison Park that he won the first of 25 Republic of Ireland caps, qualifying through ancestry.

His debut came in a friendly against Wales and though the Irish lost 3-1 he wasn't to blame. A month later he made his World Cup bow against Belgium in the Heysel Stadium in Brussels.

After a year on Merseyside he returned to Burnden Park along with £90,000 in exchange for Mike Walsh. He took his total of appearances to 274, scoring a goal in a 3-0 defeat of Burnley – before leaving Bolton a second time to join Notts County in July 1983. After playing in the NASL he had spells with Birmingham City, Gillingham, Sunderland, Scarborough, Huddersfield Town and Charlton Athletic. He then moved into management with Galway United, later taking charge of non-League cubs Spalding United, Grantham Town and Telford United.

Eamonn O'Keefe

Position	Forward
Born	Eamonn Gerard O'Keefe, Manchester, 13 October 1953
Clubs	

Stalybridge Celtic; Plymouth Argyle; Hyde United; Mossley; Everton; Wigan Athletic; Port Vale; Blackpool; St Patrick's Athletic; Chester City

International Caps	5
International Goals	1

Matches				
Year	Opponent	Result	Score	G
1981	Wales	lost	1-3	
1984	China	won	1-0	1
1985	Mexico	drew	0-0	
1985	USSR	won	1-0	
1985	England	lost	1-2	

Above: Eamonn O'Keefe

Very few players get the opportunity to fulfil the chance of becoming professional footballers: Eamonn O'Keefe got two!

Midway through the 1973-74 season, Plymouth Argyle signed the muscular Mancunian from non-League Stalybridge Celtic. After failing to impress he returned to non-League action, initially with Hyde United. He then had a brief spell in Saudi Arabia and was turning out for Mossley, when in July 1979, Everton signed him for £22,500.

Most of his three seasons at Goodison Park were spent in the club's Central League side, but he made his full international debut for the Republic of Ireland in February 1981 in the friendly against Wales. Two years earlier he had played for England's semi-pros against Scotland and Holland. According to FIFA this made him ineligible to play for Ireland. He fought FIFA's decision and eventually won his case.

In January 1982 O'Keefe left Everton and joined Wigan Athletic for a £65,000 fee. Towards the end of his first season at Springfield Park, in which the Latics won promotion to the Third Division, he netted hat-tricks against Crewe Alexandra and Mansfield Town. Revelling in his new striking role, he netted another treble the following season as Wigan beat Southend United 4-0.

In July 1983 he moved to Port Vale – in doing so, he brought an end to his three-year international exile. He celebrated his return to the national side by scoring in the Japan Cup match against China, a match the Irish won 1-0.

He later played for Blackpool and despite a long lay-off with a knee injury he surpassed himself at Bloomfield Road. After suffering a recurrence of the knee trouble, he attempted a comeback, first with St Patrick's Athletic and later Chester City, but finally had to admit defeat.

Kevin O'Callaghan

Position	Left-winger
Born	Kevin O'Callaghan, Dagenham, 19 October 1961

Clubs

Millwall; Ipswich Town; Portsmouth; Millwall; Southend United

International Caps	21
International Goals	1

Matches

Year	Opponent	Result	Score	G
1981	Czechoslovakia	won	3-1	
1981	West Germany B	lost	0-3	
1981	Poland	lost	0-3	
1982	Algeria	lost	0-2	
1982	Chile	lost	0-1	
1982	Brazil	lost	0-7	
1982	Trinidad & Tobago	lost	1-2	
1983	Iceland	won	2-0	
1983	Spain	drew	3-3	
1983	Malta	won	1-0	
1983	Spain	lost	0-2	
1984	Iceland	won	3-0	
1984	Holland	lost	2-3	
1984	Malta	won	8-0	1
1985	Mexico	drew	0-0	
1985	Norway	lost	0-1	
1985	Denmark	lost	0-3	
1985	England	lost	1-2	
1986	Switzerland	drew	0-0	
1986	USSR	lost	0-2	
1987	Brazil	won	1-0	

Above: Kevin O'Callaghan

A skilful and versatile forward, Kevin O'Callaghan started out with Millwall. He was a member of the Lions' FA Youth Cup winning side of 1978-79, a season which ended with the London club's relegation to the Third Division.

In January 1980 he was surprisingly allowed to leave The Den, joining Ipswich Town for a club record fee of £250,000. Whilst at Portman Road, O'Callaghan made his full international debut for the Republic of Ireland against Czechoslovakia. He soon became a regular in Eoin Hand's side, playing in three consecutive friendlies following his debut. It was not until his ninth cap in

the final match of 1982 that he was named in the starting line-up for a competitive international. After an outstanding game against Spain in the preliminary rounds of the 1984 European Championships, he appeared in each of the Republic's remaining six qualifiers. This culminated in his only goal for the national side in an 8-0 rout of Malta in November 1983.

O'Callaghan spent five years at Portman Road before joining Portsmouth: the initial transfer had been temporary. A hugely popular player at Fratton Park, he helped Pompey win promotion to the First Division in 1986-87, just seven seasons after the south coast club had been in the League's basement.

During the close season he rejoined Millwall and more than played his part in helping the Lions win the Second Division Championship. Plagued by a series of long-term injuries and a fall-out with manager Bruce Rioch, he moved to Southend United where he ended his first-class career.

Ronnie Whelan junior

Position	Midfield
Born	Ronald Andrew Whelan, Dublin, 25 September 1961
Clubs	

Home Farm; Liverpool; Southend United

International Caps	53
International Goals	3

Matches

Year	Opponent	Result	Score	G
1981	Czechoslovakia	won	3-1	
1982	Holland	drew	2-2	
1982	France	won	3-2	
1983	Iceland	won	2-0	
1983	Malta	won	1-0	
1983	Spain	lost	0-2	
1984	Israel	lost	0-3	
1985	USSR	won	1-0	
1985	Norway	lost	0-1	
1985	Italy	lost	1-2	
1985	Israel	drew	0-0	
1985	England	lost	1-2	
1985	Norway	drew	0-0	
1985	Switzerland	won	3-0	
1986	USSR	lost	0-2	
1986	Wales	lost	0-1	
1987	Belgium	drew	2-2	
1987	Scotland	won	1-0	
1987	Bulgaria	lost	1-2	
1987	Belgium	drew	0-0	
1987	Brazil	won	1-0	
1987	Luxembourg	won	2-0	1
1988	Luxembourg	won	2-1	
1988	Bulgaria	won	2-0	
1988	Poland	won	3-1	
1988	Norway	drew	0-0	
1988	England	won	1-0	
1988	USSR	drew	1-1	1
1988	Holland	lost	0-1	
1989	N Ireland	drew	0-0	
1989	France	drew	0-0	
1989	Hungary	drew	0-0	
1989	Spain	won	1-0	
1989	Malta	won	2-0	
1990	West Germany	drew	1-1	
1990	N Ireland	won	3-0	1
1990	Malta	won	2-0	
1990	Wales	won	1-0	
1990	Holland	drew	1-1	
1991	Morocco	won	1-0	
1991	England	drew	1-1	

Matches Continued

Year	Opponent	Result	Score	G
1992	Switzerland	won	2-1	
1993	Latvia	won	4-0	
1993	Wales	won	2-1	
1993	Lithuania	won	1-0	
1994	Lithuania	won	2-0	
1994	Spain	lost	1-3	
1994	Russia	drew	0-0	
1994	Holland	won	1-0	
1994	Germany	won	2-0	
1994	Norway	drew	0-0	
1995	Liechtenstein	drew	0-0	
1995	Austria	lost	1-3	

The son of a former international who won two full caps for the Republic of Ireland in the 1960s, he was spotted by Liverpool playing in the League of Ireland for Home Farm. He was brought to Anfield in October 1979.

Below: Ronnie Whelan

At the age of 19, having made just one League appearance for the Reds, he took his senior international bow as a substitute against Czechoslovakia at Lansdowne Road.

It was 1981-82 before Whelan won a regular place in the Liverpool side, scoring 10 League goals and two in the 1982 League Cup Final, as the Reds beat Spurs 3-1 after extra-time. In 1983 he popped up again to score the winner in extra-time as Liverpool retained the trophy by beating Manchester United 2-1. In April 1986 he netted his only hat-trick for the club in a 5-0 defeat of Coventry City, but he was never able to reproduce this kind of scoring form in a green shirt!

Under Jack Charlton, Whelan became a more industrious and resolute player. He was selected for both the European Championship Finals in West Germany in 1988 and the World Cup Finals in Italy in 1990. In the European Championship game against the USSR, Whelan scored a breathtaking goal: a long throw from Mick McCarthy eluded all the Soviet defenders and fell to Whelan, who leapt into the air to strike a perfect left-footed scissors-kick into the corner of the net. Sadly troubled by injury, he played little part in the Republic's remarkable progress to the World Cup quarter-finals.

On his return from the 1990 World Cup Finals, Whelan had two injury-plagued seasons before returning to first team action at the beginning of the 1992-93 season. However, he was later withdrawn with a thigh injury and was out for so long that many Liverpool supporters feared that it was one setback too many, and that he would never play again.

Happily he returned to duty in March 1993. His impressive displays meant that he remained a regular member of Jack Charlton's squad. In 1994 at the age of 32 he was included in his second World Cup Finals squad.

Whelan later left Anfield to join Southend United, having won six League Championship medals, two FA Cup winners' medals and a European Cup winners' medal. He later began his managerial career at Roots Hall. Sadly things started to go wrong for him and in February 1997 the club suspended him from team manager duties after an incident with match officials. Whelan later had a spell as coach of Greek club Penionis.

Paddy Bonner

Position	Goalkeeper
Born	Patrick Joseph Bonner, Clochglas, Co. Donegal, 24 May 1960
Clubs	
	Keadue Rovers; Glasgow Celtic; Kilmarnock; Glasgow Celtic
International Caps	80

Matches

Year	Opponent	Result	Score	G
1981	Poland	lost	0-3	
1982	Algeria	lost	0-2	
1984	Malta	won	8-0	
1984	Israel	lost	0-3	
1984	China	won	1-0	
1985	Italy	lost	1-2	
1985	Israel	drew	0-0	
1985	England	lost	1-2	
1985	Norway	drew	0-0	
1986	Uruguay	drew	1-1	
1986	Iceland	won	2-1	
1987	Belgium	drew	2-2	
1987	Scotland	drew	0-0	
1987	Poland	lost	0-1	
1987	Scotland	won	1-0	
1987	Bulgaria	lost	1-2	
1987	Belgium	drew	0-0	
1987	Brazil	won	1-0	
1987	Luxembourg	won	2-0	
1988	Bulgaria	won	2-0	
1988	Romania	won	2-0	
1988	Yugoslavia	won	2-0	
1988	Norway	drew	0-0	
1988	England	won	1-0	

Matches Continued

Year	Opponent	Result	Score	G
1988	USSR	drew	1-1	
1988	Holland	lost	0-1	
1989	Spain	lost	0-2	
1989	France	drew	0-0	
1989	Hungary	drew	0-0	
1989	Spain	won	1-0	
1989	Malta	won	2-0	
1989	Hungary	won	2-0	
1990	West Germany	drew	1-1	
1990	N Ireland	won	3-0	
1990	Malta	won	2-0	
1990	Wales	won	1-0	
1990	Finland	drew	1-1	
1990	Turkey	drew	0-0	
1990	England	drew	1-1	
1990	Egypt	drew	0-0	
1990	Holland	drew	1-1	
1990	Romania	drew	0-0 5-4 pen	
1990	Italy	lost	0-1	
1991	Morocco	won	1-0	
1991	Turkey	won	5-0	
1991	England	drew	1-1	
1991	Wales	won	3-0	
1991	England	drew	1-1	
1991	Poland	drew	0-0	
1991	United States	drew	1-1	
1992	Hungary	won	2-1	
1992	Poland	drew	3-3	
1992	Turkey	won	3-1	
1992	Wales	lost	0-1	
1992	Switzerland	won	2-1	
1992	Albania	won	2-0	
1992	Italy	lost	0-2	
1993	Latvia	won	4-0	
1993	Denmark	drew	0-0	
1993	Wales	won	2-1	
1993	Spain	drew	0-0	
1993	N Ireland	won	3-0	
1993	Denmark	drew	1-1	
1993	Albania	won	2-1	
1993	Latvia	won	2-0	
1993	Lithuania	won	1-0	
1994	Lithuania	won	2-0	
1994	Spain	lost	1-3	
1994	N Ireland	drew	1-1	
1994	Russia	drew	0-0	
1994	Holland	won	1-0	
1994	Bolivia	won	1-0	
1994	Czech Rep	lost	1-3	
1994	Italy	won	1-0	
1994	Mexico	lost	1-2	
1994	Norway	drew	0-0	
1994	Holland	lost	0-2	
1995	Liechtenstein	won	4-0	
1996	Mexico	drew	2-2	
1996	Bolivia	won	3-0	

career with the Bhoys, making the first of 483 League appearances against Motherwell in March 1979.

In May 1981 Bonner, who had won caps at youth and Under-21 level, was called into the senior squad for a tour of Germany and Poland. He made his full international debut on his 21st birthday. Though he wasn't to blame for any of the goals in a 3-0 defeat by the Poles, it was almost a year before he won his second cap.

With Celtic he won four League Championship badges in 1980-81, 1981-82, 1985-86 and 1987-88. He played in four Scottish League Cup Finals, all against arch-rivals Rangers, but was victorious only once, in 1983. He also won Scottish Cup winners' medals in 1985 and 1995 after victories over Dundee United and Airdrie respectively.

The arrival of Jack Charlton as Republic of Ireland team manager in 1986 proved the watershed in the international career of Paddy Bonner. The Celtic keeper proved the perfect custodian for Charlton's tactics – not only superb shot-stopping and impeccable handling but also a powerful and extremely accurate long kick. He missed just one of the Republic's qualifying matches ahead of the 1988 European Championships and played in each of the country's three matches during the tournament finals. His performance in the defeat of England in Stuttgart – especially the save late on to deny Gary Lineker – was memorable.

In the 1990 World Cup Finals in Italy Bonner conceded just two goals in the group matches, but it was his display in the second round tie against Romania for which he will always be remembered. After two hours of football, the game remained goalless and went to a penalty shoot-out. After each team had successfully converted four spot-kicks, the weary Bonner

Above: Paddy Bonner

Paddy (Packie) Bonner was Jock Stein's last signing for Celtic, when he arrived at Parkhead from Donegal junior side Keadue Rovers in 1978. He was to enjoy a 17-year produced a superb save to deny Romania's Daniel Timofte. Although the Republic lost out to the hosts in the quarter-finals, Bonner was brilliant and unlucky to concede the game's only goal after making an excellent save from Donadoni.

Back at club level, Bonner was dropped by Liam Brady, and given a free transfer by his successor Lou Macari. He subsequently joined his former Parkhead team-mate Tommy Burns at Kilmarnock. When Burns moved to Parkhead to take over from Macari, he took Bonner back with him!

In the 1994 World Cup in the United States, the Republic crashed out of the tournament after two most uncharacteristic defensive errors against Holland – the second of which left Bonner a little red-faced, after he completely misjudged the bounce of Wim Jonk's long-range shot. Bonner, who won three more caps – two as captain – later hung up his boots to concentrate on a career in coaching, initially with Celtic.

Eamonn Deacy

Position	Full-back
Born	Eamonn Stephen Deacy, Galway, 1 October 1958
Clubs	

Galway Rovers; Aston Villa; Derby County (loan); Galway United

International Caps	4
Matches	

Year	Opponent	Result	Score	G
1982	Algeria	lost	0-2	
1982	Chile	lost	0-1	
1982	Brazil	lost	0-7	
1982	Trinidad & Tobago	lost	1-2	

A strong-tackling and reliable full-back, Eamonn Deacy was a member of the Galway Rovers side during their first season as a League of Ireland club in 1977-78.

Midway through the following season, he was transferred to Aston Villa. Although he spent four years at Villa Park, he was never a first team regular. When the club won the League Championship in 1980-81, Deacy made just nine appearances.

Known as 'Chick', the former amateur international won his first full cap for the Republic of Ireland as a substitute for Kevin Moran in the 2-0 defeat by Algeria. Unfortunately for Deacy, the Republic lost all four of the internationals in which he played. His last appearance in a green shirt was the humiliating 2-1 defeat at the hands of Trinidad and Tobago in Port of Spain.

Unable to make much headway at Aston Villa, he joined Derby County on loan and in his month at the Baseball Ground impressed all concerned. However, he rejected a move to the Rams, preferring to return to his home-town League of Ireland club, who by then had changed their name to Galway United.

Again he made club history when he was a member of the first Terryland Park side to reach a major Cup Final, but the impressive Deacy was on the losing side as Shamrock Rovers triumphed in the 1985 FAI Cup Final.

Mick Fairclough

Position	Midfield/Forward
Born	Michael Joseph Fairclough, Drogheda, 22 October 1952
Clubs	

Drogheda; Huddersfield Town; Dundalk; Sligo Rovers; Newry Town

International Caps	2
Matches	

Year	Opponent	Result	Score	G
1982	Chile	lost	0-1	
1982	Trinidad & Tobago	lost	0-2	

When he burst onto the scene in the early 1970s, Mick Fairclough was hailed as the best young forward in Ireland. He was the only local player in the Drogheda side that reached their first-ever FAI Cup Final in 1971 – losing 3-0 to Limerick after the first game had been drawn.

A player renowned for his ball skills, he joined Huddersfield Town in the summer of 1971. In the early part of the 1971-72 season he broke into the Terriers' League side. During his time at Leeds Road, he saw Huddersfield drop into the Fourth Division, from the top flight four seasons before! Whilst playing for the Yorkshire club he suffered a serious knee injury, and it looked for a time as if his career was over.

He returned to Ireland and didn't play football for nigh-on five years, but then in 1980 he joined Dundalk. He was the club's leading scorer in three successive seasons including their Championship-winning season of 1981-82. He scored one of the goals in Dundalk's 2-0 win over Sligo Rovers in the 1981 FAI Cup Final and in the same year collected a League Cup winners' medal.

Fairclough had won Under-23 honours for the Republic of Ireland prior to his injury at Huddersfield. He won two full caps as a substitute against Chile and Trinidad and Tobago on the Republic's tour of South America in 1982 – a huge achievement.

He played for Dundalk until 1984 and then had brief spells with Sligo Rovers and Newry Town, until a recurrence of his knee problems forced his retirement from the game.

Sean O'Driscoll

Position	Midfield
Born	Sean Michael O'Driscoll, Wolverhampton, 1 July 1957
Clubs	
Alvechurch; Fulham; Bournemouth	
International Caps	3
Matches	

Year	Opponent	Result	Score	G
1982	Chile	lost	0-1	
1982	Brazil	lost	0-7	
1982	Trinidad & Tobago	lost	1-2	

Midfielder Sean O'Driscoll was playing non-League football for Alvechurch when he was spotted by Fulham and signed by the Craven Cottage club for a fee of £12,000 in November 1979.

His early displays for the west London club led to him winning full international honours for the Republic of Ireland, for whom he qualified under the parentage rule. O'Driscoll won three caps for the Republic, all on the disastrous tour to South America in the summer of 1982 when they were beaten by Chile, Brazil and Trinidad and Tobago.

O'Driscoll was by now a regular in the Fulham side, helping the Cottagers win promotion to Division Two in 1983-84. Midway through the following season, he lost form and joined Bournemouth on loan.

Shortly afterwards the move was made permanent: at the end of his first season at Dean Court, he won an Associate Members' Cup winners medal. He played an important role in helping the Cherries win the Third Division Championship in 1986-87. Over the next eight seasons he missed very few games for the south-coast club. Having decided to hang up his boots, he was appointed the club's physiotherapist and later took charge of the Cherries' youth side. In 1994-95 due to an injury crisis at the club, he was recalled to the side and took his total of appearances to 511 before parting company with the club.

Mike Walsh

Position	Central defender
Born	Michael Thomas Walsh, Manchester, 20 June 1956
Clubs	
Bolton Wanderers; Everton; Norwich City (loan); Burnley (loan); Fort Lauderdale Strikers (U.S.); Manchester City; Blackpool; Bury	
International Caps	4
Matches	

Year	Opponent	Result	Score	G
1982	Chile	lost	0-1	
1982	Brazil	lost	0-7	
1982	Trinidad & Tobago	lost	1-2	
1983	Iceland	won	2-0	

Mike Walsh started his career with Bolton Wanderers as a left-back but he could also play as a central defender or in midfield.

His League debut came in February 1975 when he appeared as a substitute for the experienced Tony Dunne in a 3-2 win at Nottingham Forest. For the next two seasons he continued to act as understudy, but made the headlines with a late equaliser against Fulham in the League Cup. He played in the first leg of the semi-final against Everton in place of the suspended Sam Allardyce. During

Above: Mike Walsh

Bolton's Second Division Championship-winning season of 1977-78, he missed only one game and appeared in three different positions. He was an ever-present in Bolton's two seasons back in the top flight – a run of 126 consecutive League appearances came to an end in December 1980 through injury.

During the summer of 1981 Walsh moved to Everton for £90,000 with Jim McDonagh returning to Burnden Park as part of the deal. Whilst on Merseyside, Walsh made his international debut for the Republic of Ireland when a host of high profile rivals withdrew from a summer tour of South America in 1982. His debut came in a 1-0 defeat at the hands of Chile; he then played in further defeats by Brazil and Trinidad and Tobago. His fourth and final appearance for the national side came in a European Championship qualifier against

Iceland, when the Republic recorded a 2-0 win.

Unable to hold down a regular place at Everton, he was loaned out to Norwich City and Burnley. He spent time in the NASL with Fort Lauderdale Strikers before joining Manchester City. His stay at Maine Road was brief and he was transferred to Blackpool in February 1984. Walsh spent five seasons at Bloomfield Road helping the Seasiders win promotion to Division Three in 1984-85. In 1989 he joined Bury and the following December was appointed manager at the club.

He went on to become the longest-serving manager in Division Three, taking the Shakers to three play-offs in his five years in charge. He later managed Barrow before becoming assistant-manager of Swindon Town.

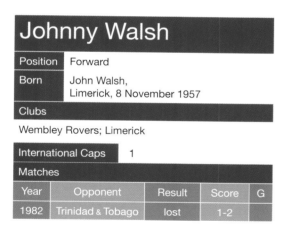

Johnny Walsh

Position	Forward
Born	John Walsh, Limerick, 8 November 1957

Clubs
Wembley Rovers; Limerick

International Caps	1

Matches				
Year	Opponent	Result	Score	G
1982	Trinidad & Tobago	lost	1-2	

After winning numerous honours with junior club Wembley Rovers, Johnny Walsh joined his local side Limerick.

In his first season with the club (1976-77) he was an FAI Cup runner-up after Limerick lost the final to Dundalk. Walsh, who never shirked a challenge, was carried off injured after just under half-an-hour of the game!

The Shannonsiders, who began as Limerick, later became Limerick United and then Limerick City. They finally reverted to the original name in the early part of the nineties. They were known as Limerick City when Walsh won a League Championship medal in 1979-80, a season after he had first won inter-League honours for the League of Ireland against a Basque selection in front of a 75,000 crowd in Bilbao. Two years later he was a member of the League of Ireland side that lined-up in front of 85,000 spectators at the River Plate Stadium against Diego Maradona's Argentina!

In 1982 he won a Cup winners' medal following Limerick's defeat of Bohemians – he was named 'Man-of-the-Match'. Following over zealous post-match celebrations he damaged his ankle, and was unable to tour New Zealand with the League of Ireland side!

A month later he was called into the Republic of Ireland side to tour South America and made the starting line-up for the game against Trinidad and Tobago.

Following Limerick's relegation, Walsh won a First Division Championship medal in 1991-92 and the following season won a League Cup winners' medal. A one-club man, Johnny Walsh spent 18 full seasons with Limerick, playing under numerous managers and refusing many offers to leave and play at a higher level.

Tony Galvin

Position	Left-winger
Born	Anthony Galvin, Huddersfield, 12 July 1956

Clubs
Goole Town; Tottenham Hotspur; Sheffield Wednesday; Swindon Town

International Caps	29
International Goals	1

Matches				
Year	Opponent	Result	Score	G
1983	Holland	lost	1-2	
1983	Malta	won	1-0	
1984	Holland	lost	2-3	
1984	Israel	lost	0-3	
1985	Mexico	drew	0-0	
1985	USSR	won	1-0	
1985	Norway	lost	0-1	
1985	Denmark	lost	0-3	
1985	Italy	lost	1-2	
1985	Norway	drew	0-0	
1985	Spain	drew	0-0	
1986	Uruguay	drew	1-1	
1986	Iceland	won	2-1	
1986	Czechoslovakia	won	1-0	
1987	Belgium	drew	2-2	
1987	Scotland	won	1-0	
1987	Bulgaria	lost	1-2	
1987	Belgium	drew	0-0	
1987	Luxembourg	won	2-0	1
1988	Luxembourg	won	2-1	
1988	Bulgaria	won	2-0	
1988	Romania	won	2-0	
1988	Poland	won	3-1	
1988	Norway	drew	0-0	
1988	England	won	1-0	
1988	USSR	drew	1-1	
1988	Holland	lost	0-1	
1989	Spain	lost	0-2	
1990	West Germany	drew	1-1	

Tony Galvin had shelved all ideas of becoming a professional footballer to take a Bachelor of Arts degree in Russian Studies at Hull University. When work permitted, he turned out for the University team. After obtaining his degree he went to Teacher Training College, and played Northern League football for Goole Town.

In January 1978 Spurs signed him for what proved a bargain £30,000. With his non-stop

Glenn Hoddle. He played a major role in the White Hart Lane club's Cup successes in the early 1980s, picking up two FA Cup winners' medals in 1981 and 1982 as Spurs overcame Manchester City 3-2 in the replayed final and Queen's Park Rangers 1-0.

His displays attracted the attention of the Republic of Ireland manager Eoin Hand, who had discovered that Galvin qualified to represent the Irish under the grandparent rule. A debut against Holland in the European Championship qualifier followed: thereafter he remained a regular in the national side.

He was outstanding for Spurs in the 1984 UEFA Cup Final against Anderlecht and went on to score 47 goals in 375 League and Cup games, before being transferred to Sheffield Wednesday for £130,000.

On the international scene, Galvin played a key role in the qualification campaign for the 1988 European Championships and was included in the starting line-ups for all three of the Republic's games in the tournament finals in Germany.

At Hillsborough he spent two difficult seasons, picking up more than his fair share of injuries before moving to Swindon Town. Winning the last of his 29 international caps at the County Ground, Galvin helped Swindon reach the First Division via the play-offs in his first season —they were subsequently relegated without taking their place in the elite due to financial irregularities.

Promoted to assistant-manager, he later took over as the Robins' caretaker boss when Ardiles left for Newcastle. With the appointment of Glenn Hoddle, he also left to renew his partnership with Ardiles, first at Newcastle and then West Bromwich Albion. Galvin, who later managed Royston Town is now a College Lecturer.

running from deep positions, ability to beat a man and produce accurate crosses, Galvin's workmanlike style was the perfect foil to the more artistic talents of Ossie Ardilles and

Kevin Sheedy

Position	Midfield
Born	Kevin Mark Sheedy, Builth Wells, 21 October 1959

Clubs

Hereford United; Liverpool; Everton; Newcastle United; Blackpool

International Caps	45
International Goals	9

Matches

Year	Opponent	Result	Score	G
1984	Holland	lost	2-3	
1984	Malta	won	8-0	1
1985	Denmark	lost	0-3	
1985	Italy	lost	1-2	
1985	Israel	drew	0-0	
1985	Switzerland	won	3-0	1
1986	Scotland	drew	0-0	
1986	Denmark	lost	1-4	
1987	Scotland	drew	0-0	
1987	Poland	lost	0-1	
1988	Israel	won	5-0	
1988	Romania	won	2-0	
1988	Poland	won	3-1	1
1988	England	won	1-0	
1988	USSR	drew	1-1	
1989	N Ireland	drew	0-0	
1989	Tunisia	won	4-0	1
1989	Hungary	drew	0-0	
1989	Spain	won	1-0	
1989	Malta	won	2-0	
1989	Hungary	won	2-0	
1990	N Ireland	won	3-0	
1990	Malta	won	2-0	
1990	Wales	won	1-0	
1990	USSR	won	1-0	
1990	Finland	drew	1-1	1
1990	Turkey	drew	0-0	
1990	England	drew	1-1	
1990	Egypt	drew	0-0	
1990	Holland	drew	1-1	
1990	Romania	drew	0-0 5-4 pen	
1990	Italy	lost	0-1	
1991	Wales	won	3-0	
1991	England	drew	1-1	
1991	Poland	drew	0-0	
1991	Chile	drew	1-1	
1991	United States	drew	1-1	
1992	Hungary	won	2-1	1
1992	Poland	drew	3-3	
1992	Turkey	won	3-1	
1992	Wales	lost	0-1	
1992	Switzerland	won	2-1	
1992	Albania	won	2-0	
1993	Latvia	won	4-0	1
1993	Wales	won	2-1	1

Above: Kevin Sheedy

Kevin Sheedy began his Football League career with Hereford United before an £80,000 move to Liverpool in the summer of 1978. However, things didn't work out for the young midfielder at Anfield and he spent most of his time in the reserves, winning four Central League Championship medals!

In June 1982 he was rescued from obscurity when Everton manager Howard Kendall paid £100,000 for his services. In his first season at Goodison, Sheedy scored 11 goals in 40 games – this earned him a call-up to Eoin Hand's Republic of Ireland squad.

Despite being born in mid-Wales, Sheedy qualified to play for the Republic through his father who was born in County Clare. His debut cap arrived when he came off the bench with eight minutes to go, during a European Championship qualifier against Holland at Dalymount Park in October 1983. Though the Irish lost 3-2, Sheedy kept his place in the side for the next game against Malta and scored in an 8-0 win.

He continued to impress for Everton, though injury forced him to miss the 1984 FA Cup Final victory over Watford. He was back the following season, playing a vital role as Everton lifted the League Championship. He also scored the Blues' third goal in the European Cup Winners' Cup Final victory over Rapid Vienna. In 1986-87 he helped Everton to another League Championship title. The following year he played his part in the Republic of Ireland's 1988 European Championship campaign, appearing in the vital qualifier against Scotland and making two appearances at the tournament finals in Germany.

He played in all five of the Republic's games in Italia '90, but it was against England in Ireland's first game that he made his greatest contribution. With England leading 1-0 and little over quarter-of-an-hour remaining, he crashed a low drive beyond Peter Shilton to register a deserved equaliser, and the Republic's first goal at a World Cup Finals.

Later in the tournament the Republic found themselves facing Romania in a penalty shoot-out – Sheedy took the first kick and scored to send the nation into the quarter-finals against Italy.

Towards the end of his career at Everton he found it difficult to hold down a place and giving up a testimonial, joined Newcastle United. He helped the Magpies win the First Division Championship before ending his career with Blackpool. Sheedy was assistant-manager to his former Republic of Ireland colleague John Aldridge at Tranmere Rovers before taking over the reins on a temporary basis following Aldridge's resignation.

Jacko McDonagh

Position	Centre-half
Born	James McDonagh, Dublin, 1960
Clubs	

Bohemians; Shamrock Rovers; Nîmes Olympic (France)

International Caps	3

Matches

Year	Opponent	Result	Score	G
1984	Malta	won	8-0	
1984	Poland	drew	0-0	
1985	Mexico	drew	0-0	

An accomplished centre-half, Jacko McDonagh was a dominant figure in the Bohemians' defence as they pressed for glory in the League of Ireland in the early-1980s. He was an FAI Cup runner-up with the Gypsies in 1982. At the start of the following season he left Dalymount Park to play for Shamrock Rovers.

Initially he was used in midfield but following the appointment of Jim McLaughlin as manager, reverted to his more customary position of centre-half.

In November 1983 after playing in a handful of Under-21 internationals, he was called up to Eoin Hand's full squad for the match against Malta. A half-time replacement for Kevin Moran, he went on to help the Republic win 8-0! He made a couple of further appearances for his country as a substitute against Poland and Mexico but with players of the calibre of Lawrenson, O'Leary, McCarthy, McGrath and Moran ahead of him in the pecking order, his collection of international caps remained at three.

With Shamrock Rovers he won League Championship medals in 1983-84 and 1984-85 – scoring nine goals in this latter campaign. The Hoops also reached the FAI Cup Final in these two seasons. Though they were surprisingly beaten by University College, Dublin in 1984, Rovers completed the double the following year by beating Galway United 1-0. After nine seasons with Shamrock Rovers, McDonagh left to end his career with French club Nîmes Olympic.

Kieran O'Regan

Position	Defender/Midfield
Born	Kieran Michael O'Regan, Cork, 9 November 1963
Clubs	

Tramore Athletic; Brighton and Hove Albion; Swindon Town; Huddersfield Town; West Bromwich Albion

International Caps	4

Matches

Year	Opponent	Result	Score	G
1984	Malta	won	8-0	
1984	Poland	drew	0-0	
1985	Mexico	drew	0-0	
1985	Spain	drew	0-0	

A versatile footballer who could operate at both full-back and midfield, Kieran O'Regan played junior football in the Munster League with Tramore Athletic.

Following a trial with Brighton and Hove Albion, he joined the Seagulls on a permanent basis, signing professional forms in April 1983. Brighton boss Jimmy Melia used him as an attacking full-back. His form in 1983-84 led to him winning the first of four caps for the Republic of Ireland in the 8-0 mauling of Malta. O'Regan's three other appearances at full international level – against Poland, Mexico and Spain – all ended in scoreless draws. His last appearance for the national side saw him come off the bench to replace Chris Hughton – within minutes he had headed a goalbound shot off the line to ensure the match remained goalless.

In August 1987 O'Regan was surprisingly allowed to leave the Goldstone Ground, and joined Swindon Town. After a season with the Wiltshire club he was on the move again, this time to Huddersfield Town. A player who had scored a hat-trick against Wales on his youth debut for the Republic, he played the majority of his 199 League games for the Yorkshire club in midfield. In June 1993 he moved to West Bromwich Albion for a tribunal-set fee of £25,000. A player with a heart of gold, never shirking a tackle, he was freed by the Baggies after a couple of seasons at the club.

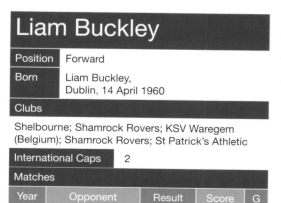

Liam Buckley

Position	Forward
Born	Liam Buckley, Dublin, 14 April 1960
Clubs	

Shelbourne; Shamrock Rovers; KSV Waregem (Belgium); Shamrock Rovers; St Patrick's Athletic

International Caps	2

Matches				
Year	Opponent	Result	Score	G
1984	Poland	drew	0-0	
1985	Mexico	drew	0-0	

One of the most feared strikers in the League of Ireland, Liam Buckley was just 18-years-old when he broke into Shelbourne's first team midway through the 1978-79 season. His impressive displays prompted Shamrock Rovers to sign him during the following season. It wasn't long before he won Under-21 honours for the Republic of Ireland against England.

A superb header of the ball and skilful on the ground, he was the Hoops' leading scorer in successive seasons from 1980-81 to 1982-83. One of the League of Ireland's most courageous players, his progress was hampered in February 1984 by a broken collar-bone. However, within a couple of months, he was back in action. With the League title already won, he scored the goal in the FAI Cup semi-final against his former club Shelbourne to put Rovers into the final, with a chance of completing the double. The Hoops though lost 2-1 to University College, Dublin, after the first meeting had been drawn.

His goalscoring prowess hadn't gone unnoticed – Eoin Hand called him into the Republic of Ireland line-up for two friendlies in the summer of 1984.

In between his two appearances for the national side, Buckley was transferred to Belgian club KSV Waregem, though he then rejoined Rovers before moving to St Patrick's Athletic, where he later became the club's assistant-manager.

Pat Byrne

Position	Midfield
Born	Patrick Joseph Byrne, Dublin, 15 May 1956
Clubs	

Bohemians; Philadelphia Fury (U.S.); Shelbourne; Leicester City; Heart of Midlothian; Shamrock Rovers; Shelbourne; Cobh Ramblers

International Caps	8

Matches				
Year	Opponent	Result	Score	G
1984	Poland	drew	0-0	
1984	China	won	1-0	
1985	Mexico	drew	0-0	
1985	Spain	drew	0-0	
1986	Denmark	lost	1-4	
1986	Wales	lost	0-1	
1986	Iceland	won	2-1	
1986	Czechoslovakia	won	1-0	

One of the League of Ireland's most influential footballers during the 1980s, Pat Byrne won every honour the Irish game has to offer.

Starting out with Bohemians, he won his first medal in 1975 as the Gypsies beat Finn Harps to win the League Cup. A year later he collected an FAI Cup winners' medal and in 1977-78, the Bohs won the League Championship.

Before the end of that most successful campaign Pat Byrne, along with team-mates Eddie Byrne and Fran O'Brien, left the club to play in the NASL for Philadelphia Fury. After a summer in the States, he returned to Ireland to play for Shelbourne, before in June 1979 signing for Leicester City.

He contributed some tenacious midfield performances to the Foxes' 1980 promotion push. He then spent the next two seasons in Scotland playing for Hearts. Though he helped them win promotion in his second season at Tynecastle, he was commuting weekly from Dublin after his wife had failed to settle in Edinburgh.

He then returned with significant success to the League of Ireland, this time playing for Shamrock Rovers. As the Hoops' skipper and playmaker, he led them as a virtual ever-present to the League Championship in 1984 and remarkably, to the League and FAI Cup double in each of the next three seasons. Not surprisingly, he was named PFAI 'Player of the Year' in 1983-84 – this accolade being followed by the Irish Footballer Writers' award in 1984-85.

Byrne (who won eight full caps for the Republic of Ireland) proved himself good enough to earn a first taste of World Cup football – albeit in the 4-1 defeat by Denmark in November 1985. Unfortunately for him, that was Eoin Hand's last match in charge. After Jack Charlton took charge, Byrne made just one more appearance for the national side.

Following his success with Shamrock Rovers, Byrne departed for Shelbourne before having a spell with Cobh Ramblers. In February 1994 he was appointed player-manager of the St James's Gate club.

Mick McCarthy

Position	Central defender
Born	Michael Joseph McCarthy, Barnsley, 7 February 1959

Clubs

Barnsley; Manchester City; Glasgow Celtic; Olympique Lyon (France); Millwall

International Caps	57
Inernational Goals	2

Matches

Year	Opponent	Result	Score	G
1984	Poland	drew	0-0	
1984	China	won	1-0	
1985	Mexico	drew	0-0	

Matches Continued				
Year	Opponent	Result	Score	G
1985	Denmark	lost	0-3	
1985	Italy	lost	1-2	
1985	Israel	drew	0-0	
1985	England	lost	1-2	
1985	Spain	drew	0-0	
1985	Switzerland	won	3-0	
1986	Switzerland	drew	0-0	
1986	USSR	lost	0-2	
1986	Wales	lost	0-1	
1986	Uruguay	drew	1-1	
1986	Iceland	won	2-1	
1986	Czechoslovakia	won	1-0	
1987	Scotland	drew	0-0	
1987	Poland	lost	0-1	
1987	Scotland	won	1-0	
1987	Bulgaria	lost	1-2	
1987	Belgium	drew	0-0	
1987	Brazil	won	1-0	
1987	Luxembourg	won	2-0	
1988	Bulgaria	won	2-0	
1988	Israel	won	5-0	
1988	Romania	won	2-0	
1988	Yugoslavia	won	2-0	1
1988	Norway	drew	0-0	
1988	England	won	1-0	
1988	USSR	drew	1-1	
1988	Holland	lost	0-1	
1989	N Ireland	drew	0-0	
1989	Tunisia	won	4-0	
1989	Spain	lost	0-2	
1989	France	drew	0-0	
1989	Hungary	drew	0-0	
1989	Spain	won	1-0	
1990	West Germany	drew	1-1	
1990	N Ireland	won	3-0	
1990	Wales	won	1-0	
1990	USSR	won	1-0	
1990	Finland	drew	1-1	
1990	Turkey	drew	0-0	
1990	England	drew	1-1	
1990	Egypt	drew	0-0	
1990	Holland	drew	1-1	
1990	Romania	drew	0-0 5-4 pen	
1990	Italy	lost	0-1	
1991	Morocco	won	1-0	
1991	Turkey	won	5-0	
1991	England	drew	1-1	
1991	United States	drew	1-1	
1992	Hungary	won	2-1	
1992	Turkey	won	3-1	
1992	Albania	won	2-0	
1992	United States	lost	1-3	1
1992	Italy	lost	0-2	
1992	Portugal	won	2-0	

Having begun his career with his hometown club Barnsley, Mick McCarthy was virtually a regular in the Tykes side throughout his time at Oakwell. He helped the Yorkshire club climb from the Fourth to the Second Division with promotions in 1978-79 and 1980-81. McCarthy's rugged, uncompromising displays at the heart of Barnsley's defence caught the attention of a number of clubs. In December 1983 he crossed the Pennines to join newly relegated Manchester City for a fee of £20,000.

The switch of clubs brought McCarthy to the attention of Republic of Ireland boss Eoin Hand. The central defender, who qualified for Ireland by virtue of his Waterford-born father, made his international debut in a friendly against Poland in May 1984. He gave a most-assured display alongside David O'Leary as the teams played out a goalless draw.

Back at Maine Road, he helped City win promotion to the First Division in 1984-85 and continued to give the club sterling service until the summer of 1987 when he joined Glasgow Celtic in a deal worth £500,000.

His first season at Parkhead ended in glory when the club claimed the 'double' of Premier League and Scottish Cup. The following campaign brought further success in the Cup, but in the League the Bhoys finished a rather disappointing third.

Following the appointment of Jack Charlton as national team manager, McCarthy found himself paired in the centre of defence with Kevin Moran. In November 1987 the Republic qualified for their first major tournament – the 1988 European Championships. McCarthy had played in six of the eight qualifiers and kept his place in the side for all three of Ireland's matches at the finals in Germany.

Mick McCarthy

McCarthy left Parkhead in April 1989 in an ill-fated move to French club Olympique Lyon, and in under a year returned to Football League action with Millwall. Though much of his time at The Den was disrupted by injuries (including surgery on his knee for a third time), he did help the Republic qualify for Italia '90.

McCarthy was Ireland's skipper: his and Jack Charlton's efforts were rewarded with a run to the last eight of the World Cup. Not surprisingly both men returned from the tournament as heroes.

In 1992, McCarthy replaced Bruce Rioch as manager of Millwall. When Charlton stood down as manager of the Republic of Ireland in February 1996, it was fitting that McCarthy should replace him. He led the Republic to the 2002 World Cup Finals before leaving to manage Sunderland, leading them into the Premiership in 2004-05 as First Division champions.

Jim Beglin

Position	Left-back
Born	James Martin Beglin, Waterford, 29 July 1963
Clubs	

Shamrock Rovers; Liverpool; Leeds United; Plymouth Argyle (loan); Blackburn Rovers (loan)

International Caps	15

Matches

Year	Opponent	Result	Score	G
1984	China	won	1-0	
1985	Mexico	drew	0-0	
1985	Denmark	lost	0-3	
1985	Italy	lost	1-2	
1985	Israel	drew	0-0	
1985	England	lost	1-2	
1985	Norway	drew	0-0	
1985	Switzerland	won	3-0	
1986	Switzerland	drew	0-0	
1986	USSR	lost	0-2	
1986	Denmark	lost	1-4	
1986	Wales	lost	0-1	
1987	Belgium	drew	2-2	
1987	Scotland	drew	0-0	
1987	Poland	lost	0-1	

Above: Jim Beglin

Jim Beglin, a left-back of the very highest quality, joined Liverpool from Shamrock Rovers for a fee of £25,000 in May 1983.

He spent his first season at Anfield in the club's Central League side but had progressed sufficiently to win a call-up from Eoin Hand for the Republic of Ireland team for two friendlies in the summer of 1984. In November of that year Beglin made his competitive debut for the Republic, in a World Cup qualifier against Denmark in Copenhagen. Though the Irish lost 3-0, Beglin played well and kept his place in the side for the next four games.

After replacing Alan Kennedy in the Liverpool side, Beglin helped the Reds win the League Championship and FA Cup in 1985-86. Just when it looked as if Beglin was destined to wear the No.3 shirt of both Liverpool and

the Republic for many years to come, disaster struck. In January 1987 during the League Cup quarter-final clash with Everton, Beglin sustained a particularly nasty leg injury – the medical diagnosis of the injury was a double compound commuted fracture. Simply, the tackle completely shattered his leg – an injury from which the 23-year-old defender would never fully recover. He was out of action for more than two years and though he recovered sufficient fitness to make a comeback, he was never able to regain his confidence or sharpness.

In the summer of 1989 he moved to Leeds United on a free transfer. Further injuries hampered his progress at Elland Road, though he did play his part in helping the Yorkshire club win the Second Division title in 1989-90. Unable to recapture the form which had made him a first team regular at Liverpool, he decided to go on loan to Plymouth Argyle and Blackburn Rovers. At the end of the 1991-92 season in which Leeds won the League Championship, he was forced into premature retirement.

Since then, like his former team-mate at both Liverpool and in the Republic of Ireland side, Mark Lawrenson, he has enjoyed success as a television pundit and commentator.

Gary Howlett

Position	Midfield
Born	Gary Patrick Howlett, Dublin, 2 April 1963
Clubs	

Home Farm; Coventry City; Brighton and Hove Albion; Bournemouth; Aldershot (loan); Chester City (loan); York City; Shelbourne

International Caps	1

Matches

Year	Opponent	Result	Score	G
1984	China	won	1-0	

A talented midfielder with an eye for goal, Gary Howlett played his early football with Home Farm before crossing the water to try his luck with Coventry City. Though he turned professional with the Highfield Road club he couldn't force his way into the Sky Blues side. In the summer of 1982 he was transferred to Brighton and Hove Albion.

He scored on his First Division debut for the Seagulls against Liverpool, and a few months later was a member of the Brighton side which drew 2-2 with Manchester United in the FA Cup Final but lost the replay 4-0. Though the south-coast club were relegated that season, Gary Howlett won four Under-21 caps for the Republic of Ireland.

Still only 21, he was given his full international debut in a Japan Cup match against China in June 1984 and though the Irish won 1-0, he made no further appearances in the green shirt.

In December 1984, Howlett was transferred to Bournemouth and in 1986-87 he helped the Cherries win the Third Division Championship. Following loan spells with Aldershot and Chester City, Howlett joined York City. Initially hampered by injury problems, he later established himself in the Minstermen's Fourth Division side. Having scored 13 goals in 101 games, his contract was somewhat surprisingly terminated and he returned to the League of Ireland to play for Shelbourne.

Following an operation to rebuild his ankle, he missed his club's appearance in the 1993 FAI Cup Final and then was left out of the side for the 1995 Final against Derry. The jinx continued the following year when he was again forced to sit out the final!

Alan Campbell

Position	Centre-forward
Born	Alan Campbell, Dublin, 1958

Clubs

Shamrock Rovers; Racing Santander (Spain)

International Caps	3

Matches

Year	Opponent	Result	Score	G
1985	Italy	lost	1-2	
1985	Israel	drew	0-0	
1985	Spain	drew	0-0	

Alan Campbell was a prolific goalscorer in the League of Ireland, coming to prominence with Shamrock Rovers.

Exceptionally quick-off-the-mark and a good header of the ball, he was the Hoops' leading scorer with 22 goals in 1979-80 – his first full season with the club. Towards the end of that season, Campbell had been joined up front by new signing Liam Buckley – the club's leading scorer for the next three seasons.

Following Buckley's departure to play his football in Belgium, Campbell again began to find the net with regularity. In 1983-84 he was the League of Ireland's top scorer with 24 goals in 26 games, helping Rovers to their first League Championship success in twenty years. The club just missed out on the 'double', losing to University College, Dublin in the 1984 FAI Cup Final.

In September 1984 Campbell parted company with the Hoops, joining Spanish club Racing Santander. He soon began to make a big impression. In February 1985 he made his full international debut for the Republic of Ireland, coming off the bench to replace John Byrne in a 2-1 defeat by Italy. He later appeared in two goalless draws against Israel and Spain, but with Jack

Charlton taking over the managerial reins shortly afterwards, Campbell's days in green were brought to a rather abrupt end.

John Byrne

Position	Forward
Born	John Frederick Byrne, Manchester, 1 February 1961

Clubs

York City; Queen's Park Rangers; Le Havre (France); Brighton and Hove Albion; Sunderland; Millwall; Brighton and Hove Albion (loan); Oxford United; Brighton and Hove Albion; Crawley Town

International Caps	23
International Goals	4

Matches

Year	Opponent	Result	Score	G
1985	Italy	lost	1-2	
1985	Israel	drew	0-0	
1985	England	lost	1-2	
1986	Uruguay	drew	1-1	
1987	Scotland	won	1-0	
1987	Belgium	drew	0-0	
1987	Brazil	won	1-0	
1987	Luxembourg	won	2-0	
1988	Luxembourg	won	2-1	
1988	Bulgaria	won	2-0	
1988	Israel	won	5-0	1
1988	Romania	won	2-0	
1988	Yugoslavia	won	2-0	
1988	Poland	won	3-1	
1990	West Germany	drew	1-1	
1990	Wales	won	1-0	
1990	Finland	drew	1-1	
1990	Turkey	drew	0-0	
1990	Malta	won	3-0	
1991	Wales	won	3-0	1
1992	Turkey	won	3-1	2
1992	Wales	lost	0-1	
1993	Wales	won	2-1	

Manchester-born forward John Byrne, who qualified for the Republic of Ireland by virtue of his Carlow-born father, began his career with York City. The powerful front man went on to score 55 goals in 175 League games for the Minstermen, including 27 in 1983-84, the season when the Bootham Crescent club won the Fourth Division Championship. Not surprisingly, Byrne was voted the Fourth

Above: John Byrne

himself in and out of the side. In May 1988 he left Loftus Road to play for French club Le Havre. Despite breaking his leg after just three months in France, he ended the 1988–89 season as the club's leading scorer.

After just two years with Le Havre, he returned to the Football League and in doing so became something of a nomad. He joined Brighton and Hove Albion and helped the Seagulls reach the Division Two play-offs in 1990-91. In October 1991 he was on the move again, this time to Sunderland, whose manager Dennis Smith paid £225,000 to take him to Roker Park.

He helped the Wearsiders go all the way to the 1992 FA Cup Final, with a goal in every round, but he failed to find the net in the final as Sunderland went down 2-0 to Liverpool. His next club was Millwall, but most of his time at The Den was spent on the treatment table. He had spells with Oxford United and Brighton (again) before moving into non-League football with Crawley Town.

Jack Charlton included him in the 1988 European Championships and 1990 World Cup squads. He was unable to make it into the line-up for any of the Republic's matches at either tournament, even though he remained a regular in the squad until the unsuccessful qualifying campaign for the 1992 European Championships.

Division 'Player of the Year'.

His prolific marksmanship brought him to the attention of scouts from a number of top clubs. In the close season, First Division Queen's Park Rangers paid £115,000 for his services.

Within four months of his arrival at Loftus Road, Byrne had been called into Eoin Hand's Republic of Ireland squad, for the game against Italy at Dalymount Park. He made a couple more appearances under Hand, both as substitute. The role was to become a familiar one to the striker throughout his international career.

With Rangers Byrne collected a League Cup runners-up medal, after they had gone down 3-0 to Oxford United in the 1986 League Cup Final. When Jim Smith replaced Alan Mullery as Rangers' boss, Byrne found

Paul McGrath

Position	Central defender/Midfield
Born	Paul McGrath, Ealing, 4 December 1959

Clubs

St Patrick's Athletic; Manchester United; Aston Villa; Derby County; Sheffield United

International Caps	83
International Goals	8

Matches

Year	Opponent	Result	Score	G
1985	Italy	lost	1-2	
1985	Israel	drew	0-0	
1985	England	lost	1-2	
1985	Norway	drew	0-0	
1985	Switzerland	won	3-0	
1986	Switzerland	drew	0-0	
1986	Denmark	lost	1-4	
1986	Wales	lost	0-1	
1986	Iceland	won	2-1	1
1986	Czechoslovakia	won	1-0	
1987	Belgium	drew	2-2	
1987	Scotland	drew	0-0	
1987	Poland	lost	0-1	
1987	Scotland	won	1-0	
1987	Bulgaria	lost	1-2	
1987	Belgium	drew	0-0	
1987	Brazil	won	1-0	
1987	Luxembourg	won	2-0	
1988	Luxembourg	won	2-1	1
1988	Bulgaria	won	2-0	1
1988	Yugoslavia	won	2-0	
1988	Poland	won	3-1	
1988	Norway	drew	0-0	
1988	England	won	1-0	
1988	Holland	lost	0-1	
1989	N Ireland	drew	0-0	
1989	France	drew	0-0	
1989	Hungary	drew	0-0	
1989	Spain	won	1-0	
1989	Malta	won	2-0	
1989	Hungary	won	2-0	1
1990	West Germany	drew	1-1	
1990	Malta	won	2-0	
1990	USSR	won	1-0	
1990	Finland	drew	1-1	
1990	Turkey	drew	0-0	
1990	England	drew	1-1	
1990	Egypt	drew	0-0	
1990	Holland	drew	1-1	
1990	Romania	drew	0-0 5-4 pen	
1990	Italy	lost	0-1	
1991	England	drew	1-1	
1991	Wales	won	3-0	
1991	England	drew	1-1	
1991	Poland	drew	0-0	

Year	Opponent	Result	Score	G
1991	Chile	drew	1-1	
1991	United States	drew	1-1	
1992	Poland	drew	3-3	1
1992	Turkey	won	3-1	
1992	Switzerland	won	2-1	
1992	United States	won	4-1	
1992	Albania	won	2-0	1
1992	United States	lost	1-3	
1992	Italy	lost	0-2	
1992	Portugal	won	2-0	
1993	Latvia	won	4-0	
1993	Spain	drew	0-0	
1993	N Ireland	won	3-0	
1993	Denmark	drew	1-1	
1993	Latvia	won	2-0	1
1993	Lithuania	won	1-0	
1994	Lithuania	won	2-0	
1994	N Ireland	drew	1-1	
1994	Germany	won	2-0	
1994	Czech Republic	lost	1-3	
1994	Italy	won	1-0	
1994	Mexico	lost	1-2	
1994	Norway	drew	0-0	
1994	Holland	lost	0-2	
1995	Latvia	won	3-0	
1995	N Ireland	won	4-0	
1995	England	won	1-0	
1995	N Ireland	drew	1-1	
1995	Portugal	won	1-0	
1995	Liechtenstein	drew	0-0	
1995	Austria	lost	1-3	
1996	Austria	lost	1-3	1
1996	Latvia	won	2-1	
1996	Portugal	lost	0-3	
1996	Holland	lost	0-2	
1996	Russia	lost	0-2	
1996	Czech Republic	lost	0-2	
1997	Wales	drew	0-0	

One of the greatest defenders ever to have worn the green shirt of the Republic of Ireland, Paul McGrath was born in Ealing, west London. He was two months old when his Irish mother took him to live in Monkstown. He played his early football for Pearse Rovers before moving to Leinster Senior League side Dalkey United. He quickly became their star player, and in the autumn of 1981 stepped up to the League of Ireland with St Patrick's Athletic. He proved a revelation at St Pat's too, and in 1981–82 was voted PFAI 'Player of the Year'.

Manchester United's late Irish scout Billy Behan liked what he saw and in April 1982 McGrath was on his way to Old Trafford for a bargain £30,000 plus extra payments for international and first team appearances. It was midway

Above: Paul McGrath

through the 1984-85 season before McGrath established himself as a first team regular with United – a season in which international recognition also came his way. He made his debut as a substitute in the match against Italy at Dalymount Park. The match ended in a 2-1 defeat but McGrath had given a polished display against the World Cup holders and won further caps in his country's next three games. At the end of that season, he claimed an FA Cup winners' medal after a commanding display at the heart of United's defence, in the 10-man victory over Everton.

When Jack Charlton was appointed Republic of Ireland manager, McGrath played in all but one of the big man's first 14 matches in charge. It was during this spell that McGrath played in a new pivotal role – a midfield sweeper playing just in front of the back four. The switch proved a huge success and the Republic qualified for the 1988 European Championships, with McGrath scoring in the last two qualifying matches against Luxembourg and Bulgaria.

During his time at Old Trafford McGrath was plagued by injury, perhaps an indication of the way he played, and in only one season managed to play more than half the matches. In 1989 just as United were about to scoop up every honour in domestic football, he moved to Aston Villa for £400,000.

His new surroundings at Villa Park seemed to agree with him however, and he was soon the fulcrum around which an impressive Villa side operated. Maintaining his fitness through a programme of exercises devised by the Villa physio, he enjoyed a seven-season run in the first team at Villa Park. In 1992-93 he helped Villa finish runners-up to Manchester United in the new Premier League and was voted PFA 'Player of the Year'.

At international level, he helped the Republic

of Ireland to the final stages of both the 1990 and 1994 World Cups. In his latter years in the national side he reverted to his preferred position of centre-half. It was from this position that he gave his greatest performance in a green shirt – the 1-0 victory over Italy at USA '94. He continued to command a place in the Republic of Ireland line-up until the end of the qualifying campaign for Euro '96. Shortly afterwards he parted company with Villa and had brief spells with Derby County and Sheffield United before hanging up his boots in 1998.

Tony Cascarino

Position	Forward
Born	Anthony Guy Cascarino, Orpington, 1 September 1962

Clubs

Crockenhill; Gillingham; Millwall; Aston Villa; Glasgow Celtic; Chelsea; Olympique Marseille (France); AS Nancy-Lorraine (France)

International Caps	88
International Goals	19

Matches

Year	Opponent	Result	Score	G
1986	Switzerland	drew	0-0	
1986	USSR	lost	0-2	
1986	Denmark	lost	1-4	
1988	Poland	won	3-1	1
1988	Norway	drew	0-0	
1988	USSR	drew	1-1	
1988	Holland	lost	0-1	
1989	N Ireland	drew	0-0	
1989	Tunisia	won	4-0	2
1989	Spain	lost	0-2	
1989	France	drew	0-0	
1989	Hungary	drew	0-0	
1989	Spain	won	1-0	
1989	Malta	won	2-0	
1989	Hungary	won	2-0	1
1990	West Germany	drew	1-1	
1990	N Ireland	won	3-0	1
1990	Malta	won	2-0	
1990	Wales	won	1-0	
1990	Finland	drew	1-1	
1990	Turkey	drew	0-0	
1990	England	drew	1-1	
1990	Egypt	drew	0-0	

Matches Continued

Year	Opponent	Result	Score	G
1990	Holland	drew	1-1	
1990	Romania	drew	0-0	
			5-4 pen	
1990	Italy	lost	0-1	
1991	Morocco	won	1-0	
1991	Turkey	won	5-0	
1991	England	drew	1-1	1
1991	England	drew	1-1	
1991	Poland	drew	0-0	
1991	Chile	drew	1-1	
1991	United States	drew	1-1	1
1992	Poland	drew	3-3	1
1992	Turkey	won	3-1	1
1992	Wales	lost	0-1	
1992	Switzerland	won	2-1	
1992	United States	won	4-1	1
1993	Wales	won	2-1	
1993	N Ireland	won	3-0	
1993	Denmark	drew	1-1	
1993	Albania	won	2-1	1
1993	Latvia	won	2-0	
1994	Lithuania	won	2-0	
1994	Spain	lost	1-3	
1994	N Ireland	drew	1-1	
1994	Russia	drew	0-0	
1994	Bolivia	won	1-0	
1994	Germany	won	2-0	1
1994	Czech Republic	lost	1-3	
1994	Holland	lost	0-2	
1995	Latvia	won	3-0	
1995	N Ireland	drew	1-1	
1995	Portugal	won	1-0	
1995	Liechtenstein	drew	0-0	
1995	Austria	lost	1-3	
1996	Austria	lost	1-3	
1996	Portugal	lost	0-3	
1996	Holland	lost	0-2	
1996	Russia	lost	0-2	
1996	Portugal	lost	0-1	
1996	Croatia	drew	2-2	
1996	Holland	lost	1-3	
1997	Liechtenstein	won	5-0	
1997	Macedonia	won	3-0	2
1997	Iceland	drew	0-0	
1997	Wales	drew	0-0	
1997	Macedonia	lost	2-3	
1997	Romania	lost	0-1	
1997	Liechtenstein	won	5-0	2
1998	Lithuania	drew	0-0	
1998	Iceland	won	4-2	
1998	Lithuania	won	2-1	2
1998	Romania	drew	1-1	1
1998	Belgium	drew	1-1	
1998	Belgium	lost	1-2	
1999	Croatia	won	2-0	
1999	Malta	won	5-0	
1999	Yugoslavia	lost	0-1	
1999	Paraguay	won	2-0	
1999	Sweden	won	2-0	
1999	N Ireland	lost	0-1	

Tony Cascarino had more than his fair share of criticism over the years but he always bounced back to let his football do the talking.

He began his Football League career with Gillingham. His form led to the 23-year-old making his international debut for the Republic of Ireland in a World Cup qualifier against Switzerland in Berne. Though the game ended goalless, the newcomer had impressed enough to keep his place for the next couple of games.

Cascarino spent six seasons at the Priestfield Stadium, being top-scorer in four of them. He had scored 78 goals in 219 League outings for the Kent club when in the summer of 1987 he was transferred to Millwall (the team he had supported as a boy) for a fee of £250,000. Linking up with Teddy Sheringham, the two of them terrorised Second Division defences. With Cascarino netting 20 goals in 39 games, the Lions won promotion to the top flight as Division Two champions.

His goalscoring feats saw Cascarino return to the Republic of Ireland side in a friendly against Poland which the Irish won 3-1. It proved enough to earn him a place in the squad for Euro '88. Cascarino was ever-present in the Republic's qualifying campaign for the 1990 World Cup Finals. On the domestic front Millwall were heading for relegation, and so in March 1990 he joined Aston Villa for £1.5 million.

The switch proved a huge disappointment, with Villa hoping to land the League Championship, Cascarino failed to score in his first eight games for the club.

Above: Tony Cascarino

There was to be more disappointment for Cascarino at the World Cup Finals in Italy during the summer. After two games without a goal, he was relegated to the bench for the Republic's next match against Holland. During the following decade, Cascarino became a specialist No.12 for the Republic. In fact, no player has made more appearances off the bench for the boys in green than Cascarino.

After another season with Aston Villa he was sold to Scottish giants Celtic for a cut-price £1.1 million. The move was ill-fated and he found himself playing second fiddle to Tommy Coyne and Charlie Nicholas. In January 1992 he joined Chelsea in a straight swap deal which took Tommy Boyd to Parkhead. In his second season at Stamford Bridge, Cascarino was laid low by two cartilage operations and found injury piling upon injury. On making a full recovery, he was freed by Chelsea. He secured a move to French club Olympique Marseille, where his career enjoyed a surprising and successful Indian summer. He finished his first season in France as the country's top scorer before moving on to enjoy further success with AS Nancy-Lorraine.

John Aldridge

Position	Forward
Born	John William Aldridge, Liverpool, 18 September 1958
Clubs	

South Liverpool; Newport County; Oxford United; Liverpool; Real Sociedad (Spain); Tranmere Rovers

International Caps	69
International Goals	19

Matches

Year	Opponent	Result	Score	G
1986	Wales	lost	0-1	
1986	Uruguay	drew	1-1	
1986	Iceland	won	2-1	
1986	Czechoslovakia	won	1-0	
1987	Belgium	drew	2-2	

Matches Continued

Year	Opponent	Result	Score	G
1987	Scotland	drew	0-0	
1987	Poland	lost	0-1	
1987	Scotland	won	1-0	
1987	Bulgaria	lost	1-2	
1987	Belgium	drew	0-0	
1987	Brazil	won	1-0	
1987	Luxembourg	won	2-0	
1988	Bulgaria	won	1-0	
1988	Poland	won	3-1	
1988	Norway	drew	0-0	
1988	England	won	1-0	
1988	USSR	drew	1-1	
1988	Holland	lost	0-1	
1989	N Ireland	drew	0-0	
1989	Tunisia	won	4-0	1
1989	Spain	lost	0-2	
1989	France	drew	0-0	
1989	Hungary	drew	0-0	
1989	Malta	won	2-0	
1989	Hungary	won	2-0	
1990	West Germany	drew	1-1	
1990	N Ireland	won	3-0	
1990	Malta	won	2-0	2
1990	Finland	drew	1-1	
1990	Turkey	drew	0-0	
1990	England	drew	1-1	
1990	Egypt	drew	0-0	
1990	Holland	drew	1-1	
1990	Romania	drew	0-0 5-4 pen	
1990	Italy	lost	0-1	
1991	Turkey	won	5-0	3
1991	England	drew	1-1	
1991	England	drew	1-1	
1991	Poland	drew	0-0	
1992	Hungary	won	2-1	
1992	Turkey	won	3-1	
1992	Wales	lost	0-1	
1992	Switzerland	won	2-1	1
1992	United States	won	4-1	
1992	Albania	won	2-0	1
1992	Italy	lost	0-2	
1992	Portugal	won	2-0	
1993	Latvia	won	4-0	3
1993	Denmark	drew	0-0	
1993	Spain	drew	0-0	
1993	Denmark	drew	1-1	
1993	Albania	won	2-1	
1993	Latvia	won	2-0	1
1993	Lithuania	won	1-0	
1994	Lithuania	won	2-0	1
1994	N Ireland	drew	1-1	
1994	Czech Republic	lost	1-3	
1994	Italy	won	1-0	
1994	Mexico	lost	1-2	1
1994	Norway	drew	0-0	
1995	Latvia	won	3-0	2
1995	N Ireland	won	4-0	1
1995	Portugal	won	1-0	
1995	Liechtenstein	drew	0-0	

Matches Continued

Year	Opponent	Result	Score	G
1996	Latvia	won	2-1	2
1996	Portugal	lost	0-3	
1996	Holland	lost	0-2	
1996	Russia	lost	0-2	
1997	Macedonia	won	3-0	

A Liverpool fan since childhood, John Aldridge harboured an ambition to step down from the terraces of the Kop to play for the Reds. After a trial as a 14-year-old he was told they would be back in touch – it took another 14 years for the phone to ring!

After playing part-time for South Liverpool, he joined Newport County in April 1979 after finishing his apprenticeship as a British Leyland toolmaker. After five seasons at Somerton Park, he took his goalscoring touch to Oxford United in a £78,000 deal. He helped the Manor Ground side win promotion from Division Three to Division One in successive seasons and victory in the League Cup Final of 1986.

International honours eluded Aldridge until he was 27, when under the grandparent rule he made his Republic of Ireland debut against Wales in Jack Charlton's first match in charge. However, to everyone's surprise, Aldridge failed to score in his first 20 internationals! Despite his lack of goals, John Aldridge was a crucial factor in the Republic of Ireland side. He played in seven of the eight qualifiers for the 1988 European Championship and appeared in all three matches at the tournament finals in Germany.

When it became clear that Liverpool's Ian Rush would be joining Juventus, the way was finally clear for Aldridge to realise his big dream: in January 1987 he joined Liverpool for £750,000. 'Aldo' flourished at Anfield

John Aldridge

where he had three highly successful seasons, scoring 61 goals in 103 League and Cup games. It was in season 1987-88 that he hit the headlines, for after scoring in the opening nine League matches, his clinical finishing brought him 29 League and Cup goals. However, though he was a ferocious and accurate penalty-taker, he was completely devastated to miss in that season's FA Cup Final against Wimbledon, as it robbed the Reds of a much-deserved 'double'! When Rush returned from Italy it became obvious that Anfield was not big enough for both of them, and Aldridge joined Spanish club Real Sociedad for £1.1 million.

It was as a Sociedad player that he travelled to Italy for the 1990 World Cup Finals. Charlton's tactics had changed since the 1988 European Championships, and though he worked tirelessly in all five games at Italia '90, Aldridge failed to find the net.

His exploits in Spain earned him the nickname 'El Zorro' after he became the first Real player to score in six consecutive matches. After two years with the club and 40 goals in 76 games, he returned to Merseyside with Tranmere Rovers. In his first season at Prenton Park, Aldridge equalled Bunny Bell's record of 1933-34 by scoring 40 goals. The move to Tranmere also preceded his best run of scoring for the Republic.

He hit six goals in 10 games during qualification for the 1994 World Cup Finals, and made three appearances during the finals in the United States. Starting the game against Mexico on the bench, he was about to replace Tommy Coyne, as the Irish trailed 2-0 – officials intervened to prevent him doing so until an administrative hitch had been resolved. After a six-minute delay during which time the Republic were down to 10-men, Aldridge entered the fray and scored with a well-taken header which

proved decisive to his team's progress to the second round. He went on to score five goals in his last nine appearances – a complete contrast to his start in international football – finishing with a highly respectable total of 19 goals.

At Tranmere he was the club's top scorer for six successive seasons before becoming player-manager in April 1996 following the departure of John King. Having scored 174 goals in 294 games for Rovers, he decided to concentrate fully on management. Despite taking them to the 2000 League Cup Final, he later parted company with the Wirral club.

Ray Houghton

Position	Midfield
Born	Raymond James Houghton, Glasgow, 9 January 1962

Clubs

West Ham United; Fulham; Oxford United; Liverpool; Aston Villa; Crystal Palace; Reading

International Caps	73
International Goals	6

Matches

Year	Opponent	Result	Score	G
1986	Wales	lost	0-1	
1986	Uruguay	drew	1-1	
1986	Iceland	won	2-1	
1986	Czechoslovakia	won	1-0	
1987	Belgium	drew	2-2	
1987	Scotland	drew	0-0	
1987	Poland	lost	0-1	
1987	Scotland	won	1-0	
1987	Belgium	drew	0-0	
1987	Luxembourg	won	2-0	
1988	Luxembourg	won	2-1	
1988	Bulgaria	won	2-0	
1988	Israel	won	5-0	
1988	Yugoslavia	won	2-0	
1988	Norway	drew	0-0	
1988	England	won	1-0	1
1988	USSR	drew	1-1	
1988	Holland	lost	0-1	
1989	N Ireland	drew	0-0	
1989	Tunisia	won	4-0	
1989	Spain	lost	0-2	

Matches Continued

Year	Opponent	Result	Score	G
1989	France	drew	0-0	
1989	Hungary	drew	0-0	
1989	Spain	won	1-0	
1989	Malta	won	2-0	1
1989	Hungary	won	2-0	
1990	N Ireland	won	3-0	1
1990	Malta	won	2-0	
1990	Finland	drew	1-1	
1990	England	drew	1-1	
1990	Egypt	drew	0-0	
1990	Holland	drew	1-1	
1990	Romania	drew	0-0	
			5-4 pen	
1990	Italy	lost	0-1	
1991	Morocco	won	1-0	
1991	Turkey	won	5-0	
1991	England	drew	1-1	
1991	England	drew	1-1	
1991	Poland	drew	0-0	
1991	Chile	drew	1-1	
1991	United States	drew	1-1	
1992	Hungary	won	2-1	
1992	Albania	won	2-0	
1992	United States	lost	1-3	
1992	Italy	lost	0-2	
1992	Portugal	won	2-0	
1993	Denmark	drew	0-0	
1993	Spain	drew	0-0	
1993	N Ireland	won	3-0	
1993	Denmark	drew	1-1	
1993	Albania	won	2-1	
1993	Latvia	won	2-0	
1993	Lithuania	won	1-0	
1994	Lithuania	won	2-0	
1994	Spain	lost	1-3	
1994	N Ireland	drew	1-1	
1994	Bolivia	won	1-0	
1994	Germany	won	2-0	
1994	Italy	won	1-0	1
1994	Mexico	lost	1-2	
1994	Norway	drew	0-0	
1994	Holland	lost	0-2	
1995	Portugal	won	1-0	
1995	Austria	lost	1-3	1
1996	Austria	lost	1-3	
1996	Czech Republic	lost	0-2	
1997	Liechtenstein	won	5-0	
1997	Romania	lost	0-1	
1997	Liechtenstein	won	5-0	
1998	Lithuania	drew	0-0	
1998	Romania	drew	1-1	
1998	Belgium	drew	1-1	
1998	Belgium	lost	1-2	1

One of the most consistent performers in the era of Jack Charlton, industrious midfielder Ray Houghton began his League career with

West Ham United but after getting few chances, he joined Fulham in 1982. An ever-present in his first season at Craven Cottage, Houghton graced Fulham's side for three seasons before Oxford United, who were then in the top flight paid £125,000 for his services.

The Manor Ground club went on to win the League Cup, Houghton scoring the second goal in the final in a 3-0 win over Queen's Park Rangers. Also in his first season with Oxford, the Scotsman won the first of 73 caps, electing to represent the Republic of Ireland, his father's homeland.

In October 1987 Houghton joined Liverpool, his value having soared to £825,000. Ending his first season at Anfield with a League Championship winners' medal, Houghton joined team-mates John Aldridge and Ronnie Whelan in the Republic of Ireland side for the 1988 European Championships.

He played in all three of the Republic's games and scored his first international goal with a much-celebrated header after five minutes of the opening game against England. The goal went on to give the Republic victory over a much-fancied England team and made Houghton a hero in his adopted country. His performances at international level prompted the interest of a number of Italian clubs but Dalglish refused to part with him.

He was in outstanding form in 1988-89, being an ever-present in the Liverpool side. They narrowly failed to take the League title but won the FA Cup, beating Everton 3-2 in the final. Sadly injuries caused Houghton to miss much of the 1989-90 season but he bounced back towards the end of the campaign to help the Liverpool cause.

Right: Ray Houghton

He appeared in all eight qualifying matches for the 1990 World Cup and was also ever-present at the finals in Italy.

Back at Anfield he did not seem to figure in Graeme Souness's plans, and was surprisingly sold to Aston Villa during the summer of 1992 for a little under £1 million. Linking up with fellow Republic of Ireland internationals Andy Townsend and Steve Staunton, he helped Villa win the League Cup before returning to London to play for Crystal Palace.

Throughout the early 1990s Ray Houghton remained a vital player for the Republic of Ireland. He missed just one of the qualifiers for the 1994 World Cup. Of course at the finals he scored the only goal of the game against Italy when he lobbed Pagliuca – a goal that would live long in the memory!

Having helped Palace regain their top-flight status via the play-offs, he joined Reading as player-coach. After new manager Tommy Boyd brought in his own coaching staff, Houghton left the Royals. Whilst with Reading he brought the curtain down on his international career with a substitute appearance in the World Cup play-off match against Belgium in 1997 – the Republic lost 2-1 but Houghton signed off by scoring their goal.

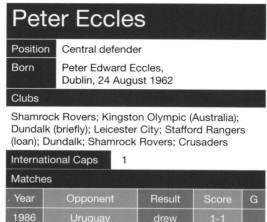

Peter Eccles

Position	Central defender
Born	Peter Edward Eccles, Dublin, 24 August 1962
Clubs	

Shamrock Rovers; Kingston Olympic (Australia); Dundalk (briefly); Leicester City; Stafford Rangers (loan); Dundalk; Shamrock Rovers; Crusaders

International Caps	1

Matches

Year	Opponent	Result	Score	G
1986	Uruguay	drew	1-1	

A tall central defender, Peter Eccles began his League of Ireland career with Shamrock Rovers, whom he joined from St Brendan's in 1981. Eccles won League Championship medals in successive seasons from 1983-84 to 1986-87, and FAI Cup winners' medals in 1987 and 1988.

The red-headed stopper holds the record for the shortest international career of any Republic of Ireland player. He came off the bench for the injured Ray Houghton in the 80th minute of Jack Charlton's second game in charge – a 1-1 draw against Uruguay at Lansdowne Road in April 1986.

After spending the summer of 1988 playing in Australia for Kingston Olympic, he joined Leicester City on a free transfer. Embarrassed by the pace of his sole Football League game – substituted at half-time – he was released by David Pleat.

He returned to Shamrock Rovers in 1991 and two years later was voted their 'Player of the Year'. In 1993-94 he captained the Hoops to the League Championship after which he moved north to play Irish League football for Crusaders. In only his fourth game for Crusaders, Eccles broke his leg, although a year later he was back in the thick of the action.

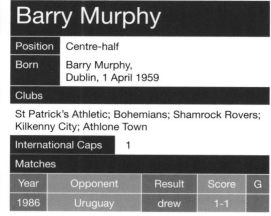

Barry Murphy

Position	Centre-half
Born	Barry Murphy, Dublin, 1 April 1959
Clubs	

St Patrick's Athletic; Bohemians; Shamrock Rovers; Kilkenny City; Athlone Town

International Caps	1

Matches

Year	Opponent	Result	Score	G
1986	Uruguay	drew	1-1	

Centre-half Barry Murphy played his early football for St Patrick's Athletic. In 1979-80 he was a member of the side that lost the FAI Cup and League Cup Finals to Waterford and Athlone Town respectively.

Within two seasons he had joined Bohemians, managed at the time by Billy Young. Though he didn't score too many goals, he netted one against Sligo in the 1983 FAI Cup Final – this proved to be a consolation strike as the Dubliners lost 2-1.

Murphy (a gas converter by trade) was surprisingly called into the Republic of Ireland side by Jack Charlton in April 1986, for the match against Uruguay. Injuries to Paul McGrath and David O'Leary, plus a recommendation by the Republic's physio Mick Byrne, saw him start the game. Lining up alongside Mick McCarthy in the heart of the Republic's defence, he had a sound game in a 1-1 draw against the South American side – sadly it proved to be his only cap.

Murphy had seen his side Bohemians finish in the top four of the League of Ireland in each of his ten seasons there. He opted for a move to Shamrock Rovers in 1988. Whilst with the Hoops he played in his third FAI Cup Final – his third on the losing side!

Towards the end of 1991, he departed for Kilkenny. Two years later, he joined Athlone Town where he ended his career.

Liam O'Brien

Position	Midfield
Born	Liam Francis O'Brien, Dublin, 5 September 1964

Clubs

Stella Maris; Bohemians; Cleveland (U.S.); Shamrock Rovers; Manchester United; Newcastle United; Tranmere Rovers

International Caps	16

Matches

Year	Opponent	Result	Score	G
1986	Uruguay	drew	1-1	
1987	Brazil	won	1-0	
1988	Israel	won	5-0	
1988	Romania	won	2-0	
1988	Yugoslavia	won	2-0	
1988	Poland	won	3-1	
1989	Tunisia	won	4-0	
1989	Spain	lost	0-2	
1992	Switzerland	won	2-1	
1993	Wales	won	2-1	
1994	Russia	drew	0-0	
1996	Croatia	drew	2-2	
1996	Holland	lost	1-3	
1996	United States	lost	1-2	
1996	Bolivia	won	3-0	
1997	Macedonia	won	3-0	

Liam O'Brien, like many Republic of Ireland internationals, began his career with junior club Stella Maris. He then had a brief spell in the League of Ireland with Bohemians and in the NASL with Cleveland Ohio. In 1983 he joined Shamrock Rovers: in each of his first three seasons with the club, they won the League of Ireland Championship.

O'Brien made his full international debut for the Republic of Ireland against Uruguay in April 1986, in Jack Charlton's second game in charge.

In October of that year he joined Manchester United for a fee of £50,000 – the Old

Above: Liam O'Brien

Trafford club also agreed to two challenge matches with the Hoops, in which O'Brien captained his new club against his old. At Old Trafford, O'Brien found it difficult to get a game on a regular basis due to the wealth of talent in United's midfield. Robson, Strachan and Whiteside formed United's engine room and so in November 1988, he left and joined Newcastle United.

The £275,000 deal was struck in somewhat controversial circumstances. O'Brien was disappointed at his lack of first team opportunities with the Reds: although United wanted him to stay, they couldn't guarantee him a starting place. Consequently the offer of a new contract was rejected in preference to signing for the Magpies.

Injuries – a broken leg and ligament problems – disrupted the early part of his

time on Tyneside but in 1992-93 he began to fulfil his potential. He was instrumental in the club winning that season's 'new' First Division Championship. Unfortunately for O'Brien, his best form had coincided with Republic of Ireland manager Jack Charlton settling on a midfield of Keane, Houghton, Townsend and Staunton.

In January 1994 O'Brien moved to Tranmere Rovers for a fee of £250,000 – he had made just six Premiership appearances for the north-east club. Whilst on the Wirral, O'Brien retained his place as an occasional player for the Republic of Ireland. He was delighted to be recalled to the international squad by new manager Mick McCarthy in 1996, and jetted off on their tour of the United States. Injuries finally caught up with the popular midfielder and in the summer of 1999 he decided to retire. Sadly, his total of 16 caps is scant recognition for a player of such undeniable talent.

Mick Kennedy

Position	Midfield
Born	Michael Francis Martin Kennedy, Salford, 9 April 1961

Clubs

Halifax Town; Huddersfield Town; Middlesbrough; Portsmouth; Bradford City; Leicester City; Luton Town; Stoke City; Chesterfield; Wigan Athletic

International Caps	2

Matches

Year	Opponent	Result	Score	G
1986	Iceland	won	2-1	
1986	Czechoslovakia	won	1-0	

An aggressive left-sided midfielder, Mick Kennedy's performances in Halifax Town's engine room quickly caught the attention of a number of First Division clubs including Everton, Liverpool and Spurs. The Yorkshire club's board said he was 'not for sale', but Kennedy refused the offer of a new contract.

In the summer of 1980 he moved to Fourth Division champions Huddersfield Town for a club record fee of £50,000.

It was while at Leeds Road that he developed his ball-winning skills, drawing admiration from many for his drive and commitment. After exactly two years with Huddersfield, he joined Middlesbrough for £100,000. In June 1984 he signed for Boro's Second Division rivals Portsmouth.

With the south coast club Kennedy got his chance in the Republic of Ireland side, playing in two successive victories over Iceland and Czechoslovakia. Having helped Portsmouth into Division One in 1987 and his next club Bradford City into the play-offs in 1988, he joined Leicester City. Showing few signs of matching his combativeness with creativity, he was on his way to Luton Town. Again, he spent just one season with the Hatters before joining Third Division Stoke City for £250,000 in August 1990. Two seasons passed at the Victoria Ground before he joined Chesterfield. Kennedy later ended his first-class career with his tenth club Wigan Athletic – although in almost all of his starts for the Latics he was substituted – prior to being released in the summer of 1994.

Niall Quinn

Position	Forward
Born	Niall John Quinn, Dublin, 6 October 1966

Clubs
Arsenal; Manchester City; Sunderland

International Caps	91
International Goals	21

Matches

Year	Opponent	Result	Score	G
1986	Iceland	won	2-1	
1986	Czechoslovakia	won	1-0	

Matches Continued

Year	Opponent	Result	Score	G
1987	Bulgaria	lost	1-2	
1987	Brazil	won	1-0	
1988	Luxembourg	won	2-1	
1988	Bulgaria	won	2-0	
1988	Israel	won	5-0	1
1988	Romania	won	2-0	
1988	Poland	won	3-1	
1988	England	won	1-0	
1989	Tunisia	won	4-0	
1989	Spain	lost	0-2	
1989	Hungary	drew	0-0	
1990	USSR	won	1-0	
1990	Malta	won	3-0	1
1990	Egypt	drew	0-0	
1990	Holland	drew	1-1	1
1990	Romania	drew	0-0 5-4 pen	
1990	Italy	lost	0-1	
1991	Morocco	won	1-0	
1991	Turkey	won	5-0	1
1991	England	drew	1-1	
1991	Wales	won	3-0	2
1991	England	drew	1-1	1
1991	Poland	drew	0-0	
1992	Hungary	won	2-1	
1992	Wales	lost	0-1	
1992	United States	won	4-1	1
1992	Albania	won	2-0	
1992	United States	lost	1-3	
1992	Italy	lost	0-2	
1992	Portugal	won	2-0	
1993	Latvia	won	4-0	
1993	Denmark	drew	0-0	
1993	Spain	drew	0-0	
1993	N Ireland	won	3-0	1
1993	Denmark	drew	1-1	1
1993	Albania	won	2-1	
1993	Latvia	won	2-0	
1993	Lithuania	won	1-0	
1994	Lithuania	won	2-0	
1994	Spain	lost	1-3	
1994	N Ireland	drew	1-1	
1995	Latvia	won	3-0	
1995	Liechtenstein	won	4-0	2
1995	N Ireland	won	4-0	
1995	England	won	1-0	
1995	N Ireland	drew	1-1	1
1995	Portugal	won	1-0	
1995	Liechtenstein	drew	0-0	
1995	Austria	lost	1-3	
1995	Austria	lost	1-3	
1996	Latvia	won	2-1	
1996	Portugal	lost	0-3	
1996	Russia	lost	0-2	
1996	Czech Republic	lost	0-2	
1996	Portugal	lost	0-1	
1996	Croatia	drew	2-2	1
1996	Holland	lost	1-3	
1996	United States	lost	1-2	
1997	Liechtenstein	won	5-0	2

Matches Continued

Year	Opponent	Result	Score	G
1998	Lithuania	won	2-1	
1998	Argentina	lost	0-2	
1999	Malta	won	5-0	1
1999	Yugoslavia	lost	0-1	
1999	Paraguay	won	2-0	
1999	Sweden	won	2-0	
1999	N Ireland	lost	0-1	
1999	Macedonia	won	1-0	1
2000	Yugoslavia	won	2-1	
2000	Croatia	lost	0-2	
2000	Malta	won	3-2	
2000	Macedonia	drew	1-1	1
2000	Turkey	drew	0-0	
2000	Czech Republic	won	3-2	
2000	Scotland	lost	1-2	
2000	Mexico	drew	2-2	
2000	United States	drew	1-1	
2000	South Africa	won	2-1	1
2001	Holland	drew	2-2	
2001	Portugal	drew	1-1	
2001	Estonia	won	2-0	
2001	Portugal	drew	1-1	
2001	Estonia	won	2-0	
2002	Holland	won	1-0	
2002	Cyprus	won	4-0	1
2002	Iran	won	2-0	
2002	Russia	won	2-0	
2002	Germany	drew	1-1	
2002	Saudi Arabia	won	3-0	
2002	Spain	drew	1-1	

Spotted by Arsenal playing junior football for Manortown United, he made his first team debut for the Gunners in December 1985, scoring a goal in a 2-0 win over Liverpool.

The young Gunner won his first cap for the Republic of Ireland against Iceland in May 1986 and became a regular on the Republic bench thereafter. Having earned a League Cup winners' medal with Arsenal in 1987, he made three substitute appearances for the Republic in the qualifying rounds of the 1988 European Championships and gained a place in the squad. His only action at Euro '88 was as a second-half substitute for Frank Stapleton in the game against England.

Following the signing of Alan Smith, Quinn's first team opportunities at Highbury were reduced and he found himself languishing in the reserves. He was eventually rescued from obscurity when signing for Manchester City for a fee of £800,000 in March 1990.

He marked his debut for the Blues with a goal in a 1-1 draw against Chelsea. Three more strikes by the end of the season secured his place in the Republic of Ireland's World Cup squad for Italy. He was on the bench for the opening game against England. A substitute appearance followed in the second match against Egypt before Quinn at last made the Republic of Ireland starting line-up. He played for the full ninety minutes against Holland, and scored the equaliser which sent the Republic into the second round of the World Cup. He kept his place for the remainder of the tournament, playing a full role in the run to the quarter-finals.

Back at Maine Road in 1990-91 he missed just one game as City climbed to fifth place in Division One and netted his first hat-trick for the club in a 3-1 win at Crystal Palace. Very few forwards caused as much havoc in the air as Niall Quinn. Coupled with his fantastic work-rate, neat distribution and the superb way he held up the ball, this made him one of the best forwards in Europe.

Playing in all 12 qualifying matches ahead of the 1994 World Cup, Quinn then ruptured a cruciate ligament and was forced to sit out not only the World Cup Finals but also a year of his career.

The 1995-96 season was to provide a double disappointment for Quinn. Not only did the Republic miss out on a place in Euro '96 after a play-off defeat by Holland but following City's relegation, he was sold to Sunderland for £1.3 million, the Wearsiders' record fee.

After a number of impressive performances in the early part of the 1996-97 season, he damaged an ankle which kept him out of

Above: Niall Quinn

first team action for seven months. Following a third knee operation, it looked as if he would miss most of the 1997-98 campaign.

He surprisingly returned to action and scored the first goal at the Stadium of Light. Quinn also scored twice in the First Division play-off final at Wembley which Sunderland lost 7-6 on penalties after drawing 4-4 with Charlton Athletic. He was outstanding the following season as the Black Cats won the First Division Championship: he seemed to be getting better with age! His partnership up front with Kevin Phillips made the transformation into the Premiership look easy!

Continuing to represent the Republic of Ireland, he scored with headers in the first two games of 2000-01 against his former clubs Arsenal and Manchester City. On the international front he was still searching for the elusive goal that would have given him his country's out-right goalscoring record. It eventually came against Cyprus in October 2001 – six months later he received a PFA Merit Award and was awarded a benefit by the north-east club. Following the Wearsiders' relegation Niall Quinn, a true Sunderland legend, decided to retire. Typical of the man, he donated all of the proceeds from his May 2002 testimonial to children's charities.

Ken De Mange

Position	Midfield
Born	Kenneth John Philip Petit De Mange, Dublin, 3 September 1964

Clubs

Home Farm; Liverpool; Scunthorpe United (loan); Leeds United; Hull City; Cardiff City (loan); Limerick; Ards; Bohemians; Dundalk

International Caps	2

Matches

Year	Opponent	Result	Score	G
1987	Brazil	won	1-0	
1989	Tunisia	won	4-0	

A combative midfield, Ken De Mange won the Irish 'Young Player of the Year' award as a 17-year-old with Home Farm before signing a three-year contract with Liverpool in 1983.

He spent four seasons at Anfield but the only time he experienced League football was when he joined Scunthorpe United on loan. On his return to Anfield he was somewhat surprisingly elevated to full international status. He made his debut for the Republic of Ireland as a second-half substitute for captain Mick McCarthy in the 1-0 win over Brazil at Lansdowne Road. Ken De Mange's second cap came in the 4-0 defeat of Tunisia in October 1988.

By now he had left Liverpool to travel across the Pennines and join Leeds United, for whom he scored on his debut against Manchester City. Though he looked to have the makings of a fine player, he was allowed to leave and joined Hull City for £65,000. In and out of the side at Boothferry Park, he was loaned to Cardiff City twice during the 1990-91 season.

After the Tigers cancelled his contract, he returned to Ireland to join Limerick. Twelve months later, he moved north to Ards, later returning to the Republic to play for Bohemians and Dundalk.

David Kelly

Position	Forward
Born	David Thomas Kelly, Birmingham, 25 November 1965

Clubs

Alvechurch; Walsall; West Ham United; Leicester City; Newcastle United; Wolverhampton Wanderers; Sunderland; Tranmere Rovers; Sheffield United; Motherwell; Mansfield Town; Derry City

International Caps	26
International Goals	9

Matches

Year	Opponent	Result	Score	G
1988	Israel	won	5-0	3
1988	Romania	won	2-0	1
1988	Yugoslavia	won	2-0	
1989	Tunisia	won	4-0	
1990	USSR	won	1-0	
1990	Malta	won	3-0	
1991	Morocco	won	1-0	1
1991	Wales	won	3-0	
1991	Chile	drew	1-1	1
1991	United States	drew	1-1	
1992	Hungary	won	2-1	1
1992	Italy	lost	0-2	
1992	Portugal	won	2-0	
1993	Denmark	drew	0-0	
1993	Wales	won	2-1	
1994	Russia	drew	0-0	
1994	Norway	drew	0-0	
1995	England	won	1-0	1
1995	N Ireland	drew	1-1	
1996	Latvia	won	2-1	
1997	Iceland	drew	0-0	
1997	Wales	drew	0-0	
1997	Macedonia	lost	2-3	1
1998	Lithuania	won	2-1	
1998	Romania	drew	1-1	
1998	Belgium	drew	1-1	

The son of a Dublin-born lorry driver, it is a miracle that David Kelly became a professional footballer. At the age of four, he fell out of a tree, fractured a leg and was diagnosed as having Perthes' disease. Neither bone nor muscle was growing in his upper left thigh and when he was eventually discharged from hospital, his left leg was four inches shorter than his right! He had to wear a brace and was aged ten before he could walk without the aid of crutches.

Despite this setback, he signed schoolboy forms for West Bromwich Albion. Manager Ron Atkinson didn't take up the option to sign him professionally, so he took up employment in the office at Cadbury's Bourneville factory and played non-League football for Alvechurch.

Spotted by Walsall manager Alan Buckley, Kelly had five fine seasons at Fellows Park, scoring 63 goals in 147 games. It was during his time with the Saddlers that he won the first of his 26 caps for the Republic of Ireland.

What a debut it was: the Third Division player netted a hat-trick in the 5-0 defeat of Israel at Dalymount Park. Ironically, the Birmingham-born player had been pencilled-in to play for the England Under-21 side against Yugoslavia. Selected by Jack Charlton for the 1988 European Championships, he didn't add to his tally of caps, though he was very much in demand.

In August 1988 in the face of attractive offers from Bayern Munich and Paris St Germain, Kelly joined West Ham United for £600,000. Playing in a far-from-fluent Hammers side, he was substituted, dropped and harshly barracked by the Upton Park faithful. To make matters worse, the Hammers were relegated at the end of his first season with the club.

Consequently in March 1990 he was allowed to move to Leicester City for £300,000. He soon offered reminders of his predatory instincts at Filbert Street, netting a hat-trick in a 5-4 win over his future club, Newcastle United. Once again it all turned sour and he joined the Magpies in December 1991.

He flourished at St James Park, netting 11 vital goals in that 1991-92 season as United battled to avoid relegation from Division Two. He was the club's top goalgetter during the following campaign with 24 strikes, as they won promotion to the top flight. Kelly netted a hat-trick against his former club Leicester in his last match for the Magpies, then moved on to Wolverhampton Wanderers for £750,000 – still in the First Division instead of sampling the Premiership with Newcastle United.

After Wolves failed to reach the Premiership, Graham Taylor placed him on the transfer list and he moved to Sunderland. After helping the Black Cats win promotion, the club were then relegated and Kelly, who was rarely left out of Jack Charlton's Republic of Ireland squads, joined Tranmere Rovers. He scored for the Wirral club in the League Cup Final at Wembley, later moving to Sheffield United, Motherwell and Mansfield Town before moving to Ireland to see out his career with Derry City.

Chris Morris

Position	Full-back
Born	Christopher Barry Morris, Newquay, 24 December 1963
Clubs	

Sheffield Wednesday; Glasgow Celtic; Middlesbrough

International Caps	35

Matches				
Year	Opponent	Result	Score	G
1988	Israel	won	5-0	
1988	Romania	won	2-0	
1988	Yugoslavia	won	2-0	
1988	Poland	won	3-1	
1988	Norway	drew	0-0	
1988	England	won	1-0	
1988	USSR	drew	1-1	
1988	Holland	lost	0-1	
1989	N Ireland	drew	0-0	
1989	Tunisia	won	4-0	
1989	Spain	lost	0-2	
1989	France	drew	0-0	
1989	Hungary	drew	0-0	
1989	Hungary	won	2-0	

Matches Continued				
Year	Opponent	Result	Score	G
1990	West Germany	drew	1-1	
1990	N Ireland	won	3-0	
1990	Malta	won	2-0	
1990	Wales	won	1-0	
1990	USSR	won	1-0	
1990	Finland	drew	1-1	
1990	Turkey	drew	0-0	
1990	England	drew	1-1	
1990	Egypt	drew	0-0	
1990	Holland	drew	1-1	
1990	Romania	drew	0-0	
			5-4 pen	
1990	Italy	lost	0-1	
1991	England	drew	1-1	
1992	Hungary	won	2-1	
1992	Poland	drew	3-3	
1992	Wales	lost	0-1	
1992	Switzerland	won	2-1	
1992	United States	won	4-1	
1992	United States	lost	1-3	
1992	Portugal	won	2-0	
1993	Wales	won	2-1	

Newquay-born Chris Morris was a natural sportsman, excelling at cricket and rugby as well as football. He looked set for a career as a PE teacher when Sheffield Wednesday manager Jack Charlton signed him for the Owls in October 1982.

Morris broke into the Yorkshire club's League side as a right-winger in 1983-84, but it was only after he switched to full-back that his true potential was revealed. He spent five seasons at Hillsborough before Celtic manager Billy McNeill paid £125,000 to take him to Parkhead in the summer of 1987.

Opting for a formation based around a sweeper and wing-backs, Chris Morris was the perfect choice to assume duties on the Bhoys' right-flank. In his first season at Parkhead, Morris' form was a revelation. Within a few months, he had won his first cap for the Republic of Ireland – his mother was born in Co. Mayo – in the 5-0 thrashing of Israel.

Looking like Celtic's answer to the loss of Danny McGrain, he helped the Bhoys win the 'double' in 1987-88, scoring a goal after just three minutes of the match against Dundee – a game that saw the Centenary Year Championship go to Parkhead.

As for the Republic of Ireland, he could not have timed his entrance on to the international stage any better. The Republic had just clinched a place at their first major tournament finals – the 1988 European Championships – and after five consecutive appearances, he travelled to Euro '88 as the team's first-choice right-back.

He continued his winning ways with Celtic and in 1988-89 netted a first-minute goal against Rangers, later helping beat the Bhoys' greatest rivals to the Scottish Cup.

He had a fine 1990 World Cup for the Republic and was seen by millions on TV shaking hands with the Romanian players before the penalty shoot-out.

Having appeared in 206 games for Celtic, Morris left to join Middlesbrough in exchange for Andy Payton. In November 1993 he damaged a cruciate ligament. This required surgery and kept him out for the rest of that season, ending his chances of playing in the USA 1994 World Cup. Though he later returned to help Boro win the First Division Championship, Morris was disappointed not to have been offered more opportunities to play in the Premiership, being released at the end of the 1996-97 season.

Kelham O'Hanlon

Position	Goalkeeper
Born	Kelham Gerard O'Hanlon, Saltburn, 16 May 1962

Clubs
Middlesbrough; Rotherham United; Carlisle United; Preston North End; Dundee United; Preston North End

International Caps	1

Matches				
Year	Opponent	Result	Score	G
1988	Israel	won	5-0	

Having had trials with Aston Villa and Derby County, goalkeeper Kelham O'Hanlon joined Middlesbrough, where he succeeded Northern Ireland international keeper Jim Platt. He later lost his place in the Boro side to former Manchester United keeper Stephen Pears, and was allowed to leave Ayresome Park. In the summer of 1985 he joined Rotherham United.

His displays for the Millers led to him winning his one and only full international cap for the Republic of Ireland against Israel in November 1987. O'Hanlon kept a clean sheet in a 5-0 win – the biggest margin of victory achieved by an Irish team under Jack Charlton – a feat later equalled against Turkey in October 1990.

Unable to displace Gerry Peyton as Packie Bonner's understudy, he continued to serve Rotherham well: in 1988-89 he helped the club win the Fourth Division Championship. In the summer of 1991 after making 304 appearances for the Yorkshire club, he was transferred to Carlisle United. At the end of his first season the PFA voted him the Fourth Division's best keeper.

In July 1993 he moved on to Preston North End where after some good displays he lost out to Steve Woods. After a spell playing in

the Scottish Premier with Dundee United, he rejoined North End as the club's assistant-manager, although he was forced back into action following an injury to the club's Finnish international Tepi Moilanen.

John Sheridan

Position	Midfield
Born	John Joseph Sheridan, Manchester, 1 October 1964

Clubs
Manchester City; Leeds United; Nottingham Forest; Sheffield Wednesday; Birmingham City (loan); Bolton Wanderers; Doncaster Rovers; Oldham Athletic

International Caps	34
Inernational Goals	5

Matches				
Year	Opponent	Result	Score	G
1988	Romania	won	2-0	
1988	Yugoslavia	won	2-0	
1988	Poland	won	3-1	1
1988	Norway	drew	0-0	
1989	Spain	lost	0-2	
1990	Wales	won	1-0	
1990	Turkey	drew	0-0	
1990	Malta	won	3-0	
1990	Italy	lost	0-1	
1991	Morocco	won	1-0	
1991	Turkey	won	5-0	
1991	Chile	drew	1-1	
1991	United States	drew	1-1	
1992	Hungary	won	2-1	
1993	Latvia	won	2-0	
1994	Spain	lost	1-3	1
1994	Holland	won	1-0	
1994	Bolivia	won	1-0	1
1994	Germany	won	2-0	
1994	Czech Republic	lost	1-3	
1994	Italy	won	1-0	
1994	Mexico	lost	1-2	
1994	Norway	drew	0-0	
1994	Holland	lost	0-2	
1995	Latvia	won	3-0	1
1995	Liechtenstein	won	4-0	
1995	N Ireland	won	4-0	1
1995	England	won	1-0	
1995	N Ireland	drew	1-1	
1995	Portugal	won	1-0	
1995	Liechtenstein	drew	0-0	
1995	Austria	lost	1-3	
1996	Austria	lost	1-3	
1996	Holland	lost	0-2	

John Sheridan began his career with Manchester City, but didn't figure in the first team at Maine Road. In March 1982 he joined Leeds United and made his League debut in a goalless draw with Middlesbrough in November of that year.

By then, he had already won Irish youth international honours – his parents were from Dublin – and soon went on to represent the Republic at Under-21, Under-23 and 'B' international level.

He was an ever-present in Leeds' 1984-85 Second Division side. Two seasons later he was a member of the Leeds side that reached the semi-finals of the FA Cup. That season Leeds also reached the Second Division play-offs, only to go down to Charlton Athletic in the final where Sheridan found the net at Elland Road. The following season he was Leeds' leading scorer. It was this form that helped him win his first cap in March 1988 in a friendly against Romania at Lansdowne Road.

He made an impressive start to his international career, winning caps in four consecutive matches and scoring in a 3-1 defeat of Poland. Finally establishing himself in Jack Charlton's squad, he remained only a fringe player due to the rapid rise of fellow midfielders Roy Keane and Andy Townsend. As a result, Sheridan made just one appearance at Italia '90, coming on in the 78th minute of the quarter-final clash with Italy.

Having left Leeds and made just one League Cup appearance for Nottingham Forest, Sheridan was now playing for Sheffield Wednesday, the Owls paying £500,000 for his services. There was a double celebration for the Owls in 1990-91. Sheridan played in every game as they won promotion to the top flight, and scored the winning goal in the Rumbelows League Cup Final that defeated

Manchester United. In 1991-92 he helped Wednesday to third spot in the First Division and the following season to a Cup Final double that saw them go down to Arsenal in both the FA and League Cup.

Sheridan was recalled to the Republic of Ireland side after an absence of 18 months, and scored in a 3-1 defeat by Spain. The Republic however qualified for the 1994 World Cup Finals. After impressive displays in the pre-tournament friendlies, he lined-up for the opening match against Italy in New York. Sheridan went on to play in all four matches and returned with his reputation much-enhanced. Having won 34 caps, his international career came to an end following the Euro '96 play-off defeats against Holland at Anfield.

After loan spells with Birmingham City and Bolton Wanderers, Sheridan joined the Trotters on a permanent basis and was a regular in their 1996-97 First Division Championship-winning side. Injuries hampered his progress the following season and in June 1998 he moved to Doncaster Rovers, before leaving the Conference new boys for Oldham Athletic.

Voted the club's 'Player of the Season' in his first year at Boundary Park, he repeated the feat in 1999-2000 and was without doubt the best passer of a ball in the lower divisions. Deciding to retire in April 2003, he remained with the Latics as the club's reserve-team coach.

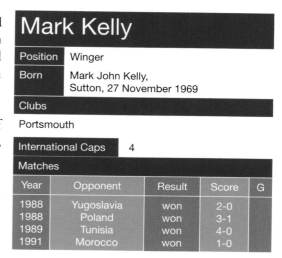

Mark Kelly

Position	Winger
Born	Mark John Kelly, Sutton, 27 November 1969
Clubs	
Portsmouth	

International Caps			4	
Matches				
Year	Opponent	Result	Score	G
1988	Yugoslavia	won	2-0	
1988	Poland	won	3-1	
1989	Tunisia	won	4-0	
1991	Morocco	won	1-0	

A skilful and adventurous winger, Mark Kelly began his playing days as an apprentice with Portsmouth before making his League debut against West Ham United in February 1988.

International recognition soon followed for the Pompey flyer. He had appeared for England at youth level but decided after talking to Jack Charlton to opt to play for the Republic of Ireland. Having represented the Irish at Under-23 and 'B' international level, he made his full debut in a friendly against Yugoslavia in April 1988. Though he helped the Republic to a 2-0 win, he had to leave the field with just one minute of the game remaining due to injury. He missed out on Charlton's squad for the 1988 European Championships, but played three more times for the Republic over the next couple of years.

After becoming a regular for Portsmouth in 1988-89 Kelly suffered a serious injury to his right knee, which resulted in him having to have the joint rebuilt. Unfortunately, each time he tried to make a comeback with Pompey's reserve side, he was knocked back by other injuries. He went on loan to Spurs but didn't appear in the North London club's League side.

Kelly made just 49 League appearances for Portsmouth, 24 of them as a substitute, and played his last game in September 1990. He remained at Fratton Park until May 1994 when his persistent injury difficulties prevented him from playing first-class football again.

Pat Scully

Position	Central defender
Born	Patrick Joseph Scully, Dublin, 23 June 1970
Clubs	

Arsenal; Preston North End (loan); Northampton Town (loan); Southend United; Huddersfield Town

International Caps	4

Matches

Year	Opponent	Result	Score	G
1989	Tunisia	won	4-0	

Centre-half Pat Scully was sent to Highbury by Arsenal's celebrated Irish scout Bill Darby as a youngster. At 18-years-old, a bright future seemed assured. In October 1988 whilst still a member of the Gunners' Football Combination side, Scully won full international honours for the Republic of Ireland, when he came off the bench to replace Chris Morris in the 4-0 defeat of Tunisia.

At Highbury he was unable to displace the likes of Tony Adams, David O'Leary and Steve Bould. He went on loan to both Preston North End and Theo Foley's Northampton Town before in January 1991 joining Southend United on a similar basis.

At the end of his spell at Roots Hall, Southend were suitably impressed by Scully's performances and he joined the club on a permanent basis for a fee of £100,000. He made an immediate impact at the heart of

the Shrimpers defence, helping them win promotion to the Second Division in 1990-91.

In March 1994 having appeared in 127 games for the Shrimpers, Scully was transferred to Huddersfield Town, again for £100,000. The following month he was a member of the Yorkshire club's side beaten in a penalty shoot-out by Swansea City in the final of the Autoglass Trophy at Wembley. The following season he helped Town win promotion to the First Division via the play-offs. Injuries and a loss of form then hindered his progress: having turned down a transfer-deadline day move to York City, he returned to Ireland.

Steve Staunton

Position	Left-back/Midfield
Born	Stephen Staunton, Dundalk, 19 January 1969
Clubs	

Dundalk; Liverpool; Bradford City (loan); Aston Villa; Liverpool; Crystal Palace (loan); Aston Villa; Coventry City

International Caps	102
International Goals	8

Matches

Year	Opponent	Result	Score	G
1989	Tunisia	won	4-0	
1989	Spain	lost	0-2	
1989	Spain	won	1-0	
1989	Malta	won	2-0	
1989	Hungary	won	2-0	
1990	West Germany	drew	1-1	
1990	N Ireland	won	3-0	
1990	Malta	won	2-0	
1990	Wales	won	1-0	
1990	USSR	won	1-0	1
1990	Finland	drew	1-1	
1990	Turkey	drew	0-0	
1990	Malta	won	3-0	
1990	England	drew	1-1	
1990	Egypt	drew	0-0	
1990	Holland	drew	1-1	
1990	Romania	drew	0-0 5-4 pen	
1990	Italy	lost	0-1	
1991	Morocco	won	1-0	
1991	Turkey	won	5-0	

Matches Continued

Year	Opponent	Result	Score	G
1991	England	drew	1-1	
1991	Wales	won	3-0	
1991	England	drew	1-1	
1991	Poland	drew	0-0	
1991	Chile	drew	1-1	
1991	United States	drew	1-1	
1992	Poland	drew	3-3	
1992	Turkey	won	3-1	
1992	Switzerland	won	2-1	
1992	United States	won	4-1	
1992	Albania	won	2-0	
1992	United States	lost	1-3	
1992	Italy	lost	0-2	
1992	Portugal	won	2-0	1
1993	Latvia	won	4-0	
1993	Spain	drew	0-0	
1993	N Ireland	won	3-0	1
1993	Denmark	drew	1-1	
1993	Albania	won	2-1	1
1993	Latvia	won	2-0	
1993	Lithuania	won	1-0	1
1994	Lithuania	won	2-0	
1994	Spain	lost	1-3	
1994	Holland	won	1-0	
1994	Bolivia	won	1-0	
1994	Germany	won	2-0	
1994	Czech Republic	lost	1-3	
1994	Italy	won	1-0	
1994	Mexico	lost	1-2	
1994	Norway	drew	0-0	
1994	Holland	lost	0-2	
1995	Latvia	won	3-0	
1995	Liechtenstein	won	4-0	
1995	N Ireland	won	4-0	
1995	England	won	1-0	
1995	N Ireland	drew	1-1	
1995	Portugal	won	1-0	1
1995	Liechtenstein	drew	0-0	
1995	Austria	lost	1-3	
1996	Latvia	won	2-1	
1996	Portugal	lost	0-3	
1996	Russia	lost	0-2	
1997	Liechtenstein	won	5-0	
1997	Macedonia	won	3-0	
1997	Wales	drew	0-0	
1997	Macedonia	lost	2-3	
1997	Romania	lost	0-1	
1997	Liechtenstein	won	5-0	
1998	Lithuania	drew	0-0	
1998	Iceland	won	4-2	
1998	Lithuania	won	2-1	
1998	Belgium	drew	1-1	
1998	Belgium	lost	1-2	
1998	Argentina	lost	0-2	
1999	Croatia	won	2-0	
1999	Malta	won	5-0	
1999	Yugoslavia	lost	0-1	
1999	Sweden	won	2-0	

Matches Continued				
Year	Opponent	Result	Score	G
2000	Yugoslavia	won	2-1	
2000	Croatia	lost	0-2	
2000	Malta	won	3-2	1
2000	Macedonia	drew	1-1	
2000	Czech Republic	won	3-2	
2000	Greece	lost	0-1	
2001	Holland	drew	2-2	
2001	Finland	won	3-0	1
2001	Andorra	won	3-0	
2001	Portugal	drew	1-1	
2001	Estonia	won	2-0	
2002	Croatia	drew	2-2	
2002	Holland	won	1-0	
2002	Cyprus	won	4-0	
2002	Iran	won	2-0	
2002	Iran	lost	0-1	
2002	Russia	won	2-0	
2002	Denmark	won	3-0	
2002	United States	won	2-1	
2002	Nigeria	lost	1-2	
2002	Cameroon	drew	1-1	
2002	Germany	drew	1-1	
2002	Saudi Arabia	won	3-0	
2002	Spain	drew	1-1	

Above: Steve Staunton

Having joined Liverpool from the League of Ireland side Dundalk during the early part of the 1986-87 season, Steve Staunton spent over a year at Anfield without first-team football. In fact, he was loaned out to Bradford City, and made his Football League debut at Valley Parade in the Yorkshire derby against Sheffield United in November 1987.

He finally broke into the Liverpool squad and wrested the left-back spot from David Burrows. An FA Cup winners' medal in 1988-89 followed Liverpool's 3-2 victory over Everton.

During the course of that season, Staunton made his full international debut against Tunisia at Lansdowne Road. Having helped the Republic to a 4-0 win, he kept his place in the side for the World Cup qualifier against Spain in Seville a few weeks later. Staunton was included in Jack Charlton's 22-man squad for the World Cup Finals in Italy in 1990. At 21 he was the youngest player at the finals.

Though by now an automatic choice for his country, he found it more difficult to hold down a regular place at Anfield during the 1989-90 season. He still won a League

Championship medal as the Reds won the title for a record-breaking 18th time.

In the summer of 1991 Staunton was transferred to Aston Villa for a fee of £1.1 million. In a dream debut for his new club, he scored the winner in a 3-2 win at Sheffield Wednesday on the opening day of the 1991-92 season. In the following campaign he helped Villa to runners-up in the first season of the Premiership.

As the Republic of Ireland kicked off their qualifying programme for the 1994 World Cup, Staunton began in his familiar left-back position, but with Sheedy injured he moved into midfield for the game against Spain. He continued in midfield throughout all the qualifiers, scoring in the games against Northern Ireland, Albania and Lithuania. Named FAI 'Player of the Year' in 1993, he unfortunately suffered more than most in the heat of Orlando, and was substituted in both of the games played there.

Gaining a League Cup winners' medal with Villa in 1994, he was outstanding in the Euro '96 qualifying campaign, missing just one game ahead of the play-off defeat against Holland at Anfield. Following the appointment of Mick McCarthy as Republic of Ireland manager, Steve Staunton was asked to revert to defence. Over the next few seasons his experience was vital, especially as McGrath and Moran had decided to retire from international football.

Occasionally captaining the national side, he had appeared in 263 games for Villa when in the summer of 1998 he rejoined Liverpool under the Bosman ruling. Despite appearing regularly for the Republic of Ireland, he struggled to hold down a place in the Liverpool side. After a loan spell with Crystal Palace, he rejoined Aston Villa.

During the 2000-01 season Staunton continued to add to his total of appearances for the Republic of Ireland. He became the all-time record holder for the number of caps, having played in 102 games. He also became the most capped player in Aston Villa's history, but in the summer of 2003 signed for Coventry City. Injuries and operations restricted his appearances for the Highfield Road club in his first season, but in 2004-05 he had fully recovered to become a regular member of the City line-up. After a spell at Walsall he was named the new Ireland manager in 2006 and Brian Kerr's replacement.

Andy Townsend

Position	Midfield
Born	Andrew David Townsend, Maidstone, 23 July 1963

Clubs

Welling United; Weymouth; Southampton; Norwich City; Chelsea; Aston Villa; Middlesbrough; West Bromwich Albion

International Caps	70
Inernational Goals	7

Matches

Year	Opponent	Result	Score	G
1989	France	drew	0-0	
1989	Spain	won	1-0	
1989	Malta	won	2-0	
1989	Hungary	won	2-0	
1990	West Germany	drew	1-1	
1990	N Ireland	won	3-0	
1990	Malta	won	2-0	
1990	Wales	won	1-0	
1990	USSR	won	1-0	
1990	Finland	drew	1-1	
1990	Turkey	drew	0-0	
1990	Malta	won	3-0	1
1990	England	drew	1-1	
1990	Egypt	drew	0-0	
1990	Holland	drew	1-1	
1990	Romania	drew	0-0 5-4 pen	
1990	Italy	lost	0-1	
1991	Morocco	won	1-0	
1991	Turkey	won	5-0	
1991	England	drew	1-1	
1991	Wales	won	3-0	
1991	England	drew	1-1	
1991	Poland	drew	0-0	

Matches Continued				
Year	Opponent	Result	Score	G
1991	Chile	drew	1-1	
1991	United States	drew	1-1	
1992	Poland	drew	3-3	1
1992	Wales	lost	0-1	
1992	United States	won	4-1	1
1992	Albania	won	2-0	
1992	United States	lost	1-3	
1992	Italy	lost	0-2	
1993	Latvia	won	4-0	
1993	Denmark	drew	0-0	
1993	Spain	drew	0-0	
1993	N Ireland	won	3-0	1
1993	Denmark	drew	1-1	
1993	Albania	won	2-1	
1993	Latvia	won	2-0	
1993	Lithuania	won	1-0	
1994	Lithuania	won	2-0	
1994	N Ireland	drew	1-1	
1994	Holland	won	1-0	
1994	Bolivia	won	1-0	
1994	Germany	won	2-0	
1994	Czech Republic	lost	1-3	1
1994	Italy	won	1-0	
1994	Mexico	lost	1-2	
1994	Norway	drew	0-0	
1994	Holland	lost	0-2	
1995	Latvia	won	3-0	
1995	N Ireland	won	4-0	1
1995	England	won	1-0	
1995	N Ireland	drew	1-1	
1995	Portugal	won	1-0	
1996	Austria	lost	1-3	
1996	Latvia	won	2-1	
1996	Holland	lost	0-2	
1996	Russia	lost	0-2	
1996	Czech Republic	lost	0-2	
1996	Portugal	lost	0-1	
1997	Liechtenstein	won	5-0	1
1997	Macedonia	won	3-0	
1997	Iceland	drew	0-0	
1997	Macedonia	lost	2-3	
1997	Romania	lost	0-1	
1997	Liechtenstein	won	5-0	
1998	Lithuania	drew	0-0	
1998	Iceland	won	4-2	
1998	Belgium	drew	1-1	
1998	Belgium	lost	1-2	

After starting his career in non-League football with Welling United of the Southern League Townsend – one of the game's best midfielders – followed his father Don (who played for Charlton Athletic and Crystal Palace in the early Sixties) into League soccer. In the summer of 1984 he joined Weymouth where his performances attracted

Above: Andy Townsend

against France in February 1989. Though the game ended goalless, Townsend did not look out of place in a Republic midfield that boasted the likes of Brady, Houghton and Whelan. By the time of the 1990 World Cup Finals, he had become an important member of the Irish side and his performances against England and Holland were very impressive.

He soon became the subject of intense transfer speculation. Within a week of the Republic of Ireland's elimination, Norwich had sold Townsend to Chelsea for £1.2 million. The job of leading the Blues was to prove good experience for a player who would go on to become the Republic's longest-serving skipper.

Townsend first wore the captain's armband at international level in the 1-0 defeat by Wales in February 1992. He was given the job on a permanent basis at the start of the qualifying campaign for the 1994 World Cup Finals.

His form at both club and international level saw him linked with a move away from Stamford Bridge, and in the summer of 1993 he joined Aston Villa for £2 million. Villa Park had become something of an Irish enclave during the early 1990s: Townsend joined fellow Republic internationals Ray Houghton, Paul McGrath and Steve Staunton at the Midlands club.

Despite missing only one game in the qualifiers, he saved his best form for the finals and against Italy in New York, where his energetic display was instrumental in his side's famous 1-0 victory.

He captained Aston Villa to success in the 1996 League Cup Final – some consolation for the Republic missing out on qualification for the 1996 European Championships. Though he retained the captaincy of the national side following the appointment of Mick McCarthy, things were changing at Villa

Park and in August 1998 he was transferred to Middlesbrough for £500,000.

He proved a big hit in his first season at the Riverside, helping Boro to promotion to the Premiership – it was as a Middlesbrough player that the Republic's longest-serving skipper won his last cap, in the second leg of the World Cup play-off against Belgium. Appointed Middlesbrough's captain for the 1998-99 Premiership season, he continued to belie his advancing years and was a perfect role model for all the other players.

Early the following season he left Boro to join West Bromwich Albion, but after a number of injury problems became player-manager of the club's reserve team. Andy Townsend now works in the media for ITV and talkSPORT Radio.

the attention of Southampton, who signed him in January 1985.

He enjoyed three full seasons at The Dell but only really established himself in the Saints' midfield in 1987-88. Surprisingly sold to Norwich City in the close season, he helped to establish the Canaries' reputation as a classy passing team. They achieved their highest-ever Football League placing of fourth and reached the FA Cup semi-final.

He also won international recognition with the Republic of Ireland, making his debut

THE 1990s

Following their success at the 1988 European Championships, the Republic of Ireland were drawn in a World Cup qualifying group alongside Spain, Hungary, Malta and Northern Ireland. With second place being good enough, there was all to play for.

Jack Charlton took an almighty gamble in arranging to start the qualifying games by visiting the three toughest teams first. Opening up against Northern Ireland in Belfast was especially tricky, even more so as the Republic's supporters would be unable to lend their massive support for security reasons – but the game had 'goalless draw' written all over it! With the Republic's squad decimated by injuries, the boys in green lost 2-0 in Spain before playing out another goalless draw in Hungary – although to be fair, the Republic did most of the attacking in a cold and windy Nep Stadium. The Republic then entertained Spain at Lansdowne Road, having yet to score a goal in the competition. An own goal by Michel gave the Irish a 1-0 win – the visitors had dropped their first points of the campaign. The Republic now faced back-to-back visits from Malta and Hungary – after a 2-0 win over Malta, the Republic played Hungary in what for both countries was tantamount to a cup final. McGrath and Cascarino found the net as the Republic recorded another 2-0 home victory. A 3-0 defeat of Northern Ireland was followed by a 2-0 win in Malta

and at the thirteenth attempt, the Republic of Ireland were set for the World Cup Finals.

In the months leading up to the finals, the Republic stretched their unbeaten run to 13 games. Having conceded just two goals, they arrived in Italy looking to cause an upset or two.

The Republic's opponents in the group games were England, Egypt and Holland. Their first game against England was played at a tremendous pace, and could not in anyway be described as a classic! England took the lead when Lineker beat two defenders to a Waddle cross, but the Republic refused to give up and pressured the England defence whenever they could. Twenty minutes from the end, substitute Steve McMahon was robbed of possession on the edge of the England area – Kevin Sheedy scored a deserved equaliser. The Irish players celebrated deep into the night but with their next opponents Egypt rarely venturing across the halfway line, Jack Charlton's side had to be content with a goalless draw. The Republic's last opponents Holland had also drawn 0-0 with England, leaving all four sides with identical records. Jack Charlton made one change to the side that faced Egypt, with Niall Quinn replacing the out-of-form Cascarino. The Dutch took the lead through Ruud Gullit but Quinn levelled the scores to ensure that both teams qualified for the second round. Lots were drawn to decide which team would be placed second and which third – the Republic took the higher place. Their opponents in the second round were Romania, who were without their star forward Lacatus. Despite creating the better chances, the Republic were unable to convert their superiority into goals. At the end of extra-time, the game remained goalless: the tie became the first one of the tournament to be decided on penalties. McCarthy lost the toss and the Romanians went first with Hagi shooting them into a 1-0 lead. The tally had reached 4-4 when Bonner saved Timofte's spot-kick. Now it was all down to the Republic's fifth penalty-taker David O'Leary. The Arsenal defender sent the keeper Lung the wrong way and sent the Irish players and fans wild. The boys in green were in the quarter-finals of the World Cup, where they would face hosts Italy. It was a thrilling encounter in which Jack Charlton's team fought well but failed to penetrate Italy's magnificent defence. As this was Italy's tenth successive game without conceding a goal, the Irish could be forgiven for their failure as Schillaci scored the winner. The Republic returned home with dignity from a World Cup competition that had exceeded all expectations.

The Republic then drew England in the European Championships of 1992 – the third consecutive major competition in which the two countries had been drawn together. The other countries in the qualifying group were Poland and Turkey. The Irish looked on course for yet another tournament final. Despite beating Turkey home and away and drawing twice with both England and Poland, a late strike by Gary Lineker against Poland took England into the Euro finals.

Though the Republic managed to avoid England in the World Cup qualifiers for USA '94, they were grouped with European Championship winners Denmark, Spain, Northern Ireland and three of the lesser footballing powers in Albania, Latvia and Lithuania. It was the only group to comprise seven teams – this meant twelve qualifying games!

The Irish made a good start, with home victories over Albania (2-0) and Latvia (4-0) followed by two goalless draws in Denmark and Spain. In the latter match in Seville, the main talking point was the linesman's flag that denied the Republic a precious goal. Even the following day's Spanish press agreed it should have been allowed to stand! Yet to concede a goal, the Republic then defeated Northern Ireland 3-0 before being held to a 1-1 draw at Lansdowne Road by Denmark. They then beat Albania, Latvia and Lithuania on their travels before beating the Lithuanians at home, in what Jack Charlton described as the worst performance since he took charge. If the Republic beat Spain, they would be through to the World Cup Finals but they were well beaten 3-1: to make matters worse, Denmark scored a late goal to take both points in their match with Northern Ireland. With two teams to qualify, there was just one point separating the top three teams prior to the Republic's final game in Belfast. The top of the table read:

	P	W	D	L	F	A	Pts
Denmark	11	7	4	0	15	1	18
Spain	11	7	3	1	26	4	17
Republic of Ireland	11	7	3	1	18	5	17

An Irish victory would secure second place, whilst a draw might be good enough if the match between Denmark and Spain didn't finish all-square. The Republic's supporters could not flock to Belfast for security reasons just as the Ulster fans couldn't descend on Dublin. Despite injuries hampering Charlton's selection, the Republic played out a goalless first-half – in fact, there had hardly been a shot on goal! News filtered through that the Danes were losing 1-0 to Spain but that mattered little when Jimmy Quinn gave the home side the lead. Only three minutes elapsed before substitute Alan McLoughlin levelled the scores – with 10-men Spain holding onto their narrow advantage, the Irish had reached their second World Cup Finals.

The Republic's first match in USA '94 was against Italy, the team that had beaten them in the quarter-finals four years before. Supported by a large part of the 74,826 who were packed into Giants Stadium, the Republic didn't take long to show the Italians that they meant business. In the 11th minute Ray Houghton ran the ball along the edge of the Italian penalty-area. Seeing Pagliuca off his line, he dipped a shot just under the bar. Italy were stunned and failed to respond with anything approaching a cohesive attack. In fact, the Italians were lucky not to concede a second goal when John Sheridan rifled a shot against the bar. The Irish retained their edge and composure and held on for a shock win. The Republic's next game against Mexico was played in the steaming heat of Orlando and is best remembered for the antics of Jack Charlton, who again found himself in confrontation with FIFA officials. Mexico were leading 2-0 when Charlton had his infamous altercation with FIFA officials, who seemed intent on preventing substitute Aldridge from taking to the field even though Coyne had already been withdrawn. Ireland fought back well and Aldridge reduced the arrears – a goal which was to prove vital in deciding their final position in the group. The Republic then played out a goalless draw with Norway to finish in second place, level on points with leaders Mexico but with an inferior goal difference. Their opponents in the last-16 were Holland but two slip-ups, one by full-back Phelan and another by goalkeeper Bonner put an end to the Republic's hopes of progressing to the quarter-finals.

Many thought that Jack Charlton would stand down but they were wrong. His final qualifying campaign was to end in disappointment, when the Republic missed out on a place at Euro '96 after a play-off match against Holland at Anfield. Eight days later, Charlton announced his resignation – he had taken Ireland to the finals of three major tournaments and to the dizzy heights of sixth place in the FIFA world rankings.

His successor was his captain Mick McCarthy. Though he started the campaign for the 1998 World Cup Finals well enough, with victories over Liechtenstein away and Macedonia in Dublin, they were followed by a goalless home draw with Iceland and a disastrous 3-2 defeat in Macedonia. Following a 1-0 defeat in Romania, the best the Republic could hope for was to finish in second place, thereby securing a play-off match against another second-placed country. The Republic recovered their form and were unbeaten in their last six matches to earn a two-legged head-to-head with Belgium. The first leg in Dublin ended all-square at 1-1 but a defeat in Brussels meant there would be no trip to France for the boys in green in 1998.

Bernie Slaven

Position	Forward
Born	Bernard Joseph Slaven, Paisley, 13 November 1960
Clubs	

Morton; Airdrieonians; Queen of the South; Albion Rovers; Middlesbrough; Port Vale; Darlington

International Caps	7
Inernational Goals	1

Matches

Year	Opponent	Result	Score	G
1990	Wales	won	1-0	1
1990	Finland	drew	1-1	
1990	Turkey	drew	0-0	
1990	Malta	won	3-0	
1991	Wales	won	3-0	
1991	Poland	drew	0-0	
1993	Wales	won	2-1	

It is difficult to estimate Bernie Slaven's status on Teeside, yet it was an unusual transfer saga that took him to Middlesbrough in October 1985. The Scot had been top-scorer in his home country in the previous season, netting 31 times for Albion Rovers. The former Morton, Airdie and Queen of the South striker had refused to re-sign for the club in the close season, and was even working as a part-time gardener!

Slaven took the step of writing to every First and Second Division side in the Football League, asking for a trial. It was Middlesbrough boss Willie Maddren who responded first, and he eventually signed Slaven for a bargain price of £25,000. He made his Boro debut against Leeds United before scoring in his first game at Ayresome Park the following week against Bradford City. His career spanned the liquidation saga at Ayresome Park and managers Maddren, Rioch, Todd and Lawrence. Though the team's fortunes fluctuated, Slaven continued to find the net on a regular basis and was the club's top scorer for six consecutive seasons.

Not surprisingly he came to the attention of former Middlesbrough boss Jack Charlton. He was picked for the Republic of Ireland after qualifying through his Irish grandfather. Slaven made his debut against Wales in March 1990, scoring the Republic's goal in a 1-0 win. This was followed by three more appearances in warm-up friendlies prior to the World Cup in Italy. Included in the Republic's squad for Italia '90, he was not used by Charlton but made three more appearances. Now on the wrong side of thirty, he was unable to establish himself in the squad for the 1992 European Championship qualifiers and was used more and more as a substitute by Middlesbrough.

Having helped the club win promotion to the Premiership, he had moved to Port Vale before they were relegated in 1992-93. After a couple of seasons with the Valiants, he returned to the north-east to link up with Darlington before being forced to retire with a persistent back injury in 1995.

Alan McLoughlin

Position	Midfield
Born	Alan Francis McLoughlin, Manchester, 20 April 1967
Clubs	

Manchester United; Swindon Town; Torquay United (loan); Southampton; Portsmouth; Wigan Athletic; Rochdale; Forest Green Rovers

International Caps	42
Inernational Goals	2

Matches

Year	Opponent	Result	Score	G
1990	Malta	won	3-0	
1990	England	drew	1-1	
1990	Egypt	drew	0-0	
1991	Morocco	won	1-0	
1991	England	drew	1-1	
1991	Wales	won	3-0	
1991	Chile	drew	1-1	
1992	Hungary	won	2-1	
1992	Wales	lost	0-1	
1992	United States	won	4-1	

Matches Continued

Year	Opponent	Result	Score	G
1992	United States	lost	1-3	
1992	Italy	lost	0-2	
1992	Portugal	won	2-0	
1993	Wales	won	2-1	
1994	N Ireland	drew	1-1	1
1994	Russia	drew	0-0	
1994	Holland	won	1-0	
1995	Liechtenstein	won	5-0	
1996	Portugal	lost	0-1	
1996	Croatia	drew	2-2	
1996	Holland	lost	1-3	
1996	United States	lost	1-2	
1996	Mexico	drew	2-2	
1996	Bolivia	won	3-0	
1997	Liechtenstein	won	5-0	
1997	Macedonia	won	3-0	
1997	Iceland	drew	0-0	
1997	Wales	drew	0-0	
1997	Macedonia	lost	2-3	1
1998	Lithuania	drew	0-0	
1998	Iceland	won	4-2	
1998	Lithuania	won	2-1	
1998	Romania	drew	1-1	
1998	Belgium	lost	1-2	
1998	Czech Republic	lost	1-2	
1999	Yugoslavia	lost	0-1	
1999	Paraguay	won	2-0	
1999	Sweden	won	2-0	
1999	N Ireland	lost	0-1	
2000	Croatia	lost	0-2	
2000	Malta	won	3-2	
2000	Macedonia	drew	1-1	

Unable to break into the first team at Manchester United, Alan McLoughlin left Old Trafford to join newly promoted Swindon Town. After making his debut for the Robins, he had a brief loan spell with Torquay United, before returning to the County Ground where he developed under the watchful eye of Ossie Ardilles.

With Swindon, McLoughlin came to be recognised as one of the most talented midfielders in British football. His excellent vision, driving energy and passing ability earned him an international call-up for the Republic's game against Malta in June 1990.

Swindon finished in fourth place in Division Two. A McLoughlin goal saw off Sunderland in the play-off final at Wembley.

The celebrations were short-lived, however: Swindon were denied their place in the top flight due to financial irregularities. In December 1990, Swindon were forced to sell their star midfielder to Southampton for £1 million – the move wasn't a success. In February 1992 he moved to Portsmouth for £400,000.

During his time at Fratton Park, McLoughlin played in two FA Cup semi-finals as well as a couple of play-off semi-finals.

In November 1993 he earned his place in the annals of Irish football. Within six minutes of coming off the bench for the World Cup qualifier against Northern Ireland, he scored a second-half equaliser – the goal that would take the Republic of Ireland to USA '94. Whilst with Pompey, McLoughlin's international fortunes were revived following the appointment of Mick McCarthy as Jack Charlton's successor. McLoughlin played in seven of the ten qualifying matches for the 1998 World Cup Finals, going on to win 42 caps for the Republic.

In December 1999 he joined Wigan Athletic, having appeared in 361 games for Portsmouth. Though he helped the Latics reach the play-offs, he was troubled by a slipped disc and eventually left to join Rochdale. Failing to win the offer of a further contract, he left to play non-League football for Forest Green Rovers.

Denis Irwin

Position	Full-back
Born	Joseph Denis Irwin, Cork, 31 October 1965

Clubs

Leeds United; Oldham Athletic; Manchester United; Wolverhampton Wanderers

International Caps	56
Inernational Goals	4

Matches

Year	Opponent	Result	Score	G
1991	Morocco	won	1-0	
1991	Turkey	won	5-0	
1991	Wales	won	3-0	
1991	England	drew	1-1	
1991	Poland	drew	0-0	
1991	United States	drew	1-1	
1992	Hungary	won	2-1	
1992	Poland	drew	3-3	
1992	Wales	lost	0-1	
1992	United States	won	4-1	1
1992	Albania	won	2-0	
1992	United States	lost	1-3	
1992	Italy	lost	0-2	
1993	Latvia	won	4-0	
1993	Denmark	drew	0-0	
1993	Spain	drew	0-0	
1993	N Ireland	won	3-0	
1993	Denmark	drew	1-1	
1993	Albania	won	2-1	
1993	Latvia	won	2-0	
1993	Lithuania	won	1-0	
1994	Lithuania	won	2-0	
1994	Spain	lost	1-3	
1994	N Ireland	drew	1-1	
1994	Bolivia	won	1-0	
1994	Germany	won	2-0	
1994	Italy	won	1-0	
1994	Mexico	lost	1-2	
1995	Latvia	won	3-0	
1995	Liechtenstein	won	4-0	
1995	N Ireland	won	4-0	
1995	England	won	1-0	
1995	N Ireland	drew	1-1	
1995	Portugal	won	1-0	
1995	Liechtenstein	drew	0-0	
1995	Austria	lost	1-3	
1996	Austria	lost	1-3	
1996	Portugal	lost	0-3	
1996	Holland	lost	0-2	
1996	Czech Republic	lost	0-2	
1997	Liechtenstein	won	5-0	
1997	Macedonia	won	3-0	
1997	Iceland	drew	0-0	
1997	Macedonia	lost	2-3	
1997	Romania	lost	0-1	
1998	Lithuania	drew	1-1	

Matches Continued

Year	Opponent	Result	Score	G
1998	Belgium	drew	1-1	1
1998	Argentina	lost	0-2	
1999	Croatia	won	2-0	1
1999	Yugoslavia	lost	0-1	
1999	Paraguay	won	2-0	1
1999	Macedonia	won	1-0	
2000	Yugoslavia	won	2-1	
2000	Macedonia	drew	1-1	
2000	Turkey	drew	1-1	
2000	Turkey	drew	0-0	

It is hard to believe that Denis Irwin once suffered the ignominy of being released on a free transfer from Leeds United.

He was quickly snapped up by Second Division Oldham Athletic, and in his first season at Boundary Park helped the Latics reach the play-offs. Irwin stayed with Oldham for four years, the highlights coming in 1989-90, his last season at Boundary Park. Oldham reached the League Cup Final, going down 1-0 to Nottingham Forest. They were involved in two thrilling FA Cup semi-finals against Manchester United before losing out to a Mark Robins goal in extra-time.

United manager Alex Ferguson was so impressed that during the 1990 close season, Irwin moved to Old Trafford in exchange for a fee of £625,000. His first season with the Reds was certainly one to remember, for not only did he win his first full international cap against Morocco but helped United win the European Cup Winners' Cup by beating Barcelona in the final. In 1991-92 he switched to left-back and helped United win the League Cup, whilst the following season he missed just two games as the Reds won the Premiership title – the trophy returning to Old Trafford after a 26-year gap.

Qualifiers for the 1994 World Cup coincided with his best form for United and it was Irwin, not the emerging Gary Kelly who travelled to the United States in possession of the No.2 shirt. He had an outstanding game against Italy in Giants Stadium, New York but after suspension against Norway, he was displaced from the right-back position.

Although his 'quiet-man' image made him one of United's least high-profile players, his overall contribution to the side was beyond reproach. In 1995-96 he helped United win the Premier League and FA Cup, once again proving to be the Reds' 'Mr Dependable'. A specialist goalscorer from set pieces, Irwin won another Championship medal the following season. Though the Republic of Ireland failed to qualify for France '98, he scored a well-taken goal in the play-offs against Belgium.

In 1998-99 a red card in the game against Liverpool ruled him out of that season's FA Cup Final, but in one of the club's best-ever campaigns, he was delighted to add a European Cup, and a fifth Premiership League winners' medal to his collection of honours. Irwin was also one of five United players selected by their fellow professionals for the PFA award-winning Premiership side. During the course of the following season, Irwin celebrated a few milestones – first becoming United's top man in Europe when he surpassed Peter Schmeichel's 17-match record in the Champions' League.

At international level, he appeared in the European Championship play-off matches against Turkey before announcing his retirement from the international game.

Winning his sixth Premiership title medal, he went on to celebrate his 500th senior game at Old Trafford on St Patrick's Day and establish a new club record with his 70th appearance in European competition. Allowed to leave Old Trafford in the summer of 2002, he joined Wolves. His first season at Molineux ended with his selection for the

PFA's First Division team of the season. He thought long and hard about retiring but gave it one more season. On 15 May 2004 he was given a tremendous ovation as he retired after a long and successful career spanning some 900-odd club appearances.

Roy Keane

Position	Midfield
Born	Roy Maurice Keane, Cork, 10 August 1971

Clubs

Cobh Ramblers; Nottingham Forest; Manchester United; Glasgow Celtic

International Caps	66
International Goals	9

Matches

Year	Opponent	Result	Score	G
1991	Chile	drew	1-1	
1992	Hungary	won	2-1	
1992	Poland	drew	3-3	
1992	Wales	lost	0-1	
1992	Switzerland	won	2-1	
1992	Albania	won	2-0	
1992	United States	lost	1-3	
1993	Latvia	won	4-0	
1993	Denmark	drew	0-0	
1993	Spain	drew	0-0	
1993	Wales	won	2-1	
1993	N Ireland	won	3-0	
1993	Denmark	drew	1-1	
1993	Albania	won	2-1	
1993	Latvia	won	2-0	
1993	Lithuania	won	1-0	
1994	Lithuania	won	2-0	
1994	Spain	lost	1-3	
1994	N Ireland	drew	1-1	
1994	Bolivia	won	1-0	
1994	Germany	won	2-0	
1994	Czech Republic	lost	1-3	
1994	Italy	won	1-0	
1994	Mexico	lost	1-2	
1994	Norway	drew	0-0	
1994	Holland	lost	0-2	
1995	N Ireland	won	4-0	1
1995	N Ireland	drew	1-1	
1996	Austria	lost	1-3	
1996	Romania	lost	0-2	
1997	Iceland	drew	0-0	
1997	Wales	drew	0-0	
1997	Macedonia	lost	2-3	
1997	Romania	lost	0-1	
1997	Liechtenstein	won	5-0	

Year	Opponent	Result	Score	G
1998	Lithuania	drew	0-0	
1998	Iceland	won	4-2	2
1998	Lithuania	won	2-1	
1999	Croatia	won	2-0	1
1999	Malta	won	5-0	1
1999	Yugoslavia	lost	0-1	
1999	Paraguay	won	2-0	
2000	Yugoslavia	won	2-1	
2000	Turkey	drew	1-1	
2000	Turkey	drew	0-0	
2000	Czech Republic	won	3-2	
2001	Holland	drew	2-2	
2001	Portugal	drew	1-1	
2001	Estonia	won	2-0	
2001	Cyprus	won	4-0	2
2001	Andorra	won	3-0	
2001	Portugal	drew	1-1	1
2002	Croatia	drew	2-2	
2002	Holland	won	1-0	
2002	Cyprus	won	4-0	1
2002	Iran	won	2-0	
2002	Russia	won	2-0	
2002	Nigeria	lost	1-2	
2004	Romania	won	1-0	
2004	Faroe Islands	won	2-0	
2005	Bulgaria	drew	1-1	
2005	Switzerland	won	3-0	
2005	France	drew	0-0	
2005	Faroe Islands	won	2-0	
2005	Israel	drew	1-1	
2005	China	won	1-0	

A footballer who provokes extreme reactions, Roy Keane was signed by Nottingham Forest manager Brian Clough from Cobh Ramblers in the summer of 1990. Typically, Clough plunged him straight into first team action – after making his debut against Liverpool at Anfield in August 1990, he finished the season playing in the FA Cup Final which Forest lost 2-1 to Tottenham Hotspur.

This disappointment was tempered somewhat four days later when he was recognised fully at international level, playing for the Republic of Ireland against Chile.

He confirmed the progress made in his initial term with another excellent season in 1991-92, when Forest reached the finals of two Cup competitions. They defeated

Above: Roy Keane

Southampton 3-2 in the Zenith Data Final but fell to Manchester United in the League Cup Final.

By the time the qualifying rounds for USA '94 kicked-off in the summer of 1992, Keane had become an established figure in the Republic's midfield. Once it became clear that Forest's days in the top flight were numbered, Keane made it clear that he intended to stay in the Premiership – an announcement which immediately alerted the big spenders. It looked as if he would join Blackburn Rovers but once Manchester United joined the chase, there was only one club in it. United originally offered £3.5 million and refused to increase the bid, while Forest insisted on a sale figure of £4 million for any transfer to go through before Keane's contract expired. The period of intransigence was broken when Alex Ferguson increased his offer by a further £250,000 – it was a British record transfer fee. In his first season at Old Trafford, Keane helped United to the League and Cup 'double'.

The midfielder played in all four of the Republic's matches at the 1994 World Cup Finals, giving a memorable display against Italy in New York. Even in the heat of Orlando, against Mexico and Holland, Keane maintained his all-action style. His efforts were recognised by RTÉ viewers, who voted him the Republic's player of USA '94. Over the next couple of years his appearances for the national side became all too rare – he played in just three of Ireland's ten Euro '96 qualifiers – a series of niggling injuries apparently being the cause of his absence.

In 1995-96 Keane was again producing brilliant competitive performances in midfield. His greatest display was reserved for the FA Cup Final against Liverpool when he won the prestigious 'Man-of-the-Match' award – he also won a Premiership Championship medal as United won their second-ever double. The following season he missed a number of games through injury but still ended the campaign as the proud possessor of a third Championship medal, as United surged to their fourth title win in five years. He was selected for the award-winning Premiership side.

The appointment of Mick McCarthy as Republic of Ireland manager saw the United midfielder sent-off in his first match in charge. The situation deteriorated even further when despite being named skipper for the 1996 US Cup, he withdrew from the trip. After an absence of over a year, he returned to the green shirt for a World Cup match against Iceland in Dublin. He found that a section of the home crowd had grown hostile to him but Roy Keane is a determined character, and it wasn't long before he'd won back both the fans and the captaincy.

He was appointed Manchester United's captain prior to the start of the 1997-98 season and named the Republic of Ireland's 'Player of the Year'. Keane suffered cruciate knee ligament damage following a challenge with Leeds United's Alf-Inge Haaland. He returned to full fitness in 1998-99, leading United to success in the FA Cup and Premiership. A yellow-card offence against Juventus in the semi-final of the European Cup ruled him out of the final. It was around this time that a huge question mark hung over Keane's future at Old Trafford: he eventually signed a new contract and led the Reds to another Premiership title. Fittingly he won both the PFA and the Football Writers' 'Player of the Year' awards. Keane won his sixth Premiership Championship medal in 2000-01 and remained a cornerstone of the Republic of Ireland team, as they made a highly promising start to qualifying for the 2002 World Cup Finals.

Controversy followed, as the well-publicised spat with Mick McCarthy saw him ruled out of the World Cup Finals, and an announcement signalled his retirement from the international scene! He quickly put the furore over his autobiography behind him and led United to another Premiership Championship. In April 2004, Keane ended his enforced absence from the Republic of Ireland side, hoping for one last chance of glory on the international stage. Having taken his total of caps to 66, Keane criticized a number of his Manchester United team-mates and parted company with the club. He signed for Glasgow Celtic in 2005 but retired at the end of the season. In August 2006 he became Sunderland manager, replacing Mick McCarthy, his former Ireland boss in an ironic twist.

Terry Phelan

Position	Left-back
Born	Terence Michael Phelan, Manchester, 16 March 1967
Clubs	

Leeds United; Swansea City; Wimbledon; Manchester City; Chelsea; Everton; Crystal Palace (loan); Fulham; Sheffield United; Charleston Battery (U.S.)

International Caps	42

Matches

Year	Opponent	Result	Score	G
1992	Hungary	won	2-1	
1992	Poland	drew	3-3	
1992	Turkey	won	3-1	
1992	Wales	lost	0-1	
1992	Switzerland	won	2-1	
1992	United States	lost	1-3	
1992	Italy	lost	0-2	
1992	Portugal	won	2-0	
1993	Latvia	won	4-0	
1993	Denmark	drew	0-0	
1993	Spain	drew	0-0	
1993	N Ireland	won	3-0	
1993	Albania	won	2-1	
1993	Latvia	won	2-0	
1993	Lithuania	won	1-0	
1994	Lithuania	won	2-0	
1994	Spain	lost	1-3	
1994	N Ireland	drew	1-1	
1994	Holland	won	1-0	
1994	Bolivia	won	1-0	
1994	Germany	won	2-0	

Matches Continued

Year	Opponent	Result	Score	G
1994	Czech Republic	lost	1-3	
1994	Italy	won	1-0	
1994	Mexico	lost	1-2	
1994	Holland	lost	0-2	
1995	England	won	1-0	
1996	Latvia	won	2-1	
1996	Holland	lost	0-2	
1996	Russia	lost	0-2	
1996	Portugal	lost	0-1	
1996	Croatia	drew	2-2	
1996	Holland	lost	1-3	
1996	United States	lost	1-2	
1996	Mexico	drew	2-2	
1996	Bolivia	won	3-0	
1997	Wales	drew	0-0	
1997	Macedonia	lost	2-3	
1998	Romania	drew	1-1	
2000	Scotland	lost	1-2	
2000	Mexico	drew	2-2	
2000	United States	drew	1-1	
2000	South Africa	won	2-1	

One of the quickest players to have worn the green shirt of the Republic of Ireland, Terry Phelan started out with Leeds United, but like Denis Irwin, was freed and joined Swansea City.

After a successful season at Vetch Field Phelan became one of Bobby Gould's first signings for Wimbledon. He kept his place in the Dons' side throughout the 1987-88 season, and won an FA Cup winners' medal following Wimbledon's surprise 1-0 defeat of Liverpool at Wembley.

International recognition was slow to arrive and it was September 1991 before he played his first game for the Republic of Ireland against Hungary. Phelan had made eight appearances for the Irish when in the summer of 1992 he joined Manchester City for a fee of £2.5 million. The move to Maine Road made Phelan the most expensive defender in Britain.

When Jack Charlton decided to push Steve Staunton into midfield, Phelan was given the No.3 shirt on a more regular basis and played in ten of the Republic's twelve qualifying matches for the 1994 World Cup. Not surprisingly he travelled to USA '94 as the national team's first-choice left-back. After playing his part in the much-celebrated victory over Italy, he was booked against Mexico and had to sit out the third game against Norway. The Republic qualified for the second round stage and Charlton decided to bring back Phelan for the match against Holland. After just 11 minutes Phelan under-hit a back-pass to Paddy Bonner, gifting the Dutch the game's opening goal. Though he continued to make occasional appearances for the boys in green, he was never again a regular.

In November 1995, Phelan joined Chelsea for a fee of £900,000. He settled in well when in the FA Cup semi-final against Manchester United, with the Blues leading 1-0, he pulled up sharply with a torn thigh muscle. Unable to force his way back into the Chelsea side, he joined Joe Royle's Everton. Like a number of his team-mates, he suffered from the injury curse which blighted the club. After a loan spell with Crystal Palace he signed for Fulham, where his performances led to his recall to the national side for a friendly with Scotland and a couple of matches in the US Nike Cup in the summer of 2000.

Sadly a pre-season injury meant that 2000-01 was a season he will want to forget, as he started just one game! Out of contract, he joined Sheffield United as cover for injuries and suspensions but on leaving Bramall Lane mid-season, joined United States 'A' League club Charleston Battery.

Liam Daish

Position	Central defender
Born	Liam Sean Daish, Portsmouth, 23 September 1968

Clubs

Portsmouth; Cambridge United; Birmingham City; Coventry City

International Caps	5

Matches

Year	Opponent	Result	Score	G
1992	Wales	lost	0-1	
1992	Switzerland	won	2-1	
1996	Czech Republic	lost	0-2	
1996	Croatia	drew	2-2	
1996	Mexico	drew	2-2	

A commanding central defender, Liam Daish began his career with his home-town club Portsmouth. Unable to force his way into the Pompey side on a regular basis, he joined Cambridge United in the summer of 1988.

His displays at the heart of the U's defence were instrumental in the club winning the Third Division Championship in 1990-91. Midway through the following season, Daish made his international debut for the Republic of Ireland under Jack Charlton, in a friendly against Wales. He won a second cap in the next game against Switzerland. With the serious business of World Cup qualification, McGrath and Moran returned to the national side.

In January 1994 Birmingham City manager Barry Fry paid £50,000 to take him to St Andrew's. Fry once said of his centre-half, that if ever a double-decker bus came along, he would head it away! This epitomised the wholehearted defender and Blues' captain, who scored a number of vital goals in leading the club to the Second Division title and the Auto Windscreen Shield victory.

His qualities forced Charlton to recall him to the Republic of Ireland squad, whilst his fellow professionals voted him into the PFA award-winning Second Division team.

In February 1996 Daish was signed by Coventry City to bolster their shaky defence. His committed displays led to him adding to his collection of international caps – his last appearance saw him sent-off in the match against Mexico in New Jersey. In January 1997 a knee injury in training intervened to bring to a premature end the career of a most promising defender.

Tommy Coyne

Position	Forward
Born	Thomas Coyne, Glasgow, 14 November 1962
Clubs	

Clydebank; Dundee United; Dundee; Glasgow Celtic; Tranmere Rovers; Motherwell; Dundee; Falkirk (loan); Clydebank; Albion Rovers

International Caps	22
Internatonal Goals	6

Matches

Year	Opponent	Result	Score	G
1992	Switzerland	won	2-1	1
1992	United States	won	4-1	
1992	Albania	won	2-0	
1992	United States	lost	1-3	
1992	Italy	lost	0-2	
1992	Portugal	won	2-0	1
1993	Latvia	won	4-0	
1993	Wales	won	2-1	1
1993	N Ireland	won	3-0	
1994	Russia	drew	0-0	
1994	Holland	won	1-0	1
1994	Bolivia	won	1-0	
1994	Germany	won	2-0	
1994	Czech Republic	lost	1-3	
1994	Italy	won	1-0	
1994	Mexico	lost	1-2	
1994	Holland	lost	0-2	
1995	Liechtenstein	won	4-0	2
1995	N Ireland	won	4-0	
1995	Austria	lost	1-3	
1996	Russia	lost	0-2	
1998	Belgium	drew	1-1	

Above: Tommy Coyne

One of the most prolific marksmen of his generation, Tommy Coyne first sprang to prominence with Clydebank and then had spells with both Dundee clubs. He made a huge impression with Dundee, bagging over 30 goals in one season. From Dundee he moved to Celtic for £500,000 to cover for Frank McAvennie's anticipated return to London. He initially failed to settle at Parkhead but once he found his feet, proved to be a consistent goalscorer. It was with the Bhoys that he came to the attention of Jack Charlton. Under the grandparent rule, he made his full international debut for the Republic of Ireland against Switzerland in March 1992, scoring in a 2-1 win.

Despite an excellent record for Celtic – 52 goals in 132 games – he was allowed to drift out of Parkhead and into English football with Tranmere Rovers. He was not long at

Prenton Park when he sadly lost his wife Alison. Deciding not to stay in England, he returned north of the border and joined Motherwell, who paid £125,000 for his services.

It was in his early days as a Well player that he experienced his greatest moment in international football. Playing as the lone striker against the Italians in the 1994 World Cup Finals, it was his tireless running that paved the way for a much celebrated 1-0 victory.

Nicknamed 'The Cobra' due to his lightning reflexes, he formed a prolific partnership at Motherwell with both Dougie Arnott and Owen Coyle – scoring 59 goals in 132 games – before rejoining Dundee. Unable to match his first period at the club, he went on loan to Falkirk before spells with Clydebank and Albion Rovers.

Eddie McGoldrick

Position	Midfield
Born	Edward John Paul McGoldrick, Islington, 30 April 1965
Clubs	

Kettering Town; Nuneaton Borough; Northampton Town; Crystal Palace; Arsenal; Manchester City; Stockport County (loan)

International Caps	15

Matches

Year	Opponent	Result	Score	G
1992	Switzerland	won	2-1	
1992	United States	won	4-1	
1992	Italy	lost	0-2	
1992	Portugal	won	2-0	
1993	Denmark	drew	0-0	
1993	Wales	won	2-1	
1993	N Ireland	won	3-0	
1993	Denmark	drew	1-1	
1994	N Ireland	drew	1-1	
1994	Russia	drew	0-0	
1994	Holland	won	1-0	
1994	Czech Republic	lost	1-3	
1995	Latvia	won	3-0	
1995	Liechtenstein	won	4-0	
1995	England	won	1-0	

Having failed to make the grade with Peterborough United, Eddie McGoldrick drifted into non-League football, initially with Kettering Town and then Nuneaton Borough. It was from there that he came into the Football League with Northampton Town. At the end of his first season at the County Ground, he had helped the Cobblers win the Fourth Division Championship, his skilful play a major contributory factor in the club's success.

After two seasons with Northampton McGoldrick signed for Crystal Palace. In his first season at the club, he was a member of the team that was promoted to the top flight via the play-offs. The next season he found himself among the long-term injured and did not regain his place in time for the FA Cup Final against Manchester United. Back in the side in 1991-92 when Palace finished third in Division One, McGoldrick won his first senior cap for the Republic of Ireland in a friendly against Switzerland – although after 45 minutes of his debut he was forced off with a knee injury. In 1992-93, the first season of the Premiership, Crystal Palace were relegated. Following the departure of manager Steve Coppell, it came as no surprise when Eddie McGoldrick was transferred to Arsenal for £1 million, with two years of his contract left.

He was a regular in the Irish side throughout qualification for the 1994 World Cup finals, and earned a place in Jack Charlton's 22-man selection for USA '94. The London-born midfielder failed to make the Republic's starting line-up. Shortly afterwards as his career with the Gunners hit hard times, his days in the green shirt of the Republic drew to a close.

Above: Eddie McGoldrick

In September 1996 he joined Manchester City on loan before signing on a permanent basis a month later. Having joined the club at its lowest ebb, he was one of the reasons that City began to make steady improvement following the New Year. Unfortunately the 1997-98 season was one of huge disappointment for McGoldrick, as niggling injuries and a bout of sciatica kept him out of the side. Following a loan spell with Stockport County, he decided to retire at the end of the campaign.

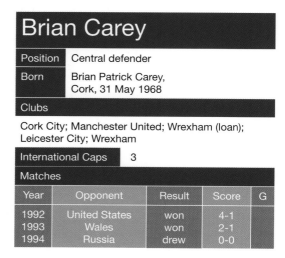

Brian Carey

Position	Central defender
Born	Brian Patrick Carey, Cork, 31 May 1968
Clubs	

Cork City; Manchester United; Wrexham (loan); Leicester City; Wrexham

International Caps	3

Matches

Year	Opponent	Result	Score	G
1992	United States	won	4-1	
1993	Wales	won	2-1	
1994	Russia	drew	0-0	

A tall and commanding central defender, Brian Carey joined Manchester United from Cork City. Before making an appearance for the Reds, he was loaned out to Wrexham and made his Football League debut at Peterborough United in January 1991. He had an even longer (three-month) stay with the Robins in 1991-92, during which he starred in their historic FA Cup victory over reigning League Champions Arsenal, and the two epic games with West Ham United in the fourth round.

The Welsh club wanted to sign him permanently but Alex Ferguson believed that he still had a future at Old Trafford. At the end of that season he was selected for the Republic of Ireland's national squad, and made a brief appearance as a substitute in a friendly against the United States. He added to his reputation when making his full debut for the Republic against Wales. Though he made a further appearance for the national side, his progress towards a regular place in the Irish side was halted by the form of McGrath and Moran.

In the summer of 1993 Carey joined Leicester City for a fee of £250,000. He helped the Foxes win promotion to the Premiership via the play-offs but his initial Premiership selection brought him dismissal against Wimbledon. Later placed on the open-to-offers list, he was sold to Wrexham for £100,000 in the summer of 1996, thus beginning his third spell with the Welsh club.

Voted the club's 'Player of the Year' in his second season at the Racecourse Ground, he then continued to impress at the heart of Wrexham's defence. Appointed club captain, he was hampered by a number of injuries including a hernia operation and a stress fracture of the foot – his experience was sorely missed. On his return to full fitness, he helped the club win promotion, before combining playing duties with coaching the Racecourse youngsters. He had appeared in 356 games for the Robins when released as a player in the summer of 2005. Brian Carey is now coach at the club.

Mike Milligan

Position	Midfield
Born	Michael Joseph Milligan, Manchester, 20 February 1967
Clubs	

Oldham Athletic; Everton; Oldham Athletic; Norwich City; Blackpool

International Caps	1

Matches

Year	Opponent	Result	Score	G
1992	United States	won	4-1	

Although Milligan started out as an associated schoolboy with Manchester City, he was not offered terms by the Maine Road club. He joined Oldham Athletic on a YTS scheme in December 1984.

After working his way up through the ranks at Boundary Park, he was inspirational to a Latics side seeking to attain First Division status. The nearest he came during his time with the club was when reaching the play-offs in 1986-87. He played a significant role in Oldham's wonderful cup runs of 1989-90, winning through to the semi-final of the FA Cup before succumbing in a replay to Manchester United, and the final of the League Cup, where they lost to Nottingham Forest.

He moved to Everton in the 1990 close season as an aspiring midfield general, but did not fit in at Goodison Park. After a season, Milligan returned to Boundary Park for a knock-down price. He played a leading role in consolidating the Latics' newly won First Division status.

After a long wait he finally broke into the Republic of Ireland team in April 1992, although only as a substitute in a low-priority friendly against the United States.

As Oldham's team captain, Milligan consistently turned in excellent performances, helping his side avoid relegation after being written off by the media. He went on to appear in 336 games for Oldham before an £800,000 transfer took him to Norwich City in the summer of 1994.

Unable to prevent the Canaries' relegation, he was then hampered by injuries, notably a serious knee complaint and a hernia operation. Whilst with Norwich, the highly competitive midfielder played the 500th game of his club career. After turning down the opportunity of becoming player-coach at Shrewsbury Town, he joined Blackpool on a free transfer but following two injury-hit seasons at Bloomfield Road, Mike Milligan decided to hang up his boots.

Alan Kernaghan

Position	Central defender
Born	Alan Nigel Kernaghan, Otley, 25 April 1967

Clubs

Middlesbrough; Charlton Athletic (loan); Manchester City; Bolton Wanderers (loan); Bradford City (loan); St Johnstone

International Caps	22
International Goals	1

Matches

Year	Opponent	Result	Score	G
1993	Latvia	won	4-0	
1993	Denmark	drew	0-0	
1993	Denmark	drew	1-1	
1993	Albania	won	2-1	
1993	Latvia	won	2-0	
1993	Lithuania	won	1-0	
1994	Lithuania	won	2-0	1
1994	Spain	lost	1-3	
1994	N Ireland	drew	1-1	
1994	Bolivia	won	1-0	
1994	Czech Republic	lost	1-3	
1995	Liechtenstein	won	4-0	
1995	England	won	1-0	
1996	Austria	lost	1-3	
1996	Portugal	lost	0-3	
1996	Holland	lost	0-2	
1996	Russia	lost	0-2	
1996	Portugal	lost	0-1	
1996	Croatia	drew	2-2	
1996	Holland	lost	1-3	
1996	United States	lost	1-2	
1996	Bolivia	won	3-0	

Above: Alan Kernaghan

He made his international debut for the Republic of Ireland in a World Cup qualifier against Latvia in September 1992, and in the next game partnered Kevin Moran against European Champions Denmark. This new central defensive pairing kept a clean sheet and for the rest of the 1994 World Cup qualifying campaign, Kernaghan understudied McGrath and Moran.

In September 1993, just days after leaving Middlesbrough for Manchester City in a £1.6 million deal, Kernaghan scored his only goal for the Republic in a 2-0 defeat of Lithuania – his celebrations left little to doubt his commitment to the Republic's cause. He was included in Jack Charlton's squad for USA '94 but failed to make an appearance in the finals.

At Maine Road, Kernaghan appeared to have lost his confidence in the Premiership. He joined Bolton Wanderers

Having won schoolboy international honours for Northern Ireland, central defender Alan Kernaghan began his career with Middlesbrough. He helped them win promotion from the Third Division in 1986–87 and in the following season helped them go up again via the play-offs.

In January 1991 he joined Charlton Athletic on loan but returned to Ayresome Park to become a member of the Boro side that won promotion to the top flight in 1991–92 as runners-up to Ipswich Town.

on loan, taking the opportunity to regain his consistency. After forcing his way back into the City side, he lost out following the appointment of Alan Ball. Following a loan spell with Bradford City, he went north of the border to join St Johnstone, where he ended his career.

Alan Kelly junior

Position	Goalkeeper
Born	Alan Thomas Kelly, Preston, 11 August 1968

Clubs

Preston North End; Sheffield United; Blackburn Rovers; Stockport County (loan); Birmingham City (loan)

International Caps	34

Matches

Year	Opponent	Result	Score	G
1993	Wales	won	2-1	
1994	Russia	drew	0-0	
1994	Germany	won	2-0	
1995	Latvia	won	3-0	
1995	N Ireland	won	4-0	
1995	England	won	1-0	
1995	N Ireland	drew	1-1	
1995	Portugal	won	1-0	
1995	Liechtenstein	drew	0-0	
1995	Austria	lost	1-3	
1996	Austria	lost	1-3	
1996	Latvia	won	2-1	
1996	Portugal	lost	0-3	
1996	Holland	lost	0-2	
1997	Macedonia	won	3-0	
1997	Iceland	drew	0-0	
1997	Macedonia	lost	2-3	
1997	Romania	lost	0-1	
1998	Romania	drew	1-1	
1998	Argentina	lost	0-2	
1999	Paraguay	won	2-0	
1999	Macedonia	won	1-0	
2000	Yugoslavia	won	2-1	
2000	Croatia	lost	0-2	
2000	Malta	won	3-2	
2000	Macedonia	drew	1-1	
2000	Turkey	drew	1-1	
2000	Czech Republic	won	3-2	
2000	Scotland	lost	1-2	
2000	United States	drew	1-1	
2001	Holland	drew	2-2	
2001	Portugal	drew	1-1	
2001	Estonia	won	2-0	
2002	Croatia	drew	2-2	

Above: Alan Kelly

The son of Republic of Ireland goalkeeping legend Alan Kelly, he followed in his father's footsteps when he joined Preston North End.

After making his League debut against Crewe Alexandra in March 1986, he kept his place until the end of the season – when North End reached their nadir of 23rd place in Division Four. In 1986-87 he shared the goalkeeping duties with David Brown as Preston's remarkable turnaround saw them win promotion to the Third Division. A long-term injury then kept him out of action before he returned to contest the No.1 jersey, first with Brown and then Simon Farnworth. After such a 'stop/start' career with a struggling Third Division club, it came as a surprise when Dave Basset signed him for Premier League

Sheffield United as cover for Simon Tracey in the summer of 1992.

Kelly became the first-ever substitute goalkeeper under new Premier League rules when he replaced Tracey for the last ten minutes of a game at Tottenham's White Hart Lane ground. When Tracey was ruled out for the remainder of the season, Kelly acquitted himself so well that he was called into Jack Charlton's Republic of Ireland squad.

He made his international debut in February 1993, replacing Bonner at half-time in a friendly game against Wales, which the Republic won 2-1. Though Bonner was back for the next game, Kelly had done enough in keeping a clean sheet to establish himself as the Celtic keeper's understudy. In May 1994 he was first included in a Republic starting line-up for a friendly against Germany and again didn't concede any goals in a 2-0 win. Rewarded with a place in Jack Charlton's squad for USA '94, he remained on the bench throughout the tournament, but later replaced Bonner as the Republic's first-choice keeper. His early form for the national side was sensational – remaining unbeaten in six hours of football. Injury prevented him from playing in any of new manager Mick McCarthy's first nine games in charge. When he had recovered, he found Shay Given had benefited from his absence.

Back at Bramall Lane, Kelly was elected to the 1995-96 PFA First Division team by his fellow professionals – an honour he received for the next two seasons. It was around this time that he began to suffer from a spate of injuries – one a cartilage injury that kept him out for three months. Kelly left the Blades in the summer of 1999, joining Blackburn Rovers for

£675,000. He began to appear on a more regular basis for the national side. However, after dropping down the pecking order at Ewood Park behind Filan and Friedel, he had loan spells with Stockport County and Birmingham City prior to retiring.

Phil Babb

Position	Central defender
Born	Philip Andrew Babb, Lambeth, 30 November 1970

Clubs

Millwall; Bradford City; Coventry City; Liverpool; Tranmere Rovers (loan); Sporting Lisbon (Portugal); Sunderland

International Caps	35

Matches

Year	Opponent	Result	Score	G
1994	Russia	drew	0-0	
1994	Holland	won	1-0	
1994	Bolivia	won	1-0	
1994	Germany	won	2-0	
1994	Czech Republic	lost	1-3	
1994	Italy	won	1-0	
1994	Mexico	lost	1-2	
1994	Norway	drew	0-0	
1994	Holland	lost	0-2	
1995	Latvia	won	3-0	
1995	Liechtenstein	won	4-0	
1995	N Ireland	won	4-0	
1995	N Ireland	drew	1-1	
1995	Portugal	won	1-0	
1995	Liechtenstein	drew	0-0	
1995	Austria	lost	1-3	
1996	Latvia	won	2-1	
1996	Portugal	lost	0-3	
1996	Holland	lost	0-2	
1996	Czech Republic	lost	0-2	
1997	Iceland	drew	0-0	
1998	Lithuania	won	2-1	
1998	Romania	drew	1-1	
1998	Argentina	lost	0-2	
1998	Mexico	drew	0-0	
1999	Croatia	won	2-0	
1999	Paraguay	won	2-0	
1999	Sweden	won	2-0	
1999	N Ireland	lost	0-1	
2000	Czech Republic	won	3-2	
2000	Scotland	lost	1-2	
2000	Mexico	drew	2-2	
2000	United States	drew	1-1	
2000	South Africa	won	2-1	
2003	Russia	lost	2-4	

Unable to get a game with Millwall, since joining as a trainee in the summer of 1987, Babb was signed by former Lions' boss John Doherty for his new club, Bradford City.

After making a scoring debut as a substitute at Valley Parade against Reading in September 1990 Babb, playing as a forward, finished the season as City's second-from-top scorer. Moved into central defence by new manager Frank Stapleton, he was surprisingly signed by Coventry City's new manager Bobby Gould for a fee of £500,000 in July 1992.

Above: Phil Babb

Following several 'Man-of-the-Match' awards, he was selected for the Republic of Ireland squad for the friendly against Albania, but had to wait until the following March before making his debut in the goalless draw with Russia. Impressing Jack

Charlton in a round of post-qualification matches for the 1994 World Cup, Babb played alongside Paul McGrath in the finals, where their partnership was one of the tournament highlights for the Republic. His displays for both the Republic and Coventry City led to him becoming the subject of intense transfer speculation during the autumn of 1994. In September he joined Liverpool for a fee of £3.75 million.

It made Phil Babb the most expensive defender in Britain. An automatic choice for the Reds as one of three central defenders, he occasionally found it difficult to come to terms with the formation, though he impressed in the 1-0 FA Cup Final defeat by Manchester United. It was then that Babb began to lose his way, both with Liverpool and the Republic of Ireland – especially at Anfield where his prospects weren't helped by the return of Steve Staunton or the arrival of new coach Gerard Houllier. He spent a month on loan with Tranmere Rovers, prior to winning back his place in the national team. After appearing in 170 games for Liverpool, he parted company with the club by moving to Sporting Lisbon. In the summer of 2002 Sunderland manager Peter Reid snapped him up on a free transfer. His performances for the Black Cats won him a surprise recall to the international set-up against Russia. Injuries then prevented him from playing for the north-east club on a regular basis and he decided to retire.

Garry Kelly

Position	Right-back
Born	Garry Kelly, Drogheda, 9 July 1974

Clubs

Home Farm; Leeds United

International Caps	52
International Goals	2

Matches

Year	Opponent	Result	Score	G
1994	Russia	drew	0-0	
1994	Holland	won	1-0	
1994	Bolivia	won	1-0	
1994	Germany	won	2-0	1
1994	Czech Republic	lost	1-3	
1994	Norway	drew	0-0	
1994	Holland	lost	0-2	
1995	Latvia	won	3-0	
1995	Liechtenstein	won	4-0	
1995	N Ireland	won	4-0	
1995	N Ireland	drew	1-1	
1995	Portugal	won	1-0	
1995	Liechtenstein	drew	0-0	
1995	Austria	lost	1-3	
1996	Austria	lost	1-3	
1996	Latvia	won	2-1	
1996	Portugal	lost	0-3	
1996	Holland	lost	0-2	
1997	Wales	drew	0-0	
1997	Romania	lost	0-1	
1997	Liechtenstein	won	5-0	
1998	Iceland	won	4-2	
1998	Lithuania	won	2-1	
1998	Belgium	drew	1-1	
1998	Belgium	lost	1-2	
1998	Czech Republic	lost	1-2	
1998	Argentina	lost	0-2	
1998	Mexico	drew	0-0	
2000	Croatia	lost	0-2	
2000	Macedonia	drew	1-1	
2000	Czech Republic	won	3-2	
2001	Holland	drew	2-2	
2001	Finland	won	3-0	
2001	Cyprus	won	4-0	1
2001	Andorra	won	3-0	
2001	Andorra	won	3-1	
2001	Portugal	drew	1-1	
2001	Estonia	won	2-0	
2002	Croatia	drew	2-2	
2002	Holland	won	1-0	
2002	Iran	won	2-0	
2002	Iran	lost	0-1	
2002	Russia	won	2-0	
2002	Denmark	won	3-0	
2002	United States	won	2-1	
2002	Nigeria	lost	1-2	

Matches Continued				
Year	Opponent	Result	Score	G
2002	Cameroon	drew	1-1	
2002	Germany	drew	1-1	
2002	Saudi Arabia	won	3-0	
2002	Spain	drew	1-1	
2003	Finland	won	3-0	
2003	Switzerland	lost	1-2	

The youngest of a family of 13, Garry Kelly joined Leeds United from Home Farm, the Dublin club that has produced a number of stars for the Yorkshire club over the years, Johnny Giles among them.

Above: Garry Kelly

He was a striker in the reserves when he was pitched into first team action as a 17-year-old winger, in a League Cup tie against Scunthorpe United in October 1991. Apart from a few appearances off the bench, he did not re-emerge until the start of the 1993-94 season. Howard Wilkinson fielded him at right-back for the opening-day fixture against Manchester City. Making the No.2 shirt his own, he matured so quickly that Jack Charlton awarded him his first full cap for the Republic of Ireland's match against Russia in March 1994.

Though he hadn't scored for Leeds, he netted in the international friendly against World Cup-holders Germany in Hanover – Charlton had seen enough and the 19-year-old Kelly headed west for USA '94. It was thought Kelly would see out the tournament on the bench. When Irwin collected a second booking in the heated match against Mexico, Kelly got his chance in the next game against Norway. In doing so, he became the youngest player to appear for the Republic of Ireland in a World Cup Finals. With Irwin and Phelan available for the final group match, Kelly retained his place for the game against Holland but the Irish lost 2-0.

It wasn't long before he was regarded as one of the best right-backs in the Premiership. Although he had a spell playing under new managers at both club level (George Graham) and at international level (Mick McCarthy) he continued to produce performances of the highest quality. Occasionally playing on the right of midfield, where his searing pace was used to good effect, Kelly also captained the United side and showed his versatility when deployed in central defence. A serious shin injury kept him out for the entire 1998-99 season. Despite United signing Danny Mills for £4 million from Charlton Athletic, Kelly won back his place and was selected by his fellow professionals in the PFA award-winning Premiership side. By the turn of the century, Kelly was Leeds United's longest-serving player, though a spate of niggling injuries reduced his first-team opportunities. Following Mills' departure to Middlesbrough Kelly regained his first team place, despite the club's relegation from the Premiership and its financial upheaval.

Kelly was capped 52 times by the Republic of Ireland and appeared in 464 games for Leeds United. He opened a cancer-care centre in his home-town of Drogheda, having donated a substantial sum from his testimonial game against Celtic in memory of his sister Mandy, who had died of the illness.

Jason McAteer

Position	Midfield
Born	Jason Wynn McAteer, Birkenhead, 18 June 1971

Clubs
Marine; Bolton Wanderers; Liverpool; Blackburn Rovers; Sunderland; Tranmere Rovers

International Caps	52
International Goals	3

Matches				
Year	Opponent	Result	Score	G
1994	Russia	drew	0-0	
1994	Holland	won	1-0	
1994	Bolivia	won	1-0	
1994	Germany	won	2-0	
1994	Czech Republic	lost	1-3	
1994	Italy	won	1-0	
1994	Mexico	lost	1-2	
1994	Norway	drew	0-0	
1994	Holland	lost	0-2	
1995	Latvia	won	3-0	
1995	Liechtenstein	won	4-0	
1995	N Ireland	won	4-0	
1995	N Ireland	drew	1-1	
1995	Liechtenstein	drew	0-0	
1996	Latvia	won	2-1	
1996	Portugal	lost	0-3	
1996	Holland	lost	0-2	
1996	Russia	lost	0-2	
1997	Macedonia	won	3-0	1
1997	Iceland	drew	0-0	
1997	Wales	drew	0-0	
1997	Macedonia	lost	2-3	
1998	Iceland	won	4-2	
1998	Lithuania	won	2-1	
1998	Romania	drew	1-1	
1999	Croatia	won	2-0	
1999	Malta	won	5-0	
1999	Yugoslavia	lost	0-1	
1999	Paraguay	won	2-0	
1999	Sweden	won	2-0	

Matches				
Year	Opponent	Result	Score	G
2000	Czech Republic	won	3-2	
2000	Scotland	lost	1-2	
2000	Mexico	drew	2-2	
2000	United States	drew	1-1	
2000	South Africa	won	2-1	
2001	Holland	drew	2-2	1
2001	Portugal	drew	1-1	
2001	Estonia	won	2-0	
2001	Finland	won	3-0	
2001	Cyprus	won	4-0	
2002	Croatia	drew	2-2	
2002	Holland	won	1-0	1
2002	Iran	won	2-0	
2002	Iran	lost	0-1	
2002	Russia	won	2-0	
2002	Denmark	won	3-0	
2002	Nigeria	lost	1-2	
2002	Cameroon	drew	1-1	
2002	Saudi Arabia	won	3-0	
2003	Finland	won	3-0	
2003	Russia	lost	2-4	
2004	Brazil	drew	0-0	

A direct hard-running footballer, Jason McAteer was spotted by Bolton Wanderers' manager Phil Neal playing for Marine Reserves in the Lancashire League. He was invited to Burnden Park for a trial. It wasn't long before he made his first-team debut, coming off the bench to replace Scott Green in a 4-0 win over Burnley in November 1992. He kept his place in the side for the next match, a second round FA Cup tie against Rochdale and scored one of the goals in another 4-0 win.

He made rapid progress and by the following February was a regular in the centre of midfield. He took part in every League game in 1993-94 and he also began to find the net – striking in both memorable FA Cup fourth-round ties against Arsenal.

He made his Republic of Ireland debut in March 1994 when he played in the goalless draw against Russia. Further impressive displays secured his participation in four of the World Cup games in the United States. McAteer became the first Bolton player to appear in a World Cup Finals competition since Tommy Banks in 1958. He then enjoyed a spectacular season with the Wanderers, which ended in promotion via the play-offs and an appearance in the League Cup Final. He had made just four Premiership appearances for the Trotters when Liverpool secured his signature for £4.5 million.

Above: Jason McAteer

At Anfield he was quickly installed in the first team, playing as an attacking wing-back on the right-hand side. In his first season he helped Liverpool reach the FA Cup Final which ended in defeat against Manchester United.

For the Republic though, he continued to play in midfield and was a regular during the qualifying rounds for Euro '96. He netted his first international goal in the 3-0 win over Macedonia in October 1996. In the return match the following April, he was red-carded for an uncharacteristically crude challenge.

The following season while playing for Liverpool, he suffered a broken left fibula and missed almost six months of action. On his return he scored twice in a 5-0 defeat of West Ham United. Though he continued to play for the Republic of Ireland, his days at Anfield were numbered.

In January 1999 he joined Blackburn Rovers for a fee of £4 million. His early days at Ewood Park were hampered by injuries and disciplinary problems though he later scored the first goal in a Blackburn-Burnley derby for 18 years! Used sparingly by Graeme Souness, McAteer opted for a move to Sunderland in October 2001, the Wearsiders paying £1 million for his services.

He made an immediate impact at the Stadium of Light before injuries took their toll, including surgery on an abdominal hernia. Starting the 2003-04 season as club captain, he led the Black Cats to the FA Cup semi-finals and earned a recall to the Republic of Ireland side before surprisingly being released by the club in the summer.

He then signed for Tranmere Rovers, where he was immediately made captain. Different recurrent injuries meant that McAteer, who has made 52 appearances for the Republic of Ireland was used tactically and carefully during the season.

Owen Coyle

Position	Forward
Born	Owen Columba Coyle, Glasgow, 14 July 1966

Clubs

Dumbarton; Clydebank; Airdrieonians; Bolton Wanderers; Dundee United; Motherwell; Dunfermline Athletic; Ross County (loan); Airdrieonians; Falkirk; Dundee United; Airdrie United; St Johnstone

International Caps			1	

Matches

Year	Opponent	Result	Score	G
1994	Holland	won	1-0	

Striker Owen Coyle began his career with Dumbarton, making his League debut against Ayr United in February 1986. After establishing himself in their side, he was the club's leading scorer in 1987-88, form that saw him transferred to Clydebank. The Bankies just missed out on promotion but Coyle (who had scored 34 goals in 68 games) became their record sale when Airdrieonians paid £175,000 for him in February 1990.

Coyle grabbed a hat-trick on his debut in a 6-0 home win over Ayr. Although he ended the season as their leading goalscorer, they missed out on promotion. In 1990-91 he set off like a house on fire, grabbing four hat-tricks in the opening seven games. He missed a number of games through injury, but ended the season as their leading scorer and helped them into the Premier League. In 1992 Airdrie reached the Scottish Cup Final where they lost 2-1 to Rangers. It was enough to give Coyle his first taste of European football the following season.

In July 1993 he joined Bolton Wanderers for a tribunal-set fee of £250,000. The slightly-built Coyle scored some vital FA Cup goals during 1993-94 that helped Wanderers reach the sixth round.

In April 1994 Owen Coyle won his only full cap for the Republic of Ireland, as a substitute for Tommy Coyne in the 86th minute of a World Cup warm-up friendly against Holland. Though Aldridge, Cascarino and Coyne were the settled strike-force, injuries robbed Coyle of further appearances, so after just four minutes, his international career was at an end.

His goal for Bolton in the play-off final against Reading at Wembley set the Lancashire club off on their comeback trail. After just a handful of appearances in the Premiership, Coyle was transferred to Dundee United.

He later moved on to Motherwell and spells followed with Dunfermline Athletic and Ross County prior to joining Airdrieonians. After topping their scoring charts, he left Broomfield Park to play for Falkirk, helping The Bairns win the First Division Championship. One of the Scottish League's most prolific scorers he then played with Dundee United and Airdrie United ending his playing days with First Division St Johnstone whom he now manages.

Jeff Kenna

Position	Full-back
Born	Jeffrey Jude Kenna, Dublin, 27 August 1970

Clubs

Southampton; Blackburn Rovers; Tranmere Rovers (loan); Wigan Athletic (loan); Birmingham City; Derby County

International Caps			27	

Matches

Year	Opponent	Result	Score	G
1995	Portugal	won	1-0	
1995	Liechtenstein	drew	0-0	
1995	Austria	lost	1-3	
1996	Latvia	won	2-1	
1996	Portugal	lost	0-3	

Matches Continued

Year	Opponent	Result	Score	G
1996	Holland	lost	0-2	
1996	Russia	lost	0-2	
1996	Czech Republic	lost	0-2	
1996	Portugal	lost	0-1	
1996	Croatia	drew	2-2	
1996	Holland	lost	1-3	
1996	United States	lost	1-2	
1997	Liechtenstein	won	5-0	
1997	Macedonia	won	3-0	
1997	Iceland	drew	0-0	
1997	Romania	lost	0-1	
1997	Liechtenstein	won	5-0	
1998	Lithuania	drew	0-0	
1998	Iceland	won	4-2	
1998	Romania	drew	1-1	
1998	Belgium	drew	1-1	
1998	Belgium	lost	1-2	
1998	Czech Republic	lost	1-2	
1998	Argentina	lost	0-2	
1999	Croatia	won	2-0	
1999	Malta	won	5-0	
2000	Turkey	drew	0-0	

Jeff Kenna had already been selected three times for the Republic of Ireland Under-21 side when he made his debut for Southampton against Derby County in May 1991. After sharing the No.2 shirt with Jason Dodd the following season, he became a regular in the Saints' side in 1992-93, becoming ever-present in 1993-94. In March 1995 Kenna was a shock signing for Blackburn Rovers who paid £1.5 million for his services.

He initially played left-back, with Graeme Le Saux moving upfield. He was later switched to wide right, wide left and finally to right-back! Just a few games short of a Championship medal, Kenna made his international debut as a substitute for Ray Houghton in the European Championship qualifier against Portugal at Lansdowne Road. He made further appearances from the bench before being drafted into the starting line-up for the last two qualifiers against Latvia and Portugal.

Kenna was often played out of position for Rovers and occasionally struggled on his weaker

surprise when he was allowed to join Derby County in March 2004. His ability to perform in any defensive position was invaluable in a team frequently disrupted by injuries. Unable to prevent the Rams' relegation he settled in to play his best football as the club made a bid to reach the play-offs.

Mark Kennedy

Position	Left-winger
Born	Mark Kennedy, Dublin, 15 May 1976

Clubs

Millwall; Liverpool; Queen's Park Rangers (loan); Wimbledon; Manchester City; Wolverhampton Wanderers

International Caps	34
International Goals	3

Matches

Year	Opponent	Result	Score	G
1996	Austria	lost	1-3	
1996	Latvia	won	2-1	
1996	Portugal	lost	0-3	
1996	Russia	lost	0-2	
1996	Czech Republic	lost	0-2	
1996	Croatia	drew	2-2	
1996	Holland	lost	1-3	
1996	United States	lost	1-2	
1996	Mexico	drew	2-2	
1996	Bolivia	won	3-0	
1997	Romania	lost	0-1	
1997	Liechtenstein	won	5-0	
1998	Lithuania	drew	0-0	
1998	Iceland	won	4-2	
1998	Romania	drew	1-1	
1998	Belgium	drew	1-1	
1998	Belgium	lost	1-2	
1998	Mexico	drew	0-0	
1999	Malta	won	5-0	
1999	Sweden	won	2-0	1
1999	N Ireland	lost	0-1	
1999	Macedonia	won	1-0	
2000	Yugoslavia	won	2-1	1
2000	Malta	won	3-2	
2000	Macedonia	drew	1-1	
2000	Czech Republic	won	3-2	
2000	Scotland	lost	1-2	1
2000	Mexico	drew	2-2	
2000	United States	drew	1-1	
2000	South Africa	won	2-1	
2001	Andorra	won	3-1	
2002	Croatia	drew	2-2	
2002	Cyprus	won	4-0	
2002	Russia	won	2-0	

side, but remained a regular in the Republic of Ireland side for the qualifiers for the 1998 World Cup Finals. He was absent for the disastrous defeat in Macedonia in April 1997.

At club level, he turned out for Rovers when not fully fit. As this obviously affected his form, he eventually lost his first team place. Still making infrequent appearances for the national side, he had to undergo two operations on an Achilles tendon injury. After recovering he went on loan to Tranmere Rovers, where his experience proved invaluable during an ultimately unsuccessful struggle against relegation. There followed another loan spell with Wigan Athletic before he joined Birmingham City in a similar capacity, prior to the move being made permanent.

Appointed the Blues' captain, he was a virtual ever-present at St Andrew's. It came as a great

Mark Kennedy first caught the eye as a lanky teenager in Mick McCarthy's Millwall team that beat both Chelsea and Arsenal in the 1994-95 FA Cup competition.

He certainly benefited by being given a wide attacking role. Following his debut for the Republic at Under-21 level, he joined Liverpool in March 1995 for a fee of £1.5 million. It made him Britain's most expensive teenager and he was soon given the opportunity to shine at Anfield.

The dream continued with his full international debut for the Republic of Ireland against Austria in a European

Championship qualifier. Though he was a fixture on the Liverpool bench throughout 1995-96, his club experience did not stop him from adding to his collection of caps at international level.

Following a loan spell with Queen's Park Rangers, the talented left-sided winger joined Wimbledon in March 1998 for £1.75 million – despite carrying a broken wrist which prevented him from playing in all but the last four games of the season. Kennedy did not have many chances the following season and while he continued to represent the Republic of Ireland, he joined Manchester City for £1 million, rising to £1.5 million after a certain number of appearances.

The scorer of a number of spectacular goals as City won promotion to the Premiership, Kennedy was recognised by his fellow professionals by selection to the award-winning PFA First Division team. On the international front, he scored in the games against Yugoslavia and Scotland, the goal against the East Europeans coming from 35 yards out to clinch a 2-1 win.

After finding life in the Premiership difficult, he suffered a number of injuries including a torn medial ligament. Unable to hold down a regular place on his return, Kennedy moved on to Wolverhampton Wanderers for £1.8 million. Helping his new side to the play-offs, he was again named in the PFA First Division side. Sadly injury forced him out of the 2002 World Cup Finals. Still not fit for the start of the following season, Kenna eventually recovered to score the vital goal in the play-off final against Sheffield United at the Millennium Stadium. Struggling to make an impact in the Premiership, although he scored against former club Manchester City, the last season or so at Molineux has seen the Dublin-born player sidelined by a spate of niggling injuries.

Shay Given

Position	Goalkeeper
Born	Seamus John Given, Lifford, Co. Donegal, 20 April 1976

Clubs

Glasgow Celtic; Blackburn Rovers; Swindon Town (loan); Sunderland (loan); Newcastle United

International Caps	71

Matches

Year	Opponent	Result	Score	G
1996	Russia	lost	0-2	
1996	Czech Republic	lost	0-2	
1996	Portugal	lost	0-1	
1996	Croatia	drew	2-2	
1996	Holland	lost	1-3	
1996	United States	lost	1-2	
1996	Bolivia	won	3-0	
1997	Liechtenstein	won	5-0	
1997	Liechtenstein	won	5-0	
1998	Lithuania	drew	0-0	
1998	Iceland	won	4-2	
1998	Lithuania	won	2-1	
1998	Belgium	drew	1-1	
1998	Belgium	lost	1-2	
1998	Czech Republic	lost	1-2	
1998	Argentina	lost	0-2	
1998	Mexico	drew	0-0	
1999	Croatia	won	2-0	
1999	Malta	won	5-0	
1999	Yugoslavia	lost	0-1	
1999	Paraguay	won	2-0	
1999	Sweden	won	2-0	
1999	N Ireland	lost	0-1	
2000	Greece	lost	0-1	
2000	South Africa	won	2-1	
2001	Finland	won	3-0	
2001	Cyprus	won	4-0	
2001	Andorra	won	3-0	
2001	Andorra	won	3-1	
2001	Portugal	drew	1-1	
2001	Estonia	won	2-0	
2002	Croatia	drew	2-2	
2002	Holland	won	1-0	
2002	Cyprus	won	4-0	
2002	Iran	won	2-0	
2002	Iran	lost	0-1	
2002	Russia	won	2-0	
2002	United States	won	2-1	
2002	Nigeria	lost	1-2	
2002	Cameroon	drew	1-1	
2002	Germany	drew	1-1	
2002	Saudi Arabia	won	3-0	
2002	Spain	drew	1-1	
2003	Finland	won	3-0	
2003	Russia	lost	2-4	
2003	Switzerland	lost	1-2	
2003	Greece	drew	0-0	

Matches

Year	Opponent	Result	Score	G
2003	Georgia	won	2-1	
2003	Albania	drew	0-0	
2003	Norway	won	1-0	
2003	Albania	won	2-1	
2003	Georgia	won	2-0	
2004	Russia	drew	1-1	
2004	Switzerland	lost	0-2	
2004	Canada	won	3-0	
2004	Brazil	drew	0-0	
2004	Czech Republic	won	2-1	
2004	Poland	drew	0-0	
2004	Romania	won	1-0	
2004	Holland	won	1-0	
2005	Bulgaria	drew	1-1	
2005	Cyprus	won	3-0	
2005	Switzerland	drew	1-1	
2005	France	drew	0-0	
2005	Faroe Islands	won	2-0	
2005	Croatia	won	1-0	
2005	Portugal	won	1-0	
2005	Israel	drew	1-1	
2005	Israel	drew	2-2	
2005	Faroe Islands	won	2-0	
2006	Sweden	won	3-0	

Goalkeeper Shay Given began his career with Glasgow giants Celtic. After turning 18 – making the bench for the Bhoys but not the team – he moved south in the summer of 1994 to join Blackburn Rovers.

His League debut came whilst on loan to Swindon Town. This was followed by another loan spell, this time with Sunderland. Displaying ultra-confidence, Given played 17 games for the then-Roker Park club, keeping 12 clean sheets. He not only picked up a First Division Championship medal but won his first full cap for the Republic of Ireland, having earlier played at Under-21 level.

He then went on to play in Mick McCarthy's first six games in charge, before losing his place because he was not playing regular first team football at Blackburn. Desperate for first team football, and out of contract at Ewood Park, Given joined Newcastle United for a tribunal-set fee of £1.5 million.

The move certainly enhanced his international prospects as he became a regular between the posts for the Republic of Ireland. Injured on international duty in November 1997, he was replaced at club level by Shaka Hislop. Given soon returned to action and played his part in helping the club reach Wembley with two excellent saves at critical points in the FA Cup semi-final. This was in contrast to the following season when after helping

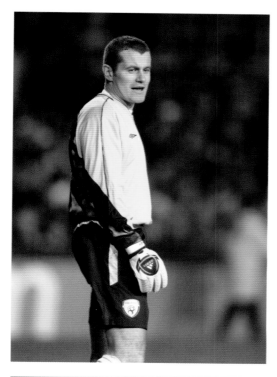

Above: Shay Given

the Magpies beat Spurs in the FA Cup semi-final, his form dipped and he lost his place to Steve Harper prior to the final at Wembley. While training with the national team in the 1999 close season, he nicked a cartilage in his right knee and had to undergo surgery. In only his second game back, he broke a bone in his wrist but following further treatment and rest, re-established himself as Newcastle's first-

choice keeper. Over the next couple of seasons he proved himself to be one of the top keepers in the Premiership. In 2001–02 his efforts were rewarded with a place in the PFA Premiership team. Having become the Magpies' most-capped player, he was outstanding for the Republic in the 2002 World Cup.

After being ever-present for the third season in succession (setting a new all-time record for consecutive appearances in the competition), his run of 140 games came to an end in November 2004, when he was absent to attend the birth of his first child. Given became the first Newcastle player to reach 50 European appearances and took his tally of international caps for the Republic of Ireland to 70. His performance in the World Cup qualifier against Switzerland was described by many as his best-ever for Ireland.

Kenny Cunningham

Position	Defender
Born	Kenneth Edward Cunningham, Dublin, 28 June 1971

Clubs

Home Farm; Tolka Rovers; Millwall; Wimbledon; Birmingham City; Sunderland

International Caps	68

Matches

Year	Opponent	Result	Score	G
1996	Czech Republic	lost	0-2	
1996	Portugal	lost	0-1	
1996	Croatia	drew	2-2	
1996	Holland	lost	1-3	
1996	United States	lost	1-2	
1996	Bolivia	won	3-0	
1997	Iceland	drew	0-0	
1997	Wales	drew	0-0	
1997	Romania	lost	0-1	
1997	Liechtenstein	won	5-0	
1998	Lithuania	drew	0-0	
1998	Iceland	won	4-2	
1998	Lithuania	won	2-1	
1998	Belgium	drew	1-1	
1998	Belgium	lost	1-2	
1998	Czech Republic	lost	1-2	
1999	Croatia	won	2-0	
1999	Malta	won	5-0	
1999	Yugoslavia	lost	0-1	
1999	Paraguay	won	2-0	

Matches Continued

Year	Opponent	Result	Score	G
1999	Sweden	won	2-0	
1999	N Ireland	lost	0-1	
1999	Macedonia	won	1-0	
2000	Yugoslavia	won	2-1	
2000	Croatia	lost	0-2	
2000	Malta	won	3-2	
2000	Macedonia	drew	1-1	
2000	Turkey	drew	1-1	
2000	Turkey	drew	0-0	
2000	Czech Republic	won	3-2	
2000	Greece	lost	0-1	
2001	Cyprus	won	4-0	
2001	Andorra	won	3-0	
2002	Iran	lost	0-1	
2002	Russia	won	2-0	
2002	Denmark	won	3-0	
2002	United States	won	2-1	
2002	Nigeria	lost	1-2	
2002	Germany	drew	1-1	
2002	Spain	drew	1-1	
2003	Finland	won	3-0	
2003	Russia	lost	2-4	
2003	Switzerland	lost	1-2	
2003	Greece	drew	0-0	
2003	Georgia	won	2-1	
2003	Albania	drew	0-0	
2003	Albania	won	2-1	
2003	Georgia	won	2-0	
2004	Australia	won	2-1	
2004	Russia	drew	1-1	
2004	Canada	won	3-0	
2004	Brazil	drew	0-0	
2004	Czech Republic	won	2-1	
2004	Poland	drew	0-0	
2004	Romania	won	1-0	
2004	Nigeria	lost	0-3	
2004	Holland	won	1-0	
2005	Bulgaria	drew	1-1	
2005	Cyprus	won	3-0	
2005	Switzerland	drew	1-1	
2005	France	drew	0-0	
2005	Faroe Islands	won	2-0	
2005	Croatia	won	1-0	
2005	Portugal	won	1-0	
2005	Israel	drew	1-1	
2005	China	won	1-0	
2005	Israel	drew	2-2	
2005	Faroe Islands	won	2-0	

Kenny Cunningham began his career as a junior with Home Farm prior to a spell with Tolka Rovers. In September 1989 he joined Millwall and by the end of the season was lining up alongside his future international manager Mick McCarthy in the top flight.

Over the next couple of seasons, Cunningham established himself as the Lions' first-choice right-back. His assured displays led to four caps for the Republic of Ireland at Under-21 level.

In November 1994, a £1.25 million deal took Cunningham and Jon Goodman to Wimbledon. Progress in the Premiership was followed by a full international debut against the Czech Republic in Prague in April 1996. During the course of 1998 Cunningham's growing importance to the national side was twice rewarded: first when he was handed the captaincy for the friendly against the Czech Republic; then towards the end of the year when he was named the FAI/Opel International Player of the Year.

A most-versatile defender, Cunningham captained the Dons. In 1999-2000 he played

in every game except the 'Black Sunday' match against Southampton at The Dell, in which the Dons were relegated from the Premiership. The hugely popular player missed most of the following campaign with a groin injury but returned to action in 2001-02 when he was again voted Wimbledon's 'Player of the Year'.

Transferred to Birmingham City for £600,000 in July 2002, he was outstanding at the heart of the Blues' defence and instrumental in the club avoiding relegation. Deservedly named the club's 'Player of the Year' in his first season at St Andrew's, he was appointed club captain. Though he initially suffered a spate of injuries, when fit he produced quiet but highly-efficient performances. An exceptional reader of the game, Cunningham appeared in 68 internationals for the Republic of Ireland, providing a steadying presence at the back during some fraught games. He retired from international football in October 2005 and was transferred from Birmingham City to Sunderland in 2006.

Curtis Fleming

Position	Defender
Born	Curtis Fleming, Manchester, 8 October 1968
Clubs	

St Patrick's Athletic; Middlesbrough; Birmingham City (loan); Crystal Palace; Darlington

International Caps	10

Matches				
Year	Opponent	Result	Score	G
1996	Czech Republic	lost	0-2	
1996	Portugal	lost	0-1	
1996	Croatia	drew	2-2	
1996	Holland	lost	1-3	
1996	United States	lost	1-2	
1996	Mexico	drew	2-2	
1996	Bolivia	won	3-0	
1997	Liechtenstein	won	5-0	
1998	Romania	drew	1-1	
1998	Mexico	drew	0-0	

Middlesbrough paid just £50,000 to pluck Curtis Fleming from St Patrick's Athletic in the summer of 1991.

One of the north-east club's most astute signings, he stepped in when Gary Parkinson was injured and helped the club win promotion to the newly formed Premiership. The arrival of Chris Moore from Celtic and the signing of £1 million right-back Neil Cox forced Fleming to show his versatility, switching from his natural position at right-back to the left side. Relegated after just one season in the Premiership, Boro returned to the top flight for the 1995-96 season.

Fleming overcame a career-threatening injury and became noted for his fine supporting runs down the flanks, as well as his excellent tackling and marking. After picking up an Under-21 cap and being selected at 'B' level during his time with St Patrick's, Fleming earned his first cap for the Republic of Ireland as a substitute for Denis Irwin against the Czech Republic in April 1996.

That month also saw him break his long goal duck – almost five years after his Middlesbrough debut – when he scored in the 2-1 home defeat by Wimbledon. After his international debut, Fleming added six more caps to his collection in the next seven weeks, but made just three further appearances during the next three years.

Back at the Riverside Fleming's progress was hampered by injuries, notably two knee operations. Though not adding to his total of international caps, he provided injury cover for the 2000 European Championship play-offs against Turkey in response to a dramatic call.

Hugely popular with Boro fans, Fleming's role in the side changed many times in his ten years and 317 appearances with the club. Following a loan spell with Birmingham City, he parted company with the north-east club, signing for Crystal Palace for £100,000.

He was made Palace captain but knee problems meant that he spent much of his time at Selhurst Park on the treatment table. Following his release by Palace, he returned to the north-east to play for Darlington, where he was a steadying influence at the heart of the Quakers' defence.

Alan Moore

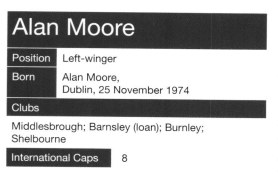

Position	Left-winger
Born	Alan Moore, Dublin, 25 November 1974
Clubs	

Middlesbrough; Barnsley (loan); Burnley; Shelbourne

International Caps	8

Matches

Year	Opponent	Result	Score	G
1996	Czech Republic	lost	0-2	
1996	Croatia	drew	2-2	
1996	Holland	lost	1-3	
1996	Mexico	drew	2-2	
1996	Bolivia	won	3-0	
1997	Liechtenstein	won	5-0	
1997	Macedonia	won	3-0	
1997	Iceland	drew	0-0	

The FAI/Opel Youth 'Player of the Year' joined Middlesbrough from Finglas Junior club Rivermount Boys and made his debut against Everton in April 1993.

The fast-raiding winger was a regular in the Boro side the following season and in 1994–95 when the Teeside club were crowned First Division champions. In the Premiership, Boro boss Bryan Robson reverted to a 5-3-2 formation and Moore often found himself out in the cold. His form for Boro had seen him play for the Republic of Ireland Under-18 and Under-21 sides, scoring on his debuts, the latter against Latvia in Riga.

He made his full international debut shortly after Mick McCarthy had taken over the reins as manager, but the Republic lost 2-0 to the Czech Republic. During 1996 Moore won eight caps in the space of seven months but then lost his place. He was unable to add to his collection of caps.

Moore was then plagued by a series of injuries and on returning to action, was loaned out to Barnsley where he was an instant hit. He then returned to the Riverside. Though his appearances were spasmodic, when he played he demonstrated some of his earlier form – jinking his way through defences, delivering telling passes and unleashing numerous goalbound shots. Two seasons in the wilderness followed before he left Middlesbrough to find a new lease of life with Burnley.

After a good first season at Turf Moor, he struggled to live up to his early promise and after being freed by the Clarets, returned to Ireland to play for Shelbourne.

Gary Breen

Position	Central defender
Born	Gary Patrick Breen, Hendon, 12 December 1973
Clubs	

Maidstone United; Gillingham; Peterborough United; Birmingham City; Coventry City; West Ham United; Sunderland

International Caps	62
International Goals	6

Matches

Year	Opponent	Result	Score	G
1996	Portugal	lost	0-1	
1996	Croatia	drew	2-2	
1996	Holland	lost	1-3	1
1996	United States	lost	1-2	
1996	Mexico	drew	2-2	
1996	Bolivia	won	3-0	
1997	Liechtenstein	won	5-0	
1997	Macedonia	won	3-0	
1997	Iceland	drew	0-0	
1997	Macedonia	lost	2-3	
1998	Lithuania	drew	0-0	
1998	Romania	drew	1-1	
1998	Czech Republic	lost	1-2	1
1998	Argentina	lost	0-2	
1998	Mexico	drew	0-0	
1999	Malta	won	5-0	1
1999	Yugoslavia	lost	0-1	
1999	Paraguay	won	2-0	
1999	Sweden	won	2-0	
1999	Macedonia	won	1-0	
2000	Yugoslavia	won	2-1	
2000	Croatia	lost	0-2	
2000	Malta	won	3-2	1
2000	Macedonia	drew	1-1	
2000	Turkey	drew	1-1	
2000	Turkey	drew	0-0	
2000	Greece	lost	0-1	
2000	Scotland	lost	1-2	
2000	Mexico	drew	2-2	
2000	United States	drew	1-1	
2000	South Africa	won	2-1	
2001	Holland	drew	2-2	
2001	Portugal	drew	1-1	
2001	Estonia	won	2-0	
2001	Finland	won	3-0	
2001	Cyprus	won	4-0	
2001	Andorra	won	3-0	
2001	Andorra	won	3-1	1

Year	Opponent	Result	Score	G
2002	Cyprus	won	4-0	
2002	Iran	won	2-0	
2002	Iran	lost	0-1	
2002	Russia	won	2-0	
2002	United States	won	2-1	
2002	Cameroon	drew	1-1	
2002	Germany	drew	1-1	
2002	Saudi Arabia	won	3-0	1
2002	Spain	drew	1-1	
2003	Finland	won	3-0	
2003	Russia	lost	2-4	
2003	Switzerland	lost	1-2	
2003	Scotland	won	2-0	
2003	Georgia	won	2-1	
2003	Albania	drew	0-0	
2003	Norway	won	1-0	
2003	Albania	won	2-1	
2003	Georgia	won	2-0	
2004	Australia	won	2-1	
2004	Russia	drew	1-1	
2004	Turkey	drew	2-2	
2004	Switzerland	lost	0-2	
2005	Bulgaria	drew	1-1	
2005	Croatia	won	1-0	

After his first club Maidstone United dropped out of the Football League, Breen left in the summer of 1993 to join Gillingham. His impressive performances for the Gills led to Peterborough United paying £70,000 for his services. In February 1996 Breen was taken to Birmingham City as replacement for Liam Daish who had left to play for Coventry City.

He won the first of 62 caps in May 1996 as an 89th minute substitute for Alan Kernaghan in the Republic's 1-0 defeat by Portugal at Lansdowne Road. With the unenviable task of filling the boots of Paul McGrath, he emerged with credit in a handful of appearances that summer. He proved himself an attacking threat with a goal in the game against Holland. By the 1998 World Cup qualifiers, Breen was the Republic's first choice centre-half.

He spent just a year at St Andrew's, as Coventry City paid £2.4 million to take him to Highfield Road. A defender who likes to bring the ball out of defence, he is also very good in the air – in 1998-99 he played a major part in City's unbeaten FA Cup run. Playing for Coventry at both right-back and in central defence, he continued to be a regular in the Republic of Ireland side. In 2000-01 he was not only voted Coventry's 'Player of the Year' but also equalled the club record for the most international appearances. Having become a cult figure at Highfield Road, his refusal to discuss a new contract somewhat soured his relationship with the fans.

Above: Gary Breen

After some fine performances for the Republic of Ireland in the 2002 World Cup Finals, Gary Breen joined West Ham United. After one season at Upton Park, he was released and joined Sunderland. His first season at the Stadium of Light was disrupted when a medial ligament injury kept him out for three months. On his return to full fitness he capped an excellent 2004-05 season by leading the Black Cats back to the Premiership and being selected in the PFA Championship team of the season.

David Connolly

Position	Forward
Born	David James Connolly, Willesden, 6 June 1977

Clubs

Watford; Feyenoord (Holland); Wolverhampton Wanderers (loan); Excelsior (Holland); Feyenoord (Holland); Wimbledon; West Ham United; Leicester City

International Caps	40
International Goals	9

Matches

Year	Opponent	Result	Score	G
1996	Portugal	lost	0-1	
1996	Holland	lost	1-3	
1996	United States	lost	1-2	1
1996	Mexico	drew	2-2	1
1997	Romania	lost	0-1	
1997	Liechtenstein	won	5-0	3
1998	Lithuania	drew	0-0	
1998	Iceland	won	4-2	1
1998	Lithuania	won	2-1	
1998	Belgium	drew	1-1	
1998	Belgium	lost	1-2	
1998	Czech Republic	lost	1-2	
1998	Mexico	drew	0-0	
1999	Yugoslavia	lost	0-1	
1999	Paraguay	won	2-0	1
1999	Sweden	won	2-0	
1999	N Ireland	lost	0-1	
1999	Macedonia	won	1-0	
2000	Turkey	drew	1-1	
2000	Turkey	drew	0-0	
2000	Czech Republic	won	3-2	
2000	Greece	lost	0-1	
2001	Holland	drew	2-2	
2001	Finland	won	3-0	
2001	Cyprus	won	4-0	
2001	Andorra	won	3-0	
2001	Andorra	won	3-1	
2002	Croatia	drew	2-2	
2002	Cyprus	won	4-0	1
2002	Iran	lost	0-1	
2002	Denmark	won	3-0	

Matches Continued				
Year	Opponent	Result	Score	G
2002	United States	won	2-1	
2002	Nigeria	lost	1-2	
2002	Spain	drew	1-1	
2003	Scotland	won	2-0	
2003	Norway	won	1-0	
2003	Albania	won	2-1	
2004	Australia	won	2-1	
2004	Turkey	drew	2-2	1
2004	Switzerland	lost	0-2	

Predatory goalscorer David Connolly burst onto the international scene in the summer of 1996. A rich run of form for Watford had seen him score eight goals in six games, including two hat-tricks. But it was too late to prevent Graham Taylor's side from dropping into the Second Division.

Having scored in Mick McCarthy's testimonial game as the Republic beat Celtic 3-0, he made his full international debut a few days later when Portugal were the visitors to Lansdowne Road. He added three more caps to his total in 1996 and opened his international goals account in the game against the United States.

Though his 1996-97 season was disrupted by persistent hamstring injuries, he scored an FA Cup hat-trick for Watford against Ashford after coming on as a substitute. In May 1997 he netted a hat-trick for the Republic of Ireland in a 5-0 win over Liechtenstein in a World Cup qualifier – all three goals coming in the space of 11 minutes prior to half-time!

Shortly after this performance, Connolly left Vicarage Road and signed for the Dutch giants Feyenoord under the Bosman ruling. The switch was to prove far from successful. After just a couple of appearances in the club's starting line-up, he returned to the Football League, joining Wolves on loan. Initially he found himself on the bench – following manager Mark McGhee's departure, he started the game against Bristol City and scored four goals in a 6-1 win!

Despite this, he found himself understudying Robbie Keane at both club and international level and returned to Holland to play for Excelsior, prior to another spell with Feyenoord.

Above: David Connolly

In July 2001 he signed for Wimbledon and immediately formed an impressive partnership up front with Neil Shipperley. Working well off the big man, he scored 18 goals and continued that form the following season as the Dons progressed up the League table.

He then joined West Ham United and set Upton Park alight with seven goals in his first 11 games and contributed greatly to the Hammers reaching the play-off final. Surprisingly, Connolly – who has won 40 caps for the Republic of Ireland – was allowed to leave. He joined Leicester City, and proved instrumental in the club retaining their Championship status.

Gareth Farrelly

Position	Midfield
Born	Gareth Farrelly, Dublin, 28 August 1975

Clubs
Home Farm; Aston Villa; Rotherham United (loan); Everton; Bolton Wanderers; Rotherham United (loan); Burnley (loan); Bradford City (loan); Wigan Athletic; Bohemians

International Caps	6

Matches				
Year	Opponent	Result	Score	G
1996	Portugal	lost	0-1	
1996	United States	lost	1-2	
1996	Bolivia	won	3-0	
1998	Czech Republic	lost	1-2	
1998	Mexico	drew	0-0	
2000	United States	drew	1-1	

A former player with Home Farm, midfielder Gareth Farrelly was taken to Aston Villa by Ron Atkinson but for a year and a half was a regular on the treatment table with a serious back injury.

Farrelly recovered and made his League debut for the Villans against Liverpool in March 1996. A couple of months later he won the first of six caps against Portugal.

Unable to win a regular place in the Villa side, Farrelly joined Everton in the summer of 1997 after the Merseyside club had paid £700,000 for his services. A player of undoubted talent, he scored the goal that secured the Blues' Premiership safety in the last match of the 1997-98 season against Coventry. He figured in only 13 minutes of an intensely frustrating 1998-99 campaign as a knee injury, which later required surgery, hampered his progress.

In November 1999 Farrelly was allowed to leave Everton and joined Bolton Wanderers on a free transfer. He scored on his debut at Sheffield United with only his second touch of the ball. In 2000-01, Farrelly had an outstanding season, showing the ability and vision to pick out the right pass almost every time. He capped a fine campaign by netting the vital first goal in the play-off final against Preston North End.

Following a catalogue of injuries and severe competition for midfield places, his first team appearances became limited and he was loaned out to Rotherham United. Having spent most of the 2003-04 season on loan at Burnley and Bradford City, Farrelly joined Wigan Athletic for the closing stages of that competition. He was not offered a new deal, and returned to Ireland to see out his career with Bohemians.

Keith O'Neill

Position	Left-winger
Born	Keith Padre Gerard O'Neill, Dublin, 16 February 1976

Clubs

Home Farm; Norwich City; Middlesbrough; Coventry City

International Caps	13
International Goals	4

Matches

Year	Opponent	Result	Score	G
1996	Portugal	lost	0-1	
1996	Croatia	drew	2-2	1
1996	Holland	lost	1-3	
1996	United States	lost	1-2	
1996	Mexico	drew	2-2	
1996	Bolivia	won	3-0	2
1997	Liechtenstein	won	5-0	1
1997	Macedonia	won	3-0	
1997	Macedonia	lost	2-3	
1999	Croatia	won	2-0	
1999	Yugoslavia	lost	0-1	
1999	N Ireland	lost	0-1	
2000	Macedonia	drew	1-1	

Tall and powerfully built, Keith O'Neill played junior football for Home Farm prior to joining Norwich City. Rapid progress at Carrow Road culminated in his debut for the Canaries as a substitute for Rob Newman, in the game against Southampton in November

1994. Any hopes of an extended run in the side were dashed when shortly afterwards he broke his ankle in a reserve game.

His form in 1995-96 led to him winning his first full cap for the Republic of Ireland as a 62nd-minute substitute for fellow debutant David Connolly against Portugal in May 1996. He was on the field from the start the following week, scoring his first international goal in a 2-2 draw with Croatia. He also scored twice in a 3-0 defeat of Bolivia – the first victory of Mick McCarthy's regime – then in August 1996 he netted his fourth goal in seven internationals in the 5-0 demolition of Liechtenstein.

With Norwich, his pace and accurate crosses caused havoc in opponents' penalty areas, until he fractured a foot and was forced to miss much of the 1997-98 campaign. On regaining full fitness, he joined Middlesbrough for a fee of £700,000 in a deal that would eventually land the Canaries £1 million.

Signed to give more bite and width to the strike force, he soon settled into life in the Premiership, forming an excellent partnership up front with Hamilton Ricard. Despite this, Boro switched him to play as a left-wing back whereupon his appearances became more restricted due to niggling injuries. When he did appear, O'Neill stamped his authority on games with his fearless tackling and impressed with some fine crossing, a legacy of having played as an orthodox winger.

O'Neill joined Coventry City for a fee of £1 million on the eve of the 2001-02 season. After impressing in his early games, he was struck down by a pelvic injury. He was sidelined until the end of the season when he suffered a double fracture of his left leg in a freak training ground incident. Sadly, despite making a brief substitute appearance in 2003-04, he was forced to announce his retirement from the game.

Dave Savage

Position	Midfield
Born	David Thomas Patrick Savage, Dublin, 30 July 1973

Clubs

Kilkenny City; Brighton and Hove Albion; Longford Town; Millwall; Northampton Town; Oxford United; Bristol Rovers

International Caps	5

Matches

Year	Opponent	Result	Score	G
1996	Portugal	lost	0-1	
1996	Croatia	drew	2-2	
1996	United States	lost	1-2	
1996	Mexico	drew	2-2	
1996	Bolivia	won	3-0	

Having started out in the League of Ireland with Kilkenny City and following a spell with Brighton and Hove Albion, he returned to Ireland to play for Longford Town. It was here that his displays prompted then Millwall manager Mick McCarthy to sign him for the Lions in the summer of 1994.

His ability to run at defenders and provide accurate crosses for the frontmen gave the London club an edge to their play for most of the 1994-95 season. He then suffered a series of injuries that kept him out of action for much of the following campaign. It was a season in which Millwall were relegated – with Savage making few appearances, it was a surprise to see him selected for the Republic of Ireland side to face Portugal in May 1996. He then went on to play in five internationals in the space of 18 days.

After playing his football on the right of midfield, Millwall switched him to a more central role before his 1997-98 season was blighted by a lower back injury. Unable to reproduce the form of his early days with the club, he was transferred to Northampton Town for a fee of £100,000.

Despite his five goals in the last five games of the campaign, the Cobblers were relegated to the League's basement. Following a change of manager at Sixfields, Savage played in a wider role, where his jinking runs brought Northampton fans to their feet as the club won promotion at the first attempt. A regular in the Cobblers' side, he had appeared in 124 games when he left Northampton in the summer of 2001 to join Oxford United, where again he missed very few games in two seasons with the U's.

His next club was Bristol Rovers where he was a regular until picking up a hamstring injury, which ruled him out of the closing stages of the 2003-04 season. Though injuries hampered his progress, he ended the following season just short of the landmark total of 400 Football League appearances.

Ian Harte

Position	Midfield
Born	Ian Patrick Harte, Drogheda, 31 August 1977

Clubs

Leeds United; Levante (Spain)

International Caps	59
International Goals	11

Matches

Year	Opponent	Result	Score	G
1996	Croatia	drew	2-2	
1996	Holland	lost	1-3	
1996	Mexico	drew	2-2	
1996	Bolivia	won	3-0	1
1997	Liechtenstein	won	5-0	1
1997	Macedonia	won	3-0	
1997	Iceland	drew	0-0	
1997	Wales	drew	0-0	
1997	Macedonia	lost	2-3	
1997	Romania	lost	0-1	
1997	Liechtenstein	won	5-0	
1998	Lithuania	drew	0-0	
1998	Iceland	won	4-2	
1998	Lithuania	won	2-1	
1998	Belgium	drew	1-1	
1998	Belgium	lost	1-2	
1998	Argentina	lost	0-2	
1998	Mexico	drew	0-0	

Matches

Year	Opponent	Result	Score	G
1999	Paraguay	won	2-0	
2000	Croatia	lost	0-2	
2000	Malta	won	3-2	
2000	Czech Republic	won	3-2	1
2001	Holland	drew	2-2	
2001	Portugal	drew	1-1	
2001	Estonia	won	2-0	
2001	Finland	won	3-0	
2001	Cyprus	won	4-0	1
2001	Andorra	won	3-0	1
2001	Andorra	won	3-1	
2001	Portugal	drew	1-1	
2001	Estonia	won	2-0	
2002	Croatia	drew	2-2	
2002	Holland	won	1-0	
2002	Cyprus	won	4-0	1
2002	Iran	won	2-0	1
2002	Iran	lost	0-1	
2002	Russia	won	2-0	
2002	Denmark	won	3-0	1
2002	United States	won	2-1	
2002	Nigeria	lost	1-2	
2002	Cameroon	drew	1-1	
2002	Germany	drew	1-1	
2002	Saudi Arabia	won	3-0	
2002	Spain	drew	1-1	
2003	Finland	won	3-0	
2003	Russia	lost	2-4	
2003	Switzerland	lost	1-2	
2003	Scotland	won	2-0	
2003	Norway	won	1-0	
2004	Australia	won	2-1	
2004	Russia	drew	1-1	
2004	Turkey	drew	2-2	
2004	Switzerland	lost	0-2	
2004	Canada	won	3-0	
2004	Czech Republic	won	2-1	1
2004	Poland	drew	0-0	
2005	Israel	drew	2-2	1
2005	Faroe Islands	won	2-0	1
2006	Sweden	won	3-0	

When 18-year-old Ian Harte came on for his Leeds United debut in the Coca Cola Cup game against Reading, it completed an amazing family double – his uncle, Gary Kelly, himself only 21, was already on the pitch. The uncle and nephew helped Leeds to a 2-1 success to take the Yorkshire club further down the road to Wembley.

Under David O'Leary's management Harte developed into a key player for United, though he had made just four first team appearances when Mick McCarthy handed

him his international debut against Croatia in June 1996. McCarthy was impressed enough to include the youngster in the Republic's next eight games: Harte rewarded his manager's faith with solid displays in the qualifiers for Euro '96.

Above: Ian Harte

His performances for club and country prompted Tottenham Hotspur to offer £2 million for his services, but this was turned down by new United boss George Graham. In 1997-98 he had the unusual distinction of making more international appearances for the Republic of Ireland than for United's first team! Despite the signing of Danny Granville from Chelsea, Harte was Leeds' first-choice left-back in 1998-99 when he was virtually ever-present. His contribution to the club's success the following season (2002-03) was recognised when he was named by fellow professionals in the PFA award-winning Premiership side.

One of the deadliest exponents of the dead-ball situation – he scored a hat-trick of free-kicks at Blackburn prior to the start of the 2000-01 season and netted in the Champions' League quarter-final against Deportivo La Coruña – he was much admired across Europe. Harte played a major role for the Republic of Ireland in the 2002 World Cup Finals before contributing three valuable goals towards the end of the following campaign as United narrowly avoided relegation. Injuries hampered his progress at Elland Road. Even when deemed fit, he failed to win a regular place in the United side.

Capped 58 times by the Republic of Ireland, Harte had played in 288 games for Leeds when he left Elland Road to play in La Liga for Spanish club Levante.

Keith Branagan

Position	Goalkeeper
Born	Keith Graham Branagan, Fulham, 10 July 1966
Clubs	

Cambridge United; Millwall; Brentford (loan); Gillingham (loan); Bolton Wanderers; Ipswich Town

International Caps	1

Matches				
Year	Opponent	Result	Score	G
1997	Wales	drew	0-0	

A virtual ever-present with his first club Cambridge United, goalkeeper Keith Branagan left the Abbey Stadium in March 1988 as Millwall paid £100,000 for his services. He couldn't force his way into the side that did well in their first season in the top flight, and he had loan spells with Brentford and Gillingham before winning a regular place in the Lions' line-up. At the end of the 1991-92 season, Millwall had six

keepers on their books. Branagan was snapped up by his former boss Bruce Rioch, who had taken over as manager of Bolton Wanderers.

He was ever-present in the Trotters' 1992-93 Second Division promotion-winning side. Though injury forced him to miss much of the following season, he was back in 1994-95 with a penalty-save in the play-off final against Reading which turned the game Bolton's way.

International recognition came his way in December 1994 when he played for the Republic of Ireland's 'B' side against England at Anfield. In February 1997 he won his first full cap, keeping a clean sheet in a scoreless friendly against Wales.

In 1996-97, Branagan kept six clean sheets in the last twelve games as the Wanderers won promotion to the Premiership as First Division Champions. He was the club's first-choice goalkeeper for seven seasons, producing a number of world-class performances that saved the Trotters a number of points. Injuries and the emergence of Jussi Jaaskelainen saw Branagan, who had played in 263 games for the Wanderers, leave the Reebok to join Ipswich Town as cover for Richard Wright. He appeared in a handful of games before a shoulder injury forced his retirement.

Jon Goodman

Position	Forward
Born	Jonathan Goodman, Walthamstow, 2 June 1971
Clubs	

Bromley; Millwall; Wimbledon

International Caps	4

Matches				
Year	Opponent	Result	Score	G
1997	Wales	drew	0-0	
1997	Macedonia	lost	2-3	
1997	Romania	lost	0-1	
1997	Liechtenstein	won	5-0	

A powerful and pacy striker, Jon Goodman joined Millwall from non-League Bromley in the summer of 1990. A hard-running and quick-thinking finisher, he went on to score 35 goals in 109 league games for the Lions before moving to Wimbledon in November 1994. Goodman scored goals whenever he had an extended run in the Dons' side. In February 1997, when he made his full international debut for the Republic of Ireland against Wales, he had only scored one League goal for Wimbledon! However, Mick McCarthy had remembered his goalscoring prowess from their days together at Millwall and handed him a late call to join the squad.

Goodman kept his place in the Republic of Ireland side for three World Cup qualifiers but before the 1997-98 season got underway, he suffered a serious injury that would sideline him for more than a year.

Even then he couldn't win a place back in the Wimbledon side due to severe injury problems for a second consecutive season. After a handful of appearances in the club's reserves – which had confirmed his talent for goalscoring – he had to retire from the game following medical advice, after four operations to his knee over a two-year period.

Kevin Kilbane

Position	Left-winger/Midfield
Born	Kevin Daniel Kilbane, Preston, 1 February 1977
Clubs	

Preston North End; West Bromwich Albion; Sunderland; Everton

International Caps	65
International Goals	5

Matches				
Year	Opponent	Result	Score	G
1998	Iceland	won	4-2	
1998	Czech Republic	lost	1-2	
1998	Argentina	lost	0-2	
1999	Sweden	won	2-0	

Matches				
Year	Opponent	Result	Score	G
1999	Macedonia	won	1-0	
2000	Yugoslavia	won	2-1	
2000	Croatia	lost	0-2	
2000	Malta	won	3-2	
2000	Turkey	drew	1-1	
2000	Turkey	drew	0-0	
2000	Czech Republic	won	3-2	
2000	Greece	lost	0-1	
2000	Scotland	lost	1-2	
2000	Mexico	drew	2-2	
2000	United States	drew	1-1	
2000	South Africa	won	2-1	
2001	Holland	drew	2-2	
2001	Portugal	drew	1-1	
2001	Estonia	won	2-0	
2001	Finland	won	3-0	1
2001	Cyprus	won	4-0	
2001	Andorra	won	3-0	1
2001	Andorra	won	3-1	1
2001	Portugal	drew	1-1	
2001	Estonia	won	2-0	
2002	Croatia	drew	2-2	
2002	Holland	won	1-0	
2002	Cyprus	won	4-0	
2002	Iran	won	2-0	
2002	Iran	lost	0-1	
2002	Russia	won	2-0	
2002	United States	won	2-1	
2002	Nigeria	lost	1-2	
2002	Cameroon	drew	1-1	
2002	Germany	drew	1-1	
2002	Saudi Arabia	won	3-0	
2002	Spain	drew	1-1	
2003	Finland	won	3-0	
2003	Russia	lost	2-4	
2003	Switzerland	lost	1-2	
2003	Scotland	won	2-0	1
2003	Georgia	won	2-1	
2003	Albania	drew	0-0	
2003	Norway	won	1-0	
2003	Albania	won	2-1	
2003	Georgia	won	2-0	
2004	Australia	won	2-1	
2004	Russia	drew	1-1	
2004	Turkey	drew	2-2	
2004	Switzerland	lost	0-2	
2004	Canada	won	3-0	
2004	Brazil	drew	0-0	
2004	Czech Republic	won	2-1	
2005	Bulgaria	drew	1-1	
2005	Cyprus	won	3-0	
2005	Switzerland	drew	1-1	
2005	France	drew	0-0	
2005	Faroe Islands	won	2-0	
2005	Croatia	won	1-0	
2005	Portugal	won	1-0	
2005	Israel	drew	1-1	
2005	China	won	1-0	
2005	Israel	drew	2-2	
2005	Faroe Islands	won	2-0	1
2006	Sweden	won	3-0	

Kevin Kilbane came up through the ranks at Preston North End. In his very first season, his ability to beat men at pace and whip in dangerous crosses saw him called up for the Republic of Ireland Under-21 squad. His form the following season saw North End receive a bid of £900,000 from West Bromwich Albion. This was rejected, but the Baggies splashed out a club record £1 million in the close season to take him to the Hawthorns.

Above: Kevin Kilbane

Quickly becoming a crowd favourite, he was elevated to the Republic of Ireland senior team, when he was preferred to Mark Kennedy for the No.11 shirt in the World Cup qualifier away to Iceland in September 1997.

Back at the Hawthorns, Kilbane lacked consistency although in 1998-99 he scored the 'Goal of the Season' against Bolton Wanderers, and netted the clincher in the tension-packed local derby win over Wolves. Such much-improved performances during the early part of the following season prompted Sunderland to pay £2.5 million for his services.

Signed to fill the void left by contract rebel Allan Johnston, it took him some time to settle and adapt to his new surroundings and the step up into the Premiership. Showing a willingness to take on defenders and tackle back when necessary, Kilbane lacked consistency during his time with the Black Cats.

Kilbane continued to be a regular for the Republic of Ireland, helping them to qualify for the 2002 World Cup. He scored the first goal of new boss Brian Kerr's reign against Scotland, whilst for Sunderland, he showed his versatility by appearing in a variety of positions. He had played in 124 games for the Wearsiders when in September 2003, Everton paid £750,000 to take him to Goodison Park.

Kilbane proved to be a spirited performer on the club's left flank, one of the major plus-points for the Blues. Capped 64 times by the Republic of Ireland, the 2004-05 season saw him become the first outfielder to figure in every Everton League game for 13 years. His consistent displays for his country in a more central role also saw him voted as the Republic of Ireland's 'Player of the Year'.

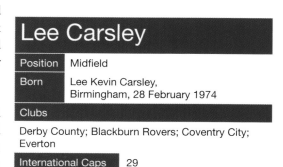

Lee Carsley

Position	Midfield
Born	Lee Kevin Carsley, Birmingham, 28 February 1974
Clubs	

Derby County; Blackburn Rovers; Coventry City; Everton

International Caps	29

Matches				
Year	Opponent	Result	Score	G
1998	Romania	drew	1-1	
1998	Belgium	drew	1-1	
1998	Belgium	lost	1-2	
1998	Czech Republic	lost	1-2	
1998	Argentina	lost	0-2	
1998	Mexico	drew	0-0	
1999	Croatia	won	2-0	
1999	Malta	won	5-0	
1999	Paraguay	won	2-0	
1999	N Ireland	lost	0-1	
1999	Macedonia	won	1-0	
2000	Yugoslavia	won	2-0	
2000	Croatia	lost	0-2	
2000	Malta	won	3-2	
2000	Turkey	drew	1-1	
2001	Finland	won	3-0	
2002	Croatia	drew	2-2	
2002	Cyprus	won	4-0	
2002	Russia	won	2-0	
2002	Saudi Arabia	won	3-0	
2003	Finland	won	3-0	
2003	Greece	drew	0-0	
2003	Scotland	won	2-0	
2003	Georgia	won	2-1	
2003	Albania	drew	0-0	
2003	Norway	won	1-0	
2003	Albania	won	2-1	
2003	Georgia	won	2-0	
2004	Russia	drew	1-1	

Lee Carsley began his career with Derby County. He proved an effective and versatile player, who could operate at the back or in midfield. Following a series of cultured displays, Carsley made his full international debut for the Republic of Ireland in a World Cup qualifier against Romania in October 1997. A 1-1 draw saw the Derby player emerge with much credit and this earned him a place in Mick McCarthy's squad.

Continued progress at League level saw him captain the Rams on a number of occasions, but he soon became the subject of various transfer rumours. It was still something of a surprise when he decided to join Blackburn Rovers in transfer deadline week, March 1999.

Rovers had paid £3.375 million for his services but were still relegated from the Premiership. Appointed Rovers' captain for

the 1999–2000 season, he flourished as the club's driving force, despite breaking a bone in his foot in the FA Cup tie with Newcastle United. Surprisingly out of favour at the start of the following season, he left Ewood Park to join Coventry City in a £2.5 million deal.

Above: Lee Carsley

Despite hitting a rich vein of personal form, he couldn't prevent the Sky Blues from losing their top-flight status. Midway through the 2001-02 season Carsley was sold to Everton for £1.95 million. Though the Blues were also fighting to avoid the drop from the Premiership, he was absolutely delighted when they retained their place in the top flight. Continuing to establish himself at international level, he played an important role in the club's rise under new manager David Moyes.

Following a spate of injuries during the 2003-04 campaign, Carsley put his international ambitions on hold in order to re-establish himself in the Everton side. Having won 29 caps for the Republic of Ireland, the feisty and committed midfielder decided to retire from international football. He became the inspirational form behind Everton's renaissance. A credit to his profession, Lee Carsley is actively involved in several charities and is the patron of the Down's Syndrome Association of Solihull.

Micky Evans

Position	Forward
Born	Michael James Evans, Plymouth, 1 January 1973

Clubs
Plymouth Argyle; Southampton; West Bromwich Albion; Bristol Rovers; Plymouth Argyle

International Caps	1

Matches				
Year	Opponent	Result	Score	G
1998	Romania	drew	1-1	

A hard-running centre-forward, Micky Evans began his career with home-town club Plymouth Argyle. After seasons of inconsistency, he benefited from a long run in the side, partnering Adrian Littlejohn up front. He caught the eye of many managers before being snapped up by Southampton's Graeme Souness in March 1997. He scored 15 goals in 41 games for the Pilgrims during the course of that campaign.

He came into a struggling Saints' side but his goals in the last few weeks of the season ensured that the south coast club would be playing Premiership football in 1997-98. He was unlucky to lose his place in the Southampton side to David Hirst, having suffered a double fracture of the cheekbone while training with the Republic of Ireland squad.

He had earlier won his first full cap against Romania but 16 days later was signed by West Bromwich Albion, who paid £750,000 for his signature. Towards the end of the season he found himself playing second fiddle to Bob Taylor, Lee Hughes and Andy Hunt before being struck down by a number of injuries that in 1998-99 saw him spend more time on the physio's couch than he did on the pitch!

Still hampered by injuries, he was allowed to join Bristol Rovers, initially on loan before the deal was made permanent. His goal tally with Rovers was a little disappointing, and it came as no surprise that before the season was out he rejoined Plymouth Argyle.

He had lost none of his confidence and in 2001-02 made an invaluable contribution to Argyle's Third Division Championship success. Often played as a sole striker, he proved very successful in holding the ball up, as well as weighing in with his fair share of goals. He continued to be a great asset at Home Park and in 2003-04 was voted the club's 'Player of the Year'. Though his goal tally was a little disappointing – scoring 34 goals in 191 games – he continues to lead the line excellently.

Rory Delap

Position	Midfield
Born	Rory John Delap, Sutton Coldfield, 6 July 1976

Clubs

Carlisle United; Derby County; Southampton; Sunderland

International Caps	11

Matches				
Year	Opponent	Result	Score	G
1998	Czech Republic	lost	1-2	
1998	Argentina	lost	0-2	
1998	Mexico	drew	0-0	
2000	Turkey	drew	1-1	
2000	Turkey	drew	0-0	
2000	Greece	lost	0-1	

Matches				
Year	Opponent	Result	Score	G
2002	United States	won	2-1	
2003	Finland	won	3-0	
2003	Greece	drew	0-0	
2004	Canada	won	3-0	
2004	Czech Republic	won	2-1	

One of the game's most versatile players, Rory Delap had played as a defender, midfielder and forward with his first club Carlisle United. This prompted Derby County manager Jim Smith to pay £500,000 for his services in February 1998.

Above: Rory Delap

Undaunted by the step up from the Third Division, Delap made his Rams' debut in a 2-1 win at Everton and kept his place in the side until the end of the season. Within a month of his move, he made his full international debut against the Czech Republic. He followed this in the summer months with another couple of appearances for the national side.

Then he suffered a mystery illness linked to the intake of energy drinks. Upon being restored to the side, a medial ligament injury forced him to miss a number of games. As his career with Derby unfolded, Delap began to find the net on a more regular basis. In 2000-01 he scored the 'Goal of the Season' with a long-range strike in the away game at Leicester.

In the summer of 2001 Southampton paid a club record fee of £3 million to take Delap to St Mary's. After a good start, he began to struggle until he was moved from right-back into midfield. His tackling, distribution and anticipation were majestic until an injury sustained at Sunderland midway through the campaign blighted what was becoming a highly successful season. In between his injuries at the south-coast club, he continued to add to his collection of international caps. Following the appointment of Harry Redknapp as manager he was given an extended run as a right-wing back.

Delap now plays for Sunderland, after a January 2006 transfer from Southampton.

Damien Duff

Position	Midfield
Born	Damien Anthony Duff, Dublin, 2 March 1979

Clubs

Lourdes Celtic; Blackburn Rovers; Chelsea

International Caps	55
International Goals	7

Matches				
Year	Opponent	Result	Score	G
1998	Czech Republic	lost	1-2	
1998	Mexico	drew	0-0	
1999	Croatia	won	2-0	

Matches				
Year	Opponent	Result	Score	G
1999	Malta	won	5-0	
1999	Yugoslavia	lost	0-1	
1999	Paraguay	won	2-0	
1999	Sweden	won	2-0	
1999	N Ireland	lost	0-1	
1999	Macedonia	won	1-0	
2000	Croatia	lost	0-2	
2000	Malta	won	3-2	
2000	Turkey	drew	1-1	
2000	Turkey	drew	0-0	
2000	Scotland	lost	1-2	
2001	Portugal	drew	1-1	
2001	Estonia	won	2-0	
2001	Cyprus	won	4-0	
2001	Andorra	won	3-1	
2001	Portugal	drew	1-1	
2001	Estonia	won	2-0	
2002	Croatia	drew	2-2	1
2002	Holland	won	1-0	
2002	Russia	won	2-0	
2002	Denmark	won	3-0	
2002	United States	won	2-1	
2002	Nigeria	lost	1-2	
2002	Cameroon	drew	1-1	
2002	Germany	drew	1-1	
2002	Saudi Arabia	won	3-0	1
2002	Spain	drew	1-1	
2003	Finland	won	3-0	
2003	Russia	lost	2-4	
2003	Switzerland	lost	1-2	
2003	Georgia	won	2-1	1
2003	Albania	drew	0-0	
2003	Norway	won	1-0	1
2003	Albania	won	2-1	
2004	Australia	won	2-1	
2004	Russia	drew	1-1	1
2004	Turkey	drew	2-2	
2004	Switzerland	lost	0-2	
2004	Canada	won	3-0	1
2004	Czech Republic	won	2-1	
2005	Bulgaria	drew	1-1	
2005	Cyprus	won	3-0	
2005	Switzerland	drew	1-1	
2005	France	drew	0-0	
2005	Faroe Islands	won	2-0	
2005	Croatia	won	1-0	
2005	Portugal	won	1-0	
2005	Israel	drew	1-1	
2005	China	won	1-0	
2005	Israel	drew	2-2	
2005	Faroe Islands	won	2-0	
2006	Sweden	won	3-0	1

the hands of Leicester City.

Although he was used sparingly the following season, he showed himself to be fast, with great control – a player who could comprehensively beat opponents. By the end of the season Duff, who had not played for the Republic of Ireland at Under-21 level, was handed a full international debut by Mick McCarthy in the game against the Czech Republic in March 1998. After impressing in the Republic's next game against Mexico, he was chosen in the side to begin the Euro 2000 qualifiers as the national team's first-choice left-winger.

Above: Damien Duff

Damien Duff joined Blackburn Rovers from Irish junior club Lourdes Celtic in March 1996. Impressive displays in the club's reserve side saw him make his debut in the last game of the 1996-97 season, a 4-2 home defeat at

He missed a month of football for Rovers near the end of that 1998-99 season when representing the Under-20 select in Nigeria. He became such an important member of the Blackburn side that the team rarely

seemed capable of any incisive movement when he was unavailable! In 2000-01 he was honoured by his fellow professionals with a place in the PFA's First Division team.

Duff has pace and quick feet and an ability to keep moving despite any body contact short of taking his legs from under him. He is doubly dangerous: he can use speed to go outside, but show him the inside and his quick feet will permit him to make huge inroads into the penalty area.

After some outstanding performances for the Republic of Ireland including a goal in the 3-0 defeat of Saudi Arabia, he had a frustrating time at Blackburn where he was hampered by recurring hamstring problems. In the summer of 2003 Duff, who had scored 35 goals in 223 games, left Rovers to join Chelsea, who paid a club record £17 million to take him to Stamford Bridge.

He signed for the Blues on the same day as Wayne Bridge and though he had an excellent first season with the London club, he suffered a dislocated shoulder at Fulham and groin and calf strains. A hamstring strain forced him to miss both legs of the crucial Champions League semi-final against Liverpool, although Carling Cup and Premiership winners' medals were a fair reward for a dazzling player who has won 54 caps for the Republic of Ireland and developed into a cult hero with the Blues fans.

Graham Kavanagh

Position	Midfield
Born	Graham Anthony Kavanagh, Dublin, 2 December 1973
Clubs	

Home Farm; Middlesbrough; Darlington (loan); Stoke City; Cardiff City; Wigan Athletic

International Caps	13
International Goals	1

Matches				
Year	Opponent	Result	Score	G
1998	Czech Republic	lost	1-2	
1999	Sweden	won	2-0	1
1999	N Ireland	lost	0-1	
2004	Canada	won	3-0	
2004	Brazil	drew	0-0	
2005	Bulgaria	drew	1-1	
2005	Cyprus	won	3-0	
2005	Switzerland	drew	1-1	
2005	Croatia	won	1-0	
2005	Portugal	won	1-0	
2005	China	won	1-0	
2005	Israel	drew	2-2	
2006	Sweden	won	3-0	

Joining Middlesbrough from Home Farm, the young midfielder was eclipsed by all the big names arriving at the Riverside. After four seasons in the north-east which included a loan spell at Darlington, he joined Stoke City in a £250,000 deal.

He soon settled into life in the Potteries and after representing the Republic of Ireland against Northern Ireland in a 'B' international, he made his full international debut against the Czech Republic in March 1998. He added two more caps to his total in 1999, scoring his first goal against Sweden in April.

Despite disciplinary problems with Stoke – he was sent-off twice in 1998-99 – he was called into the Republic of Ireland Euro 2000 squad on a couple of occasions and selected by his fellow professionals for the PFA award-winning Second Division side. The following season he helped Stoke win the Auto Windscreen Shield Final at Wembley. His name was frequently mentioned in connection with a move, but he stayed to play his part in a successful season, earning a place in the PFA Second Division side for the second season in succession. In 2000-01 he helped the Potters reach the play-offs and made the award-winning PFA side for a third season. At the end of the campaign he went on the transfer list, as he sought higher-grade football in a bid to boost his international ambitions.

Kavanagh joined Cardiff City for a fee of £1 million in July 2001. He certainly lived up to his reputation in his first season at Ninian Park, scoring 15 goals including a number of 'Goal of the Season' contenders. He was selected for the PFA award-winning team for a fourth season. After losing three successive play-off finals – two for Stoke and one for Cardiff – Kavanagh finally made it in 2002-03, leading the Welsh club to victory against Queen's Park Rangers in the final. Selected in the PFA side for a fifth successive season, he was given his first start by the Republic of Ireland against Canada, but was promptly injured!

Above: Graham Kavanagh

Transferred to Wigan Athletic in March 2005, he played a major part in the Latics' promotion to the Premiership – his performances also allowing him to add to his collection of caps for the Republic of Ireland.

Robbie Keane

Position	Forward
Born	Robert David Keane, Dublin, 8 July 1980

Clubs

Wolverhampton Wanderers; Coventry City; Inter Milan (Italy); Leeds United; Tottenham Hotspur

International Caps	62
International Goals	26

Matches

Year	Opponent	Result	Score	G
1998	Czech Republic	lost	1-2	
1998	Argentina	lost	0-2	
1998	Mexico	drew	0-0	
1999	Croatia	won	2-0	
1999	Malta	won	5-0	2
1999	Paraguay	won	2-0	
1999	Sweden	won	2-0	
1999	N Ireland	lost	0-1	
1999	Macedonia	won	1-0	
2000	Yugoslavia	won	2-1	1
2000	Malta	won	3-2	1
2000	Macedonia	drew	1-1	
2000	Turkey	drew	1-1	1
2000	Czech Republic	won	3-2	1
2000	Greece	lost	0-1	
2000	Scotland	lost	1-2	
2000	Mexico	drew	2-2	
2000	South Africa	won	2-1	
2001	Holland	drew	2-2	1
2001	Portugal	drew	1-1	
2001	Estonia	won	2-0	
2001	Finland	won	3-0	
2001	Cyprus	won	4-0	
2001	Andorra	won	3-0	
2001	Portugal	drew	1-1	
2002	Croatia	drew	2-2	
2002	Holland	won	1-0	
2002	Iran	won	2-0	1
2002	Iran	lost	0-1	
2002	Russia	won	2-0	1
2002	Denmark	won	3-0	1
2002	United States	won	2-1	
2002	Nigeria	lost	1-2	
2002	Cameroon	drew	1-1	
2002	Germany	drew	1-1	1
2002	Saudi Arabia	won	3-0	1
2002	Spain	drew	1-1	1
2003	Finland	won	3-0	1
2003	Russia	lost	2-4	
2003	Switzerland	lost	1-2	
2003	Albania	drew	0-0	
2003	Norway	won	1-0	
2003	Albania	won	2-1	1
2003	Georgia	won	2-0	1
2004	Australia	won	2-1	
2004	Switzerland	lost	0-2	

Matches Continued				
Year	Opponent	Result	Score	G
2004	Canada	won	3-0	2
2004	Brazil	drew	0-0	
2004	Czech Republic	won	2-1	1
2004	Romania	won	1-0	
2004	Nigeria	lost	0-3	
2004	Holland	won	1-0	1
2005	Cyprus	won	3-0	1
2005	Switzerland	drew	1-1	
2005	France	drew	0-0	
2005	Faroe Islands	won	2-0	2
2005	Croatia	won	1-0	1
2005	Portugal	won	1-0	
2005	Israel	drew	1-1	
2005	China	won	1-0	
2005	Israel	drew	2-2	1
2006	Sweden	won	3-0	1

Robbie Keane was just 17 when he made his League debut for Wolves against Norwich City on the opening day of the 1997-98 season. The first player to score two on his Wolves' debut since Ted Farmer in 1960, he went on to score 11 goals in 37 League games. Playing in the 'hole' behind the front two, he showed remarkable composure throughout his first campaign in the senior side.

Having progressed to the 'B' team, he became the Republic of Ireland's second-youngest full international ever, coming on for most of the second-half in Czechoslovakia, before going on to play the whole ninety minutes against Argentina. Clearly the find of the season, he was selected in the PFA divisional XI.

Having helped the Republic win the European Youth Championship in the summer of 1998, he won his fourth full international cap against Croatia and scored eight goals in Wolves' first12 games of the 1998-99 season. He also scored two for the Republic as they beat Malta 5-0 but picked up a knee injury whilst away. By March 1999 injections and illness were taking their toll. The treatment was in preparation for his trip to Nigeria for an Under-20 tournament – the Molineux club were very unhappy to lose him at this vital stage of their season.

Ironically, he made very little impact in Nigeria and the Republic did not progress much either.

Above: Robbie Keane

In August 1999 Keane left Wolves to join Coventry City for a fee of £6 million – scoring twice on his debut against Derby County. He scored 11 goals in his first 21 games despite playing alongside four different partners. Runner-up in the PFA's 'Young Player of the Year' award, he was sorely missed in the second leg of the European Championship play-off with Turkey when suspension kept him out.
In the close season Keane left Highfield Road and joined Inter Milan for £13 million, yet within a matter of months, he was back in the Football League as Leeds United paid £12 million for his services. He

made an immediate impact on a struggling side, scoring five in his first seven games – including a superb overhead kick to defeat his former club, Coventry. He netted a hat-trick during the early part of the 2001-02 season as Leeds beat Leicester 6-0 in a Worthington Cup tie at Walker's Stadium.

Continuing to be a crucial figure for the Republic of Ireland, he had a superb 2002 World Cup, netting goals in the games against Germany, Saudi Arabia and Spain.

On his return to Elland Road he found himself on the bench. After just a handful of games, he signed for Spurs for a fee of £7 million. Probably Glenn Hoddle's finest buy, he didn't take long to settle and netted a hat-trick against Everton, later ending the season as the club's leading scorer.

Sadly, the Republic of Ireland's chances of Euro 2004 qualification were blighted by his lack of availability due to injury. At White Hart Lane Keane remained an automatic choice, this in spite of the club having four top-class strikers to choose from. Consistently rising to the occasion for both club and country, Robbie Keane is the Republic of Ireland's highest-ever scorer, with 26 goals in his 62 appearances.

Mark Kinsella

Position	Midfield
Born	Mark Anthony Kinsella, Dublin, 12 August 1972

Clubs

Home Farm; Colchester United; Charlton Athletic; Aston Villa; West Bromwich Albion; Walsall

International Caps	48
International Goals	3

Matches

Year	Opponent	Result	Score	G
1998	Czech Republic	lost	1-2	
1998	Argentina	lost	0-2	

Year	Opponent	Result	Score	G
1999	Croatia	won	2-0	
1999	Malta	won	5-0	
1999	Yugoslavia	lost	0-1	
1999	Paraguay	won	2-0	
1999	Sweden	won	2-0	
1999	N Ireland	lost	0-1	
1999	Macedonia	won	1-0	
2000	Yugoslavia	won	2-1	
2000	Croatia	lost	0-2	
2000	Malta	won	3-2	
2000	Macedonia	drew	1-1	
2000	Turkey	drew	0-0	
2000	Czech Republic	won	3-2	
2000	Greece	lost	0-1	
2001	Holland	drew	2-2	
2001	Portugal	drew	1-1	
2001	Estonia	won	2-0	1
2001	Finland	won	3-0	
2001	Cyprus	won	4-0	
2001	Andorra	won	3-1	1
2001	Portugal	drew	1-1	
2001	Estonia	won	2-0	
2002	Iran	lost	0-1	
2002	Denmark	won	3-0	
2002	United States	won	2-1	1
2002	Nigeria	lost	1-2	
2002	Cameroon	drew	1-1	
2002	Germany	drew	1-1	
2002	Saudi Arabia	won	3-0	
2002	Spain	drew	1-1	
2003	Finland	won	3-0	
2003	Russia	lost	2-4	
2003	Switzerland	lost	1-2	
2003	Scotland	won	2-0	
2003	Georgia	won	2-1	
2003	Albania	drew	0-0	
2003	Norway	won	1-0	
2003	Albania	won	2-1	
2003	Georgia	won	2-0	
2004	Australia	won	2-1	
2004	Turkey	drew	2-2	
2004	Switzerland	lost	0-2	
2004	Czech Republic	won	2-1	
2004	Poland	drew	0-0	
2004	Nigeria	lost	0-3	
2004	Jamaica	won	1-0	

Having played his early football with Home Farm, midfielder Mark Kinsella joined Colchester United where he was to spend seven seasons. During that time, he helped the Layer Road club win the GM Vauxhall Conference League Championship and FA Trophy in 1991-92. After scoring 36 goals in 212 League and Cup games for Colchester, Charlton Athletic paid £150,000 for his services in September 1996. An intelligent player with a good work ethic and an eye for goal, he was made Addicks' captain. He was ever-present in 1997-98, leading the side to the Premiership via the play-offs. Not surprisingly, he was voted the club's 'Player of the Year'.

Above: Mark Kinsella

During the course of that season, having played for the Republic of Ireland 'B' side, he was called up to the full international side for the Czech Republic and Argentina games. He retained his place in the national side when Euro 2000 qualifiers got underway the following autumn – a campaign in which he was named the Addicks' 'Player of the Year' for the second successive season.

Following the Addicks' relegation, Kinsella led the club back to the top flight as First Division Champions in 1999-2000. This earned him a place in the PFA award-winning First Division side. Continuing to read the game well, Kinsella also proved his ability as an excellent passer of the ball, not afraid to hit a 40-yard pass to change the direction of play. During the course of the 2001-02 season, he was hampered by injuries – first an operation to cure a double hernia, and then a knee problem. He had scored 22 goals in 226 games for Charlton when in the summer of 2002 he left The Valley to sign for Aston Villa for a fee of £750,000.

Solid, reliable and consistent for both Villa and the Republic of Ireland in his first season in the Midlands, he then struggled with injuries. Unable to win back his first team place, he moved to Villa's neighbours West Bromwich Albion. Despite helping the Baggies win promotion to the Premiership, he was released.

Kinsella won 48 caps for the Republic of Ireland. He remained in the Midlands by signing for Walsall, for whom he featured in a role just in front of the back four.

Alan Maybury

Position	Full-back
Born	Alan Maybury, Dublin, 8 August 1978

Clubs

St Kevin's BC; Leeds United; Reading (loan); Crewe Alexandra (loan); Heart of Midlothian; Leicester City

International Caps	10

Matches

Year	Opponent	Result	Score	G
1998	Czech Republic	lost	1-2	
1999	N Ireland	lost	0-1	
2004	Czech Republic	won	2-1	
2004	Poland	drew	0-0	
2004	Romania	won	1-0	
2004	Nigeria	lost	0-3	
2004	Jamaica	won	1-0	
2004	Holland	won	1-0	
2005	Cyprus	won	3-0	
2005	China	won	1-0	

Having captained the Republic of Ireland Under-15s and -16s, Alan Maybury arrived at Elland Road in the summer of 1995. He did not make the best of starts at Leeds, suffering from homesickness and breaking his arm. He was captain of the Yorkshire club's FA Youth Cup-winning side in 1996-97 and after three appearances for the Republic of Ireland Under-21 side, made his full international debut in a friendly against the Czech Republic in March 1998.

Unable to get a game at Leeds in 1998-99, he went to Reading on loan. Maybury was unfortunate to get sent-off on his debut at home to Manchester City. He returned to Elland Road but suffered an horrendous spate of injuries prior to going out on loan again, this time to Crewe Alexandra. Finding himself on the fringes of the Leeds side, he opted for a move to the Scottish Premier League with Hearts, becoming a regular in their line-up. In a little over four years at Tynecastle, he appeared in 134 games for the Jam Tarts. Leicester City paid £100,000 in January 2005 to bring him back to the Football League.

Although able to operate in either full-back position, he was certainly more effective when overlapping on the right. He also managed to get himself on the scoresheet a couple of times. His form for the Foxes led to him winning his tenth cap for the Republic of Ireland when he was recalled to the side to play China in March 2005, a match the Irish won 1-0.

A player who likes to push forward and is confident on the ball, the only surprise about hardworking wing-back Stephen Carr's Republic of Ireland debut was that it did not come sooner.

He had been a regular in the Spurs side for three seasons, increasing in stature with each campaign, when he won his first full cap against Sweden in April 1999. Coming into the Irish squad as a replacement for the injured Denis Irwin, he had an outstanding game in a 2-0 win.

That season also saw him help Spurs to success in the Worthington Cup Final with a 1-0 defeat of Leicester City. His speed and tenacity make him a hard player to beat, and his superb ability to read the game helps him create space on the right flank from which to supply the attack. In 2000-01 he won recognition from his fellow professionals when he was selected for the Premiership's team.

Continuing to be a regular in the Republic of Ireland side, this was the season when he assumed the defensive role previously taken by Denis Irwin. Unfortunately he missed the whole of the following season with knee problems. In the opening game of the 2002-03 campaign against Everton, he pulled up with a hamstring injury which kept him out of action for another couple of months. On his return to action, he again produced performances confirming him as one of the best right-backs in the Premiership and once again won selection to the Premiership team of the season.

Stephen Carr

Position	Full-back
Born	Stephen Carr, Dublin, 29 August 1976

Clubs

Tottenham Hotspur; Newcastle United

International Caps	37

Matches

Year	Opponent	Result	Score	G
1999	Sweden	won	2-0	
1999	N Ireland	lost	0-1	
1999	Macedonia	won	1-0	
2000	Yugoslavia	won	2-1	
2000	Croatia	lost	0-2	
2000	Malta	won	3-2	
2000	Turkey	drew	1-1	
2000	Turkey	drew	0-0	
2000	Scotland	lost	1-2	
2000	Mexico	drew	2-2	
2000	United States	drew	1-1	
2000	South Africa	won	2-1	
2001	Holland	drew	2-2	
2001	Portugal	drew	1-1	
2001	Estonia	won	2-0	
2001	Andorra	won	3-1	
2001	Portugal	drew	1-1	
2001	Estonia	won	2-0	
2003	Scotland	won	2-0	
2003	Georgia	won	2-1	
2003	Albania	drew	0-0	
2003	Norway	won	1-0	
2003	Albania	won	2-1	
2003	Georgia	won	2-0	
2004	Australia	won	2-1	
2004	Russia	drew	1-1	
2004	Turkey	drew	2-2	
2004	Switzerland	lost	0-2	
2004	Canada	won	3-0	
2004	Brazil	drew	0-0	
2005	Bulgaria	drew	1-1	
2005	Cyprus	won	3-0	
2005	Switzerland	drew	1-1	
2005	France	drew	0-0	
2005	Faroe Islands	won	2-0	
2005	Israel	drew	1-1	
2005	Faroe Islands	won	2-0	

There is little doubt that Stephen Carr was the most influential player in the Spurs line-up in 2003-04. He had matured as a great leader on the pitch and taken his total of appearances for the White Hart Lane club to 272 when the new manager Jacques Santini surprisingly allowed him to join Newcastle United for a fee of £2 million.

Carr would play under six managers but despite the periods of upheaval, he was the club's most consistent player. A regular in the Magpies side, he was sidelined midway through his first season at St James Park with a knee injury which kept him out of action for three months. On his return, the squad was depleted by injuries and he found himself moved into a holding midfield role.

Left: Stephen Carr

2000+

The Republic started the qualifiers for Euro 2000 with a fine 2-0 win over Croatia. In their next game at home to Malta, Robbie Keane – aged 18 – went into the record books as Ireland's youngest-ever scorer, hitting two in three minutes in a 5-0 win. Having put up a fine display away to group favourites Yugoslavia, only to lose 1-0, the Republic made amends with a 2-1 win in the return game. They held out for a draw in Croatia only to lose to a last-gasp goal. There was heartache for the Republic in their final group game – leading Macedonia 1-0 with a little over 10 seconds remaining, they were heading for automatic qualification but on conceding an added-time equaliser, they had to try and make it through the play-offs. Their opponents were Turkey. In the first leg in Dublin, the Irish were yet again undone in the closing moments, allowing the Turks to grab an all-important equaliser from the penalty-spot in the 83rd minute, just four minutes after Robbie Keane had swept the Republic ahead. Sadly, Ireland's campaign came to a bitter end after a scoreless draw in Turkey. They failed on the away-goal rule whilst Tony Cascarino, who was involved in some unsavoury scenes at the finish, announced his retirement from the international game.

The attack-minded Republic made a good start to their 2002 World Cup campaign. They shocked the Dutch by taking a 2-0 lead in Amsterdam through Robbie Keane and Jason McAteer but wobbled late on, allowing Holland to snatch a draw. After snatching another draw in Portugal, the boys in green won four games on the trot to go top of their group. In the return game at home to Portugal, the Republic survived an early mauling to draw 1-1. Then on a rutted surface well below international standard, the Republic overcame Estonia to remain undefeated at the top of their group. Down to 10 men, the Republic pulled off

a shock 1-0 home win over favourites Holland, which effectively left the Dutch requiring miracles to make the World Cup Finals. In their final group game, 35-year-old Niall Quinn headed his way into the record books with his 21st goal for the Republic. They got the required win over Cyprus and finished joint-top with Portugal. They then had to beat Iran (the runners-up from the Asian qualifiers) in a play-off to make the finals! Following a 2-0 win in Dublin the boys in green clinched their World Cup Finals place, despite conceding a goal 30 seconds from the final whistle in Iran.

The World Cup started controversially with captain Roy Keane being sent home after an argument with manager Mick McCarthy. In their opening game of the World Cup Finals, a Matt Holland goal earned the Republic a draw with Cameroon. Four days later, Steve Staunton became the first Republic of Ireland player to earn 100 caps as Robbie Keane snatched a last-gasp equaliser against mighty Germany. The Republic then progressed to the second round by scoring three without reply against Saudi Arabia. Their opponents in this next stage of the competition were the much-fancied Spain. Ian Harte had a 62nd minute penalty saved and Kevin Kilbane hit the rebound wide, but Robbie Keane sent the game into extra-time at 1-1 with a last-minute spot-kick. There were no further goals but the Irish lost the ensuing penalty shoot-out with Holland, Connolly and Kilbane missing again! However, the squad still returned home as heroes with Robbie Keane and Damien Duff proving they will be superstars for many years to come.

The Republic didn't get off to a good start in the Euro 2004 qualifiers, losing 4-2 in Russia and then going down 2-1 at home to Switzerland. This defeat put more pressure on beleaguered boss Mick McCarthy: the following month he resigned his post as Europe's longest-serving national coach. His departure came just four months after leading the side into the last-16 of the World Cup. Two months later, Brian Kerr was named as McCarthy's successor. He had steered the Republic's Under-16s and Under-18s to European titles. Kerr's first competitive match in charge saw the Irish win 2-1 in Georgia but winger Kevin Kilbane was hit by an open penknife! After a disappointing goalless draw in Albania, the Republic snatched a last-gasp vital win over the same opponents in Dublin followed by another home victory four days later over Georgia. In the home game against Russia, the Republic lost the plot in a match full of goalkeeping errors and had to be satisfied with a 1-1 draw. Their final game in Switzerland saw them miss out on a chance of reaching the finals when they lost 2-0 to the eventual group winners – this game ended Brian Kerr's nine-game unbeaten run since starting as manager.

With no European Championships to look forward to, Kerr began planning for the World Cup qualifiers, the first of which saw Robbie Keane equal the country's goalscoring record by netting from the penalty-spot in a 3-0 win over Cyprus. The Irish then missed a host of chances before coming away from Switzerland with a point in a 1-1 draw. A goalless home draw against favourites France was followed by a 2-0 victory over the Faroes, with Robbie Keane netting both goals to overtake Niall Quinn's overall scoring record. The Republic then drew both games with Israel – matches they should have won. Another victory over the Faroes took the boys in green to the top of the group before a Thierry Henry goal was enough to defeat the Republic in the return game. A 1-0 win over Cyprus meant that the Republic needed to beat Switzerland in their final group game to qualify for the World Cup Finals in Germany. Unfortunately for the Republic, the game ended goalless and they missed out.

After Brian Kerr and his backroom staff of Chris Hughton, Pat Bonner and Noel O'Reilly were not offered new contracts, the FAI were accused by many of acting too hastily due to the lack of viable successors for the post of Republic of Ireland manager. Though the FAI vowed to take their time in making what was seen as a crucial appointment, they didn't waste much time in unveiling Steve Staunton and Sir Bobby Robson as the new Irish managerial team. At a press conference in Dublin's Mansion House, Staunton left no-one in any doubt that this was his managerial team. A comment of 'I am the boss… the buck stops with me' leaves no room for doubt in a team that also includes Kevin McDonald and Alan Kelly. Staunton also added that 'we have very talented players. We will not shirk the challenge. We're Irish.' Bobby Robson was equally direct: 'We've got some tremendously talented players and the spirit of teamwork and togetherness which has been a distinctive hallmark of successful Irish sides down the years is something which can give us an edge in the international football arena.'

Matt Holland

Position	Midfield
Born	Matthew Rhys Holland, Bury, 11 April 1974

Clubs

West Ham United; Bournemouth; Ipswich Town; Charlton Athletic

International Caps	46
International Goals	5

Matches

Year	Opponent	Result	Score	G
2000	Macedonia	drew	1-1	
2000	Mexico	drew	2-2	
2000	United States	drew	1-1	
2000	South Africa	won	2-1	
2001	Portugal	drew	1-1	1
2001	Finland	won	3-0	
2001	Cyprus	won	4-0	
2001	Andorra	won	3-0	1
2001	Andorra	won	3-1	
2001	Portugal	drew	1-1	
2001	Estonia	won	2-0	1
2002	Holland	won	1-0	
2002	Cyprus	won	4-0	
2002	Iran	won	2-0	
2002	Iran	lost	0-1	
2002	Russia	won	2-0	
2002	Denmark	won	3-0	
2002	United States	won	2-1	
2002	Nigeria	lost	1-2	
2002	Cameroon	drew	1-1	1
2002	Germany	drew	1-1	
2002	Saudi Arabia	won	3-0	
2002	Spain	drew	1-1	
2003	Finland	won	3-0	
2003	Russia	lost	2-4	
2003	Switzerland	lost	1-2	
2003	Greece	drew	0-0	
2003	Scotland	won	2-0	
2003	Georgia	won	2-1	
2003	Albania	drew	0-0	
2003	Norway	won	1-0	
2003	Albania	won	2-1	
2003	Georgia	won	2-0	
2004	Australia	won	2-1	
2004	Russia	drew	1-1	
2004	Switzerland	lost	0-2	
2004	Canada	won	3-0	
2004	Brazil	drew	0-0	
2004	Czech Republic	won	2-1	
2004	Romania	won	1-0	1
2004	Nigeria	lost	0-3	
2004	Jamaica	won	1-0	
2004	Holland	won	1-0	
2005	Portugal	won	1-0	
2005	Israel	drew	1-1	
2005	Israel	drew	2-2	

Unable to make the grade at West Ham United, midfielder Matt Holland joined Bournemouth in January 1995. In his first full season at Dean Court, he swept the board in the 'Player of the Year' awards. Playing mainly in a central midfield position, with a number of games as a sweeper, he scored 10 goals, the majority from outside the area. Appointed the Cherries' captain, he demonstrated his defensive qualities in 1996–97 when because of injuries, he played in the centre of defence.

Above: Matt Holland

In the summer of 1997 he joined Ipswich Town for a fee of £800,000 and soon became a firm favourite. Influential in Town's second-half surge up the table, he played in a variety of positions, displaying his wholehearted endeavour in every game. His most eventful experience was probably the game against Oxford United, where he took over from Richard Wright in goal while the keeper had stitches in a facial injury. Though he was powerless to prevent Kevin Francis from scoring, he scored the fourth goal himself in a 5-2 win, all before conceding a penalty! Not surprisingly he was voted 'Player of the Year' by the supporters. Instrumental in the club reaching the Premiership via the play-offs, Holland was appointed club captain.

He made his full international debut for the Republic of Ireland against Macedonia in October 1999 and also appeared in the end-of-season Nike Cup games in the United States. The following season he netted his first international goals against Andorra and Portugal, whilst at club level, he continued to epitomise all that is good about the Suffolk club – playing in the right spirit, hard but fair.

Unable to prevent the Tractor Boys' relegation from the Premiership, he remained a regular member of the Republic of Ireland squad and was picked to go to the 2002 World Cup. Ipswich Town's 'Player of the Year' for 2002–03, he was surprisingly allowed to leave Portman Road in the close season, having scored 46 goals in 314 games. He joined Charlton Athletic, who paid £750,000 for his signature.

Made club captain on his debut, he was ever-present in his first season for the Addicks, soon becoming a huge crowd favourite. He has built up a good understanding at The Valley with Danny Murphy and chipped in with some valuable goals. A regular in the Republic of Ireland side having won nearly fifty caps he announced his retirement from international football in 2006.

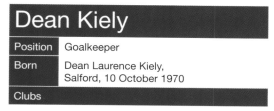

Dean Kiely

Position	Goalkeeper
Born	Dean Laurence Kiely, Salford, 10 October 1970

Clubs

Coventry City; York City; Bury; Charlton Athletic; Portsmouth

International Caps	8

Matches

Year	Opponent	Result	Score	G
2000	Turkey	drew	1-1	
2000	Turkey	drew	0-0	
2000	Greece	lost	0-1	
2000	Mexico	drew	2-2	
2002	Russia	won	2-0	
2002	Denmark	won	3-0	
2003	Finland	won	3-0	
2003	Scotland	won	2-0	

An England youth international goalkeeper, he was unable to force his way into the Coventry side and moved to York City in March 1990. Hugely popular with the Minstermen fans, he did not miss a game from December 1992 until September 1995. A serious facial injury ended a run of 150 successive senior appearances. On his return to action, he took over the captaincy and went on to play in 239 games for York before joining Bury in the summer of 1996.

Rated one of the best keepers in the lower divisions, he managed to keep 22 clean sheets in his first season at Gigg Lane and save two penalties as the Shakers won the Second Division Championship. An ever-present in 1997-98, he won a call-up to the national squad. Despite keeping 19 clean sheets for Bury, the Lancashire club were relegated. This accelerated his departure from Gigg Lane as he signed for Charlton Athletic in a £1 million deal.

He kept 19 clean sheets in his first season at The Valley – equalling a club record – and ended the season with a First Division Championship medal.

He also made his international debut for the Republic of Ireland against Turkey in November 1999 and went on to win three more caps over the course of that season.

He was impressive in the Premiership until injuring his groin, whilst in 2001–02 he was not only ever-present but voted the club's 'Player of the Year' by Addicks supporters. He was ever-present again the following season where his performances continued to prove him one of the best keepers in the Premiership. Having taken his tally of international caps to eight, he announced his retirement from international football in 2003–04. An excellent shot-stopper, he was Charlton's 'Player of the Year' for a second time in three years. Kiely continued to show his consistency, appearing in 248 games for the South London club. He left Charlton Athletic in January 2006 to join Portsmouth.

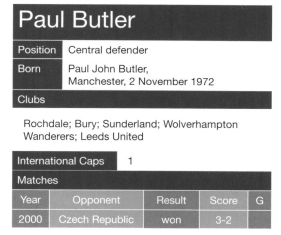

Paul Butler

Position	Central defender
Born	Paul John Butler, Manchester, 2 November 1972

Clubs

Rochdale; Bury; Sunderland; Wolverhampton Wanderers; Leeds United

International Caps	1

Matches

Year	Opponent	Result	Score	G
2000	Czech Republic	won	3-2	

Central defender Paul Butler began his career with Rochdale where he formed an excellent partnership with Peter Valentine. Voted the club's 'Player of the Year' in 1994-95 and 1995-96, he went on to appear in 188 games for the Spotland club, before Bury paid £100,000 for his services in the summer of 1996.

A constant danger at set pieces, he proved to be a shrewd capture for the Gigg Lane side as they won that season's Second Division Championship. In 1997-98 he was a revelation in a tough campaign, turning in consistent displays week in, week out and looked completely at ease at the higher level of football.

Included in Mick McCarthy's Republic of Ireland squad, he was later transferred to Peter Reid's Sunderland for a fee of £900,000. In his first season in the north-east, he picked up a First Division Championship medal. His impressive form earned him a place in the PFA First Division select, prompting Mick McCarthy to pick him for a 'B' international against the National League in February 1999. He continued to impress in the Premiership and went on to make his full international debut for the Republic of Ireland against the Czech Republic in February 2000 – becoming the first player to qualify after gaining Irish citizenship through marriage.

Following the arrival of Stan Varga and Emerson Thome at the Stadium of Light, Butler lost his place and after a loan spell with Wolves, the move was made permanent. Appointed the Molineux club's captain, he was Wolves' most consistent player over the next couple of seasons, helping them win promotion to the Premiership in 2003-04. His game was all about hard work and determination, though he couldn't prevent their relegation from the top flight.

He left Molineux on a 'Bosman' in the summer of 2004 to join Leeds United, where he was immediately made captain. His first season at Elland Road almost ended in tragedy. He swallowed his tongue in a collision with his own goalkeeper Neil Sullivan – only the prompt action of the club's physio prevented anything more serious than concussion.

Gary Doherty

Position	Central defender/Forward
Born	Gary Michael Doherty, Carndonagh, Co. Donegal, 31 January 1980
Clubs	

Luton Town; Tottenham Hotspur; Norwich City

International Caps	31
International Goals	4

Matches

Year	Opponent	Result	Score	G
2000	Greece	lost	0-1	
2000	United States	drew	1-1	
2000	South Africa	won	2-1	
2001	Cyprus	won	4-0	
2001	Andorra	won	3-0	
2001	Andorra	won	3-1	
2001	Portugal	drew	1-1	
2001	Estonia	won	2-0	
2002	United States	won	2-1	1
2003	Finland	won	3-0	
2003	Russia	lost	2-4	1
2003	Switzerland	lost	1-2	
2003	Greece	drew	0-0	
2003	Scotland	won	2-0	
2003	Georgia	won	2-1	1
2003	Albania	drew	0-0	
2003	Albania	won	2-1	
2003	Georgia	won	2-0	1
2004	Australia	won	2-1	
2004	Russia	drew	1-1	
2004	Turkey	drew	2-2	
2004	Canada	won	3-0	
2004	Czech Republic	won	2-1	
2004	Poland	drew	0-0	
2004	Nigeria	lost	0-3	
2004	Jamaica	won	1-0	
2005	Bulgaria	drew	1-1	
2005	Switzerland	drew	1-1	
2005	China	won	1-0	
2005	Israel	drew	2-2	
2005	Faroe Islands	won	2-0	

After an impressive League debut for Luton Town against Plymouth Argyle in October 1997, where he laid on a couple of goals in a 3-0 win, Doherty returned to the club's youth side. He helped them win a second consecutive South East Counties title and was joint 'Young Player of the Year'.

A regular member of the Republic of Ireland Under-18 side, he scored a number of vital goals for the Hatters the following season when playing as a striker, though at the time he preferred a central defensive role. Prior to the start of the 1999-2000 season, Doherty captained the Republic of Ireland Under-18 side in the European Championships in Sweden, returning home with a bronze medal. Virtually an ever-present in a young Luton side, he had scored five goals in successive matches when in April 2000 he was transferred to Spurs for £1 million.

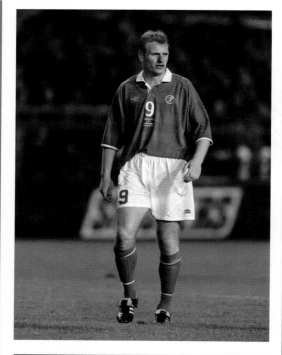

Above: Gary Doherty

He made his full international debut for the Republic when he came on as a substitute against Greece. He was then included in the starting line-up for the first time in the Nike Cup fixture with the United States in June 2000. Equally at home in attack or defence, his progress at White Hart Lane was hampered by a run of injuries. This limited his appearances which in turn meant that he missed out on a place in the Republic of Ireland squad for the 2002 World Cup Finals. Despite suffering a broken leg he proved himself one of the most versatile players in the Premiership, having played in all positions bar goalkeeper. He had appeared in 78 games for Spurs in a little over four years at White Hart Lane when he signed for Norwich City in the summer of 2004, as he went in search of regular first-team football.

Having won 31 caps for the Republic of Ireland, Gary Doherty soon settled into a good partnership at the back with Craig Fleming but was unable to prevent the Canaries' relegation from the Premiership.

Richard Dunne

Position	Defender
Born	Richard Patrick Dunne, Dublin, 21 September 1979
Clubs	

Everton; Manchester City

International Caps	24
International Goals	4

Matches

Year	Opponent	Result	Score	G
2000	Greece	lost	0-1	
2000	Scotland	lost	1-2	
2000	Mexico	drew	2-2	1
2001	Holland	drew	2-2	
2001	Portugal	drew	1-1	
2001	Estonia	won	2-0	1
2001	Finland	won	3-0	
2001	Andorra	won	3-1	
2001	Portugal	drew	1-1	
2001	Estonia	won	2-0	1
2002	Croatia	drew	2-2	
2002	Holland	won	1-0	
2002	Russia	won	2-0	
2002	Denmark	won	3-0	
2003	Greece	drew	0-0	
2003	Scotland	won	2-0	
2003	Norway	won	1-0	
2004	Australia	won	2-1	
2004	Turkey	drew	2-2	1
2004	Canada	won	3-0	
2005	Croatia	won	1-0	
2005	Portugal	won	1-0	
2005	China	won	1-0	
2006	Sweden	won	3-0	

A giant centre-half who topped 6ft 2in and 15 stone before his 16th birthday, Richard Dunne's professional progress was almost as meteoric as his physical development.

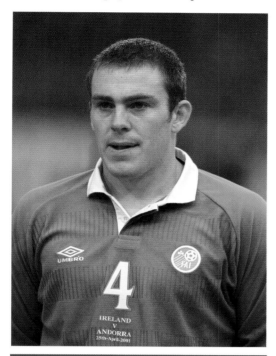

Above: Richard Dunne

The first product of Everton's sponsorship links with the Irish club Home Farm, he made history in January 1997, becoming the youngest Everton player to play in a first team match at Goodison Park. On his impressive debut in the FA Cup tie against Swindon Town, he was 17 years 106 days old. Two months later after a typically composed performance in the passion of the Merseyside derby, he was called up to the full Republic of Ireland squad. A mainstay of Everton's FA Youth Cup-winning team, Dunne represented the Republic at 'B' international level in the summer of 1998.

He helped the Republic of Ireland to a shock European Youth Championship success and was picked for the Under-21 side, but a foot injury prevented him from travelling to Nigeria for the World Youth Championships.

Establishing himself as a regular in the Everton side during 1999-2000, he made his debut for the full Republic of Ireland side against Greece in April 2000, before adding caps against Scotland and Mexico, when he scored in a 2-2 draw.

In October 2000 he surprisingly left Goodison Park to join former boss Joe Royle at Manchester City, the then Maine Road club paying £3 million for his services. Following the appointment of Kevin Keegan as manager Dunne blossomed, continuing as a regular in the Republic of Ireland side. Putting his well-documented personal problems behind him with a string of 'Man-of-the-Match' performances, Richard Dunne is now the most experienced player at the club, having played in 179 games and in 2004-05 was voted the club's 'Player of the Year'.

Steve Finnan

Position	Right-back
Born	Stephen John Finnan, Limerick, 20 April 1976
Clubs	

Welling United; Birmingham City; Notts County (loan); Notts County; Fulham; Liverpool

International Caps	36
International Goals	1

Matches

Year	Opponent	Result	Score	G
2000	Greece	lost	0-1	
2000	Scotland	lost	1-2	
2001	Portugal	drew	1-1	
2001	Estonia	won	2-0	
2001	Finland	won	3-0	1
2001	Andorra	won	3-0	
2001	Andorra	won	3-1	
2002	Croatia	drew	2-2	
2002	Holland	won	1-0	

Matches Continued

Year	Opponent	Result	Score	G
2002	Cyprus	won	4-0	
2002	Iran	won	2-0	
2002	Iran	lost	0-1	
2002	Russia	won	2-0	
2002	United States	won	2-1	
2002	Nigeria	lost	1-2	
2002	Cameroon	drew	1-1	
2002	Germany	drew	1-1	
2002	Saudi Arabia	won	3-0	
2002	Spain	drew	1-1	
2003	Russia	lost	2-4	
2003	Greece	drew	0-0	
2003	Norway	won	1-0	
2004	Australia	won	2-1	
2004	Turkey	drew	2-2	
2004	Switzerland	lost	0-2	
2004	Romania	won	1-0	
2004	Nigeria	lost	0-3	
2004	Holland	won	1-0	
2005	Bulgaria	drew	1-1	
2005	Cyprus	won	3-0	
2005	Switzerland	drew	1-1	
2005	France	drew	0-0	
2005	Faroe Islands	won	2-0	
2005	Croatia	won	1-0	
2005	Portugal	won	1-0	
2005	Israel	drew	1-1	

Discovered by Birmingham City playing non-League football for Welling United, Steve Finnan made a dramatic introduction to League football when scoring from a free-kick at Watford. Finding his opportunities limited, he had a three-month loan spell at Notts County. On his return to St Andrew's, he was selected for the Republic of Ireland Under-21 side against Norway in May 1996, scoring the equaliser in a 1-1 draw. Having impressed in his loan spell, he joined Notts County on a permanent basis in October 1996. The following season he was selected for the Republic of Ireland 'B' side and helped County win the Third Division Championship as the Meadow Lane club ran away with the title.

Playing as a winger, Finnan later left County to join Fulham for a fee of £600,000. Under Kevin Keegan, Finnan played in a variety of positions including right-wing back and central midfield. A Second Division Championship medal was the prize, as the Fulham revival continued. It is not often that a player wins Championship medals in successive seasons with different clubs, but Finnan did. He was also selected for the PFA award-winning divisional side.

In April 2000 Finnan won his first cap for the Republic of Ireland when he appeared against Greece, following this with the end-of-season friendly with Scotland.

In 2000-01 Finnan was Fulham's most outstanding player, helping the Cottagers win the First Division Championship, and winning selection for the PFA Division One side. An ever-present in Fulham's first season in the Premiership, he was named as the club's 'Player of the Season' and was selected for the PFA's Premiership team!

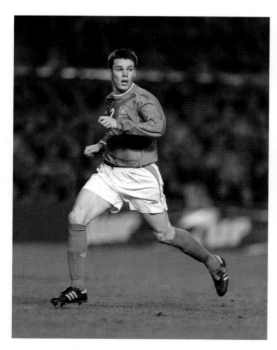

Above: Steve Finnan

Not surprisingly he was named in the Republic of Ireland squad for the 2002 World Cup Finals. Finnan had a successful World Cup, returning to Craven Cottage and showing the form that made him a target for a number of top Premiership clubs. Continuing as a regular selection for the Republic under new manager Brian Kerr, Finnan had made 207 appearances for Fulham when in June 2003 he joined Liverpool for a fee of £3.5 million.

Initially struggling to settle into his new surroundings, he enjoyed a more convincing and consistent 2004-05 season, winning a European Champions' League medal – this despite being substituted at half-time and so playing no part in Liverpool's stunning recovery!

Alan Mahon

Position	Midfield
Born	Alan Joseph Mahon, Dublin, 4 April 1978
Clubs	

Tranmere Rovers; Sporting Lisbon (Portugal); Blackburn Rovers; Cardiff City (loan); Ipswich Town (loan); Wigan Athletic

International Caps		2		
Matches				
Year	Opponent	Result	Score	G
2000	Greece	lost	0-1	
2000	South Africa	won	2-1	

An attacking midfielder who burst onto the Football League scene with Tranmere Rovers in 1995-96, the Irish youth international also made his debut for the Republic of Ireland Under-21 side during the course of that campaign.

After finding himself in and out of the side, he won a regular place towards the end of the 1997-98 season. A combination of a

recurring stomach injury and the burden of expectancy conspired to give him a frustrating time. The following season he found a rich seam of form and caused endless problems for his unfortunate markers. Developing a probing and tricky style of play, rumours began to circulate about a big-money move to the Premiership. In the summer of 2000 after making his full international debut for the Republic of Ireland against Greece, he chose to move to Sporting Lisbon.

He found it difficult to break into the side, although one of his rare appearances came in a European Champions' League game against Real Madrid.

In December 2000 he joined Blackburn Rovers, going on to produce some fine performances to assist the club in their bid for promotion. During the following season, with the exception of UEFA Cup ties, he was never in the frame at Ewood Park. In January 2003 he joined Cardiff City on loan. Though he provided the width that had been missing all season, he returned to Ewood Park shortly before the end of the season, thus missing out on the Bluebirds' play-off excitement.

In January 2004 Wigan Athletic paid £250,000 for Mahon's services. He brought balance to the Latics' midfield, helping the club win promotion to the Premiership for the first time in their history.

Barry Quinn

Position	Midfield
Born	Barry Scott Quinn, Dublin, 9 May 1979
Clubs	

Coventry City; Rushden and Diamonds (loan); Oxford United

International Caps		4

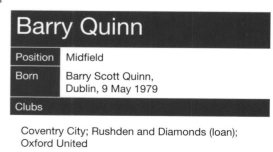

Matches				
Year	Opponent	Result	Score	G
2000	Greece	lost	0-1	
2000	Mexico	drew	2-2	
2000	United States	drew	1-1	
2000	South Africa	won	2-1	

The midfielder came to the fore during the 1998 World Under-18s Championship which the Republic of Ireland won under his captaincy.

He got his first-team chance at Coventry City, making an impressive debut during the early part of the 1998-99 season at Old Trafford. In April 1999 he captained the Republic of Ireland's Under-20 side in the World Championships in Nigeria. They reached the quarter-finals before losing on penalties to the host nation. Also that season, Quinn represented the national side at Under-21 level.

Though unable to make much progress at Highfield Road the following season, he made his full international debut against Greece and won further honours for the senior team in the US Nike Cup games in the summer. He won a regular place in the Coventry side during 2000-01. This led to him winning a recall to the Republic of Ireland's squad towards the end of the campaign. In and out of the Sky Blues side during the following two seasons, his progress wasn't helped by a spate of injuries including a broken toe.

Finding himself completely out of the first team picture at Coventry in 2003-04. Quinn had a loan spell with Rushden and Diamonds before signing for Oxford United in March 2004. A regular in the U's side throughout 2004-05, he came very close to winning the club's 'Player of the Year' award.

Dominic Foley

Position	Forward
Born	Dominic Joseph Foley, Cork, 7 July 1976

Clubs

St James' Gate; Wolverhampton Wanderers; Watford (loan); Notts County (loan); Ethnikos (Greece) (loan); Watford; Queen's Park Rangers (loan); Swindon Town (loan); Queen's Park Rangers (loan); Southend United (loan); Oxford United (loan); SC Braga (Portugal); Bohemians; KAA Ghent (Belgium)

International Caps	6
International Goals	2

Matches				
Year	Opponent	Result	Score	G
2000	Scotland	lost	1-2	
2000	Mexico	drew	2-2	1
2000	United States	drew	1-1	1
2000	South Africa	won	2-1	
2001	Estonia	won	2-0	
2001	Finland	won	3-0	

Rangy forward Dominic Foley joined Wolverhampton Wanderers from Irish team St James' Gate during the 1995 close season. The following season he came off the bench in three successive away matches, all of which were local derbies in different competitions.

His progress at Molineux was rewarded with a call-up to the Republic of Ireland Under-21 side. In 1996-97 Foley scored his first League goal for Wolves and netted for the national Under-21 side in a 4-0 defeat of Macedonia. The following season, though still a regular for the Republic's Under-21 side, he couldn't force his way into the Wolves' side on a regular basis and had a loan spell with Watford. There followed further loan spells with Notts County and Greek side Ethnikos, for whom he netted a hat-trick on his debut.

He returned to Wolves as they were not receiving his wages but despite the circumstances, he was not allowed to play until he was given international clearance.

Foley was allowed to join Watford in the summer of 1999. He suffered more than his fair share of injuries during his first season at Vicarage Road but won his first full international cap against Scotland in May 2000. Foley also made further appearances in the Nike Cup tournament the following month, scoring in the 2-2 draw with Mexico and the 1-1 tie with the United States.

In 2000-01, Foley had the misfortune to suffer a stress fracture of the fibula, but when fit, added to his tally of international caps. Allowed to leave Watford by manager Luca Vialli, he had loan spells with Swindon Town and Queen's Park Rangers in 2001-02, and with Southend United and Oxford United the following seasons before leaving to continue his career in Portugal with SC Braga in 2004–05. Foley then played a short time for Bohemians before moving to Belgium with KAA Ghent.

Stephen McPhail

Position	Midfield
Born	Stephen John Paul McPhail, Westminster, 9 December 1979

Clubs

Leeds United; Millwall (loan); Nottingham Forest (loan); Barnsley

International Caps	10
International Goals	1

Matches				
Year	Opponent	Result	Score	G
2000	Scotland	lost	1-2	
2000	United States	drew	1-1	
2000	South Africa	won	2-1	1
2002	Croatia	drew	2-2	
2002	Cyprus	won	4-0	
2003	Finland	won	3-0	
2003	Greece	drew	0-0	
2004	Turkey	drew	2-2	
2004	Canada	won	3-0	
2004	Nigeria	lost	0-3	

A member of the Leeds United side that won the FA Youth Cup in 1996-97, midfielder Stephen McPhail broke into the Yorkshire club's League side the following season. Making his full debut against Leicester City, he also came off the bench at Derby where his first touch was a superb 40-yard pass to set up Jimmy Floyd Hasselbaink for United's fifth goal! He appeared on a more regular basis in 1998-99 until picking up a niggling knee ligament injury which took some time to heal.

When the injury cleared, he was off to Nigeria with the Republic of Ireland side for the World Youth Championships. During the course of the season he made a number of appearances for the Republic of Ireland's Under-21 side.

In May 2000 he made his full international debut for the Republic of Ireland against Scotland and appeared in the Nike Cup matches in the United States. The following month he scored his first international goal in the 2-1 victory over South Africa.

The following season was an injury-ravaged one for McPhail. There was little doubt that Leeds missed his support, vision and ability to unlock defences. Injuries continued to hamper his progress in 2001-02 and he was loaned to Millwall. Unfortunately he was sent-off in his first game for the Lions and returned to Elland Road. He was in and out of the Leeds side the following season. At the start of the 2003-04 campaign he joined the former youth team manager Paul Hart at Nottingham Forest on loan.

Impressing greatly at the City Ground, he rejoined Leeds. His form over the remaining weeks of the campaign saw him recalled to the Republic of Ireland side. Surprisingly allowed to leave Leeds in the summer of 2004, having made 107 appearances, he

signed for Barnsley where he proved to be one of the most gifted footballers in the lower divisions.

Andy O'Brien

Position	Central defender
Born	Andrew James O'Brien, Harrogate, 29 June 1979
Clubs	

Bradford City; Newcastle United; Portsmouth

International Caps	22
International Goals	1

Matches

Year	Opponent	Result	Score	G
2001	Estonia	won	2-0	
2002	Croatia	drew	2-2	
2002	Holland	won	1-0	
2002	Russia	won	2-0	
2002	United States	won	2-1	
2003	Scotland	won	2-0	
2004	Australia	won	2-1	
2004	Turkey	drew	2-2	
2004	Brazil	drew	0-0	
2004	Poland	drew	0-0	
2004	Romania	won	1-0	
2004	Jamaica	won	1-0	
2004	Holland	won	1-0	
2005	Cyprus	won	3-0	
2005	Switzerland	drew	1-1	
2005	France	drew	0-0	
2005	Faroe Islands	won	2-0	
2005	Portugal	won	1-0	1
2005	Israel	drew	1-1	
2005	China	won	1-0	
2005	Israel	drew	2-2	
2006	Sweden	won	3-0	

Nicknamed 'Rash' for the way he sticks to opponents, defender Andy O'Brien signed professional forms for Bradford City in October 1996 after coming through the club's youth scheme as a trainee. Having already made his debut against Queen's Park Rangers, he showed himself to be a great prospect and was justly voted the Yorkshire club's 'Young Player of the Year'.

In 1997-98 O'Brien was selected for the Football League Under-21 side that

played its Italian counterpart at The Valley. The following season he gained his first international honours when playing for the England Under-21 side. However, later in the season, he decided to represent the Republic of Ireland – making his debut in an Under-21 friendly against Sweden. He qualified for the Republic because his father was born there.

Above: Andy O'Brien

Forming a solid partnership with David Wetherall in the centre of Bradford City's defence during 1999-2000 (his first season of Premiership football), he was voted the players' 'Player of the Year' and the supporters' 'Young Player of the Year'. After suffering a broken collarbone during the early part of the following season, he returned to a struggling Bantams side before being transferred to Newcastle United for £2 million shortly before the transfer deadline. After scoring his first goal for the Magpies in the local derby against Sunderland, he won his first full international cap for the Republic of Ireland against Estonia in June 2001.

At Newcastle, he soon established himself at the heart of the defence, giving a series of solid and dependable displays. Though continuing to be a regular member of the Republic of Ireland squad, he suffered a number of setbacks including a shin injury and a broken nose. With the Magpies he clearly benefited from playing alongside Jonathan Woodgate. Despite the increased competition for places, he kept his spot in the side.

At international level, O'Brien delivered an outstanding performance in the World Cup qualifier against Cyprus in September 2004. He scored his first goal for the national side against Portugal the following February. Since the summer of 2005, Andy O'Brien plays his football for Premiership Portsmouth.

Matches Continued				
Year	Opponent	Result	Score	G
2003	Switzerland	lost	1-2	
2003	Scotland	won	2-0	1
2004	Australia	won	2-1	1
2004	Russia	drew	1-1	
2004	Turkey	drew	2-2	
2004	Switzerland	lost	0-2	
2004	Canada	won	3-0	
2004	Brazil	drew	0-0	
2004	Czech Republic	won	2-1	
2004	Poland	drew	0-0	
2004	Romania	won	1-0	
2004	Jamaica	won	1-0	
2004	Holland	won	1-0	
2005	Bulgaria	drew	1-1	
2005	Cyprus	won	3-0	1
2005	Switzerland	drew	1-1	1
2005	France	drew	0-0	
2005	Portugal	won	1-0	
2005	Israel	drew	1-1	1
2005	China	won	1-0	1
2005	Israel	drew	2-2	
2005	Faroe Islands	won	2-0	
2006	Sweden	won	3-0	

Having scored many goals in the youth and reserve teams at Crystal Palace, Clinton Morrison was given his league debut for the last eight minutes of the final game of the 1997-98 season against Sheffield Wednesday – he scored the only goal of the game in the 90th minute!

The following season many of Palace's big names left due to the club's financial plight. Morrison moved on from being a regular on the bench to become a regular – in doing so he became the club's leading scorer. Morrison headed the club's goalscoring charts again in 1999-2000 when his form attracted the attention of a number of Premiership outfits. In 2000-1 he had his best season yet in terms of goals scored, netting 19. This led to his debut for the Republic of Ireland Under-21 side against Portugal. He followed this up with a further cap against Estonia where he had a 'goal' disallowed.

He bettered his goals tally the following season – his total of 24 led to the Republic of Ireland giving him his full international debut against Croatia in August 2001. The

following summer he became Birmingham City's record signing when he joined the St Andrew's club for £4.25 million.

Throughout his first campaign with the Blues he scored a number of vital goals at crucial moments. Despite missing the closing moments of the season through a dislocated shoulder, he added three more caps for the Republic of Ireland, scoring against both Russia and Scotland. He continued to be an important member of the Birmingham attack whether playing alongside Heskey, Pandiani or coming off the bench, scoring 16 goals in 96 games for the Midlands club. Morrison signed for First Division Crystal Palace once again in August 2006.

Clinton Morrison

Position	Forward
Born	Clinton Hubert Morrison, Wandsworth, 14 May 1979
Clubs	

Crystal Palace; Birmingham City; Crystal Palace

International Caps	31
International Goals	9

Matches				
Year	Opponent	Result	Score	G
2002	Croatia	drew	2-2	1
2002	Cyprus	won	4-0	
2002	Iran	lost	0-1	
2002	Russia	won	2-0	
2002	Denmark	won	3-0	1
2002	United States	won	2-1	
2002	Nigeria	lost	1-2	
2003	Russia	lost	2-4	1

John O'Shea

Position	Central defender
Born	John Francis O'Shea, Waterford, 30 April 1981
Clubs	

Waterford United; Manchester United; Bournemouth (loan); Royal Antwerp (Belgium) (loan); Manchester United

International Caps	25
International Goals	1

Matches

Year	Opponent	Result	Score	G
2002	Croatia	drew	2-2	
2003	Greece	drew	0-0	
2003	Scotland	won	2-0	
2003	Georgia	won	2-1	
2003	Albania	drew	0-0	
2003	Albania	won	2-1	
2003	Georgia	won	2-0	
2004	Australia	won	2-1	1
2004	Russia	drew	1-1	
2004	Switzerland	lost	0-2	
2004	Canada	won	3-0	
2004	Brazil	drew	0-0	
2004	Poland	drew	0-0	
2004	Jamaica	won	1-0	
2005	Bulgaria	drew	1-1	
2005	Cyprus	won	3-0	
2005	France	drew	0-0	
2005	Faroe Islands	won	2-0	
2005	Croatia	won	1-0	
2005	Portugal	won	1-0	
2005	Israel	drew	1-1	
2005	China	won	1-0	
2005	Israel	drew	2-2	
2005	Faroe Islands	won	2-0	
2006	Sweden	won	3-0	

John O'Shea joined Manchester United from his home-town club Waterford United in the summer of 1998. He worked his way up through the ranks to make a first team debut in the Worthington Cup game against Aston Villa in September 1999.

The following January he joined Bournemouth on loan, scoring with a powerful header in a game against Millwall before choosing to return to Old Trafford. Unable to force his way into the United side, he made a couple of appearances for the

Republic of Ireland Under-21 side in the Toulon Tournament in May 2000.

In 2001-01 he had a brief spell on loan with Royal Antwerp and continued to feature in the Republic's Under-21 side. After a number of Worthington Cup games, he eventually made United's League side in 2001-02 and won his first full cap for the Republic of Ireland against Croatia.

Above: John O'Shea

His first team opportunities at the heart of United's defence took a nose-dive following the signing of Rio Ferdinand, but he proved there were more defensive strings to his bow when he adopted full-back duties. O'Shea was more than happy to fill a variety of roles in the Reds' defence due to injuries to key players. Possessing great composure and silky defensive skills, O'Shea continues to give some solid performances. He has become one

of the team's most consistent players. Having won a Premiership League winners' medal in 2002-03 and an FA Cup winners' medal the following season, John O'Shea continues to impress for both club and country.

Steven Reid

Position	Midfield
Born	Steven John Reid, Kingston, 10 March 1981
Clubs	

Millwall; Blackburn Rovers

International Caps	14
International Goals	2

Matches

Year	Opponent	Result	Score	G
2002	Croatia	drew	2-2	
2002	Russia	won	2-0	1
2002	Denmark	won	3-0	
2002	United States	won	2-1	
2002	Nigeria	lost	1-2	1
2002	Cameroon	drew	1-1	
2002	Germany	drew	1-1	
2003	Scotland	won	2-0	
2003	Albania	drew	0-0	
2004	Russia	drew	1-1	
2004	Turkey	drew	2-2	
2004	Canada	won	3-0	
2004	Poland	drew	0-0	
2006	Sweden	won	3-0	

Having won England youth honours, Steven Reid was a product of Millwall's youth team and made his first team debut on the final day of the 1997-98 season against Bournemouth. Due to injuries, he was one of a number of local products who got their first team chance in 1998-99.

He soon forced his way into the Millwall side on a regular basis. In 2000-01 he helped them win the Second Division Championship.

During the course of that campaign, Reid made his 100th senior appearance for the Lions, and won his first Under-21 cap for the Republic of Ireland against Cyprus in

February 2001. The tall winger, who also helped out at full-back when required, soon became a regular member of the Republic of Ireland senior squad. He scored his first international goal in a 2-0 win over Russia in February 2002.

After featuring for the national side in the 2002 World Cup, he missed the first four months of the new season due to injury. He was soon back to his best – his consistency at international level was recognised when he received the FAI 'Young Player of the Year' award.

Having scored 19 goals in 167 games, he left Millwall for Blackburn Rovers for a fee of £1.8 million in July 2003. A recurrence of the hamstring injury meant four months away from football. Injuries hampered his progress in 2004-05 though when he was able to play, he proved that he possesses tremendous energy, sorely-needed when delegated to support the lone attacker.

Colin Healy

Position	Midfield
Born	Colin Healy, Cork, 14 March 1980
Clubs	

Wilton United; Glasgow Celtic; Coventry City (loan); Sunderland

International Caps	13
International Goals	1

Matches				
Year	Opponent	Result	Score	G
2002	Russia	won	2-0	
2002	Denmark	won	3-0	
2002	United States	won	2-1	
2003	Finland	won	3-0	1
2003	Switzerland	lost	1-2	
2003	Greece	drew	0-0	
2003	Scotland	won	2-0	
2003	Norway	won	1-0	
2003	Georgia	won	2-0	

Matches Continued				
Year	Opponent	Result	Score	G
2004	Australia	won	2-1	
2004	Russia	drew	1-1	
2004	Turkey	drew	2-2	
2004	Switzerland	lost	0-2	

Midfielder Colin Healy was spotted playing for Irish side Wilton United by Glasgow Celtic, joining the Parkhead club in the summer of 1998. Though his opportunities with the Bhoys were limited, he made useful contributions over the next few seasons without ever cementing a first team place.

Above: Colin Healy

In January 2002 he joined Coventry City on loan. After a quiet start, he emerged as a fine attacking central midfielder with an eye for goal. His form earned him a call-up to Mick McCarthy's Republic of Ireland squad and

he won his first cap against Russia, a match the Irish won 2-0. Healy narrowly failed to force his way into the final-23 for the World Cup Finals. It is more than likely he would have, if Roy Keane had his tantrum a day earlier!

After his spell at Highfield Road he rejoined Celtic, taking his total of appearances for the Glasgow giants to 48 before joining Sunderland in the summer of 2003. Healy made an immediate impact at the Stadium of Light but sadly his campaign ended prematurely when he suffered a double fracture of his right leg at his former loan club Coventry. Sadly the injury was so serious that he was forced to miss the entire 2004-05 campaign, and Healy has since negotiated his release from Sunderland.

Richard Sadlier

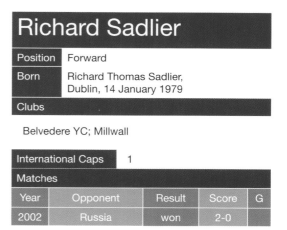

Position	Forward
Born	Richard Thomas Sadlier, Dublin, 14 January 1979
Clubs	

Belvedere YC; Millwall

International Caps	1

Matches				
Year	Opponent	Result	Score	G
2002	Russia	won	2-0	

Richard Sadlier made a promising start with Millwall during the 1997-98 season – scoring three goals in three games – sadly injury sidelined him for the rest of the campaign.

The following season he took his opportunities of regular football after an injury to Paul Shaw, grabbing his chance with some aplomb. Having helped the Lions reach the Auto Windscreen Shield Final at Wembley, it was thought he would miss the big day due to international commitments in Nigeria.

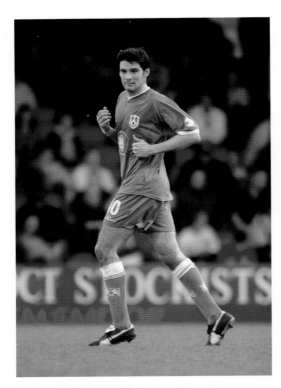

Above: Richard Sadlier

Injuries played their part the following season and then again in 2003-04, when the recurrence of the hip injury that had previously threatened his career forced his retirement from the game.

Nicky Colgan

Position	Goalkeeper
Born	Nicholas Vincent Colgan, Drogheda, 19 September 1973

Clubs

Chelsea; Brentford (loan); Reading (loan); Bournemouth; Hibernian; Stockport County (loan); Barnsley; Dundee United (loan)

International Caps | 8

Matches

Year	Opponent	Result	Score	G
2002	Denmark	won	3-0	
2003	Scotland	won	2-0	
2003	Norway	won	1-0	
2004	Australia	won	2-1	
2004	Turkey	drew	2-2	
2004	Canada	won	3-0	
2004	Poland	drew	0-0	
2004	Nigeria	lost	0-3	

Above: Nicky Colgan

The Republic were eliminated in the final stages, so he was back in time to play.

The tall, gangly forward made great progress at Millwall in 1999-2000. A player who could hold the ball up well, he developed into an excellent all-round footballer. His excellent form earned him his first cap for the Republic of Ireland Under-21s when he came off the bench in the match against Macedonia.

Sadly he then began to suffer from a spate of injuries including a broken arm and a knee complaint. He was back to his best in 2001-02 scoring 17 goals in all competitions and making his full international debut against Russia. His World Cup hopes were ended when he sustained a hip injury towards the end of the campaign.

Unable to figure at Chelsea with Dmitri Kharine, Ed de Goey and Kevin Hitchcock in front of him in the pecking order, goalkeeper Nick Colgan was loaned to both Brentford and Reading. He made his solitary League appearance for the Stamford Bridge club against West Ham United in March 1997 when all the Blues' keepers were out injured. He kept a clean sheet when representing the Republic of Ireland 'B' side but even so, he was released during the summer of 1998.

Signing for Bournemouth, he failed to make the Cherries' first team and in July 1999 went north of the border to play for Hibernian. He was the Easter Road club's first-choice keeper for three seasons, going on to make 147 appearances before losing his place to Daniel Andersson. During his time with the Scottish Premier League outfit, he won eight full caps for the Republic, making his debut

from the bench against Denmark in March 2002.

On the eve of the 2003-04 season, he joined Stockport County on loan. In spite of some outstanding displays, he returned to Easter Road. Though unable to win a place in the Hibs side, he continued to feature at international level for the Republic of Ireland.

Colgan started the 2004-05 season as first-choice keeper for Barnsley but on losing his place midway through the campaign, joined Dundee United on loan. During his time at Oakwell, he faced three penalties – saved them all – only for all three to be retaken successfully!

Graham Barrett

Position	Midfield/Forward
Born	Graham Barrett, Dublin, 6 October 1981
Clubs	

Arsenal; Bristol Rovers (loan); Crewe Alexandra (loan); Colchester United (loan); Brighton and Hove Albion (loan); Coventry City; Sheffield Wednesday (loan); Livingston

International Caps	6
International Goals	2

Matches

Year	Opponent	Result	Score	G
2003	Finland	won	3-0	1
2004	Poland	drew	0-0	
2004	Nigeria	lost	0-3	
2004	Jamaica	won	1-0	1
2004	Holland	won	1-0	
2005	Croatia	won	1-0	

Beginning his career with Arsenal, whom he captained to the FA Youth Cup in 1999-2000, striker Graham Barrett was a member of the Republic of Ireland Under-16 team that won the European title in 1998.

He won his first Under-21 cap for the Republic in February 2000 and appeared in the three Toulon tournament fixtures the following summer. Barrett made a handful of substitute appearances for the Gunners, then joined Bristol Rovers on loan. He made just one appearance, having picked up a severe throat infection, which was later diagnosed as glandular fever.

Continuing to represent the Republic's Under-21 side, he couldn't force his way into the Arsenal side. Further loan spells followed with Crewe Alexandra and Colchester United.

At the start of the 2002–03 season he made a promising bow in international football, coming off the bench to score in the Republic of Ireland's 3-0 win in Finland.

Immediately afterwards, this energetic forward joined Brighton and Hove Albion on loan and ended up staying for the whole season. In the summer of 2003 he joined Coventry City on a free transfer. Though he remained a member of the national squad, he had a mixed season for the Sky Blues. Unable to hold down a regular place at Highfield Road in 2004-05, he had a spell on loan with Sheffield Wednesday prior to rejoining Coventry. Barrett added another full international cap to his collection with an appearance against Croatia, a match the Irish won 1-0 courtesy of a Robbie Keane goal. Barrett now plays for Livingston in the Scottish Premier League.

Tommy Butler

Position	Left-winger
Born	Thomas Anthony Butler, Dublin, 25 April 1981
Clubs	

Sunderland; Darlington (loan); Dunfermline Athletic; Hartlepool United

International Caps	2

Matches

Year	Opponent	Result	Score	G
2003	Finland	won	3-0	
2003	Switzerland	lost	1-2	

Having made his first team debut for Sunderland in a Worthington Cup tie against Walsall during the early part of the 1999-2000 season, Tommy Butler went on to show great form for both the club's reserves and the Republic of Ireland youth team. This was despite suffering from inflamed tendons in his feet, an injury which kept him out of action for over a month.

He made his Premiership debut for the Black Cats towards the end of that campaign, when he came off the bench in the game against West Ham United.

The following season he had a spell on loan with Darlington and made his debut off the bench for the Republic of Ireland Under-21 side against Portugal. He then made the starting line-up for the game with Estonia, when he provided the crosses for each of the Republic's three goals.

Back at the Stadium of Light he continued to impress, and certainly did not look out of place in the top flight. Despite a series of hamstring injuries, he made his full international debut against Finland as the Republic won 3-0 in Helsinki.

With Sunderland he began to struggle to hold down a regular place, first due to a succession of loan signings and then the partnership of Arca and McCartney. Butler decided to leave the Wearsiders and joined Scottish Premier League club Dunfermline Athletic. Released midway through the 2004-05 season, he signed for Hartlepool United.

Jim Goodwin

Position	Midfield
Born	James Goodwin, Waterford, 20 November 1981
Clubs	

Tramore; Glasgow Celtic; Stockport County

International Caps	1

Matches

Year	Opponent	Result	Score	G
2003	Finland	won	3-0	

Midfielder Jim Goodwin played his early football for Tramore. He joined Glasgow Celtic in November 1997 but in almost five years at Parkhead, made just one appearance for the Scottish League giants. That came in the final game of the 1999-2000 season as the Bhoys beat Dundee United 2-0.

In the summer of 2000 Goodwin joined Stockport County on a free transfer and after netting in the 4-1 victory over Barnsley, scored the club's 'Goal of the Season' at Northampton. What he lacks in skill and natural talent, he more than makes up for with an abundance of sheer passion and aggressiveness on the pitch.

During his first season at Edgeley Park, he continued to feature for the Republic of Ireland Under-21 side. Goodwin became the ninth County player to win a full international cap when he came off the bench to replace Robbie Keane in Finland.

He continued to enjoy life with the Hatters and in 2003-04 produced a number of committed performances as well as netting six goals – including another 'Goal of the Season' contender against Bristol City. Continuing to be a virtual ever-present in the Stockport side, Jim Goodwin's versatility (which has more than compensated for his lack of skill) means that he has now appeared in 119 League and Cup games for Stockport County.

Unable to win a regular place, he spent three months of the following campaign on loan at Exeter City, playing a big part in helping the Grecians avoid relegation. He went out on loan to Cardiff City to gain further experience, and scored on his debut. A regular for the Republic of Ireland at Under-21 level, he had another spell on loan with Exeter before joining Plymouth Argyle on a short-term contract. Despite impressing in his time at Home Park, he was released in the summer of 1999 and returned to Ireland to play for Bohemians.

Over the next few seasons, Crowe proved himself to be one of the most prolific scorers in the Eircom League. This led to a couple of full international caps for the Republic of Ireland, the first in a goalless draw against Greece in November 2002. Six months later he played in the 1-0 win over Norway.

In the summer of 2004 he left Bohemians to join Shelbourne, where he teamed up with Jason Byrne – they formed one of the most feared strike partnerships in the League.

Unable to get a game at Aston Villa, Alan Lee went on loan to Torquay United and had a highly impressive spell with the Gulls, scoring a number of vital goals. A player who holds the ball up well, he had another loan spell, this time with Port Vale: it was his form for the Valiants that led to him winning international recognition for the Republic of Ireland at Under-21 level.

Above: Alan Lee

Shortly before the start of the 1999-2000 season, Alan Lee joined Burnley but made little impact at Turf Moor due to the consistency of the regular front two. Unable to make much headway, he moved on to Rotherham United where he grabbed his first-ever Football League hat-trick in a 3-1 defeat of Cambridge United. Following the club's promotion, he adjusted well to the demands of First Division football and in 2002-03 scored 17 goals, deservedly

Glen Crowe

Position	Forward
Born	Glen Crowe, Dublin, 25 December 1977
Clubs	

Wolverhampton Wanderers; Exeter City (loan); Cardiff City (loan); Exeter City (loan); Plymouth Argyle; Bohemians; Shelbourne

International Caps	2

Matches				
Year	Opponent	Result	Score	G
2003	Greece	drew	0-0	
2003	Norway	won	1-0	

Striker Glen Crowe began his career with Wolverhampton Wanderers, scoring on his first start at Charlton Athletic on the final day of the 1995-96 season.

Alan Lee

Position	Forward
Born	Alan Desmond Lee, Galway, 21 August 1978
Clubs	

Aston Villa; Torquay United (loan); Port Vale (loan); Burnley; Rotherham United; Cardiff City; Ipswich Town

International Caps	8

Matches				
Year	Opponent	Result	Score	G
2003	Norway	won	1-0	
2003	Georgia	won	2-0	
2004	Czech Republic	won	2-1	
2004	Poland	drew	0-0	
2004	Nigeria	lost	0-3	
2004	Jamaica	won	1-0	
2004	Holland	won	1-0	
2005	Cyprus	won	3-0	

receiving a call-up to the full Republic of Ireland squad.

Having scored 41 goals in 122 games, he joined Cardiff City for £850,000 – a new club record fee for the Millers. Although troubled by injury in his first season at Ninian Park, he won the first of eight caps when he played against Norway in April 2003. The sale of players at the Welsh club saw Lee partner three different players in three months. In 2004-05 he played many games whilst suffering from a groin problem, although this didn't prevent him from playing for the Republic against Cyprus. Midway through the 2005-96 campaign, Lee parted company with the Bluebirds, joining fellow Championship side Ipswich Town.

Alan Quinn

Position	Midfield
Born	Alan Quinn, Dublin, 13 June 1979
Clubs	

Cherry Orchard; Sheffield Wednesday; Sunderland (loan); Sheffield United

International Caps		6			
Matches					
Year	Opponent	Result	Score	G
2003	Norway	won	1-0	
2004	Australia	won	2-1	
2004	Jamaica	won	1-0	
2004	Holland	won	1-0	
2005	Bulgaria	drew	1-1	
2005	Croatia	won	1-0	

Signed by Sheffield Wednesday from the quaintly named Irish side Cherry Orchard in December 1997, midfielder Alan Quinn quickly became a regular in the Owls' youth team that ultimately won the FA Premier Northern Youth League in 1997-98.

After making quite an impression at Hillsborough, he was handed his first

team debut – in the final minute of the Premiership season when he came off the bench at Everton! After failing to make much impression the following season, he was one of the few promising features in 1999-2000. He also won his first cap for the Republic of Ireland at Under-21 level and added three more appearances in the Toulon Tournament.

Above: Alan Quinn

Making great strides with the Owls and establishing himself as a first-team regular, his 2000-01 season ended prematurely when he suffered a broken leg in the local derby against Sheffield United in April 2001. On his recovery he initially struggled to find his form but then came good, and was rewarded with his first full international cap against Norway in April 2003.

Despite his wholehearted approach to the game, he was allowed to go on loan to Sunderland. Before being out of contract at Hillsborough, he crossed the city to sign for Sheffield United. His impressive displays for the Blades saw the young midfielder continue to feature for the national side.

Joe Murphy

Position	Goalkeeper
Born	Joseph Murphy, Dublin, 21 August 1981
Clubs	

Stella Maris; Tranmere Rovers; West Bromwich Albion; Walsall (loan); Sunderland; Scunthorpe Utd.

International Caps		1		
Matches				
Year	Opponent	Result	Score	G
2004	Turkey	drew	2-2	

A product of Stella Maris, Tranmere Rovers' Irish nursery outfit, goalkeeper Joe Murphy made a dream debut for the Wirral club. He saved a penalty in the Worthington Cup tie of October 1999 against Oxford United. He kept his place in the side, enjoying a lengthy spell of first-team action until suffering a broken collarbone in the Worthington Cup quarter-final against Middlesbrough.

Following his return to fitness he displaced his rival John Achterberg for the Worthington Cup Final against Leicester City. His form during his first season of League football led to him winning Under-21 honours for the Republic of Ireland, when he played against Colombia and Portugal in the Toulon Tournament. Though he continued to play for the Republic's Under-21 side in 2000-01, he found himself understudying Achterberg for much of the campaign. Over the following season he played on a more regular basis but in July 2002 left Prenton Park to join West Bromwich Albion.

He saved a penalty from Liverpool's Michael Owen with his first touch in Premiership football, although most of his first season at the Hawthorns was as understudy to Russell Hoult. In 2003-04 whilst still playing most of his football for Albion's reserve side, he was rewarded with his first full cap for the Republic of Ireland as a late replacement against Turkey.

On the domestic front he found himself third-choice keeper at West Brom, and had a spell on loan at Walsall. He missed only one game until receiving a red card at Blackpool, after which he couldn't force his way back into the side. Since then he has played for Sunderland and transferred to Scunthorpe United in 2006.

Andy Reid

Position	Midfield
Born	Andrew Matthew Reid, Dublin, 29 July 1982
Clubs	

Nottingham Forest; Tottenham Hotspur

International Caps	16
International Goals	2

Matches

Year	Opponent	Result	Score	G
2004	Canada	won	3-0	
2004	Brazil	drew	0-0	
2004	Czech Republic	won	2-1	
2004	Poland	drew	0-0	
2004	Romania	won	1-0	
2004	Jamaica	won	1-0	
2004	Holland	won	1-0	
2004	Faroe Islands	won	2-0	
2005	Bulgaria	drew	1-1	1
2005	Cyprus	won	3-0	1
2005	Switzerland	drew	1-1	
2005	France	drew	0-0	
2005	Portugal	won	1-0	
2005	China	won	1-0	
2005	Israel	drew	2-2	
2005	Faroe Islands	won	2-0	

Andy Reid was a member of the Republic of Ireland team that won the UEFA Under-16 title in 1998, when he set up the winning

goal in the final. He started his Football League career with Nottingham Forest.

Above: Andy Reid

In a superb debut, he scored the second goal to clinch a 2-0 victory over Sheffield United in November 2000. Initially used as a central striker, he was switched to a wide-left midfield role where he showed vision, pace and the ability to get the ball into the box. Reminiscent of former Forest favourite John Robertson, he was a regular in the Republic of Ireland Under-21 side. In 2002-03 his excellent wing play set up many goals for David Johnson and Marlon Harewood. The following season he was Forest's only ever-present and their top scorer with 13 goals – this despite playing most of his games in midfield.

His outstanding form saw him rewarded with his full international debut for the Republic of Ireland against Canada, and named in the PFA Division One team for the season.

During the January 2005 transfer window, Reid joined Tottenham Hotspur and though continuing to represent the Republic of Ireland, has yet to realise his full potential in the top flight.

John Thompson

Position	Midfield/Right-back
Born	John Thompson, Dublin, 12 October 1981
Clubs	

River Valley Rangers; Home Farm; Nottingham Forest

International Caps	1

Matches

Year	Opponent	Result	Score	G
2004	Canada	won	3-0	

Versatile defender John Thompson made his debut for Nottingham Forest against Sheffield United in the 2001-02 season at right-back but was later moved to centre-back. He was just settling into the side when he suffered a knee injury in the game at Rotherham, which brought his season to a premature close.

A former player with Home Farm, he played much of the following season in midfield. His form led to selection for the Republic of Ireland Under-21 side. Continuing to be one of Forest's most consistent players, he made his full international debut for the Republic of Ireland against Canada in November 2003, a match the Irish won 3-0.

During the summer of 2004 John Thompson dislocated his shoulder during Forest's pre-season tour of the United States. This caused him to miss a number of games at the start of the 2004-05 campaign. His versatility enabled him to cover for a number of positions, although he appeared to play his best football in the centre of defence. Unfortunately he suffered a knee injury in the match against Sheffield United and so his season, like all the ones before ended prematurely.

Paddy Kenny

Position	Goalkeeper
Born	Patrick Joseph Kenny, Halifax, 17 May 1978
Clubs	

Bradford Park Avenue; Bury; Sheffield United

International Caps	5
Matches	

Year	Opponent	Result	Score	G
2004	Czech Republic	won	2-1	
2004	Jamaica	won	1-0	
2005	Bulgaria	drew	1-1	
2005	Croatia	won	1-0	
2005	China	won	1-0	

Above: Paddy Kenny

Liam Miller

Position	Midfield
Born	William Peter Miller, Cork, 13 February 1981
Clubs	

Ballincollig AFC; Glasgow Celtic; Manchester United

International Caps	10
International Goals	1
Matches	

Year	Opponent	Result	Score	G
2004	Czech Republic	won	2-1	
2004	Poland	drew	0-0	
2004	Romania	won	1-0	
2004	Nigeria	lost	0-3	
2005	Bulgaria	drew	1-1	
2005	Faroe Islands	won	2-0	
2005	Croatia	won	1-0	
2005	Portugal	won	1-0	
2005	China	won	1-0	
2006	Sweden	won	3-0	1

Above: Liam Miller

Following the departure of Dean Kiely to Charlton Athletic in the summer of 1998, Bury found themselves with 21-year-old Paddy Kenny, fresh from non-League football with Bradford Park Avenue as the only goalkeeper on their books.

Manager Neil Warnock handed him the No.13 shirt as he was expected to take a back seat. He started the 1999-2000 season in the first team and ended up being the Shakers' only ever-present. He enjoyed a highly consistent first season in the Football League, pulled off a number of incredible saves and was voted the supporters' 'Player of the season'. Kenny was ever-present for the second season in a row, and enjoyed a spell when he conceded just one goal in 568 minutes of football. In 2001–02 he was sent-off twice after clumsy

challenges – a season in which the club's financial problems saw him transfer-listed.

Having appeared in 150 games for Bury, Kenny joined Sheffield United, initially on loan for the injured Simon Tracey. He immediately became the club's first-choice keeper. Voted the supporters' 'Player of the Year' his performances for the Blades saw him called up into the Republic of Ireland squad, gaining his first cap as a late substitute against the Czech Republic.

Continuing as Sheffield United's first-choice keeper, he is also an important member of the current Republic of Ireland squad, demonstrating his excellence as both a shot-stopper and in one-on-one situations.

Tenacious midfielder Liam Miller was spotted playing junior football for Ballincollig AFC by Glasgow Celtic and joined the Parkhead club in October 1997.

With the Bhoys, Miller won a Scottish Premier League Championship medal in 2003-04. In all his time at Parkhead he only made 44 appearances, the majority from the bench. Although he wasn't a regular in the Celtic side, he won full international honours for the Republic of Ireland, making his debut in a 2-1 defeat of the Czech Republic in March 2004.

During the close season Miller joined Manchester United, where he was earmarked as Roy Keane's eventual successor – although Keane has since signed for Celtic!

The young Miller wasted no time in marking his debut with a telling contribution, setting up the second goal in United's Champions League qualifier against Dinamo Bucharest. The Champions' League, Carling Cup and FA Cup campaigns provided Miller with his most consistent spell in the team. As the majority of his games in the Premiership were off the bench, he needs more time to enhance his credentials as a top-class midfielder with the Reds.

One of the most prolific scorers in the National League over the past few seasons, striker Jason Byrne began his career with Bray Wanderers prior to joining Shelbourne in February 2003.

Byrne scored 64 goals in 159 games with Bray, a goalscoring record that attracted the attention of a number of clubs both in the Republic and across the water.

In April 2004, Byrne made his full international debut for the Republic of Ireland. He came off the bench in the final minute of the goalless draw against Poland in Bydgoszcz.

In 2004-05 Byrne's 25 league goals were vital to the Shels' League success. At the time of writing Byrne, who was voted the PFAI's 'Player of the Year' for the second year in a row, has scored 30 goals in just 46 appearances for Shelbourne.

It was something of a miracle that he played at all in 2001-02, following post-season surgery on a medial and cruciate ligament injury that threatened to ruin his career. As well as captaining the club's reserve side, he was called up for the Republic of Ireland Under-21 team in the Toulon Tournament in the summer of 2002.

Playing a handful of games in 2002–03, he joined Chesterfield on loan for the crucial end-of-season run-in. He scored on the last day of the season at Blackpool to help the Spireites preserve their Division Two status. The following season Douglas, who had made his full Republic of Ireland debut against Poland, spent three months on loan at Blackpool before returning to Ewood Park, where he was offered the chance of playing in the wide-left role.

Having found a regular role in the side, his willingness to work, tackle hard and cover in defence made him a favourite of the Blackburn fans. Surprisingly falling out of favour in 2004–05, he ended the campaign on loan at Gillingham prior to signing for Leeds United in the close season.

Jonathan Douglas

Position	Midfield
Born	Jonathan Douglas, Monaghan, 22 November 1981
Clubs	

Blackburn Rovers; Chesterfield (loan); Blackpool (loan); Gillingham (loan); Leeds United

International Caps			2	
Matches				
Year	Opponent	Result	Score	G
2004	Poland	drew	0-0	
2004	Nigeria	lost	0-3	

Previously capped by the Republic of Ireland at Under-16 and Under-18 levels, this promising young midfielder made his senior debut for Blackburn Rovers in the Worthington Cup tie against West Ham United in October 2000. He also featured later that season in the FA Cup third-round tie against Chester City.

Jason Byrne

Position	Forward
Born	Jason Byrne, Dublin, 23 February 1978
Clubs	

Bray Wanderers; Shelbourne

International Caps			1	
Matches				
Year	Opponent	Result	Score	G
2004	Poland	drew	0-0	

Martin Rowlands

Position	Midfield
Born	Martin Charles Rowlands, Hammersmith, 8 February 1979
Clubs	

Farnborough Town; Brentford; Queen's Park Rangers

International Caps			3	
Matches				
Year	Opponent	Result	Score	G
2004	Romania	won	1-0	
2004	Nigeria	lost	0-3	
2004	Jamaica	won	1-0	

Signed by Brentford from non-League Farnborough Town during the summer of 1998, midfielder Martin Rowlands had a fantastic first season at Griffin Park.

Not only did he earn a Third Division Championship winners' medal but he played for the Nationwide League against the Italian Serie 'B'. He was also called up for the Republic of Ireland Under-21 side. In 1999-2000 Rowlands was the supporters' 'Player of the Year', his mazy runs and teasing crosses causing havoc in opposition defences. Though he missed a number of games the following season through suspension, he won a runners-up medal in the LDV Vans Trophy after appearing for the Bees in their 2-1 defeat by Port Vale in the final of the competition.

Injuries hampered his progress over the next couple of seasons – these included a hernia operation, groin, calf and ankle problems. Towards the end of the 2002-03 campaign, he broke his leg!

On recovery Rowlands, who had made 186 appearances for Brentford, left to play for Queen's Park Rangers. Though not a prolific scorer, he netted some important strikes and finished the season with 12 goals. Voted the club's 'Player of the Year' he won the first of three international caps for the Republic of Ireland when he played against Romania. A midfield player who can play on either wing, he remains a vital member of the Loftus Road club.

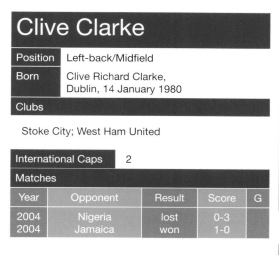

Clive Clarke

Position	Left-back/Midfield
Born	Clive Richard Clarke, Dublin, 14 January 1980
Clubs	

Stoke City; West Ham United

International Caps	2			
Matches				
Year	Opponent	Result	Score	G
2004	Nigeria	lost	0-3	
2004	Jamaica	won	1-0	

Having come through the ranks at Stoke City, the young Republic of Ireland Under-18 international left-back was given his first-team opportunity in 1998-99, though he might have won his chance earlier in the season but for injury. The following season he made the position his own, with a debut for the Republic of Ireland Under-21 side against Macedonia, after which he became a regular in the squad. He capped a fine season with a Wembley appearance, shaking off a groin injury to play in City's Auto Windscreen Shield-winning team. Whilst he continued to represent the Republic of Ireland Under-21 team, he lost out for much of the 1999-2000 season to former England full-back Tony Dorigo. Following his departure Clarke again established himself in the Potters' side, though his run of first-team games was halted by injury which sidelined him for three months.

On his return he found himself named as club captain for a number of games. His performances earned him a call-up to the Republic of Ireland senior squad. The Irish lost the match 3-0 to Nigeria in May 2004. He made a second appearance against Jamaica four days later, coming off the bench in a 1-0 win. Both of these games were played at Charlton Athletic's ground. They remain his only appearances for the national side.

He remained the club's most consistent player until his transfer to West Ham United.

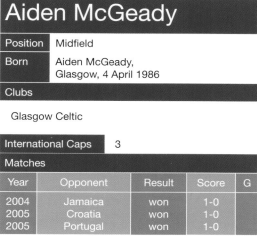

Aiden McGeady

Position	Midfield
Born	Aiden McGeady, Glasgow, 4 April 1986
Clubs	

Glasgow Celtic

International Caps	3			
Matches				
Year	Opponent	Result	Score	G
2004	Jamaica	won	1-0	
2005	Croatia	won	1-0	
2005	Portugal	won	1-0	

One of the most talked-about teenagers in Scottish football, Celtic's Aiden McGeady announced his arrival on the first-team scene in typically spectacular style, with a debut goal and man-of-the-match performance at Tynecastle.

Appearing in four games at the end of Celtic's League Championship-winning season of 2003-04, he famously opted to represent the Republic of Ireland over the country of his birth. He made his full international debut in the 1-0 defeat of Jamaica at The Valley in June 2004.

McGeady won further caps in the 1-0 victories over Croatia and Portugal during the course of the 2004-05 season, and went on to appear on a regular basis for the Bhoys. A player of prodigious talent – full of flicks, tricks and subtle touches – McGeady is arguably at his most effective in a withdrawn role behind the strikers. In 2004-05 he helped Celtic finish runners-up in the Scottish Premier League and lift the Scottish Cup, when he came off the bench in a 1-0 win over Dundee United.

Michael Doyle

Position	Midfield
Born	Michael Paul Doyle, Dublin, 8 July 1981
Clubs	

Glasgow Celtic; Coventry City

International Caps	1
Matches	

Year	Opponent	Result	Score	G
2004	Holland	won	1-0	

The tenacious left-footed midfielder started out with Glasgow Celtic. Though he won selection for the Republic of Ireland Under-21 side, he couldn't force his way into the Bhoys' side.

In the summer of 2003 he joined Coventry City on a free transfer, having previously played under Sky Blues' then-manager Eric Black when he was in charge of Celtic's youth team. A strong and ambitious player, he appeared in all four midfield positions at Highfield Road, looking most comfortable on the left. He netted several well-taken goals: his form not only earned him a contract extension but a place on the bench for the Republic of Ireland squad against Poland in April 2004. Two months later he came off the bench in the 1-0 win over Holland in Amsterdam to round off a season in which he was voted the Sky Blues' 'Young Player of the Season'.

During the close season he had a hernia operation, before returning to enjoy an excellent campaign with Coventry for whom he has now made almost 100 appearances.

Jon Macken

Position	Forward
Born	Jonathan Paul Macken, Manchester, 7 September 1977
Clubs	

Manchester United; Preston North End; Manchester City; Crystal Palace

International Caps	1
Matches	

Year	Opponent	Result	Score	G
2005	Bulgaria	drew	1-1	

Striker Jon Macken joined Preston North End from Manchester United for a fee of £250,000 in the summer of 1997. He soon became a great favourite of the North End fans with his commitment and bustling style. Modelling himself on his hero Mark Hughes, he demonstrated a good footballing brain.

The 1999-2000 season saw Macken's emergence as a striker of some quality, as he ended Preston's Second Division Championship-winning campaign as the club's top scorer. The highlights of his season included six-in-six during September and October and his 100th game for North End, when he scored the equaliser at Arsenal – the first FA Cup goal of his career. Not surprisingly he joined three team-mates in the PFA's Second Division select side.

Despite playing at a higher level in 2000-01, he was again the club's leading scorer – netting his first senior hat-trick in the Worthington Cup tie against Shrewsbury Town. Other highlights included a 19-second goal against Grimsby Town and his 50th strike for the club at Barnsley.

He became unsettled at Deepdale and in March 2002 joined Manchester City for a fee of £4 million. Macken immediately impressed, netting five times from eight appearances, including the club's record-equalling 108th goal against Portsmouth. The following season saw him struggle with injuries as he did in 2003-04, though he headed the Blues' winner in the epic FA Cup tie against Spurs.

Above: Jon Macken

He had better fortunes the following season. His club form won a call-up to the Republic of Ireland squad and he won his first cap against Bulgaria in August 2005, a match the Irish drew 1-1.

Jon Macken moved from Manchester City to Crystal Palace in the summer of 2005, but continues to suffer with a recurring back injury.

Stephen Elliott

Position	Forward
Born	Stephen William Elliott, Dublin, 6 January 1984
Clubs	

Manchester City; Sunderland

International Caps		4		
Matches				
Year	Opponent	Result	Score	G
2004	Croatia	won	1-0	
2005	China	won	1-0	
2005	Faroe Islands	won	2-0	
2006	Sweden	won	3-0	

Above: Stephen Elliot

Stephen Elliott was a prolific scorer for Manchester City at youth and reserve team level. He was on the bench for the first time against Liverpool before being given opportunities at first-team level, with cameo roles against Bolton Wanderers and Middlesbrough.

A Republic of Ireland Under-21 international, he produced some outstanding performances for the national side at the World Youth Championships in December 2003.

In the summer of 2004 Elliott joined Mick McCarthy's Sunderland. Few fans had heard his name but by the end of the season they were all predicting an extremely bright future for him. Elliott is quick and strong and possesses an excellent first touch. He is also extremely good in the air for such a small man.

His 15 goals contributed to the Black Cats winning the Championship title, and he holds the record for the most goals for the Republic of Ireland at Under-21 level, but Elliott's proudest moment was yet to come. In November 2004 he won his first full cap for the Republic in the 1-0 win over Croatia.

Kevin Doyle

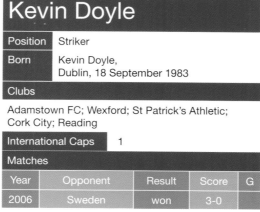

Position	Striker
Born	Kevin Doyle, Dublin, 18 September 1983
Clubs	

Adamstown FC; Wexford; St Patrick's Athletic; Cork City; Reading

International Caps		1		
Matches				
Year	Opponent	Result	Score	G
2006	Sweden	won	3-0	

Kevin Doyle started his career with Adamstown FC before joining Wexford and then St Patrick's Athletic. He moved from St Pat's to Cork City in February 2003 when boss Pat Dolan made the same move. He played in the Republic of Ireland Under-20s squad and in late 2003 in the World Youth Cup Finals in the United Arab Emirates. He then played for the Irish Under-21s at the Madeira tournament in February 2003, and finished as leading scorer as they won the competition.

In his first season with Cork he scored five goals in 39 games. In 2004 he blossomed after being switched from the right-wing to striker. He was named their player of the season in 2004-05 after top-scoring with 13 goals, including strikes in the Intertoto Cup against Nantes and NEC Nijmegen. Doyle was shortlisted for the Irish Soccer Writers' Personality of the Season as well as the Irish FA Player of the Season award. He started the 2005-06 campaign in fine form, scoring seven goals in 11 games, as well as one more in the Setanta Cup before sealing a move to Reading. An estimated crowd of 5,000 turned up to salute him when he played his last game for Cork, scoring both his side's goals in a 2-0 win over Finn Harps. Though there was interest from Aberdeen, Burnley and Stoke, Doyle opted for the Royals. Since his arrival in the Football League he has set the world alight, scoring 14 goals in 31 games at the time of writing, as Reading lead the Championship by a distance.

Joey O'Brien

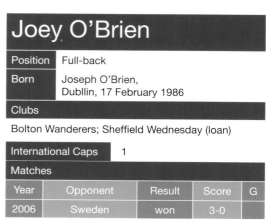

Position	Full-back
Born	Joseph O'Brien, Dublin, 17 February 1986
Clubs	

Bolton Wanderers; Sheffield Wednesday (loan)

International Caps		1		
Matches				
Year	Opponent	Result	Score	G
2006	Sweden	won	3-0	

A graduate of the Bolton youth set-up, Joey O'Brien made his first team debut as a substitute in the club's Carling Cup victory at Yeovil Town during the early stages of the 2004-05 season. To gain further experience, O'Brien was loaned out to League One team Sheffield Wednesday for the most part of the remainder of the campaign. His time at Hillsborough was most productive: he played in 15 games, scoring two goals, including one against Hull City on his debut.

His form for the Owls saw him called up to the Republic of Ireland Under-21 squad, while his last game for Wednesday saw him named as captain, in honour of his contribution during three months with the club. Upon returning to the Reebok Stadium, he made his Premiership debut against Everton in May 2005, coming on as a late substitute for Fernando Hierro. He was given his first start in Bolton colours in their away UEFA Cup first-round tie with Lokomotiv Plovdiv in September 2005. Since then, his output, skill and endeavour have endeared him to the Bolton fans, and he is now an integral part of the Premiership club's set up.

Villa's senior side but wore the No.1 jersey for their FA Youth Cup win the following year. Featuring regularly in Villa's reserve side, he had loan spells at Tamworth and Wycombe in 2003-04, playing in the last three games of the season for the Chairboys. A confident keeper, he also represented the Republic of Ireland in the World Youth Championships and also featured for the Under-21s.

In 2004-05, Henderson had two spells on loan with Notts County before returning to the Midlands club to continue his development. He impressed on a three-month loan spell at Brighton at the start of the 2005-06 season. He made his full debut in a 1-1 draw with Derby County on the opening day of the campaign – but Football League rules meant he had to return to the Midlands club at the end of the spell. In January 2006 the move was made permanent, the Seagulls paying £20,000 for his services. This will rise to £35,000 should the south-coast club remain in the Championship. Henderson made his full international debut against Sweden, replacing Shay Given for the second-half and keeping a clean sheet in a 3-0 win.

At the age of 14, he joined the youth set-up at Manchester City, and worked his way up through the ranks after impressing in the club's academy. He made his senior debut in September 2005 against local rivals Bolton Wanderers, coming off the bench. He made his first competitive start against Doncaster Rovers in the League Cup three days later. He won Man-of-the-Match on his first Premiership start against Everton, and since then has been a key player in the City side. His first few appearances were so promising that they won him a contract to keep him at the club until 2009.

He received his first senior call-up for the Republic of Ireland under new manager Steve Staunton, for the friendly against Sweden. Ireland had always maintained he would never play international football under previous manager Brian Kerr, due to a skirmish the two had over selections in an under-age Republic squad. Ireland came off the bench against Sweden to replace John O'Shea, and played a part in the build-up to Liam Miller's impressive strike.

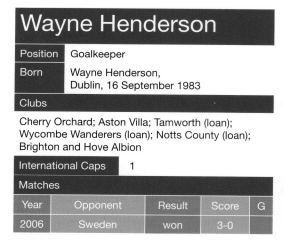

Wayne Henderson

Position	Goalkeeper
Born	Wayne Henderson, Dublin, 16 September 1983
Clubs	

Cherry Orchard; Aston Villa; Tamworth (loan); Wycombe Wanderers (loan); Notts County (loan); Brighton and Hove Albion

International Caps	1

Matches

Year	Opponent	Result	Score	G
2006	Sweden	won	3-0	

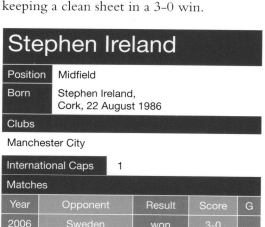

Stephen Ireland

Position	Midfield
Born	Stephen Ireland, Cork, 22 August 1986
Clubs	

Manchester City

International Caps	1

Matches

Year	Opponent	Result	Score	G
2006	Sweden	won	3-0	

Hailing from a family of goalkeepers (his father Paddy played for Shamrock Rovers and two of his brothers are also keepers), Wayne Henderson began his career with Cherry Orchard in Ireland before joining Aston Villa in 2001. He did not appear in

As a schoolboy, Stephen Ireland had trials with a number of top British clubs. Many of them were discouraged by his Osgood-Schlatter disease, a knee complaint from which he suffered during his mid-teens.

STATISTICS

REPUBLIC OF IRELAND TOP 20 POST-WAR APPEARANCES

1	Steve Staunton	102
2	Niall Quinn	91
3	Tony Cascarino	88
4	Paul McGrath	83
5	Paddy Bonner	80
6	Ray Houghton	73
7	Liam Brady	72
8=	Kevin Moran	71
	Frank Stapleton	71
	Shay Given	71
11	Andy Townsend	70
12	John Aldridge	69
13=	Kenny Cunningham	68
	David O'Leary	68
15	Roy Keane	66
16	Kevin Kilbane	65
17=	Gary Breen	62
	Robbie Keane	62
19=	Johnny Giles	59
	Ian Harte	59

REPUBLIC OF IRELAND TOP 20 POST-WAR GOALSCORERS

1	Robbie Keane	26
2	Niall Quinn	21
3	Frank Stapleton	20
4=	John Aldridge	19
	Tony Cascarino	19
	Don Givens	19
7	Noel Cantwell	14
8	Gerry Daly	13
9	Ian Harte	11
10=	Liam Brady	9
	David Connolly	9
	Roy Keane	9
	David Kelly	9
	Clinton Morrison	9
	Kevin Sheedy	9
16=	Dermot Curtis	8
	Tony Grealish	8
	Paul McGrath	8
19=	Arthur Fitzsimons	7
	Alf Ringstead	7
	Steve Staunton	7
	Andy Townsend	7

INDIVIDUAL POST-WAR SCORING FEATS

FOUR GOALS IN A GAME

Don Givens	v Turkey in Dublin	29 October 1975

THREE GOALS IN A GAME

Don Givens	v USSR in Dublin	30 October 1974
David Kelly	v Israel in Dublin	10 November 1987
John Aldridge	v Turkey in Dublin	17 October 1990
John Aldridge	v Latvia in Dublin	9 September 1992
David Connolly	v Liechtenstein in Dublin	21 May 1997

REPUBLIC OF IRELAND POST-WAR MANAGERIAL RECORD

	P	W	D	L
Mick Meagan (Sept 1969 to May 1971)	12	0	3	9
Liam Tuohy (Oct 1971 to May 1973)	10	3	1	6
Sean Thomas (June 1973)	1	0	1	0
Johnny Giles (Oct 1973 to March 1980)	37	14	9	14
Alan Kelly (April 1980)	1	1	0	0
Eoin Hand (April 1980 to Nov 1985)	40	11	9	20
Jack Charlton (Feb 1986 to Dec 1995)	94	47	30	17
Mick McCarthy (Jan 1996 to Oct 2002)	68	29	20	19
Brian Kerr (Dec 2002 to Nov 2005)	32	18	11	3
Steve Staunton (Games from Jan 2006 to March 2006)	1	1	0	0

REPUBLIC OF IRELAND COMPLETE POST-WAR RECORD

	P	W	D	L	F	A
Albania	4	3	1	0	6	2
Algeria	1	0	0	1	0	2
Andorra	2	2	0	0	6	1
Argentina	3	0	0	3	0	4
Australia	1	1	0	0	2	1
Austria	12	2	2	8	15	33
Belgium	10	1	4	5	9	18
Bolivia	2	2	0	0	4	0
Brazil	4	1	1	2	2	9
Bulgaria	7	2	2	3	8	6
Cameroon	1	0	1	0	2	2
Canada	1	1	0	0	3	0
Chile	5	2	1	2	6	5
China	2	2	0	0	2	0
Croatia	5	2	2	1	7	5
Cyprus	6	6	0	0	21	2
Czechoslovakia	11	4	0	7	12	27
Czech Republic	5	2	0	3	7	10
Denmark	12	4	5	3	16	16
Ecuador	1	1	0	0	3	2
Egypt	1	0	1	0	0	0
England	13	3	6	4	13	18
Estonia	2	2	0	0	4	0
Faroe Islands	2	2	0	0	4	0
Finland	5	3	2	0	11	2
France	12	3	4	5	11	16
Georgia	2	2	0	0	4	1
Germany	2	1	1	0	3	1
West Germany	11	4	1	6	12	20
Greece	2	0	1	1	0	1
Holland	15	6	3	6	19	20
Hungary	5	2	1	2	5	7
Iceland	7	5	2	0	16	6
Iran	3	2	0	1	4	2
N.Ireland	9	3	4	2	12	4
Israel	5	1	3	1	8	6
Italy	6	1	0	5	3	10

	P	W	D	L	F	A
Jamaica	1	1	0	0	1	0
Latvia	4	4	0	0	11	2
Liechtenstein	4	3	1	0	14	0
Lithuania	4	3	1	0	5	1
Luxembourg	4	4	0	0	9	1
Macedonia	4	2	1	1	7	4
Malta	7	7	0	0	24	2
Mexico	5	0	4	1	5	6
Morocco	1	1	0	0	1	0
Nigeria	2	0	0	2	1	5
Norway	14	7	6	1	22	10
Paraguay	1	1	0	0	2	0
Poland	20	4	8	8	20	29
Portugal	12	4	2	6	9	15
Romania	5	2	2	1	4	2
Russia	5	1	2	2	5	7
Saudi Arabia	1	1	0	0	3	0
Scotland	8	3	2	3	7	10
South Africa	1	1	0	0	2	1
Spain	22	4	6	12	17	42
Sweden	8	3	1	4	9	14
Switzerland	11	4	3	4	11	9
Trinidad & Tobago	1	0	0	1	1	2
Tunisia	1	1	0	0	4	0
Turkey	12	5	6	1	26	13
Uruguay	2	0	1	1	1	3
United States	7	3	2	2	13	11
USSR	8	3	1	4	8	8
Wales	9	3	1	5	10	10
Yugoslavia	4	2	0	2	5	6

Games Played	385
Games Won	155
Games Drawn	98
Games Lost	132
Goals Scored	610
Goals Conceded	471